RATIONALITY

RATIONALITY
CONSTRAINTS AND CONTEXTS

T.-W. HUNG
Institute of European and American Studies, Academia Sinica
Taipei, Taiwan

T.J. LANE
Taipei Medical University, Graduate Institute of Humanities in Medicine, Taipei, Taiwan; Taipei Medical University-Shuang Ho Hospital, Brain and Consciousness Research Center, New Taipei City, Taiwan; Academia Sinica, Institute of European and American Studies, Taipei, Taiwan; National Chengchi University, Research Center for Mind, Brain and Learning, Taipei, Taiwan

ELSEVIER

AMSTERDAM • BOSTON • HEIDELBERG • LONDON
NEW YORK • OXFORD • PARIS • SAN DIEGO
SAN FRANCISCO • SINGAPORE • SYDNEY • TOKYO
Academic Press is an imprint of Elsevier

Academic Press is an imprint of Elsevier
125 London Wall, London EC2Y 5AS, United Kingdom
525 B Street, Suite 1800, San Diego, CA 92101-4495, United States
50 Hampshire Street, 5th Floor, Cambridge, MA 02139, United States
The Boulevard, Langford Lane, Kidlington, Oxford OX5 1GB, United Kingdom

Library of Congress Cataloging-in-Publication Data
A catalog record for this book is available from the Library of Congress

British Library Cataloguing-in-Publication Data
A catalogue record for this book is available from the British Library

ISBN: 978-0-12-804600-5

For information on all Academic Press publications
visit our website at https://www.elsevier.com/

Publisher: Nikky Levy
Acquisition Editor: Emily Ekle
Editorial Project Manager: Timothy Bennett
Production Project Manager: Susan Li
Designer: Matthew Limbert

Typeset by Thomson Digital

Contents

V
NONHUMAN

11. Bridging the Logic-Based and Probability-Based Approaches to Artificial Intelligence

H. LIN

12. Rationality and *Escherichia Coli*

T.-W. HUNG

VI
COMMUNICATION AND EMOTION

13. Rational Belief and Evidence-Based Update

E. McCREADY

List of Contributors

T. Bayne Monash University, Melbourne, VIC, Australia

Y.-M. Fung Hong Kong University of Science & Technology, Hong Kong

I. Gold Departments of Philosophy & Psychiatry, McGill University, Montreal, QC, Canada

J. Hricko Education Center for Humanities and Social Sciences, National Yang-Ming University, Taipei, Taiwan

T.-W. Hung Institute of European and American Studies, Academia Sinica, Taipei, Taiwan

T.J. Lane Taipei Medical University, Graduate Institute of Humanities in Medicine; Taipei Medical University-Shuang Ho Hospital, Brain and Consciousness Research Center, New Taipei City; Academia Sinica, Institute of European and American Studies; National Chengchi University, Research Center for Mind, Brain and Learning, Taipei, Taiwan

N.Y. Louis Lee The Chinese University of Hong Kong, Faculty of Education, Programme for the Gifted and Talented, Hong Kong, China

T. M. Lee Department of Philosophy, Tunghai University, Taichung, Taiwan

W.C. Leong Department of General Education, Macau University of Science and Technology, Macau

H. Lin Department of Philosophy, University of California, Davis, CA, United States

E. McCready Department of English, Aoyama Gakuin University, Shibuya, Tokyo, Japan

S. Nichols Department of Philosophy, University of Arizona, Tucson, AZ, United States

G. Northoff Taipei Medical University, Graduate Institute of Humanities in Medicine; Taipei Medical University-Shuang Ho Hospital, Brain and Consciousness Research Center, New Taipei City; National Chengchi University, Research Center for Mind, Brain and Learning, Taipei, Taiwan; Institute of Mental Health Research, University of Ottawa, Ottawa, ON, Canada

R. Samuels Department of Philosophy, The Ohio State University, Columbus, OH, United States

E.H. Wang Department of Philosophy, National ChenChi University, Taipei City, Taiwan

Preface

Near the conclusion of *Songs of Myself*, Walt Whitman expresses what might be regarded as an irrational attitude toward life: "Do I contradict myself? Very well then I contradict myself." Although contradictions are paradigmatic of irrationality, to read these lines as expressing opposition to rationality would be inappropriately literal. Whitman was nobody's fool: observing the surgical treatment of war casualties and reading essayists like Emerson produced a cast of mind capable of recognizing errors in Cartesian thought, the excesses in phrenology, and the existence of counterintuitive phenomena like phantom limb. Whitman's embrace of contradiction, in addition to serving as a poetic turn-of-phrase, represents the type of rational attitude that motivates this volume: the empirical challenges to rationality that have been mounted over the past half century are best thought of not as a debunking, but as a spur to revise existing theories of rationality in light of those recent discoveries. The problem is not the acknowledgement of contradictions; the problem is to determine a proper response to recognition of those contradictions.

"Rationality" implies more than care in calculation and perspicacious reasoning over that which is familiar. It also implies a persistent tendency to lean into the unknown, a willingness to grapple with the abstruse and explore the uncharted. This tendency necessarily carries with it the risk of contradiction, for what we learn today will often contradict long-held beliefs. Many will shrink from the threat of losing their ideological compass, and some among these will seek succor in the contrived contradictions of mysticism. But a rational strain in human nature compels others to seek to learn from apparent contradiction, by revising beliefs or modifying their scope. The resort to mysticism reflects a loss of nerve; the impetus for rational deliberation reflects a capacity for recognizing ignorance and treating it as an opportunity for novel investigations that can produce new insights.

For nearly half a century rational deliberation itself has been challenged by a series of discoveries that have seemed to call into question basic assumptions about human thought. How we actually think seems to be at odds with many descriptive and prescriptive models that once held great sway in the development of modern science and scholarship. Whereas one response to these discoveries has indeed been a loss of nerve, the proper response—an assumption shared by all the essays contained here—is an active attempt to revise those models, so as to enhance their compatibility with what has been discovered, and to do so in a maximally coherent and inclusive way.

Based upon this shared assumption we have commissioned these essays and compiled this collection. In part the collection is designed so as to further an interdisciplinary reappraisal of the nature of rationality. More specifically, the intent is to contribute to development of a suitably revised, comprehensive understanding of rationality, one that befits the 21st century, one that is adequately informed by recent investigations of science, pathology, nonhuman thought, emotion, and even enigmatic Chinese texts that might previously have seemed to be expressions of irrationalism.

Some of the chapters contained here are based upon presentations delivered at the *2014 IEAS Conference on Reason and Rationality*, which was held from Aug. 14–15, in Taipei, Taiwan. For financial and administrative support provided for that conference, we are grateful to the Institute of European and American Studies at Academia Sinica and its Philosophy Group, especially Drs. Jih-Ching Ho, Norman Y. Teng, Jonathon Hricko, and Hsiang-Yun Chen. Preparations for and development of this book were sponsored in part by the Taiwan Ministry of Science and Technology (formerly, National Science Council), under Grants: 100-2410-H-038-009-MY3, 101-2410-H-001-100-MY2, 102-2420-H-038-001-MY3, 102-2420-H-038-004-MY3, 104-2420-H-038-001-MY3 and 105-2632-H-038-001-MY3. We also express our gratitude to the several anonymous reviewers for their valuable comments, to the editorial assistant at Academia Sinica, Ms Pei-Yun Lee, and to the production project manager at Elsevier, Mr Timothy Bennett, who all contributed greatly to enhancing the quality of this work.

Finally, this book is dedicated to the memory of several scientists and scholars who helped to shepherd the study of rationality through a tumultuous period in intellectual history: Carl G. Hempel, Herbert A. Simon, Paul F. Lazarsfeld, and Anthony "Tony" O'Dea. During the middle and later decades of the 20th century, this group of philosophers, social scientists, and experts in artificial intelligence worked at academic institutions in Pittsburgh, Pennsylvania. Adopting an exemplary interdisciplinary approach, they demonstrated how to begin to address the empirical challenges directed at the prevailing models of rationality. One hope for this volume is that it can serve to both celebrate and build upon their pioneering work.

T.-W. Hung, T.J. Lane
Taipei, Taiwan
Feb. 11, 2016

PART I

INTRODUCTION

For millennia philosophical works have attempted to describe, explicate, and evaluate rationality. Over the last century, new impetus was brought to this endeavor as quantification theory along with the social and behavioral sciences emerged. Yet more recently, over the last several decades, propelled by the emergence of artificial intelligence, cognitive science, evolutionary psychology, neuropsychology, and related fields, even more sophisticated approaches to the study of rationality have emerged. Intriguingly, some among these new lines of inquiry have seemed to suggest that humans are not quite the rational creatures that Aristotle imagined us to be. Indeed, our performance on rational choice experiments is suboptimal, falling short of expected utility or Bayesian prescriptions. Sometimes even experts perform at alarmingly poor levels on tests directly relevant to their areas of expertise. But what suboptimal performances imply about the nature of rationality more generally is contentious, having triggered what is in some quarters referred to as the "rationality wars." Now, however, in large part the dust from those skirmishes has settled. Informed by the turbulence of recent decades, this volume's premise is that the way to advance the project of understanding rationality is to attend to the diverse contexts in which it is realized or fails to be realized, while also attending to how it is modulated. Here we concentrate on diverse though not discrete contexts: scientific, communicative, pathological, nonhuman, ostensible irrationality in Chinese philosophy, and the modulation of reason by emotion. An important step in reassessing "rationality" is to situate it in these variegated contexts, so to better understand how belief-forming processes are shaped and constrained. Future models of rationality will need to be grounded in just such an expansive foundation if they are to further advance this seminal project.

CHAPTER

1

Rationality and its Contexts

T.J. Lane

Taipei Medical University, Graduate Institute of Humanities in Medicine, Taipei, Taiwan; Taipei Medical University–Shuang Ho Hospital, Brain and Consciousness Research Center, New Taipei City, Taiwan; Academia Sinica, Institute of European and American Studies, Taipei, Taiwan; National Chengchi University, Research Center for Mind, Brain and Learning, Taipei, Taiwan

In the centuries-long cultural project of humanity's growing awareness of its place in the universe, evaluating the extent of human rationality represents a seminal project. ***Keith E. Stanovich,*** **The Robot's Rebellion,** ***2005, 92.***

A cursory glance at the list of Nobel laureates for economics is sufficient to confirm Stanovich's description of the project to evaluate human rationality as seminal. Herbert Simon, Reinhard Selten, John Nash, Daniel Kahneman, and others were awarded their prizes less for their work in economics, per se, than for their work on rationality as such. Although philosophical works have for millennia attempted to describe, explicate, and evaluate individual and collective aspects of rationality, new impetus was brought to this endeavor over the last century as mathematical logic along with the social and behavioral sciences emerged. Yet more recently, over the last several decades, propelled by the emergence of artificial intelligence, cognitive science, evolutionary psychology, neuropsychology, and related fields, even more sophisticated approaches to the study of rationality have emerged.

Some among these new lines of inquiry, including those pursued by Kahneman (Kahneman & Tversky, 1972), have been interpreted as implying that humans are not quite the rational creatures that Aristotle imagined us to be (Piattelli-Palmarini, 1994). Indeed, it does seem to be the case that our performance in rational choice experiments is suboptimal, falling short of expected utility or Bayesian prescriptions; sometimes even experts—medical, legal, or engineering—perform at surprisingly and

Rationality. http://dx.doi.org/10.1016/B978-0-12-804600-5.00001-5

alarmingly poor levels on tests directly relevant to their areas of expertise (Kahneman & Tversky, 2000; Nisbett & Ross, 1980; Kahneman, Slovic, & Tversky, 1982). To cite just one example, trained physicians regularly and unnecessarily scare the bejeebers out of patients by committing the base rate fallacy: that is, they exaggerate the significance of positive results in diagnostic tests for relatively rare medical conditions (Hamm, 1996). But what these suboptimal performances imply about the nature of rationality more generally is contentious, having triggered what is in some quarters referred to as the "rationality wars"(Samuels, Stich, & Bishop, 2002).

It might seem that waging academic "war" over scientific findings, even if they do have important implications for how we should regard the consultations of experts, is excessive. But more is at stake than assessment of expertise. Since the assumption that humans are rational is pivotal to our understanding of the type of creature that we are, any significant challenge to that assumption might be felt demoralizing, not unlike the realizations that our species and solar system are products of evolution. Implications of these findings are, potentially, sweeping. One worry is that rationality has been thought by some to be a precondition for many of the capacities that humans exhibit (Davidson, 1984). A second, perhaps more troubling, worry is that if it is the case that we fall very far short of Aristotle's notion of rationality, such a finding might necessitate a dark reassessment of the human capacity for moral responsibility (Dahan-Katz, 2013). There was a time when concerns about moral responsibility were motivated more by the place of humans in the causal structure of the world. Recently, however, the focus of much attention has shifted to rationality and the psychological capacities that constitute its foundation (Morse, 2007), those very capacities that have been called into question. So getting clear about how to interpret the relevant scientific findings is no small thing.

We should be clear, however, about what is not contentious: substantial deviations from subjectively expected utility and Bayesian models are commonplace (Stanovich, 2010). We are not as responsive to reason when choosing beliefs or actions as may once have been thought, or at least hoped. At the personal, conscious level, we are not proficient implementers of Bayesian inference, even though it seems our brains (the subpersonal, nonconscious level) often act like a Bayesian mechanism (Hohwy, 2013). That we are susceptible to personal-level, systematic cognitive bias is no longer subject to dispute. There are limits or "bounds" to human rationality: in the context of decision-making, individual or organizational, what might be optimal is not necessarily what should be expected, for there are always constraints on information-processing capabilities (Simon, 1972, 1983). This is an instance wherein the ought-implies-can principle must be invoked: how we should reason is necessarily constrained by the capabilities of brains and their environments, no matter whether the brains are artificial, nonhuman, human, healthy or unhealthy, and irrespective of whether we are practicing science or reflecting on the seeming irrationality of recondite philosophical texts.

Many among these constraints are temporal, constraints that are most tellingly evident when agents must decide whether or how to act (practical rationality), since such decisions are made in real time. Indeed, even polynomial time greatly constrains the capacity for evaluating belief, despite the fact that within complexity theory polynomial expressions are relatively easy (Ladner, 1975). Other constraints involve the dynamic adjustment of our aspirations to features of unfolding context; decision alternatives for what to believe or how to act are not fixed or predetermined, in the way that seems to have been implied by the von Neumann–Morgenstein utility theorem or other similar normative models that characterize human beings as utility maximizers (von Neuman & Morgenstern, 1944). Instead, our aspirations are discovered in the process of searching. These, then, are adjusted upward or down, in a manner befitting the context of discovery (Selten, 2001).

Obviously, search cannot be unbounded, at least not literally. Normative models like that proposed by von Neumann and Morgenstern posit exhaustive coverage of alternatives, but neither mere mortals nor mere machines can conduct exhaustive searches, especially when it is not even clear just what might count as an alternative. Toward this end, to prune the tree of possibilities and reduce the burdens of evaluating each, we rely heavily upon rules of thumb or heuristic strategies (Gigerenzer & Goldstein, 1996). Often too, the framing of a problem (Tversky & Kahneman, 1981), conversational context (Kahneman & Tversky, 1982, pp. 132–135), and emotion (Damasio, 1999) efficiently, though not necessarily reliably, reduce search space.

Even if there is consensus on goals and their evaluation, search is not made significantly less difficult. In other words, even if we presuppose that the utilities of goals have been antecedently fixed, the problems confronted by mortals and machines do not disappear (Hempel, 1965, pp. 463–472). Deciding how to act, for example, will vary among persons, reflecting different inductive attitudes or degrees of optimism. Mathematical models of decision-making under uncertainty, like the "maximin" and "maximax" rules, reflect these differences. The former represents extreme caution, in that the maxim for action is "assume the worst possible outcome"; the latter, optimism, in that the maxim for action is expect "the best possible outcome."

Simon (1996, pp. 27–30, 119–121) neatly encapsulates many of these ideas with the felicitous, if not altogether aesthetically pleasing, term "satisfice." Rather than optimizing or maximizing, humans tend to satisfice, that is, we tend to choose between better or worse. Choosing that which is best is usually not an option because we rarely have a method of finding the optimum. Bound by practical computational limits, we cannot generate the entire list of possible alternatives nor fully evaluate the merits of those we do manage to generate. These difficulties are compounded by the fact that even were we to stumble upon the best alternative early in the search process, we could not recognize it as the best until after we had generated the entire list. So we satisfice; we conduct moderate, not exhaustive, searches until we find something acceptable, not optimal.

Naturally enough, however, the capacity to search effectively varies greatly. We differ in temperament and talent, as well as in the particular enculturation practices to which we are exposed. These differences matter although in certain important respects, we all must settle for satisficing, people exhibit better or worse capabilities for thinking up new and fruitful possibilities. Like Selten and Simon, Nozick (1993, pp. 172–181) observes that not restricting our search for alternatives to a preexisting set can be a good strategy. Even an inferior choice from among a newly generated list might be better than the best choice from a preexisting list. That which Nozick dubs "rationality's imagination" is important because lacking imagination our searches would not only fail to be exhaustive, they would be myopic. Not all who try to imagine new alternatives will succeed; more than likely a majority will fail. But rationality is as much social as it is individual (Weber, 1978; Lazarsfeld & Oberschall, 1965; Clark, 2001), and one important implication of this fact is that the costs of individual failure do not necessarily affect the group. On the other hand, successes achieved by individuals can have positive effects for the group. Thus society's capacity for insulating the group from individual failure contributes directly to promotion of rationality's more exploratory and risk-incurring features.

It should be acknowledged that von Neuman–Morgenstein utility and similar models have a well-deserved workhorse status, especially within modern economics (Karni, 2014). Nevertheless, it is clear that one among their limitations is the requirement "to abstract away aspects in the contextual environment" (Stanovich, 2005, p. 247). But the constraints that result in our suboptimal, satisficing performance make it abundantly clear that context does matter. Botterill & Carruthers (1999, p. 107) describe the implications of recent empirical and conceptual research thus: "... standards of rationality for belief-forming processes should be relativized to our needs as situated, finite, enquirers after truth." Indeed, a principal goal of this volume is to promote and assist with the task of relativizing the belief-forming processes indicative of rationality to context, features of the environment that utility maximizing models disregard.

It might be objected that enquiring "after truth," sets a goal no less impractical, or conceptually misguided, than exhaustively searching among a tree of possible alternatives. But even scholars who are wary of setting off in search of truth, like Thomas Kuhn, invoke "rationality" and tout the virtues of *rational* theory choice (Kuhn, 2000a). Kuhn is dubious about existing theories of rationality (Kuhn, 2000b, p. 159), viewing them as in need of "readjustment." But he takes explaining the success of science with respect to enhanced efficiency in puzzle solving as a possible starting point for developing new theories of rationality. A principal reason for the organization of this volume is the editors' belief that even if we assume that puzzle solving, or some similar version of "temperate" rationality (Newton-Smith, 1981, pp. 266–273), is a proper platform upon which to begin the task of "readjusting" theories of rationality, puzzle solving itself would still need to be embedded in constraint-sensitive contexts.

Of course Kuhn's discussions of rationality are confined to the context of scientific practice. Given the premise that belief-forming processes need to be contextualized, perhaps it would be better to abandon the project of investigating rationality, in general, and replace it by approaches distinctive of individual disciplines. But to take such a step would be imprudent because even though in many discussions of rationality the normative-descriptive distinction is not sharply drawn (Richardson, 1998, p. 567), there is no basis for treating "rationality" as a purely descriptive, natural kind term like, say, "fire," which underwent radical reclassification after the discovery that burning wood, rusting iron, and biological metabolism all involve oxidation, whereas the sun, lightning, northern lights, and fireflies do not (Churchland, 2002, pp. 129–131). There is no reason to anticipate discovery of an analogue to oxidation; ipso facto, there is no reason to expect that a similar compartmentalized reduction of "rationality" is in the offing.

But warning that investigations of "rationality" should not be segregated is grounded in more than an intuition that its conceptual status is unlike "fire." Although "rationality" remains somewhat diffuse, we have good reason to believe that it is a disposition shared by all cognitive agents, an important factor in marking the distinction between, say, rendering judgments and being lost in reverie (Byron, 2004). To say that rationality plays more of a role in the former than it does in the latter is to say something substantial. To a first approximation, it is that in virtue of which agents adopt or act upon beliefs, appropriately. Despite the obvious imprecision of this definition, it seems to identify a perfectly general capacity for forming true beliefs and performing successful actions, a capacity that transcends the presuppositions of any particular context or community, a capacity that is applicable to individuals or groups, to political economists or scientists, to peoples of all sociohistorical contexts, perhaps even to nonhumans (Trigg, 1993, p. 62). What is more, it is that which is lost or diminished when agents suffer from certain pathological conditions; in fact, it is often a symptom of those conditions (Bortolotti, 2010).

This general capacity seems to be what Quine (1976, p. 233) is referring to when he writes "science is itself a continuation of common sense. The scientist is indistinguishable from the common man in his sense of evidence, except that the scientist is more careful." Scientists are dependent upon a "primitive sense of evidence," that they use "carefully and systematically." Both the common man and the scientist are agents who adopt or act upon beliefs, appropriately, albeit while exhibiting contextually shaped standards for what counts as appropriate. The "primitive sense of evidence" is a reflection of our capacity for rationality; "care and system" are what enable us to overcome—in a manner that is relativized to context—the many cognitive biases that have recently been described. It is that same care and system that make possible a bootstrapping of ourselves from common sense rationality to scientific rationality.

Quine (1976, p. 234) proceeds to observe that even the very preference for simplicity "is a lay habit carried over by science." He adds that the simpler of two hypotheses is generally regarded "not only as the more desirable but also as the more probable" (1976, p. 255). The latter point, concerning the greater probability of a simpler hypothesis being true, appears to be a point at which Simon and Quine converge, satisfice and simplify find common ground. In Simon's terms, we satisfice rather than optimize, but seem none too much the worse for having done so. Perhaps our bounded rationality is of a piece with our preference for simplicity, and it is a reliable guide to navigating this uncertain world because we have developed sufficiently simple and successful strategies. These strategies are foundational, part of the common core that makes an interdisciplinary approach to rationality so apt.

Nevertheless, there is no denying that the attempt to understand rationality in a way that is not bound to any one domain or tradition is partially influenced by philosophy's predilection for an expansive approach to scholarship. In the words of Sellars (1962, p. 1), philosophy aims "to understand how things in the broadest possible sense of the term hang together in the broadest possible sense of the term." Although many of the essays collected here are animated by empirical work, this is primarily a philosophical work, one that aims to contribute to understanding how scientific, pathological, nonhuman, pedestrian, and other forms of rationality, even serious meditations on irrationality, "hang together."

To place this volume in historical context, it is an attempt to help make sense of an entire, millennia-long enterprise that has undergone an abrupt, somewhat rude awakening in recent decades. To a considerable extent, economists and philosophers have aligned with one another in a tug-of-war with psychologists over "rationality." Much but not all of the tension is more apparent than real because philosophers and economists have tended to emphasize theoretical and normative aspects (Rescher, 1988), while psychologists have tended to emphasize its practical and descriptive aspects (Kahneman, 2011). Nevertheless, it would be foolish to disregard the impact of recent psychological studies; after all, their having garnered a lion's share of Nobel Prizes for economics is not without warrant. But the evident influence of those studies does not justify wholesale refutation of positions adopted by a generation of economists and philosophers.

The proper response to conflicts over "rationality" is, instead, to call in a plumber. Midgley (2001, p. 37) opines that "when the conflicts get so bad that we do notice them, we need to call in a philosophic plumber." The rationality wars were, in their more heated, overwrought moments, just that bad. In those moments, amid the handwringing over potentially "bleak implications for human rationality" (Nisbett & Borgida, 1975), a niche was created, a need for philosophers to plumb. Now that much of the dust has settled, toward what ends should the philosophic plumbers direct their efforts?

Acknowledging that belief-forming processes are constrained does not imply that constraints cannot be satisfied locally, or in a manner that is relativized to specific contexts (Glymour, 1992, pp. 361–363). We can apply what has been learned in recent decades to specific contexts, searching for, plumbing, perhaps even correcting some erroneous beliefs and errors in belief formation. Both in spite of and because of our bounded rationality this is doable. Since search space is restricted we know where to look, and because of subjective expected utility and Bayesian models, as well as, our familiarity with cognitive bias, we know what to look for.

Although the focus of this volume is on rationality as it is realized, or fails to be realized, in specific contexts, we do as well keep an eye on how distinct pockets of localized rationality "hang together," reflecting rationality "in the broadest possible sense of the term." After all, global considerations are often called upon to override local; what is best or better provincially and provisionally might not be abiding or perdurable in the broader scheme of things. Central banks and citizens might believe printing money a good way to revive depressed economies, until inflation sets in, negating the benefits of having more currency in circulation and triggering fears among neighbors of sovereign default.

Even apparent pathologies of rationality can be informative as regards how to comprehend rationality in the broad sense of the term. It is often the case that when normal functions are damaged the nature of remaining capabilities can be seen with greater clarity (Frith, 1998). To cite just two examples, investigations of delusion can help us to better assess epistemic goodness (Bortolotti, 2015) and investigations of depression can help us to better understand the nature of belief (Lane & Flanagan, 2015). Similarly, investigations of rationality in nonhuman animals can assist with the drawing of important distinctions among types of rationality (Bermudez, 2003), while investigations of artificial intelligence can assist with understanding how knowledge relevance is or should be determined (Ford and Pylyshyn, 1996).

Of course in this broader sense we can only strive to approximate rationality, and the effort devoted to this task is carried out in the dark, so to speak, since there is no mature consensus theory of approximation. A time-honored alternative to approximation of the ideal is avoidance of error, a view associated with Pearce's "self-correcting thesis" (Mayo, 2005), a thesis no less problematic than the attempt to approximate rationality's ideal. Nevertheless, human success at having bootstrapped ourselves from common sense to science shows that taking concepts like "approximation of rationality" and "avoidance of irrationality" as rough-and-ready goals can drive progress.

But how does progress occur when the goal is inexact? Consider that every schoolboy learns to identify "north" in a rough-and-ready way by facing the sun before noontime and extending his left arm to the left side; a slightly more sophisticated technique, provided one is in the Northern Hemisphere, is to identify Polaris at Ursa Minor's handle tip. But neither of these will indicate true or geodesic north with precision; for that, surveying techniques are required. Complicating matters even more, geodesic north is distinct from magnetic north, the direction pointed to by a compass. And there are yet more distinct meanings of "north." Nevertheless, people have been finding their way north, approximately, for millennia, with methods that any child can learn.

Approximating rationality is like heading north. Human beings had probably been tilting toward rationality since the Pleistocene, long before Aristotle's theory of the syllogism, a seminal development that led to centuries of advances in rational thought, including the mathematical logic of Frege and Russell. During the last half century the pace of progress has accelerated, albeit in a way that was unanticipated. The very idea that we are rational has been challenged by findings from cognitive science, psychology, and related disciplines. Flashpoints have been many: base rate neglect, availability cascade, conjunction fallacy, belief perseverance, and so on. A modest conclusion that can be derived from these experimental findings about how humans reason is that we need a context-sensitive, carefully nuanced reassessment of rationality; a radical conclusion, as folk and scientific or scholarly models of rationality are deeply confused. This volume takes the former, not the latter, as its premise. Humans are predictably "irrational" at times, when dealing with some kinds of problems, when impaired, and when in certain contexts. But by attending closely to those varied contexts, and informed by a half century of scientific studies and philosophical efforts to achieve reflective equilibrium, the study of rationality can be rejuvenated, even applied to sober attempts at assessing irrationality.

Rationality cannot be approached asymptotically, not literally that is. Nevertheless, we can make more satisfactory our precisifications of "rationality" or its approximation. By aiming in its general direction, through analyses of some diverse contexts in which it is realized, while attending to various ways in which it is modulated, the project of understanding rationality can forge ahead. In this volume we concentrate on diverse but not discrete contexts: scientific, communicative, pathological, nonhuman, ostensible irrationality in Chinese philosophy, and the modulation of reason by emotion. This scope and variety is well suited to this early postrationality wars era. An important step in reassessing "rationality" is to situate it in variegated contexts, so to better understand how belief-forming processes are relativized and constrained. Future models of rationality, whether descriptive or normative, will need to be grounded in just such an expansive foundation, if they are to further advance this seminal project.

Acknowledgments

For the generous giving of their time to detailed discussions of rationality and its constraints, I express heartfelt gratitude to Reinhard Selten as well as to all participants in the Conference on Reason and Rationality, hosted by Academia Sinica's Institute of European and American Studies. And, for discussions of these and related matters from days passed but not forgotten, the author is also grateful to Herbert Simon, Paul Lazarsfeld, Carl Hempel, and Tony O'Dea. Funding for this research was, in part, provided by National Science Council (Ministry of Science and Technology) of Taiwan Research Grants 100-2410-H-038-009-MY3, 102-2420-H-038-001-MY3, and 104-2420-H-038-001-MY3.

References

Bermudez, J. L. (2003). *Thinking without words*. New York: Oxford University Press.

Bortolotti, L. (2010). *Delusions and other irrational beliefs*. New York: Oxford University Press.

Bortolotti, L. (2015). The epistemic innocence of motivated delusions. *Consciousness and Cognition*, *33*, 490–499.

Botterill, G., & Carruthers, P. (1999). *The philosophy of psychology*. New York: Cambridge University Press.

Byron, M. (Ed.). (2004). *Satisficing and maximizing: Moral theorists on practical reason*. New York: Cambridge University Press.

Churchland, P. S. (2002). *Brain-wise: Studies in neurophilosophy*. Cambridge, MA: The MIT Press.

Clark, A. (2001). Reasons, robots and the extended mind. *Mind and Language*, *16*(2), 121–145.

Dahan-Katz, L. (2013). The implications of heuristics and biases research on moral and legal responsibility: A case against the reasonable person standard. In N. A. Vincent (Ed.), *Neuroscience and legal responsibility* (pp. 135–161). New York: Oxford University Press.

Damasio, A. R. (1999). *The feeling of what happens*. New York: Harcourt Brace.

Davidson, D. (1984). *Inquiries into truth and interpretation*. Oxford: Clarendon Press.

Ford, K. M., & Pylyshyn, Z. W. (Eds.). (1996). *The robot's dilemma revisited: The frame problem of artificial intelligence*. New York: Praeger.

Frith, C. D. (1998). Deficits and pathologies. In W. Bechtel, & G. Graham (Eds.), *A companion to cognitive science* (pp. 380–390). Malden, MA: Blackwell.

Gigerenzer, G., & Goldstein, D. G. (1996). Reasoning the fast and frugal way: Models of bounded rationality. *Psychological Review*, *103*, 650–669.

Glymour, C. (1992). *Thinking things through*. Cambridge, MA: The MIT Press.

Hamm, R. M. (1996). Physicians neglect base rates, and it matters. *Behavioral and Brain Sciences*, *19*, 25–26.

Hempel, C. G. (1965). *Aspects of scientific explanation: And other essays in the philosophy of science*. New York: The Free Press.
Hohwy, J. (2013). *The predictive mind*. Oxford, UK: Oxford University Press.
Kahneman, D. (2011). *Thinking, fast and slow*. New York: Farrar, Straus and Giroux.
Kahneman, D., Slovic, P., & Tversky, A. (Eds.). (1982). *Judgment and uncertainty: Heuristics and biases*. Cambridge: Cambridge University Press.
Kahneman, D., & Tversky, A. (1972). Subjective probability. *Cognitive Psychology, 3*, 430–454.
Kahneman, D., & Tversky, A. (1982). On the study of statistical intuition. *Cognition, 11*, 123–142.
Kahneman, D., & Tversky, A. (Eds.). (2000). *Choices, values, and frames*. Cambridge: Cambridge University Press.
Karni, E. (2014). Axiomatic foundations of expected utility and subjective probability. In M. Machina, & K. Viscusi (Eds.), *Handbook of the economics of risk and uncertainty* (pp. 1–39). Amsterdam: Elsevier.
Kuhn, T. (2000a). Rationality and theory choice. In J. Conant, & J. Haugeland (Eds.), *The road since Structure* (pp. 208–215). Chicago, IL: The University of Chicago Press.
Kuhn, T. (2000b). Reflections on my critics. In J. Conant, & J. Haugeland (Eds.), *The road since Structure* (pp. 123–175). Chicago, IL: The University of Chicago Press.
Ladner, R. E. (1975). On the structure of polynomial time reducibility. *Journal of the Association of Computing Machinery, 22*, 155–171.
Lane, T., & Flanagan, O. (2015). Neuroexistentialism, eudaimonics, and positive illusions. In B. Kaldis (Ed.), *Mind and society: Cognitive science meets the social sciences*. Synthese Library Series: Studies in Epistemology, Logic, Methodology, and Philosophy of Science. Dordrecht, Netherlands: Springer.
Lazarsfeld, P. F., & Oberschall, A. R. (1965). Max Weber and empirical social research. *American Sociological Research, 31*(2), 185–199.
Mayo, D. G. (2005). Peircean induction and the error-correcting thesis. *Transactions of the Charles S. Peirce Society: A Quarterly Journal in American Philosophy, 41*(2), 299–319.
Midgley, M. (2001). *Science and poetry*. London: Routledge & Kegan Paul.
Morse, S. J. (2007). New neuroscience, old problems: Legal implications of brain science. In W. Glannon (Ed.), *Defining right and wrong in brain science* (pp. 195–205). Washington, DC: Dana Press.
Newton-Smith, W. H. (1981). *The rationality of science*. London: Routledge & Kegan Paul.
Nisbett, R., & Borgida, E. (1975). Attribution and the psychology of prediction. *Journal of Personality and Social Psychology, 32*(5), 932–943.
Nisbett, R., & Ross, L. (1980). *Human inference*. Englewood Cliffs, NJ: Prentice-Hall.
Nozick, R. (1993). *The nature of rationality*. Princeton, NJ: Princeton University Press.
Piattelli-Palmarinia, M. (1994). *Inevitable illusions: How mistakes of reason rule our minds*. New York: John Wiley & Sons.
Quine, W. V. (1976). *The ways of paradox and other essays, Revised and enlarged edition*. Cambridge, MA: Harvard University Press.
Rescher, N. (1988). *Rationality: A philosophical inquiry into the nature and rationale of reason*. New York: Oxford University Press.
Richardson, R. C. (1998). Heuristics and satisficing. In W. Bechtel, & G. Graham (Eds.), *A companion to cognitive science* (pp. 566–575). Malden, MA: Blackwell Publishers.
Samuels, R., Stich, S., & Bishop, M. (2002). Ending the rationality wars: How to make disputes about human rationality disappear. In R. Elio (Ed.), *Common sense, reasoning, and rationality* (pp. 236–268). New York: Oxford University Press.
Sellars, W. (1962). *Empiricism and the philosophy of mind*. London: Routledge & Kegan Paul.
Selten, R. (2001). What is bounded rationality? In G. Gigerenzer, & R. Selten (Eds.), *Bounded rationality: The adaptive toolbox* (pp. 13–36). Cambridge, MA: The MIT Press.
Simon, H. (1972). Theories of bounded rationality. In C. McGuire, & R. Radner (Eds.), *Decision and organization* (pp. 161–176). Amsterdam: North-Holland.

Simon, H. (1983). *Reason in human affairs*. Stanford, CA: Stanford University Press.
Simon, H. (1996). *The sciences of the artificial* (3rd ed.). Cambridge, MA: The MIT Press.
Stanovich, K. E. (2005). *The robot's rebellion: Finding meaning in the age of Darwin*. Chicago, IL: The University of Chicago Press.
Stanovich, K. E. (2010). *Rationality and the reflective mind*. New York: Oxford University Press.
Trigg, R. (1993). *Rationality and science: Can science explain everything?* Cambridge, MA: Blackwell.
Tversky, A., & Kahneman, D. (1981). The framing of decisions and the psychology of choice. *Science, 211*, 453–458.
von Neumann, J., & Morgenstern, O. (1944). *The theory of games and economic behavior*. Princeton, NJ: Princeton University Press.
Weber, M. (1978). *Economy and society: An outline of interpretive sociology*. Oakland, CA: University of California Press.

PART II

SCIENCE

Scientific practice is regarded by many as the best example of rational thought. But even just one day spent in a laboratory devoted to designing experiments, setting parameters, collecting data, and analyzing data is sufficient to familiarize the uninitiated with science's disheveled, occasionally even irrational, aspects. Nevertheless, science does evince standards of rationality that enable it to advance at an ever-accelerating pace. In this section our authors explore three themes: the role of simplicity in causal explanation, the difference between what scientific rationality permits and what it requires, as well as, the possibility that the discipline of psychology exhibits systematic bias.

In "Bayesian Psychology and Human Rationality" (Chapter 2), Shaun Nichols and Richard Samuels explore the implications of recent psychological research that have led some philosophers to reach pessimistic conclusions about human rationality. They counter that recent Bayesian approaches to learning and inference offer prospects for a more optimistic view. In developing this line of thought, they provide a characterization of rationality that attempts to accommodate the manifest fact that people find some Bayesian problems challenging. In developing their ideas, they explore one empirical example in detail: work on the role of simplicity in causal explanation.

In "Scientific Rationality: Phlogiston as a Case Study" (Chapter 3), Jonathon Hricko examines Hasok Chang's recent work on the chemical revolution, focusing on claims that retention of phlogiston could have benefited science. Hricko considers some of the advantages and disadvantages of retaining phlogiston and argues that it was rational for chemists to eliminate phlogiston, but it also would have been rational to retain it. He concludes that there is a sense in which scientific rationality concerns what is permissible, as opposed to what is required.

In "Cross-cultural Differences in Thinking: Some Thoughts on Psychological Paradigms" (Chapter 4), Ngar Yin Louis Lee considers to what extent human thinking reflects cross-cultural psychological differences. Critics of some psychological studies have pointed out that most research on thinking has been carried out on biased samples: Western, educated, industrialized, rich, and democratic (WEIRD) subjects. Accordingly, the universality of these findings should be challenged. Lee explores the possibility that the problems are more substantial than mere sample bias: perhaps methodologies in the psychology of thinking are inherently biased toward explaining the behavior of people whose enculturation occurred in a Western society. Taking this yet further, Lee meditates on the possibility that the discipline of psychology itself might be a product of Western culture to such a degree that its ability to uncover universal aspects of human thinking is much constrained.

CHAPTER

2

Bayesian Psychology and Human Rationality

S. Nichols, R. Samuels***

*Department of Philosophy, University of Arizona, Tucson, AZ, United States; **Department of Philosophy, The Ohio State University, Columbus, OH, United States

2.1 INTRODUCTION

Human beings make lots of mistakes. It does not take a study to show that when we are drunk, tired, or in the grip of rage, we can believe and do some very silly things. But according to an enormously influential vein of scientific research, one that has dominated the study of human judgment and decision-making for more than four decades, we are error prone in far more fundamental ways. Across a very wide range of judgment and decision-making tasks, people appear to make errors that systematically violate familiar canons of rationality (Baron, 2008; Pohl, in press). This has led many to conclude that the formal theories encoding these canons—the probability calculus and expected utility theory in particular—simply fail to describe human cognition. More generally, the evidence of deep deficiencies in human reasoning has led some philosophers and psychologists to worry that human beings are not, as previously supposed, rational beings at all—that we "lack the correct programs for many important judgmental tasks" and lack "an intellect capable of dealing conceptually with uncertainty" (Slovic et al., 1976, p. 174).

This pessimistic interpretation of the research on human inference is not, of course, without its detractors. One very common response is to criticize, on methodological grounds, the various experiments that are supposed to support such pessimism (Schwarz, 1996; Gigerenzer, 1996). Another is to reject the normative standards typically adopted by proponents of the pessimistic interpretation (Gigerenzer and Gaissmaier, 2011). But perhaps the most influential line of response comes from recent efforts

Rationality. http://dx.doi.org/10.1016/B978-0-12-804600-5.00002-7

to apply Bayesian statistics to cognition. Over the past decade, the development of Bayesian models has become pervasive across the cognitive sciences, including vision science, linguistics, memory research, developmental psychology, and the psychology of reasoning. Although these models vary considerably, one widely shared presumption is that human cognition is, in some quite fundamental sense, well described by Bayesian probability theory. Further, since Bayesian cognitive scientists—in full agreement with proponents of the pessimistic interpretation—view probability theory as a normative theory of rationality, they also contend that human cognition is in some quite fundamental sense rational. As one group of prominent researchers has put it:

> [I]t seems increasingly plausible that human cognition may be explicable in rational probabilistic terms and that, in core domains, human cognition approaches an optimal level of performance. (Chater et al., 2006)

Thus in contrast to the pessimism described earlier, Bayesian cognitive scientists tend to be optimistic when it comes to matters of human rationality.

This paper is part of a larger project in which we chart carefully the implications of Bayesian research in cognitive science for debates over the extent of human rationality. In most general terms, our question is this:

> The Vindication Question: To what extent does recent Bayesian psychological research vindicate the contention that human cognition is rational?

Addressing this question turns on triangulating three kinds of issues: (1) issues about the norms of rationality, (2) issues about the nature of Bayesian cognitive models, and (3) empirical research regarding the fit between these models and actual human performance. In the present paper, we restrict ourselves to clarifying the issue of how Bayesian norms should be construed, and to working through one particular study—due to Tania Lombrozo—which illustrates some of the complexities involved in assessing the implications of Bayesian research for claims about the extent of human rationality. Though the conclusions we reach are by necessity provisional, the position we adopt is neither as pessimistic as some would advocate, nor as optimistic as others. Judgments are more sensitive to evidence than is suggested by the pessimists, but it's far less than optimal.

2.2 THE STANDARD PICTURE AND THE STANDARD EMPIRICAL CHALLENGE

In order to assess how Bayesian research bears on issues about the extent of human rationality, we need some normative standard against which the quality of human inference can be measured: an account that specifies how one ought to make judgments and decisions. As one might expect, there is considerable debate in both philosophy and the social sciences concerning this issue. Nevertheless, there is widespread consensus among reasoning researchers in general, and Bayesians in particular, that the default standard is what the philosopher Edward Stein has called the standard picture of rationality.[1]

2.2.1 First Pass

According to the standard picture (SP):

> [T]o be rational is to reason in accordance with principles of reasoning that are based on rules of logic, probability theory and so forth. If the standard picture of reasoning [rationality] is right, principles of reasoning that are based on such rules are normative principles of reasoning, namely they are the principles we ought to reason in accordance with. (Stein, 1996, p. 4)

This characterization of SP is very widely adopted in the literature, often by quoting exactly the passage cited previously. We find a very similar description from psychologists Chase, Hertwig, and Gigerenzer (1998):

> Most researchers of inference share a vision of rationality whose roots trace back to the Enlightenment. This now classical view holds that the laws of human inference are equivalent to the laws of probability and logic (p. 206).[2]

With one significant caveat, which we discuss below, this characterization accurately captures the received view of rationality within the intellectual communities most relevant to our present discussion, though, as we will soon see, it excludes many others. Most importantly, it clearly captures the attitudes of Bayesian cognitive science. In a recent, influential paper, for example, Perfors and coworkers are quite clear that they view logic and probability theory as the normative core of a theory of rationality:

> Bayesian probability theory is not simply a set of ad hoc rules useful for manipulating and evaluating statistical information: it is also the set of unique, consistent rules for conducting plausible inference (Jaynes, 2003). In essence, it is an extension of deductive logic to the case where propositions have degrees of truth or falsity—that is, it is identical to deductive logic if we know all the propositions with 100% certainty. Just as formal logic describes a deductively correct way of thinking, Bayesian probability theory describes an inductively correct way of thinking. As Laplace (1816) said, "probability theory is nothing but common sense reduced to calculation." (Perfors et al., 2011a,b)

In short, not merely do Bayesian cognitive scientists think that probability theory is a powerful descriptive resource, they also maintain that it constitutes a core aspect of a normative theory of rationality. In what follows we assume a conception of SP incorporates Bayesian probability as a part.

Now for the caveat. It is important to notice a lacuna in the previous characterizations of SP. As a matter of fact, the aspects of the rationality debate on which philosophers have tended to focus are those concerned with theoretical reasoning: roughly, reasoning concerned with the making of judgments and revision of belief. The principles of reasoning most relevant to such tasks, and the ones foregrounded by Stein, are those derived from logic and probability theory—hence the reference to "principles of reasoning ... based on rules of logic, probability theory and so forth." But the "so forth" covers a class of principles that ought not to be ignored. For there is more to reasoning than theoretical reasoning. In addition, there is practical reasoning, which is concerned not so much with what to believe as with what to do, with the making of decisions. Despite the tendency of philosophers to focus on theoretical reasoning, it is quite clear that those psychologists and behavioral economists interested in human rationality are at least as interested in practical reasoning—with how well we make decisions. And just as there are principles of theoretical reasoning derived from the formal theories, there are also principles of practical reasoning based on formal theories, albeit expected utility theory as opposed to logic or probability theory (von Neumann & Morgenstern, 1944). Indeed much of the most important empirical work on reasoning by Kahneman and Tversky, (1979) among others, has concerned the extent to which human decision-making conforms to the dictates of expected utility theory. In view of this, a more complete characterization of SP ought to make reference to expected utility theory as well as logic and probability theory. This will be important to our discussion in later sections.

2.2.2 Accordance Conditions and the Standard Picture

It is common to note that implicit in SP is a general view about normative standards, sometimes called *deontology* (Stich, 1990; Samuels, Stich, & Bishop, 2002). What deontologists quite generally maintain is that what it is to reason correctly—what is constitutive of good reasoning—is to reason in accord with the appropriate set of rules or principles. The SP adds to this a specification of what the appropriate rules are, viz, ones based on logic, probability theory, etc.

All this is, of course, familiar territory. What is less commonly noted, however, is that this view of rationality has a crucial lacuna: there is no specification of what accordance with the rules requires. The problem is that these accordance conditions can be specified in quite different ways; and different specifications lead to quite different conclusions, both about the plausibility of SP as a normative standard, and about the extent of human rationality. In what follows we consider, and eliminate, two obvious conceptions of accordance before suggesting an alternative, more tenable view, one that we think makes better sense of Bayesian claims regarding human rationality.

2.2.2.1 *Accordance as Optimal Performance*

Let us start by eliminating a conception of accordance conditions that is obviously too strong. Imagine an agent whose beliefs, inferences, and decisions always conformed to SP. Such an agent would, for example, satisfy the coherence conditions specified by Bayesian probability theory and would always maximize expected utility. The performance of such an agent would accord precisely with that prescribed by SP. It would perform optimally by the lights of SP.

Of course, no one—not even the most ardent Bayesian—claims that humans accord with SP in this way. It is very clear that fatigue, intoxication, distraction, limits of attention and memory, and a host of other factors result in errors. That we make such performance errors is common ground between all parties (for further discussion, see Stein, 1996, Chapter 1, and Stanovich, 1999). That is not to say, of course, that disagreements about the extent of human rationality never concern performance. There are, for example, plenty of disagreements concerning the precise extent to which our inferences and judgments fit the patterns prescribed by SP. But such matters are almost invariably secondary to issues about the extent to which our underlying inferential competences are normatively appropriate (Stein, 1996). Indeed data about performance are typically of central interest only to the extent that they are considered to help assess claims about the nature of this underlying competence.

2.2.2.2 *Strong Algorithmic Accordance*

Though there are many ways to construe inferential competences,[3] when researchers are interested in whether an inferential process is normatively appropriate they very typically supposes that competences are to be construed as algorithmic level descriptions of psychological processes. This is, for example, what Slovic et al. appear to be assuming in the passage quoted earlier, when they suggest that humans "lack the correct programs for many important judgmental tasks."[4] Suppose this is so, that the relevant level of normative assessment is a Marrian algorithmic level. Then accordance with SP should also be an algorithmic requirement. Further, on such a view it is natural to think that accordance with SP requires some stepwise isomorphism between the mathematics of probability theory and the inferential process under consideration. So, for example, accordance with Bayes rule would require that a cognitive process conform, in a stepwise fashion, to the mathematical operations required to compute Bayes rule.[5]

Though seldom articulated, we suspect the present view, which we call strong algorithmic accordance, is implicit in many discussions of SP, especially among those who reject SP on the basis of familiar tractability considerations (Gigerenzer et al., 1999). As many theorists have noted, executing optimal inferential principles, such as Bayes rule, are extraordinarily, computationally demanding. For example, as Harman notes:

> If one is to be prepared for various possible conditionalizations, then for every proposition P one wants to update, one must already have assigned probabilities to various conjunctions of P together with one or more of the possible evidence propositions and/or their denials... [T]o be prepared for coming to accept or reject any of ten evidence propositions, one would have to record probabilities of over a thousand such conjunctions for each proposition one is interested in updating (Harman, 1986, 25–26)

Thus Bayesian conditionalization is intractable in the technical sense that it is superpolynomial in the size of the input.[6] But more importantly, given the computational demandingness of Bayesian calculations, we can know—even before entering the lab—that people are not doing these calculations. In which case, if the standard picture requires of rational agents that they solve these problems by actually doing the computations, the consequences appear dire for either SP or human rationality. One might accept the characterization of rationality offered by SP but deny that people are rational. Alternatively, one might maintain that SP is mistaken. Indeed, one might do so precisely because SP entails that people are not rational. For as Rysiew notes: "Insofar, then, as we wish to preserve even the possibility that humans are rational... SP seems like a pretty unsatisfactory account of what rationality requires" (Rysiew, 2008, p. 1165).

If the forementioned is correct, then a commitment to both SP and the claim that humans are rational would appear unstable. Specifically it would seem that one cannot insist, as Bayesian cognitive scientists do, that probability theory is normative and that it accurately describes human inferential processes. Yet for all the familiarity of this conclusion, we think it is mistaken. A very different but in our view more sensible reaction is to note that the dilemma turns on an uncharitable reading of SP. The claim that we cannot satisfy the norms of SP turns on assuming a strong algorithmic conception of accordance—that we would need to solve computationally difficult problems, such as belief updating, by actually doing the computations specified by SP. But if this is so, then rather than rejecting SP, we think it is reasonable merely to reject a strong algorithmic conception of SP's accordance conditions. On such a view, there is no need either to reject the rationality of human cognition or to dispense with SP. Rather, what is required is an alternative, more sensible construal of accordance conditions. What might this be?

2.2.2.3 *Weak Algorithmic Accordance*

In our view, there is a natural answer to this question, which is well motivated by how scientists explicitly handle the task of analyzing large data sets. In brief, scientists routinely confront statistical problems that cannot be solved by analytic methods. To calculate analytically the denominator in Bayes theorem, for example, one needs to sum the joint probabilities of each combination of values from each variable. And in order to do this, the number of joints that need to be calculated increases exponentially as the number of variables increases (eg, if there are 5 variables, each with 4 values, then the number of joints that need to be calculated are 4^5). In problems with many variables, this is intractable, not just for our people, but for our most powerful supercomputers.

In such instances, what do scientists do? What they do not do is throw up their hands and exclaim that no rational means of calculation is available. Instead they develop and deploy various approximation techniques. Over the last 20 years or so, researchers have developed a range of sampling methods that approximate Bayesian inference: for example, Markov Chain Monte Carlo methods such as the Metropolis Hastings algorithm. To get an intuitive sense of how such methods work, imagine there is a box in front of you that contains hundreds of dice of different denominations. Your task is to estimate the average result of a roll of a die randomly taken from the box. The analytic solution would require identifying all of the different dice, their denominations, their biases, and computing the priors for each die type and the likelihoods for each value for each die type. And even for a few dozen dice, this would vastly exceed available computational resources. Here is an alternative, more tractable strategy. Instead of seeking an analytic solution, you could just sample from the box: randomly pull out a die, roll it, record the result, replace, and repeat. This provides you with a sample from the posterior distribution; and if you collect a sufficiently large sample, you can use the average of these values to estimate the true mean. Further, the sample can be used to calculate other features of the probability distribution, such as, the error and standard deviation.

Clearly such an approximation of Bayesian inference is not an analytic solution. In a sense, it does not use Bayesian inference at all. It is not as if these kinds of method use Bayes theorem, for example. Instead, they provide reliable and general methods that enable scientists to bypass the need for analytic solutions. Further, such sampling methods are very typically the best, feasible options available to scientists; and for this reason, they have been used across a broad array of fields, including epidemiology (Hamra, MacLehose, & Richardson, 2013), population genetics (Beaumont, Zhang, & Balding, 2002), and astronomy (Van der Sluys et al., 2008). Further—and this is our main point—no one would seriously deny that it is rational for scientists to use such methods. That is, tacit in scientific practice is the presumption that such methods are rational. Indeed, we suspect that denying this presumption would be viewed by most—ourselves included—as just plain silly.

What does all this have to do with how best to construe SP? If it is rational for scientists to deploy approximation techniques to handle otherwise intractable computational problems, then we maintain it is no less rational for individual cognizers to do so. In other words, we think that, construed algorithmically, accordance with SP should require no more than good approximation methods, at any rate, not when analytic solutions are infeasible. To a first approximation, then, we propose the following construal of accordance:

> Weak Algorithmic Accordance: Where no tractable analytic solution is available, a cognitive process (or system) accords with SP—Bayesian norms, in particular—when it implements a technique that constitutes a good Bayesian approximation method.

This proposal requires some unpacking. First of all, notice that is it less demanding than strong algorithmic accordance in at least two respects. First, it does not require that we possess God-like computational abilities. This is because the runtime properties of good approximation algorithms are, more or less by definition, more feasible than those of optimal solutions. In particular, they are not superpolynomial on the size of the input. Second, though perhaps less obviously, weak algorithmic accordance is less demanding in the sense that it does not require that our inferential competences—absent performance errors—compute the Bayesian optima. Recall, on the strong algorithmic conception, an inferential competence must be isomorphic to the formal principles of SP. But since these principles define the optimal function, it also follows that a rational competence must underwrite optimal computation. In contrast, the requirement that a reasoning process implement a good Bayesian approximation method imposes no such demand, since an approximation algorithm can be very good—indeed even if it systematically deviates from the optima.

So, we have explained two respects in which weak algorithmic accordance yields a less demanding, and more tenable, construal of SP. But we also need to say more about what demands it does impose, specifically what counts as a good Bayesian approximation technique. As one might expect, there is a great deal to be said here. Indeed, there is an enormous literature in theoretical computer science regarding the desiderata on approximation techniques and how best to implement them.[7] Further, there is a very substantial literature on sampling methods, such as Monte Carlo Markov Chain methods and Gibbs filters. But for the moment, we restrict ourselves to four comments.

First, good approximation techniques are developed in such a way as ensure generality. Specifically, approximation methods are almost invariably designed to produce a result across the full range of a problem's instances, where a problem is defined by its optimal solution. In the case of Bayesian sampling methods, the problem is defined by the optimal, that is, Bayesian, means of calculating posterior probabilities. So, good Bayesian approximation techniques reliably approximate the Bayesian optima for a very wide range of cases.

Second, good approximation techniques are very typically capable, subject to resource limitations, of achieving extremely close approximations to the optima. In the case of Bayesian sampling methods, such as the Metropolis–Hastings algorithm, the result asymptotes to the optima as a function of the number of samples that are taken.

Third, and importantly for our purposes, good Bayesian approximation techniques require a sensitivity to large amounts of relevant information. Though they permit tractable computation in part by not considering every available piece of information, the dual demands of generality and close approximation to the Bayesian optima require that such methods sample very widely, and in an unbiased fashion, from the posterior distribution. In this regard, they are quite unlike many of the inferential methods recently popularized by cognitive scientists, such as the fast and frugal heuristics, well known from the work of Gerd Gigerenzer and his collaborators, which we discuss briefly in the next section. For in contrast to Bayesian sampling methods, such heuristics solve judgmental tasks despite ignoring virtually all the available information (Gigerenzer et al., 1999).

Finally, what counts as a good (ie, rational) approximation technique to use can vary across contexts. Imagine two approximation algorithms for the same problem, one is slow but highly accurate, the other is fast but less accurate. In a context where accuracy is highly valued and speed is not, then it is irrational to use the fast approximation algorithm. However, in a context where it is crucial to get an answer quickly, then it can be rational to use the less accurate algorithm. This context sensitivity of what counts as a good approximation technique is naturally accommodated in terms of expected utility. What counts as rational will depend on the utilities associated with solving the task in a particular context. If there is a high utility for speed and lower utility for accuracy, expected utility theory can say that it is rational to use the fast algorithm.

2.3 THE STANDARD CHALLENGE TO HUMAN RATIONALITY

In the previous section, we sought to develop a version of SP that provides guidelines for the assessment of human cognition without being so idealized as to fall afoul of familiar tractability objections. On a weak algorithmic conception of accordance, SP does not guarantee human irrationality. Nonetheless the elaboration of SP does little to help address the most prominent challenge to human rationality. This is because the standard challenge is an empirical one that goes far beyond saying merely that agents are hampered by various processing constraints.

2.3.1 The Challenge (a Reminder)

According to the standard challenge, there is an enormous and growing body of data which suggest that people fail to accord with SP because they systematically ignore critical information in making probabilistic inference. The key tradition here, heuristics and biases (HB), is quite well known, so we will not go into detail here. Rather, we will just present one illustration—but a compelling one—concerning the tendency for people to ignore base rate information. In a classic experiment, Kahneman and Tversky (1973) gave one group of subjects the following scenario:

> A panel of psychologists have interviewed and administered personality tests to 30 engineers and 70 lawyers, all successful in their respective fields. On the basis of this information, thumbnail descriptions of the 30 engineers and 70 lawyers have been written. You will find on your forms five descriptions, chosen at random from the 100 available descriptions. For each description, please indicate your probability that the person described is an engineer, on a scale from 0 to 100.

Another group of subjects got the same scenario, but with the base rates reversed; in this condition there were said to be 30 lawyers and 70 engineers. Subjects were then given descriptions, one of which was neutral, another was made to fit with stereotypes of lawyers, and another with the stereotype of engineers. Here is the text for the engineer stereotype:

> Jack is a 45-year-old man. He is married and has four children. He is generally conservative, careful, and ambitious. He shows no interest in political and social issues and spends most of his free time on his many hobbies which include home carpentry, sailing, and mathematical puzzles.

Now, subjects are supposed to indicate how likely it is (from 0 to 100) that Jack is an engineer. Kahneman and Tversky found that participants in both conditions gave the same, high probability estimates that Jack is an engineer. The fact that there were 70 engineers in one condition and 30 in the other had no discernible effect on subjects' responses. Moreover, when subjects were given the description that was neutral with respect to the stereotypes, people tended to say that there was a 50% chance that the person was an engineer, once more indicating that they were not using the available base rate information.

Notice: the problem here is not computational tractability. These are simple statistical problems, but people perform poorly at them. And this is just one example taken from a very large set. People show systematically bad performance on both demonstrative and nondemonstrative inference (see Stanovich, 1999, and Pohl, in press, for reviews). Moreover, Kahneman and Tversky have a systematic explanation for these reliable patterns of error: people rely on heuristics that often yield accurate results, but also deviate in systematic ways from rational norms. In the case of the lawyers and engineers problem, for example, people are relying on a representativeness heuristic whereby they estimate probability by thinking about how representative a description is of the category, without integrating the base rate information into their judgment.

2.3.2 A Consensus in the Research on Human Reasoning

The standard challenge to human rationality is very typically developed by drawing on research from the HB tradition. But it is important to note that, despite often intense criticisms, even the most prominent opponents of this tradition are in substantive agreement regarding the extent to which human cognition accords with SP (Samuels et al., 2002). Most notably, the research program associated with Gerd Gigerenzer, which promotes fast and frugal heuristics (FFH), does little to undermine this claim (Gigerenzer et al. 1999). To see why, consider one of the most effective such heuristics: *Take the Best.* Imagine you have to predict which of two cities has a higher rate of homelessness. Further, imagine you have six cues—whether the city has rent control, whether the temperature is above or below median, and so on—and that these cues are ranked in terms of how well they predict rates of homelessness. *Take the Best* says that when predicting which of two cities has the higher homelessness rate, one should initially only look at the best predictor, for example, rent control, and if one city has rent control while the other does not, one should, without considering any further information, judge the city with rent control to have a higher rate of homelessness. Only if the best predictor fails to discriminate—if the two cities both have, or both lack, rent control—should one consider the next best predictor. And only if the second cue fails to discriminate should the third best cue be considered, and so on, down the list of predictors.

Now it turns out that heuristics, such as Take the Best, do quite well on a range of prediction tasks. Indeed, Take the Best often does as well as models that take all of the cues into account (Gigerenzer, Czerlinski, & Martignon, 2002). But for all that, research within the FFH tradition yields much the same conclusion as HB regarding the extent to which human cognition accords with SP. As Michael Bishop notes, according to the FFH tradition, "people can, and often should, use very reliable FFHs that ignore lots of evidence and do not properly integrate the evidence they do consider" (Bishop, 2006, p. 217). In the homelessness case, *Take the Best* counsels us to ignore all the rest of the data once we have found the best cue that discriminates between the cities. This deliberate neglect of data is plainly at odds with SP. More generally, heuristics such as *Take the Best* are much like the heuristics proposed by HB, in that they fail to satisfy traditional epistemic demands on rationality. Here is Rysiew on this point:

> [W]e are capable of certain other, more 'coherence'-oriented forms of cognizing – checking for consistency; deliberately, even ponderously, weighing evidence; reflecting on our belief-forming processes themselves; not to mention, conducting empirical investigations into our own natural belief-forming tendencies so as, perhaps, to ultimately become better thinkers; and so on. And these sorts of more SP-type activities are the sort of thing that many epistemologists have thought to be central to epistemic rationality, and the kind of thing that's required for justified belief and knowledge. (2008, p. 1166)

Sensibly, most epistemologists do not give necessary and sufficient conditions on good reasoning. But as Rysiew's passage suggests, epistemologists often suggest necessary conditions. Internalists, in particular, maintain that good reasoning requires the agent to be attentive to possible inconsistencies among her beliefs and to be sensitive to the available evidence (Cohen, 1986, p. 575).

Despite their myriad disagreements, then, the HB and FFH traditions wholly agree that human cognitive processes very typically fail to satisfy traditional demands on rationality, and as such they agree that we fail to accord with SP. Of course, there are many ways in which philosophers and psychologists have responded to such claims (Samuels et al., 2002). In what follows, however, we want to consider one recent and extremely direct attempt to rebut the challenge. As we will see in the next section, there is a growing body of evidence that suggests that people's inferences do in fact conform to the principles of probability theory.

2.4 RATIONALITY REANIMATED

Recent work in Bayesian cognitive science provides a new possible response to worries about human rationality. In this tradition of work, one identifies a cognitive problem that needs to be solved, and then characterizes the normatively appropriate solution to the problem in terms of standard tools of probability theory, like sampling and model selection. Then one conducts experiments to measure whether human judgment and decision conforms to the normative model. Researchers within this tradition maintain that people draw inferences that conform to Bayesian models across a wide range of cognitive domains, including causal inference (Griffiths & Tenenbaum, 2009), grammar learning (Perfors et al., 2011a,b), and category learning (Kemp, Perfors, & Tenenbaum, 2007). Indeed, several studies have shown that infants make appropriate probabilistic inferences: infants are sensitive to priors (Téglás et al., 2007), are attentive to whether sampling is random or directed (Kushnir, Xu, & Wellman, 2010), and even infer overhypotheses (Dewar & Xu, 2010).

In order to discuss different aspects of how the Bayesian program impacts debate over rationality, we describe in some detail one example from recent research on probability judgments and simplicity in causal explanation. The research we discuss, by Tania Lombrozo and colleagues, draws on Bayesian theory to evaluate human performance. But the research is actually not presented as part of the Bayesian psychology program proper. We focus on it because it is especially apt for considering whether humans exhibit weak algorithmic accordance with SP.

It is a familiar theme in the philosophy of science that simpler hypotheses should be preferred. In the context of probabilistic inference, we can see one reason for this preference. More complex hypotheses risk overfitting the data. The greater flexibility of such hypotheses can mean that they extend to capture aspects of the data that should properly be construed as noise. As a result, the more complex hypothesis might do a poor job of predicting future data. In work on probabilistic inference, this issue is addressed by penalizing more complex hypotheses for their greater flexibility. For instance, there is a Bayesian form of Occam's razor that assigns complex hypotheses a lower prior probability (MacKay, 2003).[8] The data can, of course, overturn the prior probability, with the more complex hypothesis winning out. But the simpler hypothesis is favored at the starting gate. Thus we have two normative claims here: (1) all else equal, people should favor a simpler hypothesis over a more complex one; and (2) people should nonetheless reverse that preference if the data strongly favor the more complex hypothesis.

Extant work indicates that people do favor simpler hypotheses in, for example, category learning (Feldman, 2000; Griffiths, Christian, & Kalish, 2008). We will concentrate, however, on the issue of simplicity in causal explanation. In an elegant line of research, Tania Lombrozo has explored the role of simplicity in people's explanations (diagnoses) of disease when provided information about base rates (2007; Bonawitz & Lombrozo, 2012). Base rates are given by specifying the total size of the population and the *n* later specifying the number of people in the population with each disease. Simplicity is a function of the number of diseases the person might have (1 or 2). Since the proportions are stipulated, it is trivial to do the calculations to see when the simpler explanation is more probable.

The experiments present unfamiliar scenarios. In one experiment, the scenario is set on an alien planet, Zorg, and there are three diseases at issue, Tritchet's syndrome, Morad's disease, and a Humel infection. The symptoms too are unfamiliar (sore minttels, purple spots). The structure of the experiment is that disease 1 causes both symptoms, disease 2 causes one of the symptoms, and disease 3 causes the other symptom. As a result, if an alien presents with both symptoms, D1 will be simpler than the other available explanation, which is that the alien has both D2 and D3. The other factor in the decision is the base rate of the diseases in the population. In Lombrozo's experiment (study 2), the base rate information was explicitly provided to the participants. In all cases, the total population was set at 750. In one condition, each disease is present in 50 individuals; in another condition, D1 is present in 50, D2 is present in 250 individuals, and D3 is present in 220 individuals. There were a total of eight such conditions. In all conditions participants were told about an individual alien who had both symptoms, and they were asked which disease(s) the alien had.

Let us walk through an example. Suppose the incidence of each disease is 50. Since both symptoms are present, the two plausible candidate explanations are that the alien has D1 or both D2 and D3. Given the base rates, the probability that the person has D1 is 50/750, and the probability that she has both D2 and D3 is 50/750 × 50/750. This yields a probability ratio of 15 to 1 in favor of the simpler explanation. And, indeed, when participants are in this condition, they overwhelmingly favor the simpler explanation. In another condition, the base rates are 50 for D1, 610 for D2, and 620 for D3. In this condition, given the high base rates for D2 and D3, it is in fact significantly more likely that the alien has both D2 and D3 rather than D1. As a defender of SP would hope, in this condition people are more likely to judge that the individual has D2 and D3 rather than D1.

As noted previously, it is widely accepted that in probabilistic inference, simpler hypotheses should be favored, all else being equal. Earlier work had shown that, at least at some implicit level, people favor simpler hypotheses. Lombrozo's data show that at the explicit level, people also favor simpler explanations. Furthermore, Lombrozo shows that this preference for simpler explanations is moderated by base rate information. If the base rate associated with the more complex explanation is sufficiently high (compared with the simpler explanation), people will favor the more complex explanation. Furthermore, Bonawitz and Lombrozo (2012) find similar results with children, using a task involving colored chips that have different effects on a machine. The red chip causes a toy's light to activate, the green chip activates the toy's fan, and the blue chip activates both. When the child has to determine which chip(s) fell into the machine, they favor the blue chip (simple explanation) unless blue chips are very rare, in which case they favor the explanation that a red and a green chip fell in the machine.

In the foregoing example, people seem to show sensitivity to evidence in ways that would be sanctioned by our weak accordance rendering of SP. Adults and children in these tasks are sensitive to both simplicity and to base rates, as the normative theory says they should be. There is no reason to think that the subjects are throwing away data, as in the FFH cases, nor is there reason to think that the subjects are failing to integrate evidence into their judgments as in the HB cases. Moreover, these patterns of inference seem to be domain general. The tasks are pitched as abstract questions about alien diseases (Lombrozo, 2007) and colored chips (Bonawitz & Lombrozo, 2012).

2.5 RATIONALITY RECHALLENGED

Although a casual glace at the work on Bayesian inference might suggest that people exhibit something close to optimal Bayesian performance, a closer look reveals that this is far from the case. This holds for many of the classic results in the field (Kemp et al., 2007; Schulz et al., 2007; Xu & Tenenbaum, 2007). Since we already have a detailed explanation of Lombrozo's results, we will continue to focus on her work.

People should have a preference for simpler explanations, and, as we saw in the previous section, they do. In addition, people should override that preference if the data sufficiently favor a more complex explanation. Again, as we saw, they do that too. However, we omitted a very important fact about the results. People require far more evidence than they should before they will overturn their preference for the simpler explanation.

In Lombrozo's experiment, when the probability ratio is 15:1 in favor of the simpler explanation, virtually all participants prefer the simpler explanation (that the alien has just the one disease that causes two symptoms). Further, when the ratio is 10:1 in favor of the more complex explanation, the majority of participants favor the more complex explanation. But one key detail that we omitted was this: if people are Bayesian reasoners, we would expect almost everyone in this later situation—when the ratio is 10:1—to favor the more complex explanation. Yet, as a matter of fact, only 60% of participants did. More strikingly, when the ratio is 1:1, so that the objective probability (calculated by base rates and joint probabilities) of the simpler and more complex explanation is exactly the same, 90% of participants favor the simpler explanation (241). And when the ratio is 2:1 in favor of the complex explanation, nearly 70% of adults still favor the simpler explanation. Similar results were found in 5-year-old children (Bonawitz & Lombrozo, 2012). The children preferred the simpler explanation when the ratio was 2:1 in favor of the more complex explanation.[9]

So, despite initial appearances of excellence in human reasoning, performance in Lombrozo's studies is not nearly as close to the Bayesian norm as one might hope. But recall: on our preferred construal, the SP demands only weak algorithmic accordance with Bayesian norms. And to evaluate whether people in Lombrozo's experiments exhibit such accordance, we need to know more about what the algorithmic process might be. One great virtue of the Lombrozo work is that it permits a more precise understanding of the process than that afforded by much work in Bayesian psychology. As mentioned earlier, people have an excessive preference for the simpler explanations. But, as Lombrozo notes, there are two explanations for this divergence from proper Bayesian inference. The first is that participants are underweighting base rates. The second is that people have an overly strong prior bias in favor of simplicity. To place this in context, it is helpful to consider an optimal algorithm. Such an algorithm will describe a particular curve that represents responses as a function of different base rates. Let us call that the Bayesian curve. If people ignore the base rates, then we should not expect their responses to exhibit the same slope as the Bayesian curve. On the other hand, if people have a strong prior bias for simplicity, we would expect that to be manifested as a relatively constant factor that overrates simpler explanations. Of course, people might have both a simplicity bias and a tendency to neglect base rates. However, if people have a strong simplicity bias but do not ignore base rates, then we should expect the data curve to look a lot like the Bayesian curve, knocked up by a constant factor, viz., the prior bias for simplicity. As it turns out, this is precisely what Lombrozo finds. The data curve for her experiment does approximate the Bayesian curve, albeit bumped up by a constant factor (2007, pp.242 and 249).[10]

So, Lombrozo finds that people have an excessive bias for simplicity. Yet we doubt that this bias can be explained as a product of performance errors. Rather, it seems to be a feature of the algorithm itself. This means, of course, that the algorithm fails to provide a very close approximation to the optimal solution; and in that sense, it fails to meet the standards demanded of approximation algorithms in science (such as Metropolis-Hastings), where very close approximations to the optima are to expected.

Still, the process is obviously better than a coin flip. Indeed, the data suggest that the algorithm does reasonably well by the other two conditions we set for weak algorithmic accordance.

First, the algorithm is domain general, it is not dedicated only to solving problems about cheaters or incest. Rather, Lombrozo and colleagues' research indicates that the algorithm is operative in tasks involving diagnosing diseases from symptoms and in tasks involving colored chips activating a toy. This illustrates cross-domain capacity of the algorithm. Moreover, insofar as these studies involve arbitrary factors (eg, colored chips, unfamiliar symptoms of unfamiliar diseases), the algorithm itself looks to be domain general.

Second, and more importantly, the algorithm appears to do quite well by the third condition imposed by weak algorithmic accordance: that algorithms ought to be sensitive to large amounts of relevant information. Recall the algorithms from the HB and FFH traditions. For example, the *Take the Best* heuristic, developed by Gigerenzer and his colleagues is designed to ignore most of the available information. Similarly, the representativeness heuristic described by Kahneman and Tversky is supposed to completely ignore base rate information in the course of generating judgments. The algorithm implicated in Lombrozo's causal explanation tasks is clearly not like these. On the contrary, it is sensitive both to simplicity considerations and to base rate information. Moreover, Lombrozo's evidence indicates that the algorithm does not simply pit simplicity against base rates in a competition model, but actually integrates these two sources of information, leading to a nicely graded response curve.

By the standards of weak algorithmic accordance, then, the algorithm implicated in Lombrozo's task gets a mixed score. It does well by the dimensions of sensitivity and generality, but it does less well by the dimension of approximating the optima. So, how do we answer the question of whether the algorithm counts as SP rational? Without a clear proposal about how closely the algorithm must approximate the optima to count as rational, it is impossible to answer this question. Developing such a proposal is obviously beyond the ambitions of this paper. But it may well be that, at least in certain contexts, algorithms that score as well as the one implicated in Lombozo's task count as rational enough.

Acknowledgments

Both authors contributed equally to this chapter. We are grateful for feedback from members of the audiences at the Institute of European and American Studies Conference on Reason and Rationality, the University of Cincinnatti, and OSU's Center for Cognitive and Brain Sciences, especially Tim Bayne, Ian Gold, Hanti Lin, Tony Chemero, Peter Langland-Hassan, Heidi Maibom, Tom Polger, Angela Potochnik, Andrew Leber, Jay Myung, Zhong-Lin Lu, and Per Sederberg. We would also like to thank Stew Cohen, Juan Comesana, Declan Smithies, Terry Horgan, and Jonathan Weinberg for conversation about these issues. Research for this paper was supported by Office of Naval Research Grant No. #11492159 to SN.

References

Baron, J. (2008). *Thinking and deciding* (4th ed.). Cambridge University Press.

Beaumont, M. A., Zhang, W., & Balding, D. J. (2002). Approximate Bayesian computation in population genetics. *Genetics*, *162*(4), 2025–2035.

Bishop, M. A. (2006). Fast and frugal heuristics. *Philosophy Compass*, *1*(2), 201–223.

Bonawitz, E. B., & Lombrozo, T. (2012). Occam's rattle: Children's use of simplicity and probability to constrain inference. *Developmental Psychology*, *48*(4), 1156.

Chase, V. M., Hertwig, R., & Gigerenzer, G. (1998). Visions of rationality. *Trends in Cognitive Sciences*, *2.6*, 206–214.

Chater, N., Tenenbaum, J. B., & Yuille, A. (2006). Probabilistic models of cognition: conceptual foundations. *Trends in Cognitive Sciences*, *10*(7), 287–291.

Cohen, S. (1986). Knowledge and context. *The Journal of Philosophy*, *83*(10), 574–583.

Dewar, K. M., & Xu, F. (2010). Induction, overhypothesis, and the origin of abstract knowledge evidence from 9-month-old infants. *Psychological Science*, *21*(12), 1871–1877.

Feldman, J. (2000). Minimization of boolean complexity in human concept learning. *Nature*, *407*, 630–633.

Gigerenzer, G. (1996). On narrow norms and vague heuristics: a reply to Kahneman and Tversky (1996). *Psychological Review*, *103*, 592–596.

Gigerenzer, G., & Todd, P. M. the ABC Group. (1999). *Simple heuristics that make us smart*. New York: Oxford University Press.
Gigerenzer, G., Czerlinski, J., & Martignon, L. (2002). How good are fast and frugal heuristics? In T. Gilovich (Ed.), *Heuristics and biases: The psychology of intuitive judgment*. Cambridge University Press: Cambridge.
Gigerenzer, G., & Gaissmaier, W. (2011). Heuristic decision making. *Annual Review of Psychology, 62*, 451–482.
Griffiths, T. L., & Tenenbaum, J. B. (2009). Theory-based causal induction. *Psychological Review, 116*, 661–716.
Griffiths, T. L., Christian, B. R., & Kalish, M. L. (2008). Using category structures to test iterated learning as a method for identifying inductive biases. *Cognitive Science, 32*, 68–107.
Hamra, G., MacLehose, R., & Richardson, D. (2013). Markov chain Monte Carlo: An introduction for epidemiologists. *International Journal of Epidemiology, 42*(2), 627–634.
Harman, G. (1986). *Change in view: Principles of reasoning*. Cambridge, MA: MIT Press, 1986.
Kahneman, D., & Tversky, A. (1973). On the psychology of prediction. *Psychological Review, 80*, 237–251.
Kahneman, D., & Tversky, A. (1979). Prospect theory: an analysis of decision under risk. *Econometrica: Journal of the Econometric Society*, 263–291.
Kemp, C., Perfors, A., & Tenenbaum, J. B. (2007). Learning overhypotheses with hierarchical Bayesian models. *Developmental Science, 10*(3), 307–321.
Kushnir, T., Xu, F., & Wellman, H. M. (2010). Young children use statistical sampling to infer the preferences of other people. *Psychological Science, 21*(8), 1134–1140.
Lombrozo, T. (2007). Simplicity and probability in causal explanation. *Cognitive Psychology, 55*(3), 232–257.
MacKay, D. J. (2003). In *Information theory, inference, and learning algorithms* (Vol. 7). Cambridge: Cambridge University Press.
Perfors, A., Tenenbaum, J. B., Griffiths, T. L., & Xu, F. (2011a). A tutorial introduction to Bayesian models of cognitive development. *Cognition, 120*(3), 302–321.
Perfors, A., Tenenbaum, J. B., & Regier, T. (2011b). The learnability of abstract syntactic principles. *Cognition, 118*(3), 306–338.
Pohl, R. F. (Ed.). (In Press). *Cognitive illusions: Intriguing phenomena in thinking, judgment, and memory* (2nd ed.). Hove, UK: Psychology Press.
Pylyshyn, Z. W. (1984). *Computation and cognition*. Cambridge, MA: MIT Press.
Rysiew, P. (2008). Rationality disputes—Psychology and epistemology. *Philosophy Compass, 3*(6), 1153–1176.
Samuels, R., Stich, S., & Bishop, M. (2002). Ending the rationality wars: How to make disputes about human rationality disappear. In R. Elio (Ed.), *Common sense, reasoning, and rationality* (pp. 236–268). Oxford: Oxford University Press.
Schulz, L. E., Bonawitz, E. B., & Griffiths, T. L. (2007). Can being scared cause tummy aches? Naive theories, ambiguous evidence, and preschoolers' causal inferences. *Developmental Psychology, 43*(5), 1124.
Schwarz, N. (1996). *Cognition and communication: judgmental biases, research methods and the logic of conversation*. Hillsdale, NJ: Erlbaum.
Slovic, P., Fischhoff, B., & Lichtenstein, S. (1976). Cognitive processes and societal risk taking. In J. S. Carol, & J. W. Payne (Eds.), *Cognition and social behavior*. Hillsdale, NJ: Erlbaum.
Stanovich, K. (1999). Who is Rational? *Studies of individual differences in reasoning*. Mahwah, NJ: Erlbaum.
Stein, Edward (1996). *Without good reason*. Oxford: Clarendon Press.
Stich, S. (1990). *The fragmentation of reason*. Cambridge, MA: MIT Press.
Téglás, E., Girotto, V., Gonzalez, M., & Bonatti, L. L. (2007). Intuitions of probabilities shape expectations about the future at 12 months and beyond. *Proceedings of the National Academy of Sciences, 104*(48), 19156–19159.

Van der Sluys, M. V., Röver, C., Stroeer, A., Raymond, V., Mandel, I., Christensen, N., ..., & Vecchio, A. (2008). Gravitational-wave astronomy with inspiral signals of spinning compact-object binaries. *The Astrophysical Journal Letters, 688*(2), L61.

Von Neumann, J., & Morgenstern, O. (1944). *Theory of games and economic behavior*. Princeton: Princeton University Press.

Williamson, D. P., & Shmoys, D. B. (2011). *The design of approximation algorithms*. Cambridge, UK: Cambridge University Press.

Xu, F., & Tenenbaum, J. B. (2007). Sensitivity to sampling in Bayesian word learning. *Developmental Science, 10*(3), 288–297.

Endnotes

1. Even those who demure from this consensus readily acknowledge that it is the default view.
2. Though it should be noted that Gigerenzer and his collaborators are not themselves advocates of the standard picture (SP).
3. See Stein, 1996.
4. Much the same is true of Stephen Stich's well-known suggestion that the assessment of human rationality within cognitive science is principally an issue about the extent to our psycho-logic is normatively appropriate (Stich, 1990).
5. This is quite similar to what cognitive scientists have in mind when they say that a model and the process being modeled are strongly equivalent (Pylyshyn, 1984). The present suggestion then is roughly equivalent to the claim that accordance with SP norms requires human reasoning processes that are strongly equivalent to normative models of reasoning.
6. Roughly, in the worst case, the number of steps required increases exponentially (or worse) as a function of input size.
7. For an accessible introduction, see Williamson & Shmoys, 2011.
8. Technically, the way this works is a bit subtler. In Bayesian Occam's razor one does not simply assign a lower prior for the more complex hypothesis. Rather, the penalty is naturally represented as occurring in the likelihood term. We can think of the more complex hypothesis as a flexible hypothesis composed of more subhypotheses than the simpler hypothesis. And the total probability for all these subhypotheses cannot be greater than 1. When we calculate the posterior probabilities for the hypotheses, we need to accommodate all of the subhypotheses. In effect, we need to spread out the total probability of 1 across all the different subhypotheses in each hypothesis. Since the flexible hypothesis has more subhypotheses, the probability will be spread out more thinly, effectively leaving each subhypothesis of the flexible hypothesis with relatively lower probability than each subhypothesis in the simpler hypothesis.
9. This simplicity bias diverges even from what would be expected in "probability matching".
10. The adults in the Bonawitz & Lombrozo (2012) studies perform much better and do not show a simplicity bias. It is plausible that this is because in the chips task it is much easier to keep track of the base rates than it is in the aliens task. As a result, adults might not need to rely on simplicity at all to succeed at the task.

CHAPTER

3

Scientific Rationality: Phlogiston as a Case Study

J. Hricko

Education Center for Humanities and Social Sciences, National Yang-Ming University, Taipei, Taiwan

3.1 INTRODUCTION

The Chemical Revolution, to a first approximation, was an event that took place in the late 18th century and involved chemists embracing Antoine Lavoisier's oxygen theory and abandoning phlogiston-based explanations of various phenomena. The phenomena in question included combustion and the transformation of metals into oxides. For some time, chemists explained these phenomena by appealing to a substance they called phlogiston, which they posited as a component of inflammable substances and metals. According to those explanations, when an inflammable substance undergoes combustion, it loses its phlogiston; and when a metal is changed into an oxide, it loses its phlogiston. But in the late 18th century, Lavoisier did away with phlogiston and explained these phenomena in terms of oxygen. Before long, the community of chemists, as a whole, followed Lavoisier, and they eliminated phlogiston from chemistry and embraced the oxygen theory.

Today, the literature on the Chemical Revolution is so voluminous that it's difficult to say anything that hasn't already been claimed by some scholar and contested by another. Indeed, the first approximation that I offered in the previous paragraph would be unacceptable to different scholars for different reasons.[1] Considering the breadth of the literature on the Chemical Revolution, one might suspect that nothing remains to be said about it. Hasok Chang's recent work, however, shows that this is not the case. Perhaps the most exciting aspect of Chang's work concerns the bold and original conclusion for which he argues, namely, that phlogiston was killed prematurely. More specifically, Chang's view is that chemists

Rationality. http://dx.doi.org/10.1016/B978-0-12-804600-5.00003-9

should have retained phlogiston, just as they did oxygen, and that science could have benefited from this pluralistic approach.

Chang recognizes that his retelling of the story of the Chemical Revolution bears on the issue of rationality. Although he holds that the Chemical Revolution "was a fairly rational affair," he locates an element of irrationality, not in the chemists who continued to hold on to phlogiston, but in those who embraced Lavoisier's oxygen theory too readily (2012, p. 56). On Chang's understanding of rationality, if one were to admit the rationality of the response of these latter chemists, this admission would threaten Chang's claim that phlogiston was killed too soon (2012, p. 51).

In this chapter, I will examine and critically evaluate the arguments that Chang puts forward in favor of his view that chemists should have retained phlogiston. My aim in doing so is twofold—in short, I hope to shed some light on the Chemical Revolution in particular, and on scientific rationality more generally. Regarding the former, I take it that Chang is correct that it would have been rational for chemists to retain phlogiston, though my way of supporting this claim will differ from Chang's. My view will differ from Chang's in another respect, insofar as I will defend the claim that it was also rational for chemists to eliminate phlogiston. On my view, then, both the decision to retain phlogiston and the decision to eliminate it would have been rational, and the rationality of eliminating phlogiston needn't threaten Chang's claim that it would have been rational for chemists to retain it. My second aim is to use this view of the Chemical Revolution to illustrate something about scientific rationality more generally, namely, that there is a sense in which it concerns what is permissible as opposed to what is required. When it comes to deciding whether to retain or eliminate a given entity, there are cases (like that of phlogiston) in which both options are rationally permissible.

To that end, I'll proceed as follows. In Section 3.2, I'll summarize Chang's reasons for thinking that phlogiston suffered a premature death, and that science could have benefited if chemists had retained it. In Section 3.3, I'll argue that it's likely that the retention of phlogiston would not have led to the benefits that Chang discusses. These benefits would have been unlikely because a number of chemists identified phlogiston with hydrogen in the late 18th century, and, as I will argue, this identification became rather well entrenched by the early 19th century. It's likely that retaining phlogiston after this point would have brought about mixed results. It could have benefited science in ways that Chang does not discuss, but it could also have retarded scientific progress in other ways. In Section 3.4, I'll use the identification of phlogiston with hydrogen in order to draw some conclusions about the rationality of the Chemical Revolution. I'll argue that it would have been rational for chemists to eliminate phlogiston once they found that various substances thought to be rich in phlogiston contain no hydrogen. On the other hand, I'll argue that this identification could also have supported the rationality of retaining phlogiston, since insofar as it was rational to retain hydrogen, it would have been rational to retain phlogiston. Finally, in Section 3.5 I'll draw some conclusions about scientific rationality more generally.

3.2 CHANG ON RETAINING PHLOGISTON

In his recent work on the Chemical Revolution, Chang claims that phlogiston was killed prematurely and that retaining it could have benefited science.[2] Contrary to what many historians and philosophers have held, Chang argues that the Chemical Revolution did not consist in a quick conversion of the vast majority of late 18th-century chemists to Lavoisier's oxygen theory. As Chang emphasizes, there were, in fact, many anti-Lavoisierians who continued to entertain the phlogiston theory well into the 19th century (2010, pp. 62–68; 2012, pp. 29–34). Chang's claim, then, is that even after we take this into account, the death of phlogiston was still premature.

Chang's arguments for this claim come in four varieties. First of all, he argues that the elimination of phlogiston resulted in the elimination of "certain valuable scientific problems and solutions" (2012, p. 47). Chang's central example is familiar from discussions of so-called "Kuhn loss."[3] Phlogiston theorists[4] provided an explanation of the similarity of the metals in terms of their shared phlogiston oxygen theorists, on the other hand, not only failed to provide a solution, but ignored the very problem that the phlogiston theorists had attempted to solve (Chang 2012, pp. 21, 43–44). The retention of phlogiston, then, would have served as a reminder of certain problems and purported solutions.

Second, Chang argues that there were productive interactions between oxygen and phlogiston that could have continued if the latter had been retained (2012, pp. 48–50). He points out that it's unlikely that Lavoisier could have achieved what he did without building upon work by phlogiston theorists like Joseph Priestley and Henry Cavendish. Chang sees no reason why such productive interactions would have ceased if phlogiston had been retained.

Third, Chang argues that the elimination of phlogiston "close[d] off certain theoretical and experimental avenues for future scientific work" (2012, p. 47). More specifically, he argues that if chemists had retained phlogiston alongside oxygen, it would have been possible to make more rapid progress in theorizing about electricity and energy. These productive interactions, in turn, lend support to Chang's more general advocacy of pluralism in science, which involves maintaining competing systems, and his rejection of monism, which involves the elimination of all competing systems except for the winner (2011, pp. 425–428; 2012, Chapter 5).

Fourth, Chang argues that by the early 19th century, phlogiston and oxygen were on more or less equal footing, theoretically speaking. What justified chemists in retaining oxygen was really the set of operations on which they relied in carrying out various experiments. This justification, in Chang's view, would have applied equally well to phlogiston (2011, p. 420).

These latter two arguments are the most important for my purposes in the remainder of the chapter, and so I'll now turn to a more detailed discussion of each of these arguments.

3.2.1 Phlogiston, Electricity, and Energy

Chang claims that the elimination of phlogiston resulted in the elimination of various theoretical and experimental possibilities that would have been beneficial for scientists to pursue.[5] However, he believes that by retaining phlogiston, scientists could have made more rapid progress regarding electricity, on the one hand, and energy, on the other. According to Chang, if we were to engage in some truly whiggish history of science, there are two entities with which we would identify phlogiston, namely, free electrons and chemical potential energy (2009, pp. 246–250; 2011, pp. 412–423; 2012, pp. 43–48).

To begin with, there is the identification with free electrons. In Chang's view, the phlogiston theorists were correct that metals are similar to one another by virtue of some shared constituent, and that this constituent is the same thing that is released in combustion. As it turns out, it is free electrons. This isn't just a post hoc identification because, as Chang points out, many phlogiston theorists, some of whom I will discuss in more detail in Section 3.3.1, posited a connection between phlogiston and electricity. They did so, not merely out of a desire to have a grand unified theory of all of the imponderable fluids, of which phlogiston and electricity were two[6] but for experimental reasons as well. For example, Chang notes that it was known that electricity could be used to change calxes (which we know as the oxides of metals) into metals, a process that phlogiston theorists understood in terms of gain in phlogiston. He claims that if phlogiston had been retained, along with its posited connection with electricity, chemists would have continued to use any methods that they could think of in order to isolate it. He argues that it's therefore not unreasonable to think that various electrical phenomena could have been uncovered sooner. And he even speculates that if phlogiston had been retained, the discovery of the electron might have been taken for the discovery of phlogiston.

Chang also argues that if it had been retained, the concept of phlogiston would have been split, in which case it would also have been identified with chemical potential energy. His claim is that gain and loss of phlogiston can be understood in terms of gain and loss of potential energy, and that retaining phlogiston could have contributed to more rapid progress being made regarding energy. Insofar as phlogiston was conceived of as a principle, as opposed to a component, and insofar as it was conceived of as an imponderable fluid, the phlogiston theorists had a way of tracking what we would now classify as energy considerations. The oxygen theorists, on the other hand, did not. In accordance with the idea of the conservation of matter, they focused on the weights of substances before and after chemical reactions had taken place, and gain and loss of energy is not something that one can keep track of in this way.

3.2.2 Phlogiston Was Not Any Worse Than Oxygen

Chang also argues that in light of the fact that oxygen and phlogiston were on more or less equal footing by the early 19th century, it would have been rational to retain the latter as well as the former. In order to understand his argument, we must first look at Lavoisier's oxygen in a bit more detail.

As Chang emphasizes, by the early 19th century almost every theoretical claim that Lavoisier made about oxygen was proven to be false (2011, pp. 415–420; 2012, pp. 8–10).[7] Lavoisier's oxygen theory was a theory of combustion, among other things. He explained the heat and light that result from combustion in terms of the decomposition of oxygen gas, which involves the separation of oxygen base from caloric. By the early years of the 19th century, this explanation was found wanting. If oxygen gas is supposed to be the sole supporter of combustion, then Lavoisier needed an explanation for why other gases, all of which contain caloric combined with some base or other, do not support combustion. Even more damning is the fact that chemists found instances of combustion that do not involve oxygen gas at all, and so the latter could not be the sole supporter of combustion. The oxygen theory was not just a theory of combustion, though—it was also a theory of acidity. For Lavoisier (1965/1789, p. 65) oxygen was the principle of acidity, that which renders the substances with which it combines acidic. But Humphry Davy (1810b) had shown the falsity of the oxygen theory of acidity by showing that muriatic acid (hydrochloric acid, HCl) contains no oxygen.

In light of all of these theoretical failures, one might well wonder why oxygen was retained at all. Chang's answer is that the meaning of "oxygen" can, at least in part, be fixed operationally in such a way that there is continuity from Lavoisier's time to our own (2011, p. 419). His basic idea is that all of the operations by which Lavoisier produced oxygen gas work just as well today as they did in the late 18th century.

Returning now to the case of phlogiston, Chang's claim is that we can tell essentially the same story. Even in light of various theoretical failures, there is operational continuity. For example, Priestley proposed to produce phlogiston by converting metals into calxes. Although today we would understand this reaction in terms of converting metals into oxides, the operations are the same. And we can fix the meaning of "phlogiston" operationally, in terms of what is produced when a metal is converted to a calx. Chang uses these considerations to conclude that "there was no convincing reason for chemists to kill phlogiston in the late 18th century—at least no more convincing reason than there was to kill oxygen in the early 19th century" (2011, p. 420).

3.3 EVALUATING THE BENEFITS OF RETAINING PHLOGISTON

I find much with which to agree in Chang's work on the Chemical Revolution, and in the remainder of the chapter I'll indicate some of these points of agreement. My primary goal in this section, however, is to argue that if phlogiston had been retained, the benefits that Chang points to regarding electricity and energy would likely not have materialized. My argument hinges on the fact that a number of phlogiston theorists in the late 18th century identified phlogiston with hydrogen. I'll attempt to support the claim that this identification was rather well entrenched by the early 19th century. And I'll argue that, as a result, retaining phlogiston would most likely have brought about mixed results. It could have brought about some benefits that Chang does not discuss, but it could have retarded progress in various ways as well.

3.3.1 Phlogiston and Hydrogen

In the later years of the 18th century, a number of prominent phlogiston theorists identified phlogiston with inflammable air, which we now call hydrogen.[8] Cavendish was perhaps the first to make this identification. In the course of reporting the effects of various acids on various metals, he writes that "their phlogiston flies off, without having its nature changed by the acid, and forms the inflammable air" (1766, p. 145). And as early as 1782, Priestley makes this identification in a letter to Josiah Wedgwood, in which Priestley describes an experiment that, in his view, "seems to prove, that what we have called *phlogiston* is the same thing with *inflammable air in a state of combination with other bodies*" (in Bolton, 1892, p. 33).

While Cavendish may have been the first to make the identification, Richard Kirwan arguably did more than any other phlogiston theorist to defend it.[9] Kirwan first proposes this identification in the notes that he provided for the English translation of Carl Wilhelm Scheele's *Chemical observations and experiments on air and fire*. He writes of phlogiston's "properties in its purest state; which I take to be that of inflammable Air from metals" (in Scheele, 1780, p. 233). As such, Kirwan's view contrasts with that of Scheele, who claims that "*Phlogiston* is a true element and a simple principle" (1780, p. 103), but stops short of identifying it with inflammable air, which he claims "is composed of heat and phlogiston" (1780, p. 180). Two years later, Kirwan went on to develop the view that phlogiston and inflammable air are the solid and gaseous states, respectively, of the same substance. He writes:

> phlogiston... can never be produced in a *concrete state*, single and uncombined with other substances; for the instant it is disengaged from them, it appears in a fluid and elastic form, and is then commonly called *inflammable air*. (1782, pp. 195–196)

Some time later, in a striking passage from his *Essay on phlogiston and the constitution of acids*, Kirwan writes that "inflammable air, before its extrication from the bodies in which it exists in a concrete state, was the very substance to which all the characters and properties of the phlogiston of the ancient chymists [sic] actually belonged" (1789, pp. 4–5).

After identifying phlogiston with inflammable air in his *Essay*, Kirwan goes on to claim that this identification is not an idiosyncrasy of his phlogiston theory, but that it has "met the approbation of the most distinguished philosophers, both at home and abroad" (1789, p. 5). He goes on to list a number of phlogiston theorists who, he claims, also accept this identification, including "Dr. Priestley, Mr. Bewly, Mr. Bergman, Mr. Morveau, De La Metherie, Chaptal, Crell, Wiegleb, Westrumb, Hermstadt, Kaersten, &c." (1789, p. 5). To take one example from this list, Torbern Bergman puts forward a view that looks very much like Kirwan's. He writes:

> This principle, when in combination, and then it is properly called phlogiston, may be set loose by various methods; having recovered its elasticity, and gained an aerial form, by a proper increase of specific heat, it receives the name of inflammable air. (1785, pp. 219–220)

As I'll discuss later, there wasn't any universal agreement among phlogiston theorists regarding this identification, and Priestley and Cavendish in particular went on to propose other views incompatible with it. That said, there was at least some agreement regarding the identification, and a number of prominent phlogiston theorists did, at one time or another, defend it.

The oxygen theorists, on the other hand, identified inflammable air, not with phlogiston, but with hydrogen gas. This identification can be seen in the second edition of Kirwan's *Essay*, which contains both Kirwan's essay and responses from Lavoisier and his colleagues. In his commentary, Lavoisier writes of Kirwan's view that certain substances "all contain the base of inflammable air, that is to say hydrogene [sic]" (in Kirwan, 1789, p. 22). Lavoisier, in accordance with his caloric theory of heat, thereby identifies the base of inflammable air, that is, inflammable air minus caloric, with hydrogen base. It follows that hydrogen gas, for Lavoisier, is inflammable air.

There were certainly terminological differences between the oxygen theorists and the phlogiston theorists. But we can exploit one of Chang's insights (which I discussed in Section 3.2.2) in order to show a sense in which the late 18th century phlogiston theorists' identification of phlogiston with inflammable air was also an identification of phlogiston with hydrogen. If Chang is correct, then the meanings of terms like "phlogiston," "inflammable air," and "hydrogen gas" are, at least in part, fixed operationally. And if we recognize that the chemists who used these terms produced hydrogen by means of a shared set of operations, it's clear that all parties, regardless of whether they were phlogiston theorists or oxygen theorists, were talking about the same substance, namely, hydrogen. In that case, at the operational level, there's good reason to identify Kirwan's phlogiston with Lavoisier's hydrogen gas (but not hydrogen base). Though, to be sure, neither side made this identification explicitly. Moreover, given that we can produce hydrogen by means of the same set of operations today, we can identify Kirwan's phlogiston with our hydrogen.

My claim is that this identification is significant. But as Chang notes, it was one among many attempts by phlogiston theorists to identify various posits of their theories with various substances. Before arguing for the significance of this identification, it's worth briefly discussing some of these other attempts.

To begin with, as Chang points out, both Priestley and Cavendish also identified inflammable air with phlogisticated water (2012, p. 6). We can see Cavendish's view in the following passage. After stating that "inflammable air is either pure phlogiston, as Dr. Priestley and Mr. Kirwan suppose, or else water united to phlogiston," Cavendish writes: "Either of these suppositions will agree equally well with the following experiments; but the latter seems to me much the most likely" (1784, p. 137).

Chang goes on to note a similarity between Cavendish's view and another view, which suggests a link between phlogiston and electricity (2012, pp. 44, 80). On Cavendish's view, water is elementary, inflammable air is phlogisticated water, and oxygen is dephlogisticated water. Then there is Johann Wilhelm Ritter's view, which shares the commitment to elementary water, but holds that inflammable air is negatively electrified water, while oxygen is positively electrified water. If we were to identify phlogiston with negative electricity, Cavendish's and Ritter's respective views would amount to one and the same view. And, indeed, some chemists did put forward views along these lines. Chang discusses Priestley himself, who posited a connection between phlogiston and electricity (2012, pp. 80–82). After discussing a number of experiments, Priestley writes:

> These experiments favour the hypothesis of *two electric fluids*, the positive containing the principle of oxigen [sic], and the negative that of phlogiston. These united to water seem to constitute the two opposite kinds of air, viz. dephlogisticated and inflammable. (1802, p. 202)

Moreover, as Chang notes (2012, p. 80), George Smith Gibbes posits a similar connection when he claims that "[t]he principle of the negative side of the galvanic apparatus resides in all combustible bodies,... and answers exactly to the Phlogiston of Scheele" (1809, p. 13). And without giving up the identification of phlogiston with inflammable air, Kirwan speculates "that phlogiston, in a state perhaps 100 times rarer than inflammable air, and consequently containing much more fire, may possibly constitute the electric fluid" (1782, p. 210).

To evaluate the benefits of retaining phlogiston, the crucial issue comes down to the extent to which the identifications between phlogiston and various substances became entrenched in the practice of chemistry. My claim is that the identification of phlogiston with hydrogen became rather well entrenched, while the other identifications did not. To be sure, a full justification of this claim would require more work than I will do here, which will be limited to the discussion of a single but important source of evidence, namely, the work of Humphry Davy, to which I'll now turn.

3.3.2 Davy's Phlogistic and Electrochemical Speculations

Davy's work is important to consider because, as Chang notes, he was one of a number of chemists who engaged in some "relatively maverick attempts to employ phlogiston again for various scientific purposes" (2012, p. 65). And of all the chemists working in the early 19th century, Chang singles out Davy as "[p]erhaps the most interesting case of the new generation of anti-Lavoisier chemists" (2012, p. 33). One might suspect that Davy's enthusiasm for phlogiston, combined with his work in electrochemistry, provided the perfect conditions for identifying phlogiston with electricity in a way that would become entrenched in the practice of chemistry. Indeed, Chang references Davy's phlogistic speculations with this possibility in mind (2012, p. 80). But Davy, in fact, maintained the identification of phlogiston with hydrogen throughout his work. And often he doesn't even bother to make this identification explicit to his readers. Such passages provide evidence for the claim that this identification was fairly well entrenched, not just for Davy, but for his audience as well. At this point, I'll briefly discuss Davy's phlogistic and electrochemical speculations to make this point clear.

To begin with, as Chang points out, Davy does engage in some speculation regarding phlogiston in his 1807 Bakerian Lecture. Davy writes:

> A phlogistic chemical theory might certainly by [sic] defended, on the idea that the metals are compounds of certain unknown bases with the same matter as that existing in hydrogene [sic]; and the metallic oxides, alkalies and acids compounds of the same bases with water... (1808a, p. 33)

Davy goes on to consider the limitations of such a theory immediately after introducing it. But the fact that he mentions it at all shows that he does display some enthusiasm for phlogiston. This passage is notable for another reason, though: if one did not have the identification of phlogiston with hydrogen in mind when reading this passage, it would be completely unclear why this theory is supposed to be a phlogiston theory. Hence, this passage shows that at this stage of his thinking, if Davy identified phlogiston with anything, it was with hydrogen. Moreover, it shows that he expected that his audience had made the same identification; otherwise, he would have been more explicit about the identification and the reasons for it.

Davy continues his phlogistic speculations in another paper, published in 1808. After emphasizing the superiority of the oxygen theory, he claims that "the only good arguments in favour of a common principle of inflammability, flow from some of the novel analogies in electrochemical science" (1808b, p. 363). He goes on to spell out what he has in mind:

> Oxygene [sic] is the only body which can be supposed to be elementary, attracted by the positive surface in the electrical circuit, and all compound bodies, the nature of which is known, that are attracted by this surface, contain a considerable proportion of oxygene [sic]. Hydrogene [sic] is the only matter attracted by the negative surface, which can be considered as acting the opposite part to oxygene [sic]; may not then the different inflammable bodies, supposed to be simple, contain this as a common element? (1808b, p. 363)

If we keep in mind the identification of phlogiston with hydrogen, we can see these "novel analogies" as suggesting a kind of phlogiston theory. And indeed, Davy goes on to identify phlogiston with hydrogen more explicitly later in the paper, when, in the course of speculating on the nature of metals, he writes of "the adherence of their phlogiston or hydrogene [sic]" (1808b, p. 364).

Shortly after this passage, Davy engages in some further speculation and considers "[o]ther hypotheses [which] might be formed upon the new electrochemical facts, in which still fewer elements than those allowed in the antiphlogistic or phlogistic theory might be maintained" (1808b, p. 368). This way of framing his electrochemical speculations makes it clear that for Davy, these hypotheses are not elaborations of either the oxygen (ie, "antiphlogistic") theory or the phlogiston theory. That said, Davy's motivation for engaging in these electrochemical speculations appears to be the same as his motivation for engaging in various phlogistic speculations. Robert Siegfried (1964, pp. 118–119) has argued that Davy entertained various phlogistic theories because of his desire to reduce the number of chemical elements, and the same point applies to the hypotheses that Davy mentions here.

The particular hypothesis that Davy goes on to consider is based on his observations of a coincidence between chemical states and electrical states. Acids, being attracted to the positive surface in an electric circuit, are negative, while the alkalies and inflammable substances are positive. Moreover, acids lose their acidic properties when they are positively electrified, while the alkalies lose their alkaline properties when negatively electrified. Davy concludes that "[i]n these instances the chemical qualities are shewn [sic] to depend upon the electrical powers; and it is not impossible that matter of the same kind, possessed of different electrical powers, may exhibit different chemical forms" (1808b, p. 368). Such a hypothesis, then, would admit fewer elements, since the very same element may exhibit different properties depending on its electrical powers.

In a footnote to this passage (1808b, pp. 368–369), and in some unpublished notes (quoted in John Davy, 1836, pp. 405–406), Davy engages in some additional electrochemical speculation, again with the goal of reducing the number of chemical elements. He considers the idea that water is an element and entertains a view that is the opposite of Ritter's, namely, that hydrogen is positively electrified water and that oxygen is negatively electrified water. The metals, charcoal, sulfur, phosphorus, and nitrogen are constituted of unknown bases and hydrogen, while the acids, oxides, alkalies, and earths are constituted of unknown bases and oxygen. The elements on this theory, then, are water and these unknown bases.

Given that Davy engaged in these electrochemical and phlogistic speculations, one might expect him to posit some kind of connection between phlogiston and electricity of the kind put forward by Priestley, Gibbes, and Kirwan. Davy's phlogistic and electrochemical speculations both involve the idea that metals and inflammable substances contain hydrogen. And since Davy identifies phlogiston with hydrogen, and since he often makes use of the idea that hydrogen is positively charged, one might expect him to identify phlogiston with some kind of electrical power. But an examination of Davy's work frustrates these expectations. For some time, Davy continued to entertain the phlogistic idea that inflammable bodies contain hydrogen (1809, p. 103; 1810a, p. 69). And his electrochemical speculations also appear in subsequent work (1810a, p. 62). But Davy never identifies phlogiston with electricity or indeed with anything other than hydrogen. One plausible explanation for this fact is that for both Davy and his audience, the identification of phlogiston with hydrogen was already too well entrenched to consider displacing.

At this point, if I've established anything at all, it's that Davy identified phlogiston with hydrogen throughout his phlogistic speculations, and that he wrote as if he expected his audience to have the same identification in mind. While I take it that Davy's work provides evidence for my claim that this identification was, by the early 19th century, more well entrenched than any other, I acknowledge that this claim requires additional work to fully support. That said, in the remainder of the chapter I will take this claim for granted and see what follows from it. But before moving on, it's worth briefly discussing the shape of the further work required to support this claim, and in doing so I'll indicate some reasons to be optimistic about the prospects.

As Chang notes, Davy was one of a number of anti-Lavoisierian chemists working in the early 19th century (2010, pp. 63–68; 2012, pp. 30–34). A complete justification for my claim would therefore involve looking at these other chemists. Among them are some whom I've already discussed in Section 3.3.1, for example, Ritter, Priestley, and Gibbes. Ritter is unlikely to have been able to establish a more well entrenched identification of phlogiston with something other than hydrogen, since, as Chang points out, his work on elementary water was rejected by most chemists (2012, pp. 87–94). It's not clear that Priestley's posited connection between phlogiston and electricity would have fared any better, since, as Chang notes, it's not clear how much attention his 1802 paper received (2012, p. 82). And while Chang lists Gibbes as one of the anti-Lavoisierians, he does not include Gibbes in a subsequent figure that focuses on "salient figures" from the previously mentioned list (2012, pp. 31, 34). If Chang's judgment regarding salience is correct, Gibbes would not have had the influence necessary to entrench his posited connection between phlogiston and electricity. Chang lists a number of other anti-Lavoisierians, but Davy surely stands out as one of the most prominent and influential. And given his phlogistic and electrochemical speculations, his work is likely the most significant when it comes to supporting my claim regarding the entrenchment of the identification of phlogiston with hydrogen. So although I've only discussed a single source of evidence for my claim, it's a significant one.

3.3.3 Benefits and Harms of Retention

At this point we can evaluate Chang's claim that if chemists had retained phlogiston, science could have benefited. If I am right that the identification of phlogiston with hydrogen was well entrenched by the early 19th century, then if phlogiston had been retained, so would its identification with hydrogen. And so, if we are to engage in an evaluation of the benefits of retaining phlogiston, we must keep this identification in mind.

To begin with, I think Chang is correct about some of the benefits that he discusses. Even if we keep the identification of phlogiston with hydrogen in mind, it's likely that the retention of phlogiston would have served as a useful reminder of unsolved problems and potential solutions. Chang gives the example of the phlogiston theorists' explanation of the similarity of the metals, which appealed to their shared phlogiston. Though metals do not contain hydrogen, the reminder of the problem is useful. Moreover, if retaining phlogiston would have reminded oxygen theorists of various unsolved problems, such reminders would have counted as a kind of productive interaction between the phlogiston and oxygen theories. Hence, I think Chang is also correct that retaining phlogiston would have likely lead to subsequent productive interactions.

That said, if the identification with hydrogen was well entrenched by the early 19th century, it's unlikely that retaining phlogiston would have led to the other benefits that Chang discusses, namely, more rapid progress regarding energy and electricity. There doesn't seem to be any kind of direct path from phlogiston qua hydrogen to these benefits, and so it's likely that they would not have materialized.[10] There may have been a more indirect path to such benefits, for example, one that took into account various electrochemical phenomena, like the fact that hydrogen is attracted to the negative surface in an electric circuit. However, even if there were such an indirect path, it's not clear that the retention of phlogiston would be needed for following that path, since oxygen theorists could also recognize these electrochemical phenomena. More generally, in order for the retention of phlogiston to have the benefits for which Chang argues, it had to have been possible for chemists working in the early 19th century to identify phlogiston with energy and/or electricity. And if my argument in Section 3.3.2 is correct, the identification of phlogiston with hydrogen was so well entrenched that it would have been difficult, but perhaps not impossible, for an identification with electricity, energy, or anything else to catch on.

Some unaddressed issues still remain. It's possible that the retention of phlogiston, along with its identification with hydrogen, could have brought about some benefits that Chang does not discuss. And it's also possible that retaining phlogiston could have brought about harms. In my view the retention of phlogiston would most likely have brought about both benefits and harms. In order to see this, a useful starting point is Kirwan's framing of what is at issue in the opposition between the phlogiston theorists and the oxygen theorists:

> The controversy is therefore at present confined to a few points, namely, whether the *inflammable principle* be found in what are called phlogisticated acids, vegetable acids, fixed air, sulphur, phosphorus, sugar, charcoal, and metals. (1789, pp. 6–7)

Kirwan held that the inflammable principle (ie, phlogiston or hydrogen) is a constituent of all of these substances, and we can inquire into the benefits and harms of retaining a view like this.

As for the benefits of retention, acids do contain hydrogen, and so the expectations of phlogiston theorists like Kirwan would have paid off.[11] That said, it's difficult not to conclude that the oxygen theory of acidity retarded progress in determining the composition of acids. It encouraged chemists to look for oxygen (the principle of acidity) in acids like muriatic acid (hydrochloric acid, HCl) and prussic acid (hydrocyanic acid, HCN) that do not contain it. In contrast, phlogiston theorists were in a better position to grasp the nature of such acids. A case in point is Scheele, who was the first to isolate chlorine by decomposing muriatic acid, and who held that the components of that acid are chlorine and phlogiston (1931/1774, pp. 29–30). In the course of presenting his own results on muriatic acid, Davy claims that Scheele's view "may be considered as an expression of facts," while the oxygen theory "rests in the present state of our knowledge, upon hypothetical grounds" (1810b, p. 237). Perhaps if some kind of phlogiston theory had been more widely held and the oxygen theory had been less widely held, chemists would have determined the composition of muriatic acid and prussic acid more quickly than they, in fact, did. I take it that this is a plausible benefit of retaining phlogiston.

Although some phlogiston theorists may have been in a better position to grasp the nature of acids that do not contain oxygen, it's debatable whether the theories of acidity that phlogiston theorists offered were much of an improvement over Lavoisier's oxygen theory. Kirwan's theory of acidity is a kind of hybrid phlogistonist/oxygenist theory. According to his theory, the principle of acidity is fixed air, which we know as carbon dioxide (CO_2), but which Kirwan held to be a compound of phlogiston and oxygen (1789, pp. 39, 78, 80). And on the phlogistic theory that Davy entertains in his 1807 Bakerian Lecture, acids are compounds of certain unknown bases and water (1808a, p. 33). Since both water and Kirwan's fixed air contain oxygen, there is a sense in which these theories are just as misguided as Lavoisier's oxygen theory of acidity.

That said, there's also a sense in which these phlogiston theories of acidity are much closer to the truth than the oxygen theory. Since both water and Kirwan's fixed air also contain hydrogen, these theories entail that acids contain hydrogen. And based on two of our three current definitions of acidity, namely, the Arrhenius definition and the Brønsted–Lowry definition, it is hydrogen ions, and not oxygen, that play an essential role in acids. It's admittedly a long shot to conclude that retaining phlogiston would have enabled chemists to recognize this essential role more quickly than they, in fact, did. But it's at least worth considering, and it may represent another potential benefit of retaining phlogiston.

As for the harms of retention, fixed air, sulfur, phosphorus, charcoal, and the metals do not contain hydrogen, and so the expectations of phlogiston theorists would have been frustrated. Just as the oxygen theory retarded progress regarding the composition of acids, it's likely that retaining phlogiston would have retarded progress regarding the composition of these substances. After all, it would have guided chemists to continue to attempt to isolate the hydrogen that these substances purportedly contain. It's plausible, then, that eliminating phlogiston actually benefited the scientific investigation into the composition of these substances.

3.4 THE RATIONALITY OF ELIMINATING/ RETAINING PHLOGISTON

Now that we've seen that the retention of phlogiston would likely have brought about both benefits and harms, we can examine the issue of rationality. To be sure, these are distinct issues. An evaluation of the rationality of deciding whether to retain phlogiston in the early 19th century must be independent of any subsequent benefits and harms of doing so, which were largely unknown at the time of the decision. That said, in this section, I'll draw on some of the historical details from my discussion of the benefits and harms of retention in order to argue that it was rational for chemists to eliminate phlogiston and that it also would have been rational for them to retain it. But first I'll discuss what Chang has to say regarding the rationality of the Chemical Revolution, since I'll be concerned to replace his view of rationality with my own.

3.4.1 Chang on the Rationality of the Chemical Revolution

According to Chang (2012, p. 51), if it was rational for chemists to abandon phlogiston and embrace Lavoisier's oxygen theory, then Chang's own claim that phlogiston suffered a premature death would be invalidated. For this reason, he devotes a fair amount of discussion to the rationality of the Chemical Revolution. He begins by making the following three points, which admittedly fall short of a comprehensive theory of rationality:

> Firstly, rationality is not a matter of truth; rather, rationality is about good ways of making judgments and decisions, given what one knows or believes at the time... Secondly, rational thinking or discourse follows some rules or methods that are agreed within the relevant community, to the extent that there is conscious deliberation at all. Thirdly, the minimal condition of rationality is instrumental: at least, a rational action must either achieve some stated aim of the agent, or at least be intended by the agent as contributing toward a certain aim. (2012, p. 51)[12]

In my view, these points suffice for the purposes of his discussion, and I'll adopt them in what follows.

Although Chang holds that the Chemical Revolution "was a fairly rational affair," there was an element of irrationality, which he locates "not in the refusal of some chemists to go along with Lavoisier, but in the readiness of too many others to do so" (2012, p. 56). He considers, and ultimately rejects, a number of arguments in the literature that purport to show that such a conversion was rational (2010, pp. 49–61; 2012, pp. 51–56). On Chang's understanding of rationality, to sustain the claim that phlogiston was killed prematurely, it cannot be the case that it was rational for these chemists to abandon phlogiston and convert.[13] Chang's overall view of rationality thus entails that the rationality of eliminating phlogiston precludes the rationality of retaining it and vice versa. Unless Chang had this view of rationality in mind, he wouldn't be concerned with objecting to various arguments purporting to show the rationality of abandoning phlogiston and converting to the oxygen theory. It's also worth noting that the three points with which Chang prefaces his discussion do not entail his overall view of rationality. Chang's view of rationality is one that I wish to question, and ultimately replace, in what follows, and I now turn to that task.

3.4.2 Eliminating and Retaining Phlogiston Are Both Rational

My own view is that it was rational to eliminate phlogiston, and it also would have been rational to retain it. I'll now attempt to show why both elimination and retention would have been rational, and in doing so I'll once again make use of the identification of phlogiston with hydrogen.

I'll consider the rationality of elimination first. Once again, Kirwan's (1789, pp. 6–7) account of the controversy will serve as a useful way to frame my discussion. As I've already noted previously, Kirwan held that fixed air (carbon dioxide, CO_2), sulfur, and the metals all contain hydrogen. By 1791 Kirwan's failure to isolate the hydrogen that he presumed these substances to contain led him to abandon his phlogiston theory:

> I know of no single clear decisive experiment by which one can establish that fixed air is composed of oxygen and phlogiston, and without this proof it seems to me impossible to prove the presence of phlogiston in metals, sulphur or nitrogen... (quoted in Partington, 1961, p. 664)

It would surely be rational for chemists to eliminate phlogiston for the reasons that Kirwan cites. More specifically, if phlogiston qua hydrogen was supposed to be a shared component of these substances, as the evidence against the existence of hydrogen in these substances grew, it would have been rational to eliminate phlogiston while retaining hydrogen.

While I take it that the identification of phlogiston with hydrogen supports the rationality of eliminating phlogiston, I also see a way in which this same identification supports the rationality of retaining it. In short, the basic idea is that insofar as it was rational for chemists to retain hydrogen, it would have been rational for them to retain phlogiston. To be sure, the lack of phlogiston qua hydrogen in the substances discussed in the previous paragraph would have frustrated the expectations of phlogiston theorists. But these substances are only a subset of the substances that Kirwan mentions in his account of the controversy. He also mentions acids and sugar, which do contain hydrogen. Phlogiston theorists needn't have held that all of the substances that Kirwan lists must contain hydrogen in order for the controversy to be settled in their favor. It would have been rational for them to retain phlogiston and conclude that it was somewhat different from what they had initially theorized. They might have even gotten to work on determining the role of phlogiston in acids, which could have brought about the benefits I discussed in Section 3.3.3.

If this conclusion seems implausible, it's worth recalling some of the points that Chang makes regarding oxygen, which I discussed in Section 3.2.2. In particular, chemists retained oxygen even after they discovered that it is not the principle of acidity, that it is not the sole supporter of combustion, and that the heat and light that result from combustion are not due to the decomposition of oxygen gas into oxygen base and caloric. These discoveries represented a significant departure from Lavoisier's oxygen theory, and yet it was still rational for chemists to retain oxygen. In that case, it would also have been rational for chemists to retain a modified form of phlogiston after acknowledging that various discoveries had shown that their initial theories were, in various respects, incorrect.

My attempt to justify the rationality of retaining phlogiston differs from Chang's, though I do think that I can appeal to one of Chang's insights in order to strengthen my argument. In Section 3.2.2 I discussed Chang's idea that the retention of oxygen was justified by the operations chemists used to produce it. And given that phlogiston theorists also had operations for producing phlogiston, Chang concludes that there was no more reason to eliminate phlogiston than there was to eliminate oxygen. One issue with Chang's proposal is that he considers a number of distinct and mutually incompatible phlogiston theories, including "Kirwan's "inflammable air" theory, Priestley's "electric fluid" theory, and Cavendish's "elementary water" theory". In that case, determining the set of operations for producing phlogiston may prove difficult. But if I am right that, by the early 19th century, the identification of phlogiston with hydrogen was well entrenched, then we would have a way of determining the operations by which chemists at the time produced phlogiston: they are just the same operations by which they produced hydrogen. In that case, Chang's operational justification for retaining phlogiston applies even more forcefully once one takes into account the well-entrenched nature of the identification of phlogiston with hydrogen.

One may object that what I've pointed to here are actually considerations that must be weighed in the course of determining whether elimination or retention is rational, rather than considerations that show both decisions to be rational. There may be reasons in favor of elimination and reasons in favor of retention. But rationality requires weighing these reasons against one another in order to determine the optimal decision. It may be the case that such reasons are, indeed, equally good, which allows for the possibility that the two decisions can be equally rational. But if this is, indeed, the case, then perhaps I need to do more in order to show that the reasons on each side are equally good.

In order to respond to this objection, it's sufficient to point out that there may be no privileged perspective from which one can weigh these reasons. As Chang emphasizes, rationality is, at least in part, about making good decisions based on what one believes. Furthermore, as I'll now argue, the outcome of weighing these reasons depends on the beliefs of those who weigh them. To see this, we can consider the following two beliefs:

(1) Phlogiston is found in acids.
(2) Phlogiston is found in metals.

And we'll consider two fictional early 19th century phlogiston theorists (chemist A and chemist B), while keeping in mind that the identification of phlogiston with hydrogen was, by this point, well entrenched.

Suppose that chemist A and chemist B both believe (1) and (2), but they differ from one another regarding the beliefs that they are likely to abandon in light of new evidence. Chemist A is more willing to abandon (2) than to abandon (1), and in that sense, takes phlogiston's role in acids to be more central than its role in metals. In contrast, chemist B is more willing to abandon (1) than to abandon (2), and in that sense, takes phlogiston's role in metals to be more central than its role in acids. Now suppose that both discover that acids, but not metals, contain hydrogen. Given their beliefs, the reasons in favor of retaining phlogiston will appear stronger to chemist A than to chemist B. Moreover, the reasons in favor of eliminating phlogiston will appear stronger to chemist B than to chemist A. Hence, given their beliefs, we can see that if chemist A were to decide to retain phlogiston, and chemist B to eliminate it, both decisions would be rational.

It may be objected that this conclusion merely shows that we must move from considering the rationality of decisions to the rationality of beliefs. Once we can show that one chemist's set of beliefs is more rational than the other's, we can show that one decision is more rational than the other. However, in the case under consideration, this objection does not have much force since, given the state of chemistry in the early 19th century, both sets of beliefs were rational. We can grasp this point by reference to Davy's work. Davy entertained both (1) and (2), and even if he didn't believe either, the fact that he entertained both shows that, at the time, (1) and (2) were live possibilities. It's therefore difficult to convict either chemist A or chemist B of irrationality on the basis of having these beliefs. It's also difficult to say that it would have been irrational to have a stronger belief in (2) than in (1) or vice versa. And since both sets of beliefs were rational, we cannot appeal to those beliefs in order to argue that one decision would have been less rational than the other.

At this point I'm in a position to state my conclusions regarding the rationality of retaining and eliminating phlogiston. Both decisions were rational, not because chemists lacked decisive empirical evidence, but because what looked to one chemist like decisive evidence for elimination may not have looked decisive from the perspective of some other chemist. When confronted with the same set of experimental results, one chemist could have seen decisive reasons for eliminating phlogiston, while another could have seen decisive reasons for concluding that phlogiston, much like oxygen, is very different from what chemists had initially theorized. Hence, at the level of individual chemists, it was rational for them to eliminate phlogiston, and it also would have been rational for them to retain it. When it comes to the community of chemists more generally, I take it that it was rational for them, as a whole, to eliminate phlogiston. But it's also possible that those individual chemists in favor of retaining phlogiston could have reached the critical mass required for the community, as a whole, to retain it, and I see no reason why it would be irrational of them to do so. It also would have been rational for the community to embody the kind of pluralism for which Chang argues, according to which some chemists would develop the oxygen theory, and others would develop phlogiston theories or hybrid theories that employ both oxygen and phlogiston. In short, when it comes to phlogiston, both retention and elimination would have been rational.

3.5 SCIENTIFIC RATIONALITY MORE GENERALLY

I'll now make some brief remarks about how the arguments that I've presented bear on the issue of scientific rationality more generally. If those arguments are correct, then we must admit that when scientists are faced with a decision between retaining and eliminating a given entity, it may be the case, at least sometimes, that both decisions are rational. Rationality alone may not dictate whether scientists ought to respond to some particular empirical results by eliminating an entity or by retaining it in some modified form. It's not always the case that one decision is rationally required while the other is forbidden. Both decisions may be rationally permissible, and an adequate account of scientific rationality must be able to accommodate such cases.

I won't attempt to develop an account of scientific rationality that accommodates such cases. Instead, I'll discuss a couple of extant views of rationality, due to Bas van Fraassen (1989) and P.D. Magnus (2014) that, in my view, hold some promise for accommodating such cases. Both views are broadly pragmatist in nature, and both hold that rationality concerns what is permitted, as opposed to what is required. On van Fraassen's (1989, pp. 171–172) view, "what it is rational to believe includes anything that one is not rationally compelled to disbelieve." And since distinct sets of beliefs can be consistent with this prescription, van Fraassen's account allows for the possibility that "rational persons with the same evidence can still disagree in their opinion" (1989, p. 175). In a similar vein, Magnus's view "allows for some people to rationally believe *P* and others to rationally believe ~*P*" (2014, p. 134). Magnus can thus acknowledge that "rationality must allow agents in comparable circumstances to come to different beliefs; that is, epistemology must be *permissive*" (2014, p. 132). Both views thus allow for the possibility that rational scientists could have disagreed regarding, say, their beliefs in the existence of phlogiston. And to that extent, both views hold some promise for accommodating cases in which retention and elimination are both rational decisions.

There are, however, two respects in which these views would need to be developed further in order to fully accommodate such cases. First of all, both views concern the rationality of beliefs, and they would need to be extended to cover the rationality of decisions, like the decision between retaining and eliminating a given entity. Second, both views concern individual rationality as opposed to collective rationality, and to accommodate my conclusions about the rationality of the community of chemists as a whole, it's necessary to say something about collective rationality. Magnus is not silent on this issue: he puts forward his view in an attempt to show that collective rationality does not require scientists to violate individual rationality. He begins with the idea that collective rationality may require scientists to adopt different beliefs in the same circumstances. While some philosophers[14] hold that collective rationality thus requires scientists to violate individual rationality, Magnus argues that it can be rational for individual scientists to adopt different beliefs in the same circumstances. It would involve a further step to draw the same conclusion about collective rationality and show that, say, different communities (perhaps subcommunities or counterfactual communities) can rationally adopt different beliefs, or make different decisions, in the same circumstances. Taking this further step would be necessary to accommodate cases like the one I discussed. That said, I suspect that, with a bit of work, a view of the kind that Magnus and van Fraassen defend can be extended to decisions and to collective rationality.

3.6 CONCLUSIONS

My primary goal in this chapter has been to argue that it was rational to eliminate phlogiston, but that it also would have been rational to retain it. In doing so, I framed my arguments as a response to Chang's work on the Chemical Revolution. I also attempted to show that the identification of phlogiston with hydrogen, as made by a number of prominent phlogiston theorists in the late 18th century, became rather well entrenched by the early 19th century. I employed this identification to evaluate the benefits and harms of retaining and eliminating phlogiston, respectively, and to evaluate the rationality of these two decisions. And I concluded that, more generally, scientific rationality concerns what is permissible, as opposed to what is required.

Acknowledgments

Thanks to Tzu-Wei Hung, Timothy Lane, and the participants of the 2014 IEAS Conference on Reason and Rationality for stimulating my thinking on the topic of rationality; and to David Jacobs, Derek Leben, and Karen Yan for comments on previous drafts. Much of the research for this chapter was completed during my time as a postdoctoral fellow at the Institute of European and American Studies at Academia Sinica, and so I thank the institute, and especially my sponsor, Jih-Ching Ho.

References

Bergman, T. (1785). *A dissertation on elective attractions*. Edinburgh: John Murray.

Boantza, V. (2008). The phlogistic role of heat in the Chemical Revolution and the origins of Kirwan's 'ingenious modifications... into the theory of phlogiston'. *Annals of Science, 65*(3), 309–338.

Bolton, H. C. (Ed.). (1892). *Scientific correspondence of Joseph Priestley: Ninety-seven letters addressed to Josiah Wedgwood, Sir Joseph Banks, Capt. James Keir, James Watt, Dr. William Withering, Dr. Benjamin Rush, and others*. New York: Collins Printing House.

Cavendish, H. (1766). Three papers, containing experiments on factitious air. *Philosophical Transactions, 56*, 141–184.

Cavendish, H. (1784). Experiments on air. *Philosophical Transactions of the Royal Society of London, 74*, 119–153.

Chang, H. (2009). We have never been whiggish (about phlogiston). *Centaurus, 51*(4), 239–264.

Chang, H. (2010). The hidden history of phlogiston: how philosophical failure can generate historiographical refinement. *HYLE, 16*(2), 47–79.

Chang, H. (2011). The persistence of epistemic objects through scientific change. *Erkenntnis, 75*(3), 413–429.

Chang, H. (2012). *Is water H_2O? Evidence, realism and pluralism*. Dordrecht: Springer.

Davy, H. (1808a). The Bakerian Lecture [for 1807]: On some new phenomena of chemical changes produced by electricity, particularly the decomposition of the fixed alkalies, and the exhibition of the new substances which constitute their bases; and on the general nature of alkaline bodies. *Philosophical Transactions of the Royal Society of London, 98*, 1–44.

Davy, H. (1808b). Electro-chemical researches, on the decomposition of the earths; with observations on the metals obtained from the alkaline earths, and on the amalgam procured from ammonia. *Philosophical Transactions of the Royal Society of London, 98*, 333–370.

Davy, H. (1809). The Bakerian Lecture [for 1808]: An account of some new analytical researches on the nature of certain bodies, particularly the alkalies, phosphorus, sulphur, carbonaceous matter, and the acids hitherto undecompounded; with some general observations on chemical theory. *Philosophical Transactions of the Royal Society of London, 99*, 39–104.

Davy, H. (1810a). The Bakerian Lecture for 1809. On some new electrochemical researches, on various objects, particularly the metallic bodies, from the alkalies, and earths, and on some combinations of hydrogene. *Philosophical Transactions of the Royal Society of London, 100*, 16–74.

Davy, H. (1810b). Researches on the oxymuriatic acid, its nature and combinations; and on the elements of the muriatic acid. With some experiments on sulphur and phosphorus, made in the laboratory of the Royal Institution. *Philosophical Transactions of the Royal Society of London, 100*, 231–257.

Davy, J. (1836). *Memoirs of the life of Sir Humphry Davy* (Vol. 1). London: Longman, Rees, Orme, Brown, Green, & Longman.

Gibbes, G. S. (1809). *A phlogistic theory ingrafted upon M. Fourcroy's philosophy of chemistry*. Bath: W. Meyler and Son.

Kinzel, K. (2015). State of the field: are the results of science contingent or inevitable? *Studies In History and Philosophy of Science, 52*, 55–66.

Kirwan, R. (1782). Continuation of the experiments and observations on the specific gravities and attractive powers of various saline substances. *Philosophical Transactions of the Royal Society of London, 72*, 179–236.

Kirwan, R. (1789). *An essay on phlogiston and the constitution of acids* (2nd ed.). London: J. Johnson.

Kitcher, P. (1990). The division of cognitive labor. *The Journal of Philosophy, 87*(1), 5–22.

Klein, U. (2015). A revolution that never happened. *Studies In History and Philosophy of Science, 49*, 80–90.

Kuhn, T. S. (2012/1962). *The structure of scientific revolutions* (50th anniversary ed.). Chicago, IL: University of Chicago Press.

Kusch, M. (2015). Scientific pluralism and the Chemical Revolution. *Studies In History and Philosophy of Science, 49*, 69–79.

Lavoisier, A. L. (1965). *Elements of chemistry*. New York: Dover (Original work published 1789).

Magnus, P. D. (2014). Science and rationality for one and all. *Ergo, 1*(5), 129–138.

Mauskopf, S. H. (2013). Historicizing H_2O. *Studies In History and Philosophy of Science, 44*(4), 623–630.

McEvoy, J. G. (1997). Positivism, whiggism and the Chemical Revolution: a study in the historiography of chemistry. *History of Science, 35*, 1–33.

Partington, J. R. (1961). *A history of chemistry* (Vol. 3). London: Macmillan.

Priestley, J. (1802). Observations and experiments relating to the pile of Volta. *A Journal of Natural Philosophy, Chemistry, and the Arts, by William Nicholson, 1*, 198–204.

Radick, G. (2008). Introduction: Why what if? *Isis, 99*(3), 547–551.

Reiss, J. (2009). Counterfactuals, thought experiments, and singular causal analysis in history. *Philosophy of Science, 76*(5), 712–723.

Samuels, R., Stich, S., & Faucher, L. (2004). Reason and rationality. In I. Niiniluoto, M. Sintonen, & J. Woleński (Eds.), *Handbook of epistemology* (pp. 131–179). Dordrecht, The Netherlands: Springer.

Scheele, C. W. (1780). *Chemical observations and experiments on air and fire*. With a prefatory introduction by Torbern Bergman; translated from the German by J. R. Forster; to which are added notes by Richard Kirwan; with a letter to him from Joseph Priestley. London: J. Johnson.

Scheele, C. W. (1931). On manganese or magnesia; and its properties. In: *The collected papers of Charles Wilhelm Scheele, translated from the Swedish and German originals by Leonard Dobbin* (pp. 17–49). London: G. Bell and Sons (Original work published 1774).

Siegfried, R. (1964). The phlogistic conjectures of Humphry Davy. *Chymia, 9*, 117–124.

Siegfried, R. (1988). The Chemical Revolution in the history of chemistry. *Osiris, 4*, 34–50.

Soler, L. (2008). Are the results of our science contingent or inevitable? *Studies In History and Philosophy of Science, 39*(2), 221–229.

Stewart, J. (2012). The reality of phlogiston in Great Britain. *HYLE, 18*(2), 175–194.

van Fraassen, B. C. (1989). *Laws and symmetry*. Oxford: Clarendon Press.

Zollman, K. J. S. (2010). The epistemic benefit of transient diversity. *Erkenntnis, 72*(1), 17–35.

Endnotes

1. To take one example, Ursula Klein (2015) argues that the changes that Lavoisier inaugurated shouldn't be understood as constituting a revolution at all.
2. Chang is thus consciously engaging in counterfactual history of science (2012, pp. 62–65), and he thus advocates the view that the results of science are contingent as opposed to inevitable (2012, p. 288). In this chapter, I'll follow him in both of these respects. [For more on counterfactual history, see Radick (2008) and Reiss (2009). For more on whether the results of science are contingent or inevitable, see Soler (2008) and Kinzel (2015).]
3. For Kuhn's own discussion of this example, see Kuhn (2012/1962, p. 156).
4. Who often defended distinct and mutually incompatible phlogiston theories, some of which I will discuss in Section 3.3.1.
5. It's worth noting that he thinks these benefits have since been realized "by some very circuitous routes" without phlogiston (2012, p. 47).
6. Or three, if one prefers a two-fluid theory of electricity.
7. Chang draws support from similar claims made by McEvoy (1997, pp. 22–23) and Siegfried (1988, p. 35).
8. For a detailed discussion of this identification, see Stewart (2012).
9. Boantza (2008, p. 332) emphasizes Kirwan's contribution in this regard, and dismisses Cavendish's earlier identification as a "fleeting observation" and an "isolated instance."
10. Seymour Mauskopf (2013, p. 625) and Martin Kusch (2015, p. 75) both make a similar evaluation when they claim that Kirwan's phlogiston theory, which identified phlogiston with hydrogen, did not have the potential to bring about the benefits that Chang discusses.
11. To be sure, though, a caveat is in order here—Arrhenius acids and Brønsted–Lowry acids contain hydrogen, while Lewis acids needn't.
12. These latter two points correspond to the deontological and consequentialist conceptions of rationality that are often discussed in the literature on that topic. [See Samuels, Stich, and Faucher (2004, p. 166) for a good introduction to these two conceptions.]
13. Kusch (2015, p. 74) sees the issue in quite the same way, and claims that Chang's argument requires him to show that it was irrational for chemists working in the late 18th century to abandon phlogiston.
14. For example, Kitcher (1990) and Zollman (2010).

CHAPTER

4

Cross-Cultural Differences in Thinking: Some Thoughts on Psychological Paradigms

N.Y. Louis Lee

The Chinese University of Hong Kong,
Faculty of Education, Programme for the Gifted and Talented,
Hong Kong, China

4.1 INTRODUCTION: A UNIVERSAL MIND GAME

The first decade of the present century saw the popularity of a deductive problem-solving game, Sudoku. In a typical example, the problem solver is presented with a puzzle grid of nine cells by nine cells. The grid is further divided into nine boxes, each three cells by three cells, with each box having its own boundary. Certain digits are already present in the puzzle grid. The problem solver's job is to fill in all empty cells with digits from one to nine, subject to the following constraint:

1. Each column must contain each of the numbers 1 to 9 once and only once;
2. Each row must contain each of the numbers 1 to 9 once and only once;
3. Each box must contain each of the numbers 1 to 9 once and only once.

Fig. 4.1 shows a typical problem. Sudoku is therefore a puzzle calling for deduction from premises with multiple quantifiers.[1] Since its introduction in the United Kingdom in 2004, Sudoku has become extremely popular worldwide; Sudoku problems still feature in many daily newspapers.

Sudoku is therefore an interesting psychological phenomenon: its "universal" popularity suggests that not only diverse populations (both

Rationality. http://dx.doi.org/10.1016/B978-0-12-804600-5.00004-0

		1		9		2	7	
		9			2		5	
2					3			
3				1	4			2
	8						4	
1			2	8				5
			9					7
	1		3			9		
	4	6		7		5		

FIGURE 4.1 **A typical Sudoku problem.** One of the problems tested in Lee, Goodwin, and Johnson-Laird (2008).

agewise and culturewise) are capable of drawing deductions with few instructions but they also enjoy doing them. Indeed, the present authors and colleagues discovered that participants sampled from two different populations spontaneously develop different and more advanced sorts of deductive strategies as they gather Sudoku experience (Lee et al., 2008).

Cognitive scientists studying higher cognition have as their aim in discovering universal principles about human cognition, regardless of theoretical tradition, the following: mental rules (Rips, 1994; Braine & O'Brien, 1998), mental models (Johnson-Laird, 2006), Bayesian theories (Oaksford & Chater, 2007), or cognitive architecture (Newell, 1973, 1990; Anderson & Lebiere, 1998). Recently, cross-cultural psychologists have queried the universal validity of theories in cognitive science. Some of these authors, most notably Richard Nisbett and his colleagues (Nisbett, 2003; Nisbett, Peng, Choi, & Norenzayan, 2001), argue that individuals from different cultures employ different modes of thought because of sociohistorical differences. The main distinction they draw is that between Westerners and East Asians, with the former more likely to engage in "analytic thinking," and the latter more likely to "think holistically," such as accepting seeming contradictions (henceforth, the East vs West theory). They have demonstrated noticeable differences in reasoning tasks between Western and East Asian samples (Norenzayan, Smith, Kim, & Nisbett, 2002; Peng & Nisbett, 1999). In another recent advance, one of those authors coauthored an article, provocatively entitled *The weirdest people in the world?*, suggesting that most psychological experiments (not limited to those in the psychology of thinking) employ participants who are Western, educated, industrialised, rich, and coming from democratic societies (WEIRD) (Henrich, Heine, & Norenzayan, 2010).

They argue that while psychological theories purport to explain universal rules about human behavior, WEIRD participants are hardly representative of mankind; in fact, they are sometimes the least representative. They therefore advocate that psychologists scale down the scope of their theoretical claims: "... we need to be less cavalier in addressing questions of *human* (sic.) nature on the basis of data drawn from this particularly thin, and rather unusual, slice of humanity" (p. 61), and that comparative work should be encouraged by universities and funding agencies alike, so as to build "a more complete understanding of human nature" (p. 82).

Henrich et al.'s (2010) paper therefore serves as a good platform for discussion on the universality of existing cognitive theories (henceforth the "cognitive universals" issue). On one hand, the present author acknowledges the necessity of cognitive scientists to be more sensitive. On the other hand, the cognitive universals issue appears to be a conundrum arising from the incommensurability of different research paradigms as well as intellectual traditions. This paper therefore presents certain observations about the subject.

Its aims are modest: it does not make any attempt to present a comprehensive review of theories and findings in related domains: epistemology, philosophy of science, hermeneutics, philosophy, intellectual history, anthropology, postmodernism, and so on. Likewise, it does not offer a clear solution to the issue: such solution (not resolution) is both implausible and unnecessary. Rather, it details, to a certain extent, the "intellectual conflicts" of the author as both a trained cognitive psychologist in the Western empirical tradition and a culturally aware individual with Chinese cultural roots.

4.2 PIECEMEAL INTELLECTUAL ENDEAVOURS

In 1973 the late cognitive scientist Allen Newell gave a symposium speech, subsequently published as a conference paper entitled *You can't play 20 questions with nature and win*, that was amusing, notorious, and illuminating in equal measure (Newell, 1973). Newell argued that cognitive scientists typically conducted experiments investigating narrowly defined, specific aspects of cognition which, while well designed and having yielded interesting findings, would not just simply add up to form a comprehensive theory about cognition (henceforth, the "unified cognition" issue). He therefore argued for the need of building cognitive architectures: theories of how cognition functions as a whole. He and his colleagues' Soar model (Newell, 1990), as well as other cognitive architectures (eg, ACT-R, Anderson & Lebiere, 1998), are learning models that rely on "production systems," in which cognitive operations or actions are carried out once specified conditions are matched. (The philosopher of mind Jerry Fodor (1983) also famously pointed at the nonmodularity of mind: to put it simply, a "compartmentalised" cognitive system with discrete cognitive processes does not exist). While cognitive architectures have accounted successfully for an impressive range of cognitive phenomena, critics have pointed out that they have the computational power of a universal Turing machine and hence are more similar to a program language than empirically testable theories (Johnson-Laird, 1988, p. 172).

Cross-cultural psychologists who argue that existing theories of cognition ought to account for findings drawn from a wider range of samples are in fact arguing that either (1) it is possible to construct universal cognitive theories after taking into account cultural differences, or (2) it is impossible to construct theories that are universal, because different peoples employ different cognitive processes (regardless of whether those processes are known). In either case, there is a clear and weird (no pun intended) parallel between the "cognitive universals" issue and the "unified cognition" issue: piecemeal research fails to yield universal theories.

In the present author's view, the "cognitive universals" issue may be tackled by examining two key questions: (1) Are current methodologies in the psychology of thinking inherently biased toward explaining Western behavior? and (2) Is the discipline of psychology an all-revealing intellectual apparatus for understanding universal aspects of human thinking?

4.3 IS THE PSYCHOLOGY OF THINKING INHERENTLY CULTURALLY BIASED TOWARD EXPLAINING WESTERN BEHAVIOR?

That psychological elements are present in folk or formal philosophy in a particular culture does not mean that the intellectual field of psychology is necessarily the best mode of enquiry for uncovering processes of human thinking. I take one example: the "three-character classic" (三字經 is a text that young Chinese school children had to recite and memorise. Its authorship and first publication date was not clear, although many attributed authorship to either 王應麟 or 區適子 in the Song Dynasty (宋 AD 960–1279), and many Chinese scholars subsequently edited and modified the text since (黃沛榮 1992). The text comprises pairs of short sentences, each of three-character length (for easy rhyming and memorising by children), and contain foundational Chinese knowledge, including moral teaching, titles of classical Chinese texts, and a chronology of Chinese history, among others. It was considered important enough for the pioneering

Sinologist-cum-missionary James Legge to translate it into English. The first lines of the text are (author's translation):

> 人之初，性本善，性相近，習相遠。
> At birth, men are good-natured;
> Their natures are similar, their habits different.
>
> 苟不教，性乃遷，教之道，貴以專。
> Left uneducated for long, man's nature changes;
> The way to education, lies in dedication.

Although the focus of these lines, as well as of the text in general, is holistic moral education (instilling the right learning attitude of the young), their contents should no doubt impart to the Western reader the flavour of behaviorism, according to which human behavior is shaped predominantly, if not solely, by education and subsequent nurturing after birth. So goes the classic quotation by the American behaviorist John B. Watson, much beloved and cited by modern introductory psychology textbooks:

> Give me a dozen healthy infants, well-formed, and my own specified world to bring them up in and I'll guarantee to take any one at random and train him to become any type of specialist I might select – doctor, lawyer, artist, merchant-chief and, yes, even beggar-man and thief, regardless of his talents, penchants, tendencies, abilities, vocations, and race of his ancestors. (Watson, 1930, p. 82)

In other words, the basic tenet of behaviorism emerged in China several centuries before Watson laid down his own, systematically, explicitly, analytically, and in a way that allows scrutiny by empirical studies, at the start of the 20th century in the United States.

What is the moral here? While the study (not necessarily empirical) of aspects of human behavior and cognition has featured in many cultures and schools of thought, the discipline of psychology, and its subset the psychology of thinking, is essentially "Western," taking root in Western philosophical thought.

While ancient Greek philosophers also had psychological ideas and intuitions that were not put to empirical test, because of the lack of the much clichéd "scientific method" back then, their ideas and intuitions, together with contemporary advances in other scientific fields, gave rise to psychology in the late 19th century.

Scholars in the cultural psychology tradition, most notably the American psychologist Michael Cole, famously traced the development of modern psychology back to early distinctions of two sorts of psychology, one focussing on basic, rule-based mental operations such as visual perception, which were readily amenable to laboratory testing, and the other, Völkerpsychologie (folk psychology), which acknowledges the role of culture and language in shaping higher level mental operations and thoughts (see Cole, 1996, Chapter 1). These scholars, following the groundwork laid out by early Russian psychologists such as Vygotsky and Luria, acknowledge the importance of the cultural context of human thinking and take a decidedly developmental tilt in their research programs. While there is much to admire in such research, it is hard to envisage how universal cognitive processes (if any) may be uncovered beyond a descriptive level.

4.4 A HOLISTIC ANALYSIS OF HOLISTIC VERSUS ANALYTIC THINKING

Consider the following syllogism: all tall athletes have large foot size; famous basketball players have large foot size; famous basketball players are tall athletes.

To anybody with logical training, it should be obvious that this syllogism is invalid; in other words, the truth of the two premises does not yield the truth of the conclusion. One classic finding in the psychology of thinking literature, the "belief bias" effect, suggests that participants are more likely to judge invalid syllogisms to be valid when the conclusion is itself a real world belief (eg, it is indeed true that famous basketball players are tall athletes) than when it is not. Norenzayan et al. (2002) compared the performances of an American (WEIRD) sample and Korean (at least half WEIRD) sample on the task, and hypothesised that because East Asians were more likely to engage in holistic reasoning, their Korean sample should display a stronger belief bias compared with their American counterparts. Indeed, they found such a pattern of results, which they took as empirical support for the distinction between East Asian's holistic thinking and Westerner's analytic thinking. The authors argued that "people in all cultures are likely to possess both [holistic and analytical] reasoning systems" (p. 654) and regard holistic and analytic thinking as preferred thinking styles rather than entrenched processes.

If it were true that people in all cultures are likely to possess both holistic and analytical reasoning systems, and that these "reasoning systems" were merely preferred thinking styles, then it would be reasonable for the reader to assume that if deductive validity had been explicitly defined for Norenzayan et al.'s (2002) Korean sample, those East Asians would have displayed a much weaker belief bias effect (psychologists are knowledgeable of fine instructional effects on experimental performance; Hudson (1966), for instance, demonstrated that English schoolboys belonging to the arts study stream naturally did not think like those in the science study stream, but readily did so when instructed to think like science students, and vice versa).

Furthermore, if Norenzayan et al.'s assertions were right, then there would be (to put it lightly) severe theoretical implications on cognitive science. Experiments such as Norenzayan et al. (2002) have yielded valuable evidence in support of the East vs West theory: qualitative differences in reasoning across cultures (the East vs West theory in fact covers other cognitive domains such as attention and categorisation, but this paper shall stick to its focus of reasoning processes). Yet, the East versus West theory is merely descriptive and makes no attempt to specify any concrete cognitive operations as orthodox cognitive science models do. To cite two obvious questions: (1) How does the magic switch between holistic versus analytical thinking operate? and (2) How do monocultural individuals acquire "the other" thinking style, and which universal cognitive processes drive such acquisition? As a corollary, which cognitive processes could possibly be universal, how could we arrive at them, and why?

4.5 SOME THOUGHT EXPERIMENTS

To address the two questions posed toward the end of Section 4.2, I will resort to several thought experiments.

Thought experiment 1a [the "biased psychologists" experiment (a)]: Have researchers on psychology of thinking (whether they conduct cross-cultural studies or not) complete a culturally fair (let us just assume there can be a good one) holistic versus analytic thinking style questionnaire and compute the proportion of holistic versus analytic thinkers.

Thought experiment 1b [the "biased psychologists" experiment (b)]: Compile statistics of Chinese psychologists by research specialty domain and compare them with, for instance, those of psychologists from any "Western" population (probably best if America, since cross-cultural experiments typically employ American participants). For each domain, compare also the relative proportion of psychologists in both samples, having made significant theoretical advances, controlling for base rates and so on.

Thought experiment 2 (the "mind games" experiment): Present classic psychological findings in reasoning (or other domains in psychology, for that matter) to university-educated individuals around the world. Describe corresponding explanatory theories to them. Ask them to indicate how much they believe those theories explain their thinking and compare these scores across different populations.

Thought experiment 3 (the "historical" experiment): If we could press a magic button and delete the past one hundred years' worth of psychological research and start carte blanche, what would we do, and what sort of psychology would we achieve in say 10 years' time?

Thought experiment 4 (the "historical revision" experiment): According to the United Nations Department of Economic and Social Affairs (2014), over half of the world's population (54%) is already urbanised, compared with 30% in 1950. Moreover, the world's urban population is projected to be at 66% in 2050. Many authors—including Nisbett himself—have pointed at the effects of education and globalisation on thinking (Nisbett, 2003, Chapter 8). Will current findings in cognitive science become more universally valid (as the world turns more WEIRD) by 2050, and were they even less valid than now back in 1950?

Thought experiment 5 (the "socio-political context" experiment): One of the 20th century's classic advances in psychology is Amos Tversky and Daniel Kahneman's research program on decision-making, in which they demonstrated the nonlinearity of utility functions for humans: individuals are notoriously risk averse when it comes to gains, and risk seeking when it comes to losses (Tversky & Kahneman, 1981). How might these findings be attenuated in societies less democratic than WEIRD locations?

These experiments range from plausible (experiment 1b), to highly implausible (experiment 3), to outright impossible (eg, experiment 5). Of course, I am by no means advocating conducting them. I shall now comment on each of the experiments.

4.5.1 Are Psychologists Themselves a WEIRD Population?

This author's predictions for experiment 1 (the "biased psychologists" experiment) are that most psychologists are analytic thinkers (analytic as defined in the Western way), and the ratio of psychologists having made big theoretical advances in cognitive psychology to those in, say, social psychology would be much larger among Americans than Chinese. In other words, Chinese psychologists would contribute relatively much more to social psychology than cognitive science compared with Americans. (Ironically enough, the latter prediction, superficially interpreted, would be supportive of the East vs West theory.)

4.5.2 Is Psychology for Real?

The inspiration behind experiment 2 was the idea that experiments in the psychology of thinking were but a "mind game," as suggested to me by individuals involved in the psychology business, ranging from innocent participants to world-renowned professors. Its goal is simple: to see how "epistemologically compatible" psychology is different in lay populations (hence, complementary to experiment 1). Of course, differences between East Asian and Western populations do not necessarily undermine the truth of the theories presented. Rather, the measure is indicative of how much psychological enquiries are embedded in a culture at large. The measure is also likely to tell if certain psychological notions, as operationalized by researchers (in particular cross-cultural researchers), are in fact misrepresentations or even fantasies. The author offers two cases in point. (1) Perhaps as a reaction to Peng and Nisbett's (1999) reductionist view of Chinese dialectical thinking (both folk and philosophical), my colleague W.C. Wong delineated many different sorts of dialectical thinking (Wong, 2006). The author's best guess, of course, is that Peng and Nisbett's theory would hardly be taken seriously on these shores. (2) The American psycholinguist Alfred Bloom gathered much notoriety in his study on counterfactual abilities among the Chinese people (Bloom, 1981). Bloom argued that, unlike English, the Chinese language does not have a specific grammatical syntax indicating counterfactuals, and hence counterfactual thinking was hampered among the Chinese. Bloom's (1981) naïve and grandiose claim was swiftly and readily dismissed by a study by Au (1983), who employed more accurately translated experimental materials (see also Au, 1984, and Bloom, 1984, for a follow-up exchange). (As all Chinese speakers would know, counterfactuals in Chinese are indicated instead by temporal markers.) While Au's rebuttal (1983) might have caused a stir in the United States in the 1980s, imagine how Chinese scholars would have laughed at both the necessity and importance of such a rebuttal to Bloom's "psychological theory."

It is blindingly obvious that a psychologist's own cultural background is part of the cultural context of psychological studies itself.

4.5.3 How Might Psychology Have Been?

Experiment 3 is not completely novel. In their call for more diverse sampling in psychological experiments, Medin and Bang (2008) began with the following question: "What would the field of psychology look like if its beginnings had been in China?" Yet, individuals knowledgeable of Chinese intellectual history would have known that Chinese epistemology would not have given birth to "psychology" [see the seminal work of Chi'en, (1953/2001), Chapter 1]. To the present author, Medin and Bang's question is little different from "What would the field of Chinese medicine look like if its beginnings had been in Britain?"

If psychology were to start today instead, cognitive psychologists would likely have "carved up" cognitive processes in vastly different ways. The popular usage of mobile devices, such as the iPhone, would likely alter theorising of attentional processes, and the dynamism of contemporary society might well be even more sympathetic and encouraging to the theories of bounded rationality and adaptive rationality (Gigerenzer & Selten, 2001). A more "diverse" set of human behavior, thanks to globalisation and advances in information technology, would surely give rise to different research questions and foci in psychological investigations. Experiments 4 and 5 further highlight how much the discipline of psychology itself is itself shaped by sociocultural factors, if not a culture in itself.

4.6 WHAT OF COGNITIVE UNIVERSALS?

Does the above paint a rather gloomy picture of the potential of our understanding cognitive universals? Scientific enquiries rest on both existing theories and assumptions. Cognitive science has given rise to frameworks of understanding human behavior: in the absence of alternative proposals (cf. Section 4.3), humans will have to make do with current theorising about human reasoning processes. (One may also point at linguistic similarities among different peoples as grounds to believe in the universality of reasoning processes; see, eg, Chomsky, 1995; Hauser, Chomsky, & Fitch, 2002.) I invite the reader to revisit the Sudoku phenomenon referred to in Section 4.1. However contrived or well-defined Sudoku puzzles are as instances of human reasoning, as sceptics of formal reasoning research (Voss, Perkins, & Segal, 1991) would argue, that different participant samples are capable of and enjoy solving them is indicative. East Asians also readily draw deductions. Their, together with Westerner's, Sudoku solving abilities also need accounting for. The present author and colleagues explained the findings by means of an existing framework, the mental model theory (Johnson-Laird, 2006).

Interestingly, Henrich et al. (2010) in fact acknowledge the existence of standard rationality theories. They argue that the use of WEIRD samples is justified, because "counter-examples to standard rationality predictions could come from any sample in the world" (p. 81). I concur with this Popperian idea: piecemeal attacks on existing theories are useful in clarifying the theories. Yet, it is not immediately clear, in Henrich et al.'s view, what "standard rationality" constitutes. In a manuscript review, A. Norenzayan (2008) suggested that Peng and Nisbett (1999) "in their *seminal paper* (italics mine) did not claim that the Chinese do not or cannot detect logical consistency. Their claim is that Chinese cultural circumstances encourage a tolerance of apparent contradiction (logical or not)." Is "tolerance of apparent contradiction" some sort of metacognitive operation (in cognitive science parlance) then? What sorts of additional cognitive processing does such tolerance entail? There is, alas, no "standard rationality" in the psychology of thinking research: Bayesian theorists, for instance, hold very different views about rationality from those of, say, mental model researchers. Yet the descriptive, behavioral cross-cultural findings that Henrich et al. (2010) cite do call for reanalyses of rationality. (Think, for instance, if "considering both sides of an argument" were a cultural prerogative of the East; then only doing so would be adaptively rational.) Precisely because I agree with Henrich et al. (2010) suggestion that generalisation is dangerous for science, I am all the more inclined to consider that taking one theory of cognition and then generalizing it to *the* theory of cognition as all the more dangerous.

4.7 RESOLUTIONS

This paper has outlined several problems about problems with current psychology of thinking paradigms; it is therefore, if it may be termed such, a second-order critique. Critiques can, of course, run ad infinitum, with the irony of being driven by a cognitive apparatus, the operation of which is yet unknown.

In their critique of the current state of psychology, Henrich et al. (2010) recommended a restructuring of the discipline, such that journal editors would "press authors to both explicitly discuss and defend the generalisability of their findings" (p. 82). These authors are right in their call for cognitive psychologists to be more sensitive to cultural differences and sample variability in their experimentation and theorising, and to be more alert to theoretical contexts so as to avoid blind adherence to monolithic research paradigms.[2] Yet, psychological studies, whether drawing from cross-cultural samples or only WEIRD participants, whether experimental or observation, are necessarily time bound. All psychological studies, including, of course, those in thinking, are but snapshots of human behavior and thinking in a grand social and historical narrative of human culture(s), with some snapshots more durable and informative than others. It is this fact that psychologists must realize.

The psychology of thinking is perhaps necessarily a fragmented science: a comprehensive picture of the real workings of cognitive processes is hard to get at (re: both the cognitive universals and unified cognition issues), for reasons outlined above. Cognitive scientists may therefore wish to live with this fact. One way to advance psychology may actually be less reliance on existing theoretical frameworks and more reliance on immediate intuition about specific aspects of cognition, as far as research questions are concerned. Cognitive scientists hailing from less WEIRD parts of the world should pay particular effort to identify psychological concepts related to human thinking embedded in their own cultures, and design possible ways to investigate them without blind adherence to existing mainstream psychological frameworks (re: Section 4.3). While back translation now may well be a commonly adopted and accepted methodology for cross-cultural psychological research (Brislin, 1970), that a notion can be understood clearly does not mean it "speaks" to the population (re: experiments 1 and 2). The sizeable literature and long discourse on the Sapir-Whorf hypothesis (Whorf, 1964) have discussed interesting pragmatic effects, as well as other effects on higher cognition (Wierzbicka, 1992).

If there were any truth that a psychologist's own cultural background played any role in their theoretical conceptions about human thinking, Henrich et al. (2010) construal of the cognitive universals problem would be but only one version of the real problem itself, limited by their very own version of WEIRD psychology training. Academic multilingualism, and academic multiculturalism, would therefore be another advice to students of human thinking.

References

Anderson, J. R., & Lebiere, C. (1998). *The atomic components of thought*. Mahwah, NJ: Lawrence Erlbaum Associates.

Au, T. K. (1983). Chinese and English counterfactuals: the Sapir-Whorf hypothesis revisited. *Cognition, 15*, 155–187.

Au, T. K. (1984). Counterfactuals: In reply to Alfred Bloom. *Cognition, 17*, 289–302.

Bloom, A. H. (1981). *The linguistic shaping of thought: A study in the impact of language of thinking in China and the West*. Mahwah, NJ: Lawrence Erlbaum Associates.

Bloom, A. H. (1984). Caution—the words you use may affect what you say: A response to Au. *Cognition, 17*, 275–287.

Braine, M. D. S., & O'Brien, D. P. (Eds.). (1998). *Mental logic*. Mahwah, NJ: Lawrence Erlbaum Associates.

Brislin, R. W. (1970). Back-translation for cross-cultural research. *Journal of Cross-Cultural Psychology, 1*, 185–216.

錢穆 Chi'en M. (1953/2001). 中國思想史 (Chinese intellectual history). 台北：蘭臺出版社。

Chomsky, N. (1995). *The minimalist program*. Cambridge, MA: MIT Press.

Cole, M. (1996). *Cultural Psychology: A once and future discipline*. Cambridge, MA: Belknap.

Fodor, J. (1983). *The modularity of mind*. Cambridge, MA: MIT Press.

Gigerenzer, G., & Selten, R. (Eds.). (2001). *Bounded rationality: The adaptive toolbox*. Cambridge, MA: MIT Press.

Hauser, M., Chomsky, N., & Fitch, W. T. (2002). The language faculty: What is it, who has it, and how did it evolve? *Science, 298*, 1569–1579.

Henrich, J., Heine, S. J., & Norenzayan, A. (2010). The weirdest people in the world? *Behavioural and Brain Sciences, 33*, 61–135.

Hudson, L. (1966). *Contrary imaginations: A psychological study of the English schoolboy*. London: Methuen.

Johnson-Laird, P. N. (1988). *The computer and the mind: An introduction to cognitive science*. London: Fontanta Press.

Johnson-Laird, P. N. (2006). *How we reason*. Oxford: Oxford University Press.

Lee, N. Y. L., Goodwin, G. P., & Johnson-Laird, P. N. (2008). The psychological puzzle of Sudoku. *Thinking and Reasoning, 14*, 342–364.

Medin, D. & Bang, M. (2008). Perspective taking, diversity and partnerships. *American Psychological Association*, 22. http://www.apa.org/science/about/psa/2008/02/medin.aspx

Newell, A. (1973). You can't play 20 questions with nature and win: Projective comments on the papers of this symposium. In W. G. Chase (Ed.), *Visual information processing* (pp. 283–308). New York: Academic Press.

Newell, A. (1990). *Unified theories of cognition*. Cambridge, MA: Harvard University Press.

Nisbett, R. E. (2003). *The geography of thought: How Asians and Westerns think differently… and why*. New York: Free Press.

Nisbett, R. E., Peng, K., Choi, I., & Norenzayan, A. (2001). Culture and systems of thought: Holistic vs. analytic cognition. *Psychological Review, 108*, 291–310.

Norenzayan, A., Smith, E. E., Kim, B. J., & Nisbett, R. E. (2002). Cultural preferences for formal versus intuitive reasoning. *Cognitive Science, 26*, 653–684.

Oaksford, M., & Chater, N. (2007). *Bayesian rationality: The probabilistic approach to human reasoning*. Oxford: Oxford University Press.

Peng, K., & Nisbett, R. E. (1999). Culture, dialectics, and reasoning about contradiction. *American Psychologist, 54*, 741–754.

Perry, W. G., Jr. (1968/1999). *Forms of ethical and intellectual development in the college years: A scheme*. San Francisco, CA: Jossey-Bass.

Rips, L. J. (1994). *The psychology of proof*. Cambridge, MA: MIT Press.

Tversky, A., & Kahneman, D. (1981). The framing of decisions and the psychology of choice. *Science, 211*, 453–458.

United Nations Department of Economic and Social Affairs (2014). *World urbanisation prospects (highlights)*. United Nations, New York: United Nations. Available at: http://esa.un.org/unpd/wup/Highlights/WUP2014-Highlights.pdf

Voss, J. F., Perkins, D. N., & Segal, J. W. (1991). *Informal reasoning and education*. Hillsdale, NJ: Lawrence Erlbaum Associates.

Watson, J. B. (1930). *Behaviourism (rev. ed.)*. Chicago, IL: University of Chicago Press.

Whorf, B. L. (1964). In J. B. Carroll (Ed.), *Language, thought, and reality: Selected writings of Benjamin Lee Whorf*. Cambridge, MA: MIT Press.

Wierzbicka, A. (1992). *Semantics, culture, and cognition: universal human concepts in culture-specific configurations*. Oxford: Oxford University Press.

Wong, W. C. (2006). Understanding dialectical thinking from a cultural-historical perspective. *Philosophical Psychology, 19*, 239–260.

Endnotes

1. Theoretically, it is possible to solve Sudoku puzzles by pure trial and error, but the "problem space" for even the easiest kinds of puzzles available is so big that such a strategy is practically implausible. A variant of trial and error is to enter digits randomly until contradictions are found.
2. Interestingly enough, a landmark Harvard study by educational psychologist William Perry (1968/1999) found that undergraduates gradually shifted from epistemological dualism (believing there are concrete rights and wrongs in knowledge) to epistemological relativism over the course of their studies.

PART III

PATHOLOGY

Those among us who work with psychiatric patients on a regular basis are often struck by certain aspects of their thought that suggest they do care about and are sensitive to evidence. A colleague of one of the editors has a young male patient who suffers from schizophrenic delusions, delusions that include belief that he is the son of the Japanese emperor. Upon being asked how he knows he is the emperor's son, he replies that every morning he appears in the entranceway of a local Japanese department store where he is loudly greeted by a large group of people who are bowing toward him and speaking Japanese. Of course he neglects to offer that, as is the custom of Japanese department stores, they bow to and loudly greet all new customers at the start of each day. In this section our authors explore three themes, two related to delusions and one to ruminations: whether delusional thought results from a failure of systems designed for belief fixation, whether certain delusions serve as evidence that some beliefs are modular, and whether depressive ruminations are in some respects rational.

In "Flying Solo: Delusions, Rationality and Doxastic Solipsism" (Chapter 5), Tim Bayne observes that delusions are typically regarded as failures of rationality. According to this epistemic view, what distinguishes delusional from nondelusional thought is the degree to which persons depart from the norms of good reasoning. Bayne examines a number of objections to this epistemic conception and explores an alternative that centers on the notion of proper function. According to the proper function view, delusions occur when the systems responsible for belief fixation fail to function in the ways for which they were designed.

In "Rationality and Delusion," (Chapter 6), Ian Gold observes that some evolutionary psychiatrists suggest persecutory delusions are an effect of social threats in the evolutionary past. Gold explores this proposal in the context of a general approach to delusions and develops a model of persecution that attempts to explain how delusions develop and why they are retained in the face of conflicting evidence. He suggests that one consequence of this model is that some beliefs, at least some pathological beliefs, are modular.

In "Is Depressive Rumination Rational?" (Chapter 7), Timothy Lane and Georg Northoff assess the relationship between depressive rumination and rationality. They observe that while most mental disorders affect only a small segment of the population, depression is unique in that it is both prevalent and costly. This has led some researchers to propose evolutionary explanations that treat depression as an adaptation. Lane and Northoff consider and reject one such explanation, namely, the "analytical rumination hypothesis" (ARH), which postulates that depression's crucial adaptive trait is rumination—negative, intrusive thoughts. According to ARH, depressive ruminations are not indications of a disorder; rather, they are a rational trade-off because they help solve dilemmas, albeit at the cost of inducing anhedonia. Lane and Northoff argue that ARH is unlikely to be true. In developing their critique of ARH, they appeal to recent imaging studies of depression that show resting state hyperactivity in anterior midline regions of the brain correlates with abnormal levels of self-focus. It seems that on the personal level, patients are trapped within themselves, isolated from the external world; on the subpersonal level, patterns of resting state activity reflect these experiences of self-absorption and isolation. Lane and Northoff conjecture that rational responses to social dilemmas are those that strike a balance between internal and external concerns.

CHAPTER

5

Delusion and the Norms of Rationality

T. Bayne

Monash University, Melbourne, VIC, Australia

5.1 INTRODUCTION

Among the many propositions that human beings are capable of believing, some stand out as being particularly strange and outlandish. Some people believe that a close relative—their wife or husband, for example—has been replaced by a qualitatively identical imposter (Capgras & Reboul-Lachaux, 1923; Young, Reid, & Wright, 1993). Some people believe that a part of their body—an arm or a leg, for example—which is still clearly attached to them is no longer theirs but belongs to someone else, such as the physician examining them (Bisiach & Geminiani, 1991). And some people believe that a malicious agent—a television news anchor, for example—is inserting thoughts into their mind (Frith, 1992). Beliefs of the first kind are known as Capgras delusions, beliefs of the second kind are known as delusions of somatoparaphrenia, and beliefs of the third kind are known as delusions of thought insertion.[1]

Delusions appear to be paradigmatic instances of irrationality, and one might well be forgiven for assuming that anyone with the beliefs just mentioned must be flouting the norms of epistemic rationality. Not only do the agents in question not appear to have any evidence for their beliefs, they also appear to have a great deal of evidence against them. The literature on delusions certainly assumes that delusions are, in essence, disorders of rationality. Consider the following much-cited characterization of delusion:

> Delusion: A false belief based on incorrect inference about external reality that is firmly sustained despite what everyone else believes and despite what constitutes incontrovertible or obvious proof or evidence to the contrary. (DSM IV-TR, 2000)

Rationality. http://dx.doi.org/10.1016/B978-0-12-804600-5.00005-2

Many aspects of this characterization have come in for widespread criticisms—delusions need not be false, they need not be based on inference, and they need not concern external reality (Davies, Coltheart, Langdon, & Breen, 2001)—but few theorists have taken issue with the claim that delusions are held in the face of "incontrovertible or obvious proof or evidence to the contrary."[2] Despite its intuitive appeal and undoubted influence, the epistemic conception of delusions is open to criticism on a number of fronts. This paper examines three of the central criticisms facing the epistemic account and explores an alternative view of delusion that centers on the notion of proper function.[3]

5.2 THE EPISTEMIC CONCEPTION OF DELUSION

Let us begin with the notion of epistemic rationality. To be epistemically rational is to adhere to the norms of epistemic rationality.[4] What precisely those norms are is a matter of dispute (Gigerenzer, 1991; Goldman, 1986; Harman, 1986; Kaplan, 1996; Rescher, 1988), but we can assume that any list of epistemic norms will include the norm of proportioning one's belief according to one's evidence. One is epistemically irrational in believing *P* insofar as one lacks adequate evidence for *P*.

Epistemic rationality must be distinguished from instrumental rationality. It can be instrumentally rational to believe a proposition for which one lacks evidence if believing that proposition contributes toward the realization of one's goals. Believing that a business venture will succeed might be epistemically irrational if one's evidence indicates that it will fail, but it might be instrumentally rational insofar as believing that it will succeed is likely to increase its chance of success.

Many of the questions surrounding the notion of epistemic rationality center on the notion of evidence. One such question concerns the types of mental states that can provide evidence for or against a belief. Although some theorists have claimed that "nothing can count as a reason for holding a belief except another belief" (Davidson, 1986, p. 310), it is surely plausible to regard perceptual experience and bodily sensations as providing reasons for belief in their own right. Seeing a dog gives one reason to believe that there is a dog in front of one and feeling pain gives one reason to believe that one has suffered bodily damage. The epistemic status of an agent's belief is a function not only of what beliefs they have but also of their experience.

Experiences function as a source of evidence in virtue of their representational content. Thus any account of epistemic rationality must address the question of what kinds of contents can be presented in experience. This is a contentious issue, and there is little agreement on the kinds of properties that can be experientially encoded. Some theorists hold that perception is restricted to "low-level" properties such as shape, colour, and spatial location; others hold that it can also include "high-level" properties such as biological properties, causal properties, and mental properties (Bayne, 2009; Siegel, 2006; Hawley & Macpherson, 2011).

Might there be propositions that are epistemically (ir)rational in and of themselves, that is, independent of the agent's other mental states? One might think so. Arguably, it would be rational to both accept self-verifying propositions (such as "I believe that I have beliefs") and reject self-refuting propositions (such as "I believe that I have no beliefs") irrespective of one's other mental states. But self-verifying and self-refuting propositions are rather unusual. What about propositions, which are neither self-verifying nor self-refuting? Consider the proposition that emeralds are grue, where grue is the property of being green if examined before some future time *t* and blue if examined thereafter (Goodman, 1973). David Lewis (1986) once claimed that it would be "utterly unintelligible and nonsensical" to believe that emeralds are grue. Lewis is surely right to suggest that there is something decidedly odd for a human being to believe that emeralds are grue, but it is far from clear that this is a verdict which an account of epistemic rationality should deliver (as Lewis himself noted). One can certainly imagine a scenario in which gruesome beliefs might be held without flouting the norms of rationality. (On planets in which emeralds are indeed grue, natural selection might well have fashioned creatures to spontaneously form the belief that emeralds are grue.) So, if there is a sense of "irrationality" according to which it is irrational to believe that emeralds are grue, this must be a nonepistemic sense of the term.

So much for epistemic rationality—how exactly might an appeal to epistemic rationality ground an account of delusion? The basic idea is that delusions are formed and maintained in the face of the agent's evidence—evidence that is not merely accessible to the agent in some extended sense of the term, but evidence that the agent actually grasps and should recognize as evidence against the relevant claim. However, this basic idea is clearly in need of supplementation, for it is possible to violate the norms of epistemic rationality without being delusional. When are violations of epistemic rationality delusional rather than simply examples of everyday irrationality?

There are two approaches that one might consider here: a *kinds* approach and a *capacities* approach. The kinds approach attempts to distinguish delusions from everyday instances of irrationality by appealing to the kinds of violations that occur in the two contexts: on this view, everyday instances of irrationality involve relatively minor violations of the norms of epistemic rationality, whereas delusions involve major or gross violations of those norms. The DSM implicitly assumes this position in characterizing delusion as belief in the face of "incontrovertible or obvious proof or evidence to the contrary" (DSM IV-TR). The capacities conception however, focuses on the agent's cognitive capacities in distinguishing delusional irrationality from everyday irrationality. One of the striking features of delusions is that we tend not to blame individuals for their delusional beliefs; we think of delusions as states that afflict individuals as opposed to exercises of judgment for which they might be held responsible. By contrast, we typically hold individuals responsible for nondelusional instances of irrationality: for engaging in wishful thinking, for jumping to conclusions, and for ignoring evidence. One explanation for our contrasting attitudes here is that we assume that those guilty of everyday irrationality are capable of avoiding their errors, whereas those guilty of delusional irrationality are not. But although the kinds and capacities approaches are conceptually distinct, I suspect that in practice the latter will collapse back into the former, for attempts to determine whether a person has the capacity to reason in accordance with the norms of epistemic rationality are likely to rely on their patterns of reasoning: are their departures from the norms of epistemic rationality relatively minor and corrigible, or are they deep and incorrigible?

So much for epistemic rationality—let me turn now to the first of three challenges that confront the epistemic approach to delusion.

5.3 THE ABSENCE OF REASONING DEFICITS

If delusions involve violations of the norms of epistemic rationality, then one would expect the reasoning patterns of delusional individuals to show systematic departures from the norms of epistemic rationality. However, there is rather little evidence that this is the case.

Let us begin with deductive reasoning. Anecdotally, many delusional individuals appear to retain the capacity to follow deductive arguments. Consider, the following interview with a patient suffering from somatoparaphrenia, who denied ownership of his left hand. The examining physician placed the patient's left hand between his own hands and asked, "Whose hands are these?"

> Patient: Your hands.
> Examiner: How many of them?
> Patient: Three
> Examiner: Ever seen a man with *three* hands?
> Patient: A hand is the extremity of an arm. Since you have three arms, it follows that you must have three hands. (Bisiach, 1988, p. 469)

Such anecdotal reports are reinforced by the failure to find any general deficit in the capacity of delusional individuals to reason deductively

(Cutting, 1997; Maher, 1992). Indeed, studies have found that when common sense and deductive validity come into conflict, schizophrenic individuals are more influenced by validity than nondelusional controls are (Owen, Cutting, & David, 2007).

Of course, deduction is only one aspect of everyday reasoning, and it is arguably a rather marginal element of it at that. To the extent that delusions involve departures from the norms of epistemic rationality it is likely that those departures concern inference to the best explanation or *abduction* (Lipton, 2004). In abductive reasoning, one proposition recommends itself as belief-worthy (or at least, as more worthy of belief than a competing proposition) in virtue of its capacity to explain a particular datum. For example, one might conclude that it rained last night on the grounds that there is water in the street. Here, the hypothesis that it rained is justified on the grounds that it accounts for the datum (water in the streets) better than competing hypotheses (eg, that a water pipe burst) do.

Might delusional individuals fail to reason in accord with the norms of abduction? In an important study, Huq, Garety, & Hemsley (1988) discovered an association between delusions and what has become known as a jumping to conclusions (JTC) reasoning bias (Garety & Hemsley, 1994; Garety et al., 2005; see also Dudley & Over, 2003; Fear & Healy, 1997; Fine, Gardner, Craigie, & Gold, 2007). A JTC reasoning bias is paradigmatically tested with the beads task, in which participants are presented with a series of beads that they have been told are drawn from only one of two jars. The jars contain beads of two colours in complementary ratios, for example, 85:15 red to green and 85:15 green to red. Participants are required to guess which of the two jars the beads are being drawn from. Individuals who guess more quickly—or with more certainty—than is typical are said to have a JTC reasoning bias.

Although it is intriguing, the finding that delusional individuals appear to exhibit a JTC bias provides little justification for the epistemic approach. For one thing, the relationship between a JTC bias and the presence of delusions is far from straightforward. A JTC bias has been found in nondelusional schizophrenic individuals (Moritz & Woodward, 2005), in patients whose delusions had remitted (Peters & Garety, 2006), and in the nondelusional relatives of individuals with delusions (Van Dael et al., 2006). More importantly, those who display a JTC bias need not be violating the norms of epistemic rationality. Consider a subject who is disposed to make a judgment about which urn the beads are being drawn from on the basis of a single draw. Such judgments will be correct 85% of the time, and that does not seem to be an unreasonable basis on which to form a belief.[5]

Of course, the beads task taps only one form of abductive reasoning, and it is entirely possible that delusions are associated with systematic deficits or biases in other forms of abductive reasoning. But even if that were the case, it would be a further question whether those biases involve violations of the norms of epistemic rationality. Discussion of this issue is problematized by the fact that the evaluation of abductive inferences is far from straightforward. The beads task lends itself to a straightforward Bayesian solution, for its structure supports precise probability assignments. But few domains share the formal features exhibited by the beads case, and questions about whether a particular abductive inference is legitimate will often be contested.[6]

Although the considerations just adduced put some pressure on the epistemic conception, they are obviously not decisive, and the advocate of the view could argue that delusional individuals have systematic reasoning deficits that simply have not been identified. However, any such response needs to be accompanied by an account of why these deficits might have escaped detection. One possibility is that they are relatively subtle. However, they cannot be too subtle given our capacity to distinguish delusional irrationality from everyday irrationality. Another possibility is that they have escaped detection because they are domain specific. But here too the advocate of the epistemic approach must tread carefully, for the domains in terms of which reasoning is structured are unlikely to be as specific as those that characterize (monothematic) delusions. (It is unlikely that there is a module dedicated to reasoning about the identity of close family members.) There is clearly a great deal more to be said on these issues, but the considerations presented here suggest that the epistemic approach faces something of a challenge in explaining away the lack of general reasoning deficits in individuals with (monothematic) delusion.

5.4 THE CHALLENGE FROM COGNITIVE NEUROPSYCHIATRY

A second challenge to the epistemic conception derives from cognitive neuropsychiatry itself, for some of the leading accounts of delusions provided by cognitive neuropsychiatry are not easily squared with the epistemic account.

Let me illustrate this point with reference to what is arguably the poster child of contemporary cognitive neuropsychiatry: the Capgras delusion. Central to contemporary treatments of the Capgras delusion is a model of vision according to which there are two pathways from the face recognition system, one of which involves affective processing and one of which involves semantic processing concerning the identity of particular individuals (Ellis & Lewis, 2001; Ellis & Young, 1990). The Capgras delusion is thought to involve damage to the affective pathway: although the patient is able to recognize the faces of family members, this recognition is not accompanied by the normal feeling of familiarity. In order to explain this anomaly, the patient forms the belief that the person they are looking at is not the family member who they claim to be but is instead an imposter. This model has been confirmed by the finding that the physiological response to familiar faces in Capgras patients is abnormally reduced (Brighetti, Bonifacci, Borlimi, & Ottaviani, 2007; Ellis, Lewis, Moselhy, & Young, 2000; Ellis, Young, Quayle, & de Pauw, 1997; Hirstein & Ramachandran, 1997).

Assuming that this model is basically on the right lines, what should we say about the patient's epistemic situation? Given his anomalous affective experience, is he flouting the norms of epistemic rationality in forming (and then maintaining) the belief that the woman he sees is not his wife?

To address this question we must consider two issues, the first of which concerns the nature of the patient's experience of his wife. What impact does the damage to the affective pathway have on the patient's conscious life? Does it give rise to a generic sense that "something isn't right"? Does it give rise to a specific experience of his wife as an imposter (Bayne & Pacherie, 2004a,b)? Or is the impact of the damage on consciousness restricted to the thought, "Perhaps this woman is not my wife" (Coltheart, Menzies, & Sutton, 2010)? One cannot take a stand on the degree to which Capgras patients flout the norms of epistemic rationality without addressing these issues, for the content of an individual's experience of the world has a direct impact on the kinds of beliefs that they are rationally permitted to form.

The second issue in need of clarification concerns the role of the patient's background knowledge of the world. Evaluating the plausibility of the Capgras belief requires determining not only the patient's experience but also his background beliefs about such things as the possibility of imposter scenarios. It is not implausible to suppose that such considerations will defeat whatever evidence the patient's experience provides for the Capgras hypothesis. As Coltheart and his collaborators put it:

> Capgras patients exhibit nonstandard reasoning in the sense that they do not efficiently use the right subset of background beliefs, or check their hypothesis effectively against other information available to them. As a result, their abductive reasoning isn't reliable. (Coltheart et al., 2010, p. 276)

By "nonstandard" Coltheart and colleagues mean not (just) that the Capgras patient fails to reason in a way that a cognitively unimpaired human being would reason, but that their reasoning is normatively inappropriate, that they ignore "obvious proof or evidence to the contrary."

This position is certainly tempting but it is not irresistible. One problem is that it is far from obvious how one ought to weigh current experience against background belief for the purposes of belief revision (Davies & Egan, 2013; McKay, 2012; Stone & Young, 1997). Perhaps it is rational (or at least not irrational) to privilege the testimony of persistent immediate experience over that of background belief or the claims of medical professionals (Hohwy & Rosenberg, 2005). Furthermore, it is unclear whether the kinds of additional information with which the patient might be confronted—"that trusted friends and family believe the person is his wife, that this person wears a wedding ring that has his wife's initials engraved in it, that this person knows things about the subject's past life that only his wife could know" (Coltheart et al., 2010, p. 279)—entails that the imposter hypothesis is "absurd," "preposterous," or "unbelievable"; in fact, given all the other evidence that the patient has, it may not even render the imposter hypothesis unreasonable. After all, any imposter worth her salt would be able to fool friends and family, would have a wedding ring with the correct initials engraved on it, and would know anything that the patient's wife would know. The very nature of the imposter hypothesis ensures that clear and compelling evidence against it will be difficult to procure.

How might the advocate of the epistemic account respond to the considerations provided in this section? One option would be to suggest that these considerations do not tell against the epistemic account of delusions, but instead show that the Capgras delusion is not a genuine delusion. I think this line of response should be taken seriously. Our pretheoretical judgments about the kinds of beliefs that are (and are not) delusional are not sacrosanct but are revisable in light of developments in cognitive neuropsychiatry. It is also worth noting that the amount of attention the Capgras delusion has received from cognitive neuropsychiatry is out of all proportion with its prevalence. Delusions of persecution, jealousy, grandiosity, and reference are vastly more common, and we have not yet seen any reason to deny that these delusions involve serious violations of the norms of epistemic rationality.

These points are not without merit, but their force must be tempered by the following considerations. First, although the Capgras delusion may not be particularly common it does seem to be a paradigmatic example of a delusion, and any account of delusion ought to vindicate our judgments about paradigmatic instances of the category. Second, and more importantly, the challenge posed by cognitive neuropsychiatry concerns not only the Capgras delusion but extends to a number of other monothematic delusions, for experience-based accounts have been offered of the Cotard delusion, the Fregoli delusion, the delusion of alien control, reduplicative paramnesia, the delusion of mirrored misidentification, the delusion of thought insertion, and anosagnosia for hemiplegia (see Davies et al., 2001, and Coltheart, 2007, for reviews). The advocate of the epistemic conception who is tempted to endorse the response considered here might find that they are forced to adopt an implausibly restrictive conception of the domain of the delusional.

5.5 THE DEMARCATION CHALLENGE

A third challenge to the epistemic approach concerns the task of demarcating delusional beliefs from ordinary nondelusional beliefs that are (also) held in the face of "incontrovertible or obvious proof or evidence to the contrary." Whereas the previous two objections focused on the idea that violating the norms of epistemic rationality is a necessary condition on being a delusion, this objection focuses on the claim that it is not a sufficient condition.

As we noted in Section 5.2, it is natural for the advocate of the epistemic approach to distinguish delusional irrationality from ordinary instances of irrationality by appealing to the degree to which the belief flouts the norms of epistemic rationality: unlike everyday irrationality, delusional irrationality involves believing in the face of obvious evidence to the contrary, where what is obvious is not the evidence itself but the fact that it makes the delusional thought extremely unlikely. But although this proposal might enable us to demarcate delusional belief from certain kinds of everyday instances of irrationality, it struggles to demarcate delusional belief from many culturally sanctioned beliefs.

Consider the Uduk of Sudan, who believe that ebony trees can overhear human conversation, and that by burning an ebony twig in water and reading its ashes one can decipher the secret plans of witches (James, 1988). These beliefs appear to violate the norms of epistemic rationality in striking ways. Surely, one is tempted to think, the Uduk have independent (and, one might think, conclusive) reasons to deny that trees can hear and that the plans of witches can be divined in the traces left by ashes. Yet it is also clear that these beliefs are not delusional, at least not when they are held in the context of Uduk culture. (It might, of course, be delusional for a contemporary Westerner to hold these beliefs.) Instances of nondelusional irrationality are rife within our own culture, although their familiarity blinds us to their existence. Consider the widespread belief that one will be subject to bad luck if a black cat crosses one's path on Friday the 13th. From an epistemic point of view this belief appears to be no worse off than the belief that the world is about to end because a black car has stopped in front of one's house, yet the former belief is a culturally sanctioned superstition whereas the latter would be regarded as delusional (Spitzer, 1990). Does the epistemic approach have the resources to distinguish genuine delusions from culturally sanctioned exercises of irrationality? Call this the demarcation challenge.

One response to the demarcation challenge is to reject the assumption that there is a genuine distinction between delusions and culturally sanctioned exercises of irrationality. From a scientific point of view—this line of response continues—there is no difference between those beliefs that are typically regarded as delusional and those culturally sanctioned beliefs that are held "in the face of obvious proof or evidence to the contrary." But although this position might resonate with some authors—consider Richard Dawkins's (2006) description of religious belief as delusional—I see little reason to take it seriously. Clinical assumptions about the domain of the delusional are not beyond scrutiny but they should be taken seriously, and it is clear that culturally sanctioned beliefs of the kind described here fall outside their scope.

The DSM attempts to meet the demarcation challenge by appending the following clause to its characterization of delusion: "The belief is not one ordinarily accepted by other members of the person's culture or subculture (eg, it is not an article of religious faith)." This response is clearly an ad hoc attempt to save the epistemic view by fiat and does nothing to address the core challenge. To have any plausibility the epistemic approach must be able to demarcate delusional belief from culturally sanctioned beliefs on the basis of epistemic considerations alone.

A third response to the demarcation challenge involves an appeal to testimony. Consider the following passage from Richard Samuels:

> When I believe that there is an all-powerful God, I do so in part on the basis of widespread access to testimony: (putative) experts—eg, priests and rabbis—television shows, popular opinion, and so on. The belief may well be false, and such testimony may ultimately be subject to defeaters. But there is little doubt that testimony is a genuine source of warrant, and there is little doubt that in societies where theism is widespread, many such lines of testimony exist, and most of us are exposed to it from an early age. (Samuels, 2009, p. 70)

This line of thought is far and away the most promising response to the demarcation challenge, but I am not persuaded that it is completely successful.

First, even if culturally sanctioned beliefs are sustained by testimony, it does not follow that they are not also endorsed in the face of "obvious proof or evidence to the contrary." One might argue that the sheer implausibility of many religious beliefs—their lack of coherence with the agent's background knowledge of the world—renders their acceptance fundamentally irrational even when they receive the endorsement of one's community. Second, whether or not religious belief (or indeed any other culturally sanctioned belief that we would want to distinguish from delusion) is sustained by "testimony" depends on what exactly testimony involves. As standardly understood, testimony involves a background belief to the effect that the source in question is an epistemic authority. We treat the traveller's reports as a form of testimony, for they have been to places where we have not trod. But although religious belief *can* rest on an appeal to testimony, acquiring the religious beliefs of one's community seems to be less a matter of evidence transfer and more a matter of contagion and imitation: people acquire the religious beliefs of their community in much the way in which they acquire its habits of speech, mores, and social norms. Perhaps "testimony" of some kind does indeed play a pivotal role in demarcating culturally sanctioned belief from delusion, but if so then it is not a notion of testimony that should be understood in purely epistemic terms.

Let me review the three challenges to the epistemic view that I have considered. The first challenge centered on the fact that there is little evidence that delusional individuals have general difficulties in conforming to the norms of epistemic rationality. The second challenge concerned an apparent tension between the epistemic approach and the account of the Capgras delusion provided by cognitive neuropsychiatry. The third challenge is that of justifying the demarcation between delusions and those culturally sanctioned beliefs that are (also) held in the face of obvious evidence to the contrary. Although none of these challenges refutes the epistemic approach—the open-ended nature of the relevant concepts surely renders any such talk inappropriate—they do put considerable pressure on it. Perhaps we ought to approach delusions from another angle.

5.6 THE FUNCTIONAL CONCEPTION OF DELUSION

The norms of epistemic rationality tell you what you ought to do insofar as you are a rational agent. But there is another set of norms to which we might appeal in thinking about what is distinctive of delusions: functional norms.[7] The functional norms of belief revision tell you what you ought to do insofar as you are a normally functioning agent. The functional norms that apply to a particular creature depend on its cognitive architecture, on how it has been designed. Just as the visual system is designed to generate certain kinds of experiences when stimulated in certain ways, so too the belief-forming system is designed to generate certain kinds of beliefs when stimulated in certain ways. The functional approach conceives of delusions as the doxastic counterparts to the visual agnosias: they are caused by the failure of a psychological system to function in accordance with its design specifications.[8]

Although there is a clear conceptual distinction between the functional approach and epistemic approach, one might worry that the distinction is *merely* conceptual, and that the functional norms of belief formation should be identified with the epistemic norms of belief formation. In other words, one might think that the norms which specify how a properly functioning human being will form and revise its beliefs should be identified with the norms which specify how a rational agent should form and revise its beliefs. According to this perspective, the functional approach would not be an alternative to the epistemic approach but would instead provide its philosophical foundations (as it were). But although this view is widely (if implicitly) held, it is also deeply mistaken, and there are a number of powerful reasons to think that the functional norms of belief formation are not coeval with the epistemic norms of belief formation.

First, it is unlikely that evolution *could have* selected for mechanisms that perfectly conform to the norms of epistemic rationality. We are the products of natural selection, and evolution has fashioned our cognitive capacities from whatever materials were ready to hand (Stich, 1990). Moreover, there is no particular reason to think that evolution would have selected for mechanisms that operate in accord with the norms of epistemic rationality even if it could have done so. From an evolutionary perspective, the point of belief formation is not to equip the organism with a true and complete picture of the world but to improve its fitness, and there is no particular reason to assume that fitness is always (or even generally) maximized by a cognitive architecture that cleaves to the norms of epistemic rationality. On the contrary, there is good reason to suspect that organisms may be best served by mechanisms of belief fixation that depart from those norms in systematic ways (McKay & Dennett, 2009; Sperber & Mercier, 2012).[9]

In light of these considerations, it should be no surprise to discover that neurotypical human beings are indeed systematically irrational (Samuels & Stich, 2004; Samuels, Stich, & Bishop, 2002). We struggle with the Wason (1966) selection task, we ignore base rates (Kahneman & Tversky, 1973), we are willing to believe that a conjunction is more probable than its conjuncts (Tversky & Kahneman, 1982), and we are prone to form beliefs that portray ourselves in a flattering manner (Alicke, Vredenburg, Hiatt, & Govorun, 2001; Taylor & Brown, 1988). In short, there is every reason to think that the functional norms of human belief fixation are not coeval with the norms of epistemic rationality.

The functional conception might depart from the epistemic conception in substantive ways, but why think that it is superior to it? Delusions might often be described as "pathologies of belief" (Coltheart & Davies, 2000), but do such descriptions get to the heart of the matter?

Let us begin with the fact that delusional individuals do not appear to have general reasoning deficits. As we noted in Section 5.3, this fact poses a challenge to the epistemic approach, for if delusions are essentially violations of epistemic rationality, then one would expect delusional individuals to display failures of epistemic rationality in nondelusional contexts. But the fact that delusional individuals do not display systematic departures from the norms of epistemic rationality does not put the same kind of pressure on the functional approach, for the functional approach involves no commitment to the idea that delusions are essentially violations of epistemic rationality. In saying this I do not mean to suggest that delusions *do* generally conform to the norms of epistemic rationality—in fact, most delusions probably violate such norms in fundamental ways—but simply that we should not assume that delusions are epistemically irrational.

What about the challenge from cognitive neuropsychiatry? Let us return to the Capgras delusion. As we noted in Section 5.4, there are various ways to think about current models of the Capgras delusion from the perspective of epistemic rationality. On some interpretations of the data, Capgras patients flout the norms of epistemic rationality, but on other interpretations of the data they do not. Deciding between these interpretations is far from straightforward, for it requires taking a position on a number of contested issues, such as how the patient experiences his wife (does he experience her as an imposter?), and how one should weigh the testimony of first-person experience against that of background belief and the claims of others. So, on the epistemic view of delusions there are real questions concerning whether the Capgras delusion is indeed a delusion.

From a functional perspective, the central question is whether the Capgras patient departs from the functional norms of belief formation. If the model of the Capgras delusion provided by cognitive neuropsychiatry is on the right lines, then Capgras patients do indeed depart from those norms (widely construed), for a properly functioning cognitive agent would not hold the Capgras belief in the contexts in which the Capgras patient does.

But perhaps the strongest argument for the functional conception concerns its capacity to meet the demarcation challenge. There are two strands to the functional response to this challenge. The first strand involves the idea that certain kinds of thoughts come naturally to human beings, whereas others occur only to human beings who are cognitively impaired in some way. Religious beliefs clearly belong in the first category. We may not be designed to endorse any particular set of religious (superstitious, moral, or political) beliefs—evolution does not, in general, operate at that level of granularity—but we are naturally disposed to look for signs of supernatural agency (Barrett, 2000; Guthrie, 1995). By contrast, believing that a close relative has been replaced by an imposter, that a part of one's own body is in fact a part of someone else's body, and that malicious agents are inserting thoughts into one's mind does not come naturally to human beings, at least not in quite the same way.[10] We might compare delusional beliefs with the "gruesome beliefs" mentioned in Section 5.2: although they might be functionally appropriate for the members of some possible species, they do not appear to fit the functional profile of human beings.

The second strand in the functionalist response to the demarcation challenge concerns the role of a person's social context in shaping their beliefs. As Murphy notes, "it's normal for people to pick up beliefs that we find weird from the culture around them, and not normal for them to arrive at equivalently weird beliefs all by themselves in cultures that provide no support for such beliefs" (2013, p. 119). We might also add that it is not normal for people to cling to beliefs that are regarded as deviant by the members of their community. One might appeal to an epistemic notion of testimony at this point (as we observed earlier), but I doubt that any such appeal will do justice to the wide range of ways in which an individual's social context sculpts their doxastic profile.[11]

5.7 CONCLUSIONS

I opened this essay with the observation that delusions appear to be paradigmatic instances of irrationality: they strike us as canonical examples of beliefs that violate the norms of epistemic rationality. We have seen that vindicating this observation has proven to be rather more challenging than we might have anticipated. I have suggested that instead of trying to patch up the epistemic view of delusions we should think of delusions in functional terms: what makes a belief delusional is the fact that a human being with a normally functioning belief-forming system would not have endorsed it (at least, not with delusional conviction). Although delusions may (and often will) flout the epistemic norms of belief formation, they need not.

Let me end with some brief reflections on what this approach might entail with respect to the question of whether delusions qualify as a "natural kind" (Gilleen & David, 2005; Samuels, 2009; Radden, 2011). In this essay I have followed orthodoxy in assuming that delusions qualify as a unitary kind in some relatively robust sense. But we should recognize that this assumption is far from secure. Psychiatric taxonomy is not in good shape (Stich & Murphy, 2000; Poland, Von Eckardt, & Spaulding, 1994), and it is entirely possible that the category of delusions will not be retained by a mature science of mental disorder. From the perspective of the functional approach the central question here is whether the various ways in which human beings depart from the functional norms of belief formation might be usefully bundled together. Arguably the central "fault lines" in an overarching theory of delusion should be structured not in terms of delusional content but in terms of the ways in which the agent in question has departed from the functional norms of belief formation. This perspective might motivate us to group together delusions with different contents should they turn out to involve the same kind of doxastic dysfunction, and to regard delusions with the same content as instances of distinct delusional types should they turn out to involve different kinds of doxastic dysfunction (Breen, Caine, & Coltheart, 2001). In other words, the functional perspective might have an impact not only on our conception of delusions as such, but also on our view of what it is for two beliefs to count as instances of the same type of delusion.

References

Alicke, M. D., Vredenburg, D. S., Hiatt, M., & Govorun, O. (2001). The "better than myself effect". *Motivation and Emotions, 25*, 7–22.

American Psychiatric Association. (2000). *Diagnostic and statistical manual of mental disorders* (4th ed., text rev.). Washington, DC: Author.

American Psychiatric Association. (2013). *Diagnostic and statistical manual of mental disorders* (5th ed.). Washington, DC: Author.

Barrett, J. L. (2000). Exploring the natural foundations of religion. *Trends in Cognitive Sciences, 4(1)*, 29–34.

Bayne, T. (2009). Perception and the reach of phenomenal content. *Philosophical Quarterly, 59(236)*, 385–404.

Bayne, T., & Pacherie, E. (2004a). Bottom-up or top-down?: Campbell's rationalist account of monothematic delusions. *Philosophy, Psychiatry & Psychology, 11(1)*, 1–11.

Bayne, T., & Pacherie, E. (2004b). Experience, belief, & the interpretive fold. *Philosophy, Psychiatry & Psychology, 11(1)*, 81–86.

Bisiach, E. (1988). Language without thought. In L. Weiskrantz (Ed.), *Thought without language* (pp. 464–484). Oxford University Press.

Bisiach, E., & Geminiani, G. (1991). Anosognosia related to hemiplegia and heminopia. In G. P. Prigatano, & D. L. Schachter (Eds.), *Awareness of deficit after brain injury: Clinical and theoretical issues* (pp. 17–39). Oxford: Oxford University Press.

Boyer, P. (2010). Intuitive expectations and the detection of mental disorder: a cognitive background to folk-psychiatries. *Philosophical Psychiatry, 23(6)*, 821–844.

Breen, N., Caine, D., & Coltheart, M. (2001). Mirrored-self misidentification: two cases of focal onset dementia. *Neurocase, 7(3)*, 239–254.

Brighetti, G., Bonifacci, P., Borlimi, R., & Ottaviani, C. (2007). Far from the heart far from the eye: evidence from the Capgras delusion. *Cognitive Neuropsychiatry, 12*, 189–197.

Capgras, J., & Reboul-Lachaux, J. (1923). L'illusion des 'soises' dans un délire systématisé chronique. *Bulletin de la Société Clinique et Médicine Mentale, 11*, 6–16.

Cherniak, C. (1986). *Minimal rationality*. Cambridge, MA: MIT Press.

Coltheart, M. (2007). The 33rd Sir Frederick Bartlett Lecture: Cognitive neuropsychiatry and delusional belief. *The Quarterly Journal of Experimental Psychology, 60(8)*, 1041–1062.

Coltheart, M., & Davies, M. (2000). *Pathologies of belief*. Oxford: Wiley-Blackwell.

Coltheart, M., Menzies, P., & Sutton, J. (2010). Abductive inference and delusional belief. *Cognitive Neuropsychiatry, 15*(1–3), 261–287.

Cummins, R. C. (1975). Functional analysis. *Journal of Philosophy, 72*, 741–764.

Cutting, J. (1997). *Principles of psychopathology*. Oxford: Oxford University Press.

Davidson, D. (1986). A coherence theory of truth and knowledge. In E. LePore (Ed.), *Truth and interpretation: Perspectives on the philosophy of Donald Davidson*. Oxford: Blackwell.

Davies, M., Coltheart, M., Langdon, R., & Breen, N. (2001). Monothematic delusions: towards a two-factor account. *Philosophy, Psychiatry and Psychology, 8*(2/3), 133–158.

Davies, M., & Egan, A. (2013). Delusion: Cognitive approaches—Bayesian inference and compartmentalisation. In K. W. M. Fulford, M. Davies, R. G. T. Gipps, G. Graham, J. Sadler, G. Stanghellini, & T. Thornton (Eds.), *The Oxford handbook of philosophy and psychiatry* (pp. 689–730). Oxford: Oxford University Press.

Dawkins, R. (2006). *The God delusion*. London: Transworld Publishers.

Dudley, R. E. J., & Over, D. E. (2003). People with delusions jump-to-conclusions: a theoretical account of research findings on the reasoning of people with delusions. *Clinical Psychology & Psychotherapy, 10*, 263–274.

Ellis, H. D., & Lewis, M. B. (2001). Capgras delusion: A window on face recognition. *Trends in Cognitive Sciences, 5*, 149–156.

Ellis, H. D., & Young, A. W. (1990). Accounting for delusional misidentifications. *British Journal of Psychiatry, 157*, 239–248.

Ellis, H. D., Lewis, M. B., Moselhy, H. F., & Young, A. W. (2000). Automatic without autonomic responses to familiar faces: Differential components of covert face recognition in a case of Capgras delusion. *Cognitive Neuropsychiatry, 5,* 255–269.

Ellis, H. D., Young, A. W., Quayle, A. H., & de Pauw, K. W. (1997). Reduced autonomic responses to faces in Capgras delusion. *Proceedings of the Royal Society, Series B: Biological Sciences, 264,* 1085–1092.

Fear, C. F., & Healy, D. (1997). Probabilistic reasoning in obsessive-compulsive and delusional disorders. *Psychological Medicine, 27,* 199–208.

Fine, C., Gardner, M., Craigie, J., & Gold, I. (2007). Hopping, skipping or jumping to conclusions? Clarifying the role of the JTC bias in delusions. *Cognitive Neuropsychiatry, 12(1),* 46–77.

Frith, C. (1992). *The cognitive neuropsychology of schizophrenia.* Hove: Psychology Press.

Garety, P. A., Freeman, D., Jolley, S., Dunn, G., Bebbington, P. E., Fowler, D. G., Kuipers, E., & Dudley, R. (2005). Reasoning, emotions, and delusional conviction in psychosis. *Journal of Abnormal Psychology, 114,* 373–384.

Garety, P. A., & Hemsley, D. R. (1994). *Delusions: Investigations into the psychology of delusional reasoning.* Oxford: Oxford University Press.

Gigerenzer, G. (1991). On cognitive illusions and rationality. *Poznan Studies in the Philosophy of the Sciences and the Humanities, 21,* 225–249.

Gilleen, J., & David, A. S. (2005). The cognitive neuropsychiatry of delusions: From psychopathology to neuropsychology and back again. *Psychological Medicine, 35,* 5–12.

Gold, J., & Gold, I. (2014). *Suspicious minds: How culture shapes madness.* New York: Free Press.

Gold, I., & Hohwy, J. (2000). Rationality and schizophrenic delusion. *Mind and Language, 15(1),* 146–167.

Goldman, A. (1986). *Epistemology and cognition.* Cambridge, MA: Harvard University Press.

Goodman, N. (1973). *Fact, Fiction, and Forecast* (3rd ed.). Indianapolis, IN: Bobbs-Merrill.

Griffiths, P. (1993). Functional analysis and proper functions. *British Journal for the Philosophy of Science, 44,* 409–422.

Guthrie, S. (1995). *Faces in the clouds.* New York: Oxford University Press.

Harman, G. (1986). *Change in view.* Cambridge, MA: MIT Press.

Hawley, K., & Macpherson, F. (2011). *The admissible content of experience.* Oxford: Wiley.

Hirstein, W., & Ramachandran, V. S. (1997). Capgras syndrome: A novel probe for understanding the neural representation of the identity and familiarity of persons. *Proceedings of the Royal Society, Series B: Biological Science, 264,* 437–444.

Hohwy, J., & Rosenberg, R. (2005). Unusual experiences, reality testing and delusions of alien control. *Mind & Language, 20*(2), 141–162.

Huq, S. F., Garety, P. A., & Hemsley, D. R. (1988). Probabilistic judgements in deluded and non-deluded subjects. *Quarterly Journal of Experimental Psychology, A, 40,* 801–812.

James, W. (1988). *The listening ebony. Moral knowledge, religion and power among the Uduk of Sudan.* Oxford: Clarendon Press.

Kahneman, D., & Tversky, A. (1973). On the psychology of prediction. *Psychological Review, 80,* 237–251.

Kaplan, M. (1996). *Decision theory as philosophy.* Cambridge: Cambridge University Press.

Lewis, D. (1986). *On the plurality of worlds.* Oxford: Oxford University Press.

Lipton, P. (2004). *Inference to the best explanation* (2nd ed.). London: Routledge.

Maher, B. A. (1992). Delusions: Contemporary etiological hypotheses. *Psychiatric Annals, 22,* 260–268.

McKay, R. (2012). Delusional inference. *Mind and Language, 27(3),* 330–355.

McKay, R., & Dennett, D. (2009). The evolution of misbelief. *Behavioral and Brain Sciences, 32(6),* 493–561.

Millikan, R. (1993). *White queen psychology and other essays for Alice.* Cambridge, MA: MIT Press.

Moritz, S., & Woodward, T. S. (2005). Jumping to conclusions in delusional and non-delusional schizophrenic patients. *British Journal of Clinical Psychology, 44,* 193–207.

Murphy, D. (2013). Delusions, modernist epistemology and irrational belief. *Mind and Language, 28(1)*, 113–124.

Neander, K. (1991). Functions as selected effects: the conceptual analysis defense. *Philosophy of Science, 58*, 168–184.

Owen, G., Cutting, J., & David, A. S. (2007). Are people with schizophrenia more logical than healthy volunteers? *British Journal of Psychiatry, 191*, 453–454.

Pargetter, R. (1984). The scientific inference to other minds. *Australasian Journal of Philosophy, 62*, 158–163.

Peters, E., & Garety, P. (2006). Cognitive functioning in delusions: a longitudinal analysis. *Behaviour, Research & Therapy, 44*, 481–514.

Poland, J., Von Eckardt, B., & Spaulding, W. (1994). Problems with the DSM approach to classifying psychopathology. In G. Graham, & G. L. Stephens (Eds.), *Philosophical psychopathology* (pp. 235–261). Cambridge, MA: MIT Press.

Radden, J. (2011). *On delusion*. London: Routledge.

Rescher, N. (1988). *Rationality*. Oxford: Oxford University Press.

Sadock, B. J., & Sadock, V. A. (2007). *Kaplan and Sadock's synopsis of psychiatry*. Baltimore, MD: Lipincott Williams and Wilkins.

Samuels, R. (2009). Delusion as a natural kind. In L. Bortolotti, & M. Broome (Eds.), *Psychiatry as cognitive neuroscience: Philosophical perspectives* (pp. 49–79). New York: Oxford University Press.

Samuels, R., & Stich, S. (2004). Rationality and psychology. In A. Mele, & P. Rawling (Eds.), *The Oxford handbook of rationality* (pp. 279–300). Oxford: Oxford University Press.

Samuels, R., Stich, S., & Bishop, M. (2002). Ending the rationality wars: how to make disputes about human rationality disappear. In R. Elio (Ed.), *Common sense, reasoning and rationality* (pp. 236–268). New York: Oxford University Press.

Siegel, S. (2006). Which properties are represented in perception? In T. Szabo Gendler, & J. Hawthorne (Eds.), *Perceptual experience* (pp. 481–503). Oxford: Oxford University Press.

Sperber, D., & Mercier, H. (2012). Reasoning as a social competence. In H. Landemore, & J. Elster (Eds.), *Collective wisdom: Principles and mechanisms* (pp. 368–392). Cambridge: Cambridge University Press.

Spitzer, M. (1990). On defining delusion. *Comprehensive Psychiatry, 31(5)*, 377–397.

Stich, S. (1990). *The fragmentation of reason*. Cambridge, MA: MIT Press.

Stich, S., & Murphy, D. (2000). Darwin in the madhouse: Evolutionary psychology and the classification of mental disorders. In P. Carruthers, & A. Chamberlain (Eds.), *Evolution and the human mind: Modularity, language, and meta-cognition* (pp. 62–92). Cambridge: Cambridge University Press.

Stone, T., & Young, A. (1997). Delusions and brain injury: the philosophy and psychology of belief. *Mind and Language, 12*(3/4), 327–364.

Taylor, S. E., & Brown, J. D. (1988). Illusion and well-being: a social psychological perspective on mental health. *Psychological Bulletin, 103*, 193–210.

Tversky, A., & Kahneman, D. (1982). Judgments of and by representativeness. In D. Kahneman, P. Slovic, & A. Tversky (Eds.), *Judgment under uncertainty: Heuristics and biases* (pp. 84–98). Cambridge: Cambridge University Press.

Van Dael, F., Versmissen, D., Janssen, I., Myin-Germeys, I., van Os, J., & Krabbendam, L. (2006). Data gathering: Biased in psychosis? *Schizophrenia Bulletin, 32(2)*, 341–351.

Vul, E., Goodman, N., Griffiths, T. L., & Tenenbaum, J. B. (2014). One and done? Optimal decisions from very small samples. *Cognitive Science, 38(4)*, 599–637.

Wason, P. C. (1966). Reasoning. In B. M. Foss (Ed.), *New horizons in psychology* (pp. 106–137). Harmondsworth, England: Penguin.

Young, A. W., Reid, I., & Wright, S. (1993). Face processing impairments and the Capgras delusion. *British Journal of Psychiatry, 162*, 695–698.

Endnotes

1. I will restrict my attention to monothematic delusions and leave to one side the important (but tricky) question of whether the considerations advanced here apply also to polythematic delusions.
2. The most recent edition of the DSM replaces the phrase "incontrovertible or obvious proof or evidence to the contrary" with the claim that delusions are "fixed beliefs that are not amenable to change in light of conflicting evidence" (DSM-5, 2013). I will focus on the wording of DSM IV-TR on the grounds that it better captures what I regard as the dominant view of delusion in the clinical literature (see eg, Sadock & Sadock, 2007, p. 505).
3. See Gold & Hohwy (2000) for a criticism of the epistemic account from another perspective.
4. These norms are also known as the norms of "procedural" or "instrumental" rationality.
5. See Vul, Goodman, Griffiths, & Tenenbaum (2014) for an interesting discussion of the ways in which belief formation on the basis of very small samples can be rational.
6. This challenge can perhaps be best appreciated by considering various forms of philosophical skepticism, such as the claim that there is no good reason to believe in the existence of minds other than one's own. In response to such skeptical challenges, advocates of common sense have often appealed to abduction: belief in the existence of other minds—it is claimed—is rationally permitted (or perhaps even required) because it provides the best explanation of a range of behavioral data that would otherwise go unexplained (Pargetter, 1984). But although such claims are plausible they are not uncontroversial, and sceptics down the ages have argued that various skeptical scenarios provide explanations of the relevant data that are at least as good as—if not superior to—those that are provided by common sense.
7. I will leave to one side the important (but tricky!) question of what it is for a psychological system to have the function that it does. For some discussion of how biological and psychological functions should be understood see Cummins (1975), Griffiths (1993), Millikan (1993), and Neander (1991).
8. For other discussions of delusion that are sympathetic to what I am calling the functional approach, see Boyer (2010), McKay and Dennett (2009), and Murphy (2013).
9. Indeed, there are good reasons to think that no viable cognitive architecture could operate in accord with the norms of epistemic rationality, as Cherniak (1986) points out.
10. The qualification 'at least not in quite the same way' is intended to capture the fact that delusional themes are not randomly distributed but are structured by the mind's functional architecture. See Gold & Gold (2014) for an important discussion of this issue.
11. I explore this theme in more detail in a companion piece to this paper entitled "'Flying Solo': Delusions, Dreams and Doxastic Solipsism".

CHAPTER

6

Outline of a Theory of Delusion: Irrationality and Pathological Belief

I. Gold

Departments of Philosophy & Psychiatry, McGill University, Montreal, QC, Canada

6.1 DELUSIONS

Consider some strange beliefs:

The NSA is listening to my conversations.
My boyfriend is cheating on me with Sarah Palin.
My actions are being controlled by the CEO of Apple.
Vladimir Putin is putting thoughts into my head.
I can fly.
I am the chief disciple of the Buddha.
George Clooney is madly in love with me.
Having been bitten by a dog, I am pregnant with puppies.
I caused the earthquake in Haiti.
I am dead.
The television is sending me messages.
There is a stranger living in my bathroom mirror.

These pathological beliefs, known as delusions, are symptoms of some 75 different psychiatric and neurological illnesses, endocrine disorders and infections, as well as side effects of medication, alcohol and drug abuse (Manschreck, 1979), and a core symptom of psychotic illness, notably schizophrenia (American Psychiatric Association, 2013), though they may also be present in high-functioning individuals with other forms of psychotic illness (Munro, 1999). Some disorders are typically characterized by "monothematic" delusions—those concerned with a single ideational

Rationality. http://dx.doi.org/10.1016/B978-0-12-804600-5.00006-4

motif—whereas delusional patients with schizophrenia typically suffer from multiple forms of delusion and are severely impaired both cognitively and socially (Coltheart, 2013).

What kind of belief are a delusions? Some proposals have been made, but the challenge of definition has turned out to be surprisingly difficult. The best known of these is that of the *Diagnostic and Statistical Manual of Mental Disorder* (4th ed.; DSM-IV-TR) which characterized a delusion as a "false belief based on incorrect inference about external reality that is firmly sustained despite what almost everyone else believes and despite what constitutes incontrovertible and obvious proof or evidence to the contrary" (American Psychiatric Association, 2000, p. 821). Unfortunately, this definition suffers from a significant number of weaknesses; indeed, there are counterexamples to just about all of the conditions of the definition (Coltheart, 2007). As a result, perhaps, the latest edition of the DSM, DSM-5, has opted for a minimalist characterization of delusions as "fixed beliefs that are not amenable to change in light of conflicting evidence" (American Psychiatric Association, 2013, p. 87). While roughly correct, this characterization is of very little practical use given that it is no less true of a vast number of nonpathological beliefs as it is of delusions.

However, the category of delusional belief is picked out, it is hardly contentious that delusions are a paradigm of irrationality. That is to say, any theory of rationality that has delusions come out as rational beliefs will be suspect. It is surprising, therefore, that it is far from obvious how to characterize delusional irrationality. This is largely because the contemporary theory of rationality understands rational thought in terms of the standards of reasoning (Cherniak, 1986; Gold & Hohwy, 2000), but—*pace* the DSM-IV-TR definition—there is little evidence of reasoning abnormalities in people with delusions. The most extensively studied domain of reasoning and delusion is that of probabilistic reasoning, and the standard paradigm for investigating that form of reasoning in delusion is the "beads task." In this task, the participant is told that she will be shown beads from one of two jars. The first contains 85% red beads and 15% black beads and the second contains 85% black beads and 15% red beads. The participant's task is to decide from which jar the beads are being drawn (Peters & Garety, 2006). The primary finding of this research is that patients tend to come to a decision sooner than healthy participants (Fine, Gardner, Craigie, & Gold, 2007). They thus exhibit what has been called a "jumping to conclusions" reasoning bias.

Despite this finding, there are reasons to doubt that it supports the view that the irrationality of delusion can be located in abnormal reasoning. First, reasoning about probabilities is generally difficult, and many healthy individuals do it poorly (Baron, 2007). Second, the difference in reasoning behavior between patients with delusions and healthy participants in the beads task tends to be quite small and seems inadequate to support the florid irrationality of delusional beliefs. Most importantly, however, an application of Bayes theorem to the beads task reveals that if the first two beads in the sequence are red (say), the probability is about .97 that they came from the jar with mostly red beads. It is plausible that most healthy people who were aware of the probabilities would think it was rational to make a choice in the beads task (but not necessarily in other circumstances, for example, having to choose a dangerous medical procedure for their child) on the basis of a probability of .97. This is in fact what people with delusions tend to do, whereas healthy controls tend to wait for more information before coming to a decision about the jars. Although patients with delusions differ from healthy controls, therefore, it strains the notion of rationality to claim that the delusional reasoners, who behave in accordance with the Bayesian norms that most healthy people would take to be rational, are irrational, whereas those reasoners who deviate from the Bayesian norms they themselves accept are the rational ones (Maher, 2001). Locating the irrationality of delusional belief in reasoning abnormalities, therefore, is going to require more evidence than is currently available.

In the absence of an obvious strategy for characterizing delusional irrationality, it is natural to suppose that a successful theory of delusion might illuminate the issue. Unfortunately, there is currently no consensus on what a psychological or neurobiological theory of delusion would look like. My aim, therefore, is to sketch a hypothesis about delusion that has implications for the question of irrationality. Even if the theory turns out to be incorrect, it may nonetheless provide one model for how to approach the question when better theories become available.

6.2 A SOCIAL THEORY OF DELUSION

6.2.1 The Phenomena to be Explained

In the absence of a definition of delusion, a theory of delusion must have a working account of which beliefs are delusional. Given the significant problems associated with this definition, and the nonspecific replacement offered by DSM-5, the most conservative strategy is to rely on expert opinion. Expert opinion can of course be wrong and may eventually be revised by a theory. As a way of getting a theory off the ground, however, I will take delusions to be whichever beliefs psychiatrists and other practitioners take to be delusions.

Before addressing the question of which beliefs those are, we have to make a distinction between two senses of "delusion." Suppose that an American psychiatrist sees a patient who believes that the NSA is hacking into his computer. At the same time, an Australian psychiatrist sees a patient who believes that ASIO (the Australian Security Intelligence Organization) is bugging his phone. In one sense of "delusion," these two beliefs are distinct delusions because the thoughts expressed are distinct. In another sense, however, it is plausible that they are the same delusion dressed up in different details because they express the same basic motif. We will call the specific idea expressed by a delusion its *content* and the theme or motif of the delusion its *form* (Berrios, 2008). In what follows we will be concerned primarily with form rather than content.

The DSM definitions characterizes delusions in terms of their formal[1] properties: they are false, the result of incorrect reasoning, resistant to change, and so on. No restriction is placed on the content of delusional belief. As a result the DSM definitions are consistent with the prediction that delusional belief should be as varied as belief itself; delusional belief, in short, could in principle be about anything. Psychiatrists and other practitioners, in contrast, make rather fine distinctions among strange beliefs. A patient who believes that the NSA has implanted a microphone in his tooth is likely to be thought to have a persecutory delusion, but one who believes that the NSA is implanting microphones in other people's teeth is more likely to be thought to have a nonpsychotic belief in a conspiracy theory. Prima facie, these two beliefs are very similar. Clinically, however, they are classified differently.

DSM-5 mentions a number of delusional forms (Stompe et al., 2003), and the psychiatric literature confirms that over time and across cultures, only a relatively small number of thoughts are recognized as delusions. Table 6.1 summarizes the frequency of delusional forms in a number of different locales. Although the classificatory schemes differ somewhat from study to study, there is considerable overlap among them. For example, persecutory delusions appear everywhere and are always the most common form of delusion.

Although different taxonomies are consistent with these data, the following is one version of an exhaustive list of the forms of delusion:

1. *Persecutory delusions:* fears of being harmed by others;
2. *Referential delusions:* beliefs that external events have a special meaning for the delusional person;
3. *Grandiose delusions:* beliefs according to which one is special or has particular powers;
4. *Erotomanic delusions:* beliefs that someone, usually of high social status, is in love with the delusional person;
5. *Nihilistic delusions:* beliefs concerned with an imminent catastrophe or with nonexistence;

TABLE 6.1 Forms of Delusion Across Culture

Form	English	African	Jamaican	Continental Europeans	English speaking non-Europeans*	Asian	Middle Eastern	Far Eastern	Caribbean
Persecutory	26	45	37	14	11	22	9	7	31
Reference	16	11	9	8	3	12	6	13	11
Grandiose and religious	11	19	21	8	8	8	6	7	8
Sexual and fantastic	14	6	15	7	3	4	0	27	10

* *North Americans, White South Africans, Australians, and New Zealanders.*

Form	Sydney
Persecutory	80.0
Religious	26.7
Grandiose	23.3
Reference	15.6
Somatic	14.4
Mind Control	4.4
Guilt	4.4
Mind reading	4.4
Thought broadcasting	3.3
Transmitting devices	3.3
Thought withdrawal	3.3
Believing that a stranger is a close relative	2.2
Believing that they are someone else	2.2
Believing someone is in love with them	2.2
Extraterrestrial	2.2
Other delusions	6.7

Form	Tokyo	Vienna	Tubingen
Persecution/ injury	75.9	70.3	72.7
Poisoning	8.0	14.9	18.0
Jealousy	1.9	1.0	6.0
Being stolen from	4.9	2.0	2.7
Parasitosis	0.9	3.0	2.0
Mission/grandeur/ special ability	19.4	19.8	18.7
Erotomania	6.5	5.9	6.7
Descent	2.8	1.0	0.7
Pregnancy	0.9	3.0	0.7
Resurrection	0	1.0	0
Invention	0.3	0	0.7
Hypochondria/ dying	8.6	19.8	9.3
Guilt/sin	4.9	20.8	15.3
Being dead	0.3	5.9	0.7

Form	Seoul	Shanghai	Taipei
Persecutory	72.3	78.9	79.1
Reference	6.0	54.2	59.0
Grandiose	48.2	27.5	38.8
Control	35.5	23.9	30.9
Somatic	23.4	14.1	24.5
Guilt	31.2	4.9	5.8
Jealousy	17.0	8.5	3.6
Poverty	2.1	4.2	5.0
Nihilism	0.7	2.1	3.6

Form	Western Turkey	Central Turkey
Persecutory	74.6	83.7
Reference	57.7	70.9
Poisoning	9.5	26.2
Religious	10.9	20.9
Grandiosity	10.0	19.8

(*Continued*)

TABLE 6.1 Forms of Delusion Across Culture (*cont.*)

Form	Tokyo	Vienna	Tubingen
Poverty	0	1.0	2.0
Death of relations	3.4	1.0	2.7
World catastrophe	2.5	2.0	4.7
Separation of being	1.5	3.0	1.3
Homosexual	0	0	0
Others	5.9	10.9	8.0
Religious	6.8	19.8	21.3

Form	White	British Pakistani	Pakistani
Persecution	48	60	62
Control	50	26	13
Reference	48	43	11
Grandiose ability	26	19	28
Grandiose identity	14	23	42
Religious	14	21	11
Sexual	14	13	16
Depersonalisation	18	11	2
Hypochondriacal	8	17	5
Misinterpretation	8	6	8

Form	Western Turkey	Central Turkey
Being controlled	6.0	19.8
Mind reading	4.5	17.4
Jealousy	3.5	14.0
Guilt/sin	0.5	13.4
Hypochondria	1.0	12.2
Erotomania	2.5	9.3
Thought broadcasting	0.5	11.1
Thought insertion	1.0	9.3
Nihilistic	4.0	5.2
Thought withdrawal	0.5	5.2
Nobility	0	3.5
Inferiority	0	3.5
Homosexual	0	3.5
Parasitosis	0	1.2
World catastrophe	0	1.2
Resurrection	0	1.2
Others	4.5	0.6

(Redrawn from Brakoulias, V., & Starcevic, V. (2008). A cross-sectional survey of the frequency and characteristics of delusions in acute psychiatric wards. Australasian Psychiatry 16, 87–91; Gecici, O., Kuloglu, M., Guler, O., Ozbulut, O., Kurt, E., Onen, S., Ekinci, O., Yesilbas, D., Caykoylu, A., Emul, M., Alatas, G., & Albayralc Y., (2010). Phenomenology of delusions and hallucinations in patients with schizophrenia. Bulletin of Clinical Psychopharmacology 20, 204–212; Kim, K., Hwu, H., Zhang, L.D., Lu, M.K., Park, K.K., Hwang, T.J., Kim, D., & Park, Y.C., (2001). Schizophrenic delusions in Seoul, Shanghai and Taipei: a transcultural study. Journal of Korean Medical Science 16, 88–94; Ndetei, D., & Vadher, A., (1984). Frequency and clinical significance of delusions across cultures. Acta Psychiatrica Scandinavica 70, 73–76; Suhail, K., & Cochrane, R., (2002). Effect of culture and environment on the phenomenology of delusions and hallucinations. International Journal of Social Psychiatry 48, 126–138; and Tateyama, M., Asai, M., Hashimoto, M., Bartels, M., & Kasper, S. (1998). Transcultural study of schizophrenic delusions. Psychopathology 31, 59–68.)

6. *Somatic delusions:* anxieties about health or bodily function;
7. *Delusions of thought:* beliefs (among others) that thoughts are being inserted into, or withdrawn from, one's mind or that one's thoughts are being read;
8. *Delusions of control:* beliefs according to which one's actions or bodily movements are being manipulated by another agent;
9. *Delusions of jealousy:* beliefs about infidelity;
10. *Religious delusions:* beliefs being persecuted by supernatural forces or that one is a religious figure or on a divine mission;
11. *Delusions of guilt* or *sin:* beliefs that one is responsible for a terrible event; and
12. *Misidentification delusions:* beliefs concerned with one's own identity or the identity of others.

The most striking thing about this list of forms is that, as Richard Bentall (1994) points out, delusions are almost all concerned with the social world (including oneself and one's body) and one's place in it. Moreover, there appear to be unifying subthemes even within this short list. Jealousy is a form of persecution in the sense that two people—the partner and his or her lover—are conspiring, or have conspired, to act in a way that is harmful to the victim. Delusions of control have a persecutory flavor insofar as they represent some agent as manipulating the delusional person, implicitly against his wishes. Similar remarks could be made about at least some forms of delusions of thought. The notion of interfering with someone's thought suggests a particular method of control or manipulation. Certainly the manipulation of behavior or thought is not experienced as having the benefit of the victim as its goal and is thus unwelcome. One theme of delusional belief, therefore, is the threat of harm posed by other people. Call this theme "social threat."

A second theme is the abilities or talents of the delusional person. Grandiosity is sometimes expressed as beliefs to the effect that one is special or particularly capable— "I am a successful DJ," or "I have the cure to cancer"—and sometimes in terms of the relation of the victim to important others, for example, "I am the cousin of Tony Blair," (Knowles, McCarthy-Jones, & Rowse, 2011, p. 685). This latter form of expression asserting one's social relations suggests that grandiosity and erotomania are linked because erotomanic delusions typically express the belief that someone of high social status is in love with the delusional person. One way to characterize grandiose and erotomanic delusions, therefore, is to say that they represent the patient as having a high social status in virtue of their abilities or social connections. Call this delusional theme "social power."

Notice that although religious delusions are typically classified as an independent form of delusion, that is probably inaccurate. These delusions fall into the category either of persecutory or grandiose beliefs.

They appear distinct only in virtue of the supernatural entities or forces to which they refer. There are cultures, however, in which supernatural beings are elements of the social world (Boyer, 2001; Kopytoff, 1971). The idea that religious delusions are an autonomous form is, therefore, likely to be an artefact of contemporary culture.

A third theme is, in some sense, the converse of grandiosity. Somatic delusions, some nihilistic delusions—especially the Cotard delusion, the belief that one's organs are rotting or that one is dead—and delusions of guilt or sin, represent the delusional person as particularly damaged, weak, or vulnerable. We can call this theme "social inferiority."

Ten of the twelve forms of delusion thus cluster around three themes. The small number of delusional forms, their social content and internal relations seem unlikely to be coincidences. At any rate, these patterns deserve investigation. The hypothesis I will explore is that delusions are disordered versions of thoughts that function as warning signals about dangerous others as well as distorted thoughts that function as strategies to combat these social threats. In the next section, I articulate two questions for a theory of delusion and then turn to the evolutionary motivation behind the social theory to be developed.

6.2.2 Central Questions

Although a satisfactory theory of delusion will have to be able to answer a great many questions, including the definitional one, two have driven recent research in the field. The first is, How do delusions arise? That is, how is the implausible or bizarre thought formed in the first place? Call this the problem of delusion development. The second question is, Why are delusions retained despite their intrinsic implausibility and in the face of counter-evidence? Call this the problem of delusion retention. We will return to these questions below.

6.2.3 Evolutionary Background: The Social Brain Hypothesis

The relatively large brains of primates, including humans, presents a puzzle because brain tissue is energetically expensive; the brain represents about 20% of the body's total energy use but only 2% of its weight (Raichle & Gusnard, 2002). It is widely agreed that the hypothesis about brain evolution best supported by the evidence is that the large primate brain evolved to cope with the complexities of social life, a view known as the "social brain hypothesis" (Dunbar, 1993, 1998). One line of evidence in support of the hypothesis is that in primates there is a linear relation between the ratio of neocortical volume to total brain volume on the one hand and social group size on the other (Fig. 6.1; Dunbar & Shultz, 2007).

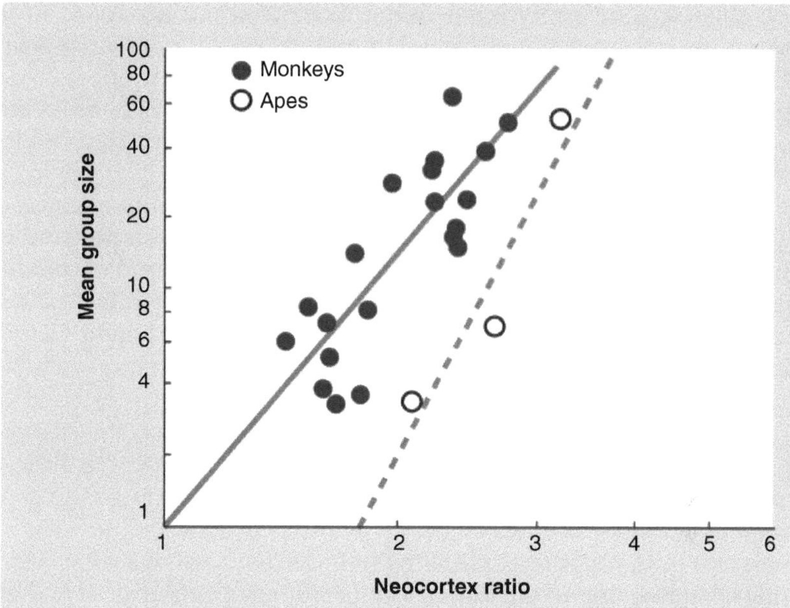

FIGURE 6.1 **The relationship between brain size and group size.** *(Redrawn from Dunbar and Shultz, 2007, p. 1344.)*

The central advantage of living in large social groups is defense against predation (Dunbar, 1988), but the affiliative relationships that arise in primate social groups are likely to have laid the foundation for the cooperative endeavors that support the benefits inaccessible to more solitary animals. As social group size grows, however, the risk of exploitation by others in the group also increases (Neuberg, Kenrick, & Schaller, 2011). Indeed, in many human societies most of the dangers in the environment come from other people rather than the physical environment, and this is true even though human beings' violent exploitation of one another has been dramatically reduced over human history (Muchembled, 2012; Pinker, 2011).

In what follows, my focus will be nonviolent social threats. One form of this kind of exploitation is free riding, in which one benefits from social life without contributing to it. A game-theoretic model of cooperation developed by Enquist and Leimar (1993) shows that when the territory in which a community lives is sufficiently large, free riding becomes a significant obstacle to cooperation. The increase in territory makes it possible for free riders to exploit conspecifics and then move far enough away to find new strangers to exploit. More importantly, once free riding becomes common enough in a social group, the rational strategy is to refrain from engaging in cooperative behavior altogether. Social exploitation, therefore, threatens to undermine some of the most important benefits that large social groups deliver.

The challenge for individuals living in large social groups is to find a way to benefit from social life while minimizing the risks associated with it (Neuberg et al., 2011). Enquist and Leimar (1993) propose two behavioral adaptations that might have evolved for this purpose. One is gossip (Dunbar, 2004). Interest in reports about others that focus on their faults is one way to raise the probability that free riders become known to potential victims. A second strategy is suspicion, a family of conscious or unconscious mental states that signal the risk of exploitation and motivate one to avoid those who threaten it. Suspicion, in effect, provides a one way to distinguish more promising potential cooperative partners from less promising ones and thereby reduce the risk of falling victim to exploitation.

6.2.4 The Suspicion System

I posit the existence of a cognitive system whose purpose is to generate suspicion in response to evidence of social threats; call this the suspicion system. In order to explore the possible features of such a system, consider defense against predation as an analogous evolutionary adaptation (Blanchard et al., 2011; Woody & Szechtman, 2011). Overt physical threats do not present a particular cognitive challenge, but when physical attack is stealthy, an animal has to be sensitive to subtle and ambiguous cues—such as the rustle of leaves—and be able to interpret them as signals of potential danger (Blanchard et al., 2011). These cues must also capture attention, suppress competing concerns, and motivate the individual to act appropriately. In addition, cognition of this sort should be calibrated in the direction of generating false positives, given the overwhelming disadvantages of missing genuine evidence of threat (Haselton & Nettle, 2006).

Social dangers are not typically threats to life and limb, though they may reduce one's fitness and, therefore, be as significant in the long run. A partner's infidelity, for example, may prevent one from having offspring which, in evolutionary terms, is no different from death. A cognitive system evolved to detect social threats is likely to share some of the features of a system concerned with physical attack. It is likely to be sensitive to subtle and ambiguous clues, and given the pervasive possibility of exploitation by means of deception, such clues may be deliberately hidden. Cues to social threat are likely, therefore, to be subtle and ambiguous. These clues must be interpretable as signs of social threat, and, like the cues to physical threat, should capture attention, suppress competing concerns, and motivate defensive action.

As an illustration, consider jealousy (Buss, 2000). Seeing Cassio in possession of Desdemona's handkerchief, Othello takes this to be evidence of Desdemona's infidelity. He comes to that conclusion quickly and without consciously entertaining the many steps in the chain of reasoning leading to it. The thought that Desdemona is unfaithful comes full-blown into consciousness, captures his attention, and is highly motivating. Jealousy is thus a highly adaptive mental state because it represents the possibility of a certain kind of social threat in the environment, and it motivates one to mobilize whatever resources one has to defend against it (Neuberg et al., 2011).

Finally, the suspicion system is likely to be particularly sensitive to intentions to carry out exploitation. There are two reasons for this. First, whereas the intentions to engage in physical attack often do not arise much before the attack itself, social exploitation—especially when deception is involved—is typically preceded by exploitative intentions with a significant time lag. Since the ultimate purpose of the suspicion system is to defend against social threats, the lag between intention and action provides the time to engage in defense (Neuberg et al., 2011).

Second, there are forms of exploitation that are not obvious even when one has been exploited. Suppose that your café chain offers you a loyalty card that gives you a discount on your coffee. Using the loyalty card makes it possible for the chain to collect information about your buying practices, and this gives them the ability to target their advertising to you more effectively and to sell you more coffee. As a consequence, it is quite conceivable that the loyalty card will lead you to spend more money on coffee than you save with the loyalty card. That fact, however, will not be apparent in the behavior of any of the baristas you encounter. Your café chain has not harmed you overtly, or even deceived you, but they have (arguably) exploited you, and you will not know this unless you have formed some ideas about the intentions that lie behind the behavior. In short, there are some forms of exploitation that are going to be much more readily identifiable by the intentions that lie behind behavior than from any behavior itself.

6.2.5 Some Evidence

What evidence is there for the existence of the suspicion system? Two lines of evidence come from studies of face perception. Human faces are a rich source of information about other people's dispositions, including about whether they are potentially threatening (Adams et al., 2011), and humans are capable of making rapid judgments of complex social features from faces. For example, subjects make convergent judgments about how likeable, aggressive, or competent someone is based on a picture of their face (Todorov, Mandisodza, Goren, & Hall, 2005; Willis & Todorov, 2006). People make even quicker judgments about threats from faces. Bar, Neta, & Linz (2006), for example, showed subjects pictures of faces and asked them to make judgments based on their "gut reaction" concerning how threatening the person appeared to be. They found a strong correlation between judgments made at 39 ms and those made at 1700 ms. In contrast, judgments of likeability, aggressiveness, or competence cannot be reliably made that rapidly (Todorov et al., 2005; Willis & Todorov, 2006).

Individuals who are not threatening can be thought of as trustworthy. In an elegant series of studies making use of artificial face stimuli, Todorov and colleagues (Oosterhof & Todorov, 2008; Todorov, Pakrashi, & Oosterhof, 2009) have explored the perception of trustworthiness in faces. With an exposure of 33 ms, subjects made reliable judgments of trustworthy and untrustworthy faces, and at 167 ms the judgments were not significantly different from those made with long exposures. In addition, they found that subjects made finer discriminations among untrustworthy faces than among trustworthy ones. Since small differences in untrustworthiness may represent greater differences in risk than small differences in trustworthiness, this is what one would predict (Fig. 6.2).

Notice that the judgments being made in these experiments are not of occurrent mental states. The face stimuli are not exhibiting expressions that can be used to make inferences about states of mind. Nor is there a social context or narrative that can be used to make mental state inferences. Thus the judgments being made are not products of a Theory of Mind (Apperly, 2011) capacity in the familiar sense. Rather, subjects are making something like a judgment of personality traits—about whether someone appears to have a friendly disposition in general. Someone who is clearly expressing anger or fear signals in an unambiguous way a threat of some kind. Judgments of threat or trustworthiness, in contrast, attempt to represent a stable, latent feature of the mind of the other person. The fact that judgments of threat and trustworthiness are made more rapidly than other complex social features provides some support for the hypothesis that these judgments are underpinned by a cognitive mechanism that is distinct from those that subserve other trait judgments such as competence or likeability.

A second line of evidence for the existence of a suspicion system comes from lesion studies. The amygdala is traditionally characterized as a brain structure that supports emotional function, especially fear detection. The fact that the amygdala is responsive to fear suggests that it is sensitive to ambiguous stimuli. Someone expressing anger is conveying an explicit threat. Someone expressing fear, however, is signaling the presence of something threatening in the environment but does not indicating whether that threat is also a threat to the viewer (Adams et al., 2012).

Animal studies have revealed that the amygdala also subserves social cognition. In an early study, Dicks, Myers, & Kling (1969) lesioned the amygdala in rhesus monkeys and found that the animals became socially indifferent. They stopped seeking out social activity, lost interest in social interactions, and were "retarded in their ability to foresee and avoid dangerous confrontations" (p. 71). Further, lesions to the amygdala made shortly

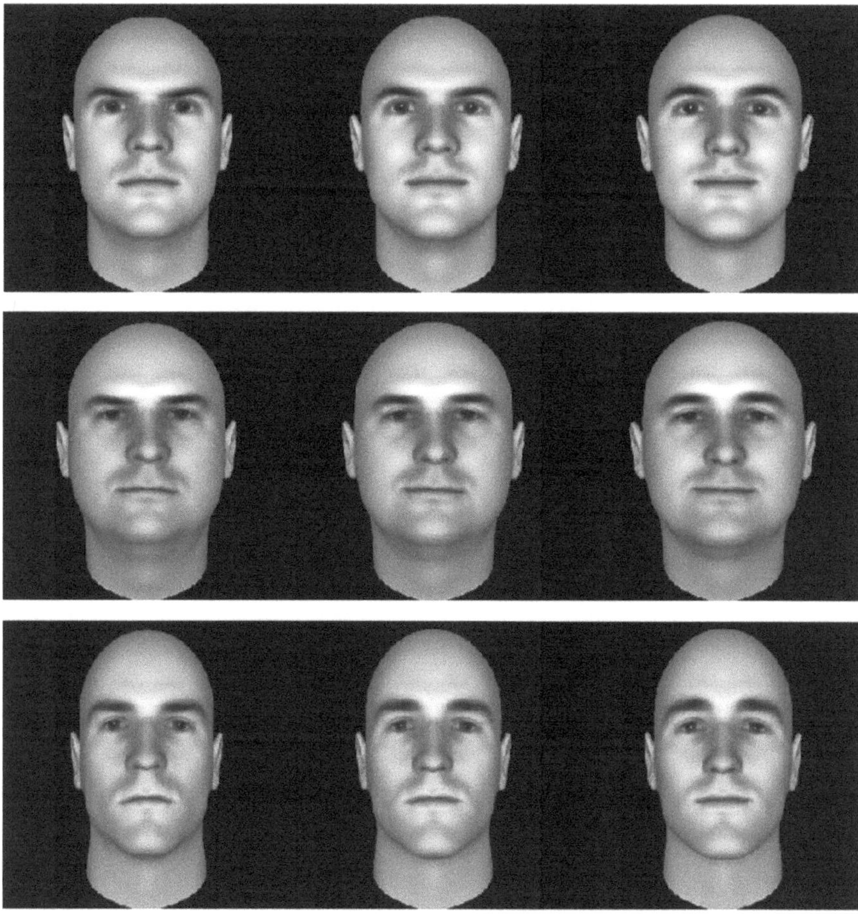

FIGURE 6.2 **More and less trustworthy faces.** *(From Todorov, Pakrashi, & Oosterhof, 2009, p. 823.)*

after birth produce animals that have a deficit in evaluating and responding to social threats (Bauman, Bliss-Moreau, Machado, & Amaral, 2011).

Amygdala lesion studies have been carried out in humans as well, in particular in a patient known as SM who has focal bilateral amygdala lesions as a consequence of the rare genetic disorder known as Urbach–Wiethe disease (Tranel & Hyman, 1990). SM is intellectually normal, though she has a slight executive function deficit, but is dramatically impaired in recognizing facial expressions of fear and mildly impaired in recognizing other negative emotions such as disgust, anger, and sadness (Adolphs, Tranel, Damasio, & Damasio, 1994; Buchanan, Tranel, & Adolphs, 2009). In addition, she does not seem to feel fear. In a recent study, she was taken into a haunted house, shown frightening movies, and exposed to spiders. She did not display fear and reported that she did not experience it (Feinstein, Adolphs, Damasio, & Tranel, 2011).

As in the animal studies, however, amygdala lesions in humans seem to be social as well as emotional (Buchanan et al., 2009). Adolphs, Tranel, & Damasio (1998) asked SM and other amygdala patients to judge faces as more or less "approachable" or trustworthy. SM's judgments agreed with those of healthy subjects for the trustworthy faces, but increasingly diverged with greater apparent untrustworthiness as judged by healthy subjects. In a second study, Tranel, Gullickson, Koch, & Adolphs (2006) had SM evaluated by two psychotherapists who were unaware of her neurological condition. The therapists agreed that she did not exhibit any psychopathology, but one of them commented that "she did not seem to have a normal sense of distrust and 'danger'" (p. 219). The parents of another amygdala patient known as AP say that "she tends to 'trust' people too easily," and they have encouraged her to be "more wary of strangers" (Buchanan, Tranel & Adolphs, 2009, p. 301).

In fact, SM is capable of detecting fear when she is instructed to pay attention to the eye region of faces. Of all the emotions, fear seems to be most dependent on the eyes for its expression and detection, and SM does not spontaneously attend to this region. For this reason, Buchanan, Tranel & Adolphs (2009) hypothesize that the purpose of the amygdala is to explore the social environment rather than to detect its features. A narrower interpretation is also consistent with the data; the amygdala may be seeking out evidence of social threats in the environment, in effect doing the work of a suspicion system.

6.2.6 A Dual-Process Account

The studies of Bar, Todorov, and their colleagues show that subjects are capable of making judgments of whether a face appears trustworthy extremely quickly. This provides some evidence that the suspicion system is what is often referred to by "dual process" theories as a "System 1" form of cognition. Dual-process theories (Evans, 2008, 2010; Kahneman, 2011) posit the existence of two parallel cognitive systems addressed to a single cognitive problem or domain. System 1 tends to be unconscious, automatic, effortless, and fast. In contrast, "System 2" cognition tends to be conscious, controlled, effortful, and slow. System 1 is typically thought to provide rule-of-thumb solutions to cognitive problems under conditions of limited time and information, whereas System 2 cognition is thought to evaluate a broader range of evidence more flexibly, systematically, and thoroughly.

The suspicion system is a form of System 1 cognition designed to act as a quick-and-dirty "early warning system" for social threats (Green & Phillips, 2004; Zolotova & Brune, 2006). System 2 social threat cognition,

TABLE 6.2 A Comparison of Some Characteristic Features of System 1 and System 2

	System 1	System 2
Cluster 1 *Consciousness*	Unconscious (preconscious)	Conscious
	Implicit	Explicit
	Automatic	Controlled
	Low effort	High effort
	Rapid	Slow
	High capacity	Low capacity
	Default process	Inhibitory
	Holistic, perceptual	Analytic, reflective
Cluster 2 *Evolution*	Evolutionary old	Evolutionary recent
	Evolutionary rationality	Individual rationality
	Shared with animals	Uniquely human
	Nonverbal	Linked to language
	Modular cognition	Fluid intelligence
Cluster 3 *Functional characteristics*	Associative	Rule based
	Domain specific	Domain general
	Contextualized	Abstract
	Pragmatic	Logical
	Parallel	Sequential
	Stereotypical	Egalitarian
Cluster 4 *Individual differences*	Universal	Heritable
	Independent of general intelligence	Linked to general intelligence
	Independent of working memory	Limited by working memory capacity

(Redrawn from Evans, 2008, p. 257.)

in contrast, engages with all of the evidence in order to provide a more reliable evaluation of the actual risk of threat. Once the suspicion system sounds the alarm, System 2 is engaged to determine whether the early warning is justified or not (Asp & Tranel, 2013; Speechley & Ngan, 2008).

As Table 6.2 indicates, System 1 cognition is often thought to be subserved by cognitive "modules." Fodor (1983; see also Coltheart, 1999) characterizes modules as having some or all of seven typical (but not necessary) features. They are domain specific (restricted to operating on one kind of stimulus or cognitive content); innately specified; not assembled from simpler cognitive components; hardwired; computationally autonomous (ie, do not share cognitive resources such as memory); fast, and informationally encapsulated (ie, they are to some degree or other prevented from getting access to information in other cognitive systems). Paradigm modules are perceptual systems, and the relative insulation of perceptual systems from top-down effects, as in visual illusions, for example, provide familiar illustrations of informational encapsulation.

The suspicion system is likely to have some, but not all, of these properties. As we have seen, it is fast. It is likely to be innately specified and hardwired to the extent that some of the cognitive functions on which it likely depends—detecting eye gaze (Emery, 2000) and facial emotion (Baron-Cohen et al., 1996), interpreting body movements (Gobbini, Koralek, Bryan, Montgomery, & Haxby, 2007), or hand orientation (Tessari, Ottoboni, Mazzatenta, Merla, & Nicoletti, 2012), all of which may carry information about social threat—are likely to develop rather than be learned (Ullman, Harari, & Dorfman, 2012). As a result, however, it is (at least to some extent) assembled from simpler components or, at any rate, is the recipient of information from those systems. In addition, because memory of social threat is very likely to be relevant to the function of the suspicion system, it is not computationally autonomous. The suspicion system is informationally encapsulated to a high degree, and this feature of the system is, as we will see, a significant part of the explanation of the phenomenology of persecutory delusions, and, in particular, why they are resistant to revision.

Finally, in one sense at least the suspicion system is domain specific in that it is concerned exclusively with the social. However, clues to the social domain can include input from any or all of the senses and may depend on complex social information. These cues can be thought of as falling into two broad categories: direct and indirect. Direct evidence comes from the observation of the threatening person herself. The briefest exposure to Angela Lansbury's Mrs. Iselin in *The Manchurian Candidate,* for example, generates a clear feeling that this is someone best avoided. Indirect evidence comes from nonbehavioral sources—for instance, a written communication that contains information suggesting that one is the target of someone's malign intention—or from the behavior of others. The latter often occurs in complex social situations. Consider, for example, a well-known scene from the film *The Godfather.* The character of Frank Pentangeli is captured by the FBI and pressured to testify against Michael Corleone. In order to threaten Pentangeli, the mob kidnaps his brother, Vincenzo, and brings him into the courtroom. As soon as Frank sees Vincenzo, he immediately understands Vincenzo's presence as evidence of a threat: testify and your family will be harmed.

Notice that it is the mere presence of Vincenzo in the courtroom that signals the threat. Although Frank immediately infers the existence of intentions to harm his brother, and the cues to the threat emerge in a social situation, no behavior is being "interpreted." Thus although Frank is exercising his Theory of Mind capacity by forming beliefs about the mental states of others, the intentions are not inferred from facial expressions, linguistic behavior, or any immediate source of information about other people's minds. Moreover, although there are a great many inferential steps between the visual perception of his brother and the idea that if he testifies his family will be harmed, it appears that the recognition of social threat happens quickly and more or less automatically. Of course, this situation is not precisely analogous to the case of suspicion because here the threat is *meant* to be clearly understood by the target of the threat, whereas suspicion is the state one is in when one has evidence of malicious intentions that are typically going to be hidden. Nonetheless, where the two cases are analogous is in the fact that a complex social situation, together with background information, can be used to infer the threatening intentions of a dangerous other.

Before engaging in the labor-intensive process of mobilizing defenses against a putative social threat, it makes good sense to engage in a more detailed and systematic investigation to ensure the threat is real. The purpose of System 2 suspicion is to evaluate the evidence of social threat in a way that is deliberate and careful. If System 2 concludes that there is indeed evidence of threat, it confirms the need to engage in defensive behavior. So, for example, when Othello sees Cassio in possession of Desdemona handkerchief, he immediately interprets this as evidence of a threat, a result of the activity of the suspicion system. When system 2 is engaged to review all of the putative evidence, he (incorrectly, of course) comes to the conclusion that his feeling of jealousy is justified. If, in contrast, System 2 had concluded that there was insufficient evidence in support of the presence of a threat, it would have suppressed the activity of the suspicion system and the feeling of jealousy and thoughts of infidelity would have subsided.

6.2.7 Hypothesis

The general hypothesis at the heart of the social theory of delusion is that delusions are manifestations of disorders (of various kinds) to the suspicion system and to its connections to other cognitive functions. Although detailed models of each of the forms of delusion are beyond the scope of this paper, we can say something about the relation of the suspicion system to the three themes that characterize 10 of the 12 delusional forms: social threat, social power, and social vulnerability.

The social theory of delusion posits that delusions concerned with social threat are manifestations of a suspicion system that is not appropriately calibrated with respect to the evidence of the threats in the environment, in short, that the suspicion system is detecting threats that are not there. Some evidence for this suggestion comes from research on schizophrenia. People with schizophrenia are different from healthy controls in the perception of emotion (Amminger et al., 2012; Kohler, Walker, Martin, Healey, & Moberg, 2010), and some features of these deficits can be interpreted as bearing on the question of threat perception. Pinkham, Brensinger, Kohler, Gur, & Gur (2011), for example, found that actively paranoid subjects tend to perceive neutral faces as expressing anger—an emotion signaling possible threat—in comparison with nonactively paranoid subjects. Green, Williams, & Davidson (2003a, b) compared the visual scanpaths of healthy, delusion-prone, and frankly delusional participants and found that people with persecutory delusions pay more attention than healthy controls to threat-related words and remember more threat-related sentences (Bentall & Kaney, 1989; Bentall, Kaney, & Bowen-Jones, 1995; Kaney, Wolfenden, Dewey, & Bentall, 1992). They are also indistinguishable in their thoughts about social situations from people with social phobia, a mental disorder characterized by a fear of being scrutinized and negatively evaluated by other people (Newman Taylor & Stopa, 2013). Moreover, there is reason to think that these threat-related impairments are causes rather than effects of psychosis. Emotion recognition deficits may persist even when a psychotic episode has remitted; individuals at high risk for schizophrenia, but who have not had a psychotic episode, show similar impairments; and healthy biological siblings of people with schizophrenia may also exhibit some of these deficits (Amminger et al., 2012; Kee, Horan, Mintz, & Green, 2004).

The social theory posits that the themes of social power and social vulnerability are central to the forms of delusion as responses to social threat. First, let us take grandiosity. In response to physical threats, animals often make themselves look bigger: elephants stick out their ears, zebras huddle together, puffer fish blow themselves up, and so on (Eibl-Eibesfeldt, 1970). In human culture, social power is typically more important than physical power, and threats from others are often met with evidence of one's social status or social relationships. As in the physical domain, the assertion of social power represents an effort to get the aggressor to carefully consider the risks associated with the aggression. Evidence that retaliation is possible, either by the victim himself or by his social connections, may move the aggressor to withdraw the threat or target a different victim. On the social theory, grandiose delusions are distorted versions of assertions of social power aimed at rebuffing social threat.

Assertions of social vulnerability may also act as a defense against social threat in the way that acts of submission in the animal kingdom do.

Animals produce characteristic behaviors, such as prostrating themselves before a more dominant animal, the effect of which is to neutralize potential aggression (Eibl-Eibesfeldt, 1970). In a similar fashion, self-depreciation is used in human social exchanges to signal deference and thereby mollify an aggressor. According to the social theory, delusions of social vulnerability are distorted versions of self-deprecatory behaviors, the purpose of which is to defend against social threat by appeasing threatening individuals.

6.2.8 Central Questions Again

As indicated above, a theory of delusion must address two central questions, the first about delusion formation and the second about retention. We will consider the formation question first. Some delusions are simply irrational; there are few circumstances in which a belief that a loved one has been replaced by a duplicate would be reasonable, and no conditions in which the belief that one is dead would be. Others, however, do not express intrinsically strange or improbable ideas. As recent history has revealed all too clearly, for example, the belief that powerful institutions are invading our privacy can be both normal and pathological. These latter nonbizarre delusions may sometimes be formed as a result of a normal functioning of the suspicion system and only become pathological because they are inappropriately retained.

It is also possible that some delusions are formed in a pathological fashion to begin with, and there are at least two obvious ways in which this could happen. First, the suspicion system could become hypersensitive so that inconsequential events are taken to be evidence of social threat. There are any number of trivial reasons why someone might not be invited to a working lunch, for example, but a hypersensitive suspicion system might interpret that event as evidence of a conspiracy on the part of one's coworkers. Second, the interpretation of events might go awry in such a way that an event is inappropriately taken to be evidence of social threat. Whereas it is not hard to imagine a scenario in which not being invited to a working lunch might constitute evidence of social threat, there are very few circumstances in which the color of the boss's tie could count as such evidence. A suspicion system that produces a warning signal in response to the tie is malfunctioning. The first case of malfunction is an excessive response to an appropriate stimulus, the second is a response to an inappropriate stimulus.

Let us turn now to the question of delusion retention. The answer to the question why delusions are not rejected once they have been formed requires an appeal to the dual-process account sketched above. Many healthy people have paranoid thoughts that are immediately seen as implausible. One might have a fleeting thought of conspiracy in response to being left out of a work lunch, but, all things being equal, that thought is typically rejected more or less immediately. As a form of System 1 cognition, the suspicion system responds to a narrow range of input and classifies the event of being left out as threatening. In contrast, System 2 has access to a wide range information, context, past history, and so on and can interpret the isolated occurrence as almost certainly harmless. The paranoid thought is abolished, therefore, by the intervention of System 2 thought about social threat. Once System 2 determines that the suspicion system has produced a false alarm, in inhibits it, and the thought of threat is abolished.

Paranoid and other pathological thoughts are retained when System 2 cannot inhibit the activity of the suspicion system, and there are at least three ways in which this could happen. One possibility is that the threshold for activation of the suspicion system is abnormally low, as mentioned above. Under these conditions, the suspicion system might continue to produce warning signals even in the presence of an inhibitory intervention by System 2. A second possibility is that there is no disorder to the suspicion system but rather a functional disconnection between it and System 2. Under these conditions, suppose a normal warning signal is produced by the suspicion system, as in the case of being excluded from a work lunch. System 2 is activated and concludes that there is no evidence of real threat. However, because the suspicion system cannot be inhibited it continues to produce a warning signal. A third possibility is a combination of the two, a hypersensitive suspicion system and a functional disconnection between it and System 2.

Notice that in all three of these scenarios, one would expect there to be a period during which someone with delusion-like thoughts (originating in the suspicion system) will also have the thought (originating in System 2) that the thought is not justified. And indeed this is precisely what occurs during the prodromal phase of schizophrenia (Yung & McGorry, 1996). During this period patients have delusion-like thoughts but retain insight (Amador & David, 2004) into the implausibility of the thought. Eventually the insight disappears, and the patient develops a full-blown commitment to their delusion. A dual-process model account of this change might run as follows. In the presence of two contradictory thoughts—the persecutory thought and its negation—some form of arbitration is called into play to adjudicate between the two, and the delusional thought wins out. This may be the case for either or both of two reasons. First, each time the suspicion system produces a novel warning signal this will be taken as fresh evidence of threat, and the accumulating evidence may eventually come to outweigh the output of System 2. Second, because it is safer to err on the side of oversensitivity to social threat, repeated threat warnings may trump the System 2 judgment that no threat is present.

Once the output of the suspicion system is deemed to have identified a true threat, it is likely that the role of System 2 changes. Given that it is now an established "fact" that there is a threat in the environment, the task of System 2 shifts to address the challenge of understanding it better and making it as coherent as possible with the rest of the patient's beliefs. System 2 thus tries to answer questions about who the persecutors are, why they are persecuting the patient, and so on. It is at this stage that the social and cultural environment becomes relevant. At a moment when the NSA has been discovered to be spying on American citizens, that fact might provide a natural answer to the question of the identity of the persecutors. In a culture where the NSA does not play the role of a possible persecutor, it would not be integrated into a delusional narrative. It is natural to hypothesize, therefore, that the dozen or so forms of delusion are stable across time and culture because they reflect the function (or malfunction) of the suspicion system which, as an old, hardwired, and modular form of cognition, is not plastic. The variability of delusional contents, in contrast, can be traced to the function of System 2 and its capacity to draw on information of all kinds in elaborating delusional ideas.

6.3 RATIONALITY REDUX: FORMULATING THE PROBLEM

Two aspects of the social theory of delusion appear to be relevant to characterizing the irrationality of delusional belief. The first aspect is the theory's identification of the origin of delusions in a module that is inadequately connected, or responsive to, other more global, reflective, or informative cognitive sources. This view assimilates delusions to other belief states constrained by cognitive limitations; paradigm cases can be found in the biases and heuristics literature (Kahneman, Slovic and Tversky, 1982). Unfortunately, whether or not *these* beliefs deserve to be thought of as rational or irrational is itself a contentious matter (Gigerenzer & Brighton, 2009). Nonetheless, progress in the latter debate may be of use in better understanding the status of delusions.

A second aspect of the social theory that is relevant to the question of rationality is the theory's emphasis on the centrality of the content of delusional thoughts. Under the influence of the DSM, contemporary psychiatry has tended to focus on the presence or absence of symptoms, including delusions, and on their formal features. Thinking about mental disorders has tended to abstract away from the particular contents of delusional thought, obsessive rumination, depressive ideation, and the like. In contrast, the present approach depends on taking the contents of delusional forms seriously. This raises the possibility that the irrationality of delusion will have to be handled by what Lewis (1986) identifies as the irrationality of the contents of mental states (Gold & Hohwy, 2000):

> ...instrumental [i.e.] procedural rationality, though it is the department of rationality that has proved most tractable to systematic theory, remains only one department among others. We think that some sorts of belief and desire... would be unreasonable

> in a strong sense. .. Think of the man who for no special reason, expects unexamined emeralds to be grue. Think of Anscombe's (1957) example. .. of someone with a basic desire for a saucer of mud. .. (Lewis, 1986, p. 38)

To appeal to "content irrationality" in the context of delusions is, unfortunately, no more than to formulate a question about delusions, not to provide a theory of their irrationality. If delusions are irrational on the grounds that they have an irrational content, the question to be answered is what makes such contents irrational. And that question—though somewhat narrower than the general question with which we started—seems, at this stage, no less difficult.

References

Adams, R., Ambady, N., Nakaya, K., & Shimojo, S. (Eds.). 2011. *The Science of Social Vision*, Jr., N Ambady, K Nakayama, S Shimojo (Eds.). Oxford: Oxford University Press.

Adams, R., Franklin, R., Kveraga, K., Ambady, N., Kleck, R., Whalen, P., Hadjikhani, N., & Nelson, A. (2012). Amygdala responses to averted vs direct gaze fear vary as a function of presentation speed. *Social Cognitive and Affective Neuroscience*, *7*, 568–577.

Adolphs, R., Tranel, D., & Damasio, A. (1998). The human amygdala in social judgment. *Nature*, *393*, 470–474.

Adolphs, R., Tranel, D., Damasio, H., & Damasio, A. (1994). Impaired recognition of emotion in facial expressions following bilateral damage to the human amygdala. *Nature*, *372*, 669–672.

Amador, X., & David, A (Eds.). (2004). *Insight and psychosis* (2nd ed.). Oxford: Oxford University Press.

American Psychiatric Association. (2000). *Diagnostic and statistical manual of mental disorders* (4th ed.). text revision (DSM-IV-TR). Washington, DC: American Psychiatric Publishing.

American Psychiatric Association. (2013). *Diagnostic and statistical manual of mental disorders* (5th ed.). (DSM-5). Washington, DC: American Psychiatric Publishing.

Amminger, G., Schäfer, M., Papageorgiou, K., Klier, C., Schlögelhofer, M., Mossaheb, N., Werneck-Rohrer, S., Nelson, B., & McGorry, P. (2012). Emotion recognition in individuals at clinical high-risk for schizophrenia. *Schizophrenia Bulletin*, *38*, 1030–1039.

Apperly, I. (2011). *Mindreaders*. Hove, England: Psychology Press.

Asp, E., & Tranel, D. (2013). False tagging theory: Toward a unitary account of prefrontal cortex function. In D. Stuss, & R. Knight (Eds.), *Principles of frontal lobe function* (pp. 383–416). Oxford: Oxford University Press.

Bar, M., Neta, M., & Linz, H. (2006). Very first impressions. *Emotion*, *6*, 269–278.

Baron, J. (2007). *Thinking and deciding*. Cambridge: Cambridge University Press.

Baron-Cohen, S., Riviere, A., Fukushima, M., French, D., Hadwin, J., Cross, P., Bryant, C., & Sotillo, M. (1996). Reading the mind in the face: A cross-cultural and developmental study. *Visual Cognition*, *3*, 39–59.

Bauman, M., Bliss-Moreau, E., Machado, C., & Amaral, D. (2011). The neurobiology of primate social behavior. In J. Decety, & J. Cacioppo (Eds.), *The Oxford handbook of social neuroscience* (pp. 683–701). New York: Oxford University Press.

Bentall, R. (1994). Cognitive biases and abnormal beliefs: Towards a model of persecutory delusions. In A. David, & J. Cutting (Eds.), *The neuropsychology of schizophrenia* (pp. 337–360). Hillsdale, MI: Lawrence Erlbaum.

Bentall, R., & Kaney, S. (1989). Content specific information processing and persecutory delusions: An investigation using the emotional Stroop test. *British Journal of Medical Psychology*, *62*, 355–364.

Bentall, R., Kaney, S., & Bowen-Jones, K. (1995). Persecutory delusions and recall of threat-related, depression-related, and neutral words. *Cognitive Therapy and Research*, *19*, 445–457.

Berrios, G. (2008). Descriptive psychiatry and psychiatric nosology during the nineteenth century. In E. Wallace, & J. Gach (Eds.), *History of psychiatry and medical psychology* (pp. 353–379). New York: Springer.

Blanchard, D., Griebel, G., Pubbe, R., & Blanchard, R. (2011). Risk assessment as an evolved threat detection and analysis process. *Neuroscience and Biobehavioral Reviews, 35,* 991–998.

Boyer, P. (2001). *Religion explained.* New York: Basic Books.

Brakoulias, V., & Starcevic, V. (2008). A cross-sectional survey of the frequency and characteristics of delusions in acute psychiatric wards. *Australasian Psychiatry, 16,* 87–91.

Buchanan, T., Tranel, D., & Adolphs, R. (2009). The human amygdala in social function. In P. Whalen, & E. Phelps (Eds.), *The human amygdala* (pp. 289–318). New York: Guilford Press.

Buss, D. (2000). *The dangerous passion.* New York: Free Press.

Cherniak, C. (1986). *Minimal rationality.* Cambridge, MA: MIT Press.

Coltheart, M. (1999). Modularity and cognition. *Trends in Cognitive Science, 3,* 115–120.

Coltheart, M. (2007). The 33rd Sir Frederick Bartlett Lecture: Cognitive neuropsychiatry and delusional belief. *The Quarterly Journal of Experimental Psychology, 60,* 1041–1062.

Coltheart, M. (2013). On the distinction between monothematic and polythematic delusions. *Mind & Language, 28,* 103–112.

Dicks, D., Myers, R., & Kling, A. (1969). Uncus and amygdala lesions: Effects on social behavior in the free-ranging rhesus monkey. *Science, 165,* 69–71.

Dunbar, R. (1988). *Primate social systems.* Ithaca, NY: Cornell University Press.

Dunbar, R. (1993). Coevolution of neocortical size, group size and language in humans. *Behavioral and Brain Sciences, 16,* 681–694.

Dunbar, R. (1998). The social brain hypothesis. *Evolutionary Anthropology, 6,* 178–190.

Dunbar, R. (2004). Gossip in evolutionary perspective. *Review of General Psychology, 8,* 100–110.

Dunbar, R., & Shultz, S. (2007). Evolution in the social brain. *Science, 317,* 1344–1347.

Emery, N. (2000). The eyes have it: The neuroethology, function and evolution of social gaze. *Neuroscience and Biobehavioral Reviews, 24,* 581–604.

Eibl-Eibesfeldt, I. (1970). *Ethology: The Biology of Behavior* (E. Kinghammer, Trans.). New York: Holt, Rinehart, and Winston.

Enquist, M., & Leimar, O. (1993). The evolution of cooperation in mobile organisms. *Animal Behaviour, 45,* 747–757.

Evans, J. (2008). Dual-processing accounts of reasoning, judgment, and social cognition. *Annual Review of Psychology, 59,* 255–278.

Evans, J. (2010). *Thinking twice.* Oxford: Oxford University Press.

Feinstein, J., Adolphs, R., Damasio, A., & Tranel, D. (2011). The human amygdala and the induction and experience of fear. *Current Biology, 21,* 34–38.

Fine, C., Gardner, M., Craigie, J., & Gold, I. (2007). Hopping, skipping or jumping to conclusions? Clarifying the role of the JTC bias in delusions. *Cognitive Neuropsychiatry, 12,* 46–77.

Fodor, J. (1983). *The modularity of mind.* Cambridge, MA: MIT Press.

Gecici, O, Kuloglu, M., Guler, O., Ozbulut, O., Kurt, E., Onen, S., Ekinci, O., Yesilbas, D., Caykoylu, A., Emul, M., Alatas, G., & Albayrak, Y. (2010). Phenomenology of delusions and hallucinations in patients with schizophrenia. *Bulletin of Clinical Psychopharmacology, 20,* 204–212.

Gigerenzer, G., & Brighton, H. (2009). Homo heuristicus: Why biased minds make better inferences. *Topics in Cognitive Science, 1,* 107–143.

Gobbini, M., Koralek, A., Bryan, R., Montgomery, K., & Haxby, J. (2007). Two takes on the social brain: A comparison of theory of mind tasks. *Journal of Cognitive Neuroscience, 19,* 1803–1814.

Gold, I., & Hohwy, J. (2000). Rationality and schizophrenic delusion. *Mind and Language, 15,* 146–167.

Green, M., & Phillips, M. (2004). Social threat perception and the evolution of paranoia. *Neuroscience and Biobehavioral Reviews, 28,* 333–342.

Green, M., Williams, L., & Davidson, D. (2003a). Visual scanpaths and facial affect recognition in delusion-prone individuals: Increased sensitivity to threat? *Cognitive Neuropsychiatry, 8*, 19–41.
Green, M., Williams, L., & Davidson, D. (2003b). Visual scanpaths to threat-related faces in deluded schizophrenia. *Psychiatry Research, 119*, 271–285.
Haselton, M., & Nettle, D. (2006). The paranoid optimist: an integrative evolutionary model of cognitive biases. *Personality and Social Psychology Review, 10*, 47–66.
Kahneman, D. (2011). *Thinking, fast and slow*. New York: Farrar, Straus & Giroux.
Kahneman, D., Slovic, P., & Tversky, A. (Eds.). (1982). *Judgment under uncertainty: Heuristics and biases*. Cambridge: Cambridge University Press.
Kaney, S., Wolfenden, M., Dewey, M., & Bentall, R. (1992). Persecutory delusions and recall of threatening propositions. *British Journal of Clinical Psychology, 31*, 85–87.
Kee, K., Horan, W., Mintz, J., & Green, M. (2004). Do the siblings of schizophrenia patients demonstrate affect perception deficits? *Schizophrenia Research, 67*, 87–94.
Kim, K., Hwu, H., Zhang, L., Lu, M., Park, K., Hwang, T., Kim, D., & Park, Y. (2001). Schizophrenic delusions in Seoul, Shanghai and Taipei: a transcultural study. *Journal of Korean Medical Science, 16*, 88–94.
Knowles, R., McCarthy-Jones, S., & Rowse, G. (2011). Grandiose delusions: A review and theoretical integration of cognitive and affective perspectives. *Clinical Psychology Review, 31*, 684–696.
Kohler, C., Walker, J., Martin, E., Healey, K., & Moberg, P. (2010). Facial emotion perception in schizophrenia: A meta-analytic review. *Schizophrenia Bulletin, 36*, 1009–1019.
Kopytoff, I. (1971). Ancestors as elders in Africa. *Africa, 41*, 129–142.
Lewis, D. (1986). *On the plurality of worlds*. Oxford: Oxford University Press.
Maher, B. (2001). Delusions. In P. B. Sutker, & H. E. Adams (Eds.), *Comprehensive handbook of psychopathology*. New York: Kluwer Academic/Plenum Publishers.
Manschreck, T. (1979). The assessment of paranoid features. *Comprehensive Psychiatry, 20*, 370–377.
Muchembled, R. (2012). A History of Violence *(J. Birrell, Trans.)*. Cambridge: Polity Press.
Munro, A. (1999). *Delusional disorder*. Cambridge: Cambridge University Press.
Ndetei, D., & Vadher, A. (1984). Frequency and clinical significance of delusions across cultures. *Acta Psychiatrica Scandinavica, 70*, 73–76.
Neuberg, S., Kenrick, D., & Schaller, M. (2011). Human threat management systems: self-protection and disease avoidance. *Neuroscicnce and Biobehavioral Review, 35*, 1042–1051.
Newman Taylor, K., & Stopa, L. (2013). The fear of others: A pilot study of social anxiety processes in paranoia. *Behavioural and Cognitive Psychotherapy, 41*, 66–88.
Oosterhof, N., Todorov, A. (2008). The functional basis of face evaluation. *Proceedings of the National Academy of Sciences* 105:11087–11092.
Peters, E., & Garety, P. (2006). Cognitive functioning in delusions: A longitudinal analysis. *Behaviour Research and Therapy, 44*, 481–514.
Pinker, S. (2011). *The better angels of our nature*. New York: Viking.
Pinkham, A., Brensinger, C., Kohler, C., Gur, R., & Gur, R. (2011). Actively paranoid patients with schizophrenia over attribute anger to neutral faces. *Schizophrenia Research, 125*, 174–178.
Raichle, M., Gusnard, D. (2002). Appraising the brain's energy budget. Proceedings of the National Academy of Science of the United States of America 99:10237–10239.
Speechley, W., & Ngan, E. (2008). Dual-stream modulation failure: A novel hypothesis for the formation and maintenance of delusions in schizophrenia. *Medical Hypotheses, 70*, 1210–1214.
Stompe, T., Ortwein-Swoboda, G., Ritter, K., & Schanda, H. (2003). Old wine in new bottles? Stability and plasticity of the contents of schizophrenic delusions. *Psychopathology, 36*, 6–12.
Suhail, K., & Cochrane, R. (2002). Effect of culture and environment on the phenomenology of delusions and hallucinations. *International Journal of Social Psychiatry, 48*, 126–138.

Tateyama, M., Asai, M., Hashimoto, M., Bartels, M., & Kasper, S. (1998). Transcultural study of schizophrenic delusions. *Psychopathology, 31*, 59–68.

Tessari, A., Ottoboni, G., Mazzatenta, A., Merla, A., & Nicoletti, R. (2012). Please don't! The automatic extrapolation of dangerous intentions. *PLoS One, 7*, e49011.

Todorov, A., Mandisodza, A., Goren, A., & Hall, C. (2005). Inferences of competence from faces predict election outcomes. *Science, 308*, 1623–1626.

Todorov, A., Pakrashi, M., & Oosterhof, N. (2009). Evaluating faces on trustworthiness after minimal time exposure. *Social Cognition, 27*, 813–833.

Tranel, D., Gullickson, G., Koch, M., & Adolphs, R. (2006). Altered experience of emotion following bilateral amygdala damage. *Cognitive Neuropsychiatry, 11*, 219–232.

Tranel, D., & Hyman, B. (1990). Neuropsychological correlates of bilateral amygdala damage. *Archives of Neurology, 47*, 349–355.

Ullman, S., Harari, D., Dorfman, N. (2012). From simple innate biases to complex visual concepts. *Proceedings of the National Academy of Science* 109:18215–18220.

Willis, J., & Todorov, A. (2006). First impressions: Making up your mind after a 100-ms exposure to a face. *Psychological Science, 17*, 592–598.

Woody, E., & Szechtman, H. (2011). Adaptation to potential threat: the evolution, neurobiology, and psychopathology of the security motivation system. *Neuroscience and Biobehavioral Reviews, 35*, 1019–1033.

Yung, A., & McGorry, P. (1996). The initial prodrome in psychosis: Descriptive and qualitative aspects. *Australian and New Zealand Journal of Psychiatry, 30*, 587–599.

Zolotova, J., & Brune, M. (2006). Persecutory delusions: Reminiscence of ancestral hostile threats? *Evolution and Human Behavior, 27*, 185–192.

Endnote

1. This sense of "form" is the traditional one, not the sense of form—meaning motif—just described.

CHAPTER

7

Is Depressive Rumination Rational?

T.J. Lane[*,**,†,‡], *G. Northoff*[*,**,‡,¶]

***Taipei Medical University, Graduate Institute of Humanities in Medicine, Taipei, Taiwan; **Taipei Medical University-Shuang Ho Hospital, Brain and Consciousness Research Center, New Taipei City, Taiwan; †Academia Sinica, Institute of European and American Studies, Taipei, Taiwan; ‡National Chengchi University, Research Center for Mind, Brain and Learning, Taipei, Taiwan; ¶Institute of Mental Health Research, University of Ottawa, Ottawa, ON, Canada**

...he who learns must suffer. And even in our sleep pain that cannot forget, falls drop by drop upon the heart, and in our own despite, against our will, comes wisdom to us... ***(Hamilton, Trans., 1958, p. 170)***

7.1 INTRODUCTION

Nearly half a century ago Hempel (1965, p. 150) opined that "classifications of mental disorders will increasingly reflect theoretical considerations." More than three decades later Murphy & Stich (2000), in addition to claiming that clinical practice is based upon false theory, lamented that little progress had been made along the lines that Hempel anticipated. They contended that evolutionary psychology has a natural and central role to play in the development of a new taxonomy that is grounded in natural science. One goal of such a project is the determination of just "what conditions count as disorders at all" (2000, p. 71).

Surveying candidate theoretical developments, Murphy and Stich cited several theories of depression, all of which concern problems pertaining to social relations (2000, pp. 74–84): (1) malfunction of a reciprocal altruism module, (2) social competition switching strategies, and (3)

Rationality. http://dx.doi.org/10.1016/B978-0-12-804600-5.00007-6

defection. As for the first among these, McGuire and Troisi (1998) argue that depression results from a tendency to overestimate one's own contributions to social relationships while underestimating the contributions of others. Because of their chronic misestimates they feel exploited and therefore choose to avoid social interaction. As for the second, Nesse (2000) hypothesizes that depression is an evolved response to the loss of status, an introspective marker that indicates a need to switch social strategies. And, as for the third, Watson and Andrews (2002) argue that depression is a means by which persons can derive more investment from their social network, as in the case of postpartum depression when mothers feel unable to nurture their children unless conspecifics lend more assistance.

Even those who voice skepticism of "social theories of depression" (Raison & Miller, 2013) accord some recognition to the possibility that social stressors may have played a significant evolutionary role. These authors argue that risk alleles for depression have been retained in the human genome because they encode for an "integrated suite" of immunological and behavioral responses that promote defense against infection, especially during infancy when the immune system is not fully operational and when selection pressures from infection are strongest. The idea is that depression is associated with elevated immune inflammatory responses, and these elevated responses are critical to fighting infection.[1] This seems to sit well with the social theories, because psychosocial stress puts people at risk for developing depression, even while that same stress serves as a potent activator of immune defense by increasing inflammation. But the authors argue that social concerns, per se, are secondary: what matters most is that "in ancestral environments, the association between stress perception and risk of subsequent wounding was reliable enough that evolution operated by…(favoring) organisms that prepotently activated inflammatory systems in response to a wide array of environmental threats and challenges" (Raison & Miller, 2013, p. 22). These stressors would have, incidentally, included psychosocial stressors.

But many problems append to these "evolutionary psychology" approaches to explaining depression. Not only can they be found wanting on conceptual grounds (Woodward & Cowie, 2004), the standard for an ideally complete adaptation explanation is extremely difficult to satisfy (Brandon, 1990). Yet more problematically, there is a dearth of experimental evidence showing that humans possess the psychological mechanisms posited by theories based upon evolutionary psychology (Buller, 2005).

Very recently, some among those who presuppose an adaptive advantage for dealing with social pressures that might be derived from depression have turned their attention to this problem, the dearth of experimental evidence concerning the posited psychological mechanisms. They have argued that work on the typical animal models, mice and rats, can mislead, because they do not have the right kind of social organization (Hendrie & Pickles, 2009). Next, turning their attention to humans, they hypothesize that a specific brain region, the third ventricle,[2] which appears to mediate many behaviors associated with depression—sleep-wake cycles, appetite for food and sex, social affiliations, and fear or defensive behaviors—can help focus experimental work, especially with regard to development of more drug-based therapies (Hendrie & Pickles, 2010).

Whether experimental work focused on the third ventricle will succeed remains to be seen. But what does seem clear is that one can acknowledge the utility of negative emotional states when responding to stressors, without proclaiming that those states necessarily confer an adaptive advantage. Such negative states might be more like height: for men reproductive fitness increases steeply with increasing height, up to the point at which musculoskeletal and other health problems begin to outweigh the social and mating advantages of being tall (Nettle, 2004). In other words, there is only a thin adaptive peak between being too tall or too short, and in every generation there is a normal distribution of statures around that peak. On this view, one could argue that increasing height—or a disposition to respond to certain stressors with depression—is selected for because of the beneficial effects limned earlier, until that is the negative effects begin to outweigh the positive.[3] Depression then would arise "because of the tendency of the affect system, in extreme deviations from center, to go into a self-reinforcing cycle, at both the neurobiological and psychological level, which traps it at pathological negativity" (Nettle, 2004, p. 99). In a word, depression might not be an adaptation so much as it is dysregulation of mechanisms underlying normal variation.

Still, certain nagging facts about depression continue to suggest that it is best thought of as an adaptation. Especially noteworthy is that depression is unique among mental health problems in being so commonplace (Hagen, 2011, p. 720). Lifetime prevalence of disorders like schizophrenia or autism is about 1% or less, while it exceeds 20% for major depressive disorder (MDD). What makes this difference even more striking is that, when epidemiological estimates are based on longitudinal data, lifetime risks for succumbing to depression approach 50% (Blanco et al., 2008). It is this extremely high incidence rate, inter alia, which suggests to some theorists that some distinctive feature of depression—for example, rumination—is the manifestation of a properly functioning stress response mechanism, not a biological malfunction. Therefore, in the next section we present this most recent attempt at formulating an evolutionary explanation, a formulation that emphasizes depression's ruminative cognitive style.

7.2 THE ANALYTICAL RUMINATION HYPOTHESIS

Andrews and Thomson (2009) argue that unipolar depression's ruminations should be thought of as analogous to fever: that is, both are mechanisms that have evolved so as to produce effective responses to stressors.[4] On this view, organisms evolve stress response mechanisms that are triggered by specific stressors. Because resources cannot be devoted to all problems at once, stress response mechanisms prioritize fitness-related goals, coordinate trade-offs among body and mental functions—physiology, immune functions, attention and cognition, etc.—and allocate resources in such a way as to reflect priorities and trade-offs.

According to the Andrews and Thomson "Analytical Rumination Hypothesis" (ARH), the intrusive, persistent ruminating over social problems so characteristic of depression is not, per se, a good thing.[5] Nevertheless, it is an evolutionary adaptation. For adaptations, as can be seen from the example of fever, trade-offs are commonplace. Fever has costs: it is metabolically expensive and it can have deleterious effects upon work, sexual function, social relations, and so forth. But fever also enables organisms to coordinate aspects of the immune system in response to a stressor, infection (Kluger, 1986). Impairments associated with fever, thus understood, are not the result of a disorder; rather, they are the outcome of an adaptive trade-off, a trade-off that is necessary in order to produce an effective response to the stress of infection.

As for depression, consistent with the evolutionary theories discussed in the previous section, here the salient stressor is usually a social problem. Depression's costs are similar to those of fever: correlating with the sad mood and anhedonia are a host of deleterious effects on sexual functioning, work, sleeping, eating and social relations. But like fever, according to the Andrews and Thomson "design analysis" argument, there is an upside as well. In developing their argument, they presuppose that if a trait's features "proficiently promote" a specific effect, this very fact can be taken to support the claim that the effect is an evolved function of the trait, because of the unlikelihood that the trait's features could be wholly attributable to chance.

The effects they believe to be proficiently promoted by sadness or depression are four: (1) an analytical reasoning style, (2) accompanied by coordination of body systems to promote ruminative analysis of the triggering problem, (3) that aids development and evaluation of potential solutions, and (4) that diminishes resources available for other cognitive tasks, thereby resulting in the decrements often exhibited when depressed patients perform problem solving or cognitive tasks in the laboratory. The positive effect of the trade-off then is enhanced likelihood of being able to solve a serious social problem, at the cost of diminished performance in other domains. What is unique about the intrusive thoughts associated with rumination is that they involve analysis (Andrews & Thomson, 2009, p. 629). And, as is the case with fever, depressed moods are not pleasant, but they are claimed to proficiently promote a gene-propagating effect.

Why does this matter? Among other things, it goes to the heart of whether people suffering from depression should be treated with medication. ARH suggests that psychotherapies that can assist people to identify and solve problems should be favored, for example, having patients write about the thoughts and feelings associated with depressed episodes (Andrews & Thomson, 2009, p. 635). Andrews and Thomson argue (2009, p. 645) that people should "stop trying to quickly resolve their pain with simple solutions, transition to a slower, analytical approach to problem solving, and *learn how to endure the pain until the problem is solved*."[6] ARH proposes that it is the emotional pain and extended nature of depressive rumination that should be valued: were it not for these characteristics, people would not be motivated to devote the long-term effort essential to solving complex problems.[7] What is needed—what should not be avoided or medicated away—is a slow, problem-solving approach that includes learning how to endure pain. Learning to endure and make use of the pain associated with depression might be part of depression's evolutionary heritage, a heritage that explains the "venerable philosophical traditions that view emotional pain as the impetus for growth and insight into oneself and the problems of life" (Andrews & Thomson, 2009, p. 645)

7.3 RUMINATION

The ARH emphasizes the importance of rumination, but "rumination" is a multi-dimensional concept, admitting of distinct modes. According to the "response style theory" (RST), the type of rumination that accompanies depression is "a mode of responding to distress that involves repetitively and passively focusing on symptoms of distress and on the possible causes and consequences of these symptoms" (Nolen-Hoeksema, Wisco, & Lyubomirsky, 2008, p. 400; cf. Nejad, Fossati, & Lemogne, 2013). RST holds that such passive, repetitive rumination can neither salve feelings nor solve problems. On the contrary, it has multiple deleterious consequences: it aggravates depressed moods by activating negative thoughts and memories, it interferes with problem solving by making thought more pessimistic and fatalistic, it interferes with instrumental behavior, and it causes loss of social support which further fuels depression.[8]

More generally, rumination may be thought of as a disposition to dwell on negative stimuli or memories and inhibit processing of or accessing of positive stimuli (Nolen-Hoeksema et al., 2008, pp. 411–412). For example, when rumination is induced in subjects—commonly by asking that they think about a recent, stressful event, like a fight or the death of a loved one—these negative dispositions become especially evident. After 10 min of thinking about unpleasant interpersonal exchanges or loss, subjects exhibit negative biases in retrieving autobiographical information, predicting the future, and distributing attentional resources. Dot probe tasks of attention, whether auditory or visual,[9] reveal dispositions among ruminators to attend to the negative more than the positive, whether the stimuli are task relevant or task irrelevant (Foland-Ross et al., 2013).

Rumination is assessed by a 22-item scale that describes responses to depressed mood that are self-focused, symptom-focused, and focused on potential consequences of one's mood. Examples include the following: "I think, 'Why do I react this way?'; "I think about how hard it is to concentrate"; and, "I think I won't be able to do my job if I don't snap out of this' (Nolen-Hoeksema et al., 2008, p. 401). Tendencies measured by this scale tend to be relatively stable, even for persons whose depressive symptoms change significantly.

If rumination is indeed so stable though, how is it related to depression, especially MDD? One possibility is that rumination contributes to a person's descent from dysphoria into MDD, "but once an individual is in an episode, other autonomous self-perpetuating processes emerge that determine the duration of episodes" (Nolen-Hoeksema et al., 2008, p. 404). Among these processes are elevated peripheral levels of norepinephrine metabolites, increased phasic REM sleep, poor sleep maintenance, hypercortisolism, decreased cerebral blood flow and glucose metabolism within anterior cortical structures accompanied by increased blood flow, and glucose metabolism in paralimbic regions.[10] Even if these processes themselves did not trigger MDD symptoms, they may help to maintain and extend those symptoms.

But is it ruminations of any type that trigger, extend, or maintain depression? As mentioned previously, "rumination" is multidimensional, admitting of constructive and nonconstructive types.[11] The former, variously referred to as "pondering," "self-reflective," or "adaptive," is concrete and process-focused; the latter, variously referred to as "brooding," "passive," or "maladaptive," is abstract and associated with a strong negative bias (Nejad et al., 2013, pp. 1–2; Nolen-Hoeksema et al., 2008, pp. 413–414; Trapnell & Campbell, 1999; Treynor, Gonzalez, & Nolen-Hoeksema, 2003; Watkins, & Moulds, 2005). Clinical-scale items that target brooding reflect abstract forms of self-focus that emphasize obstacles to overcoming problems: for example, "I think, 'what am I doing to deserve this?" or "I think, 'why can't I handle problems better?" It is this—brooding—that has been found to positively correlate with depression, both concurrently and longitudinally.

The profile for pondering is different. For pondering, typical clinical-scale items include, for example, "I go someplace alone to think about my feelings" or "I analyze recent events to try to understand why I am depressed." Unlike brooding, pondering is positively correlated only with concurrent depression; it is negatively correlated with depression longitudinally (Treynor et al., 2003). Brooding, therefore is a trait, while pondering is not.

In a review of recent studies attempting to flesh out the distinction between these two, Nolen-Hoeksema et al. (2008, p. 414) conclude that pondering is "a form of self-reflection that may be emotionally distressing in the short-run, but *adaptive in the long run* because it leads to successful problem solving."[12] For those who do become clinically depressed pondering is a constructive response. Brooding, on the other hand, appears to be a trait that can trigger, maintain, or aggravate depressive moods. In sum, it appears that pondering—but not brooding—is that which can play a role of the sort envisioned by advocates of the ARH.

7.4 RUMINATION AND THE RESTING STATE HYPOTHESIS OF MDD

The relevance of this distinction between the different types of ruminative cognition to MDD's neural substrate has recently been established by Hamilton et al. (2011). The authors discovered that dominance by the brain's "default mode network" (DMN) positively correlates with elevated levels of brooding, but with only low levels of pondering (cf., Hamilton, Chen, & Gotlib, 2013). It seems, thereby, that the neuronal activity in virtue of which people are caused to suffer the symptoms of depression is not related to the type of rumination that the ARH requires. And this link between brooding and the DMN can serve as a point of departure for showing why it is not likely that depressive rumination is an adaptation, and why it does not afford a rational path "for growth and insight into oneself and the problems of life."

The concept, DMN, was introduced by Raichle et al. (2001) to describe a set of dispersed brain regions[13] that exhibit a stable pattern of resting state metabolic activity and blood flow. This resting state "connectivity" pattern—as manifest by signal fluctuations that covary—is identifiable when subjects undergo functional magnetic resonance imaging (fMRI). High levels of DMN activity occur when people are daydreaming, mind wandering, or otherwise not engaged in tasks that involve attending to or responding to specific external stimuli.[14] Hence it is thought of as a default mode (Raichle, 2010).

This resting state or default mode is particularly intriguing because the expenditure of energy when the brain reacts to external stimuli is only slightly more than what is required when it is "at rest" or, say, daydreaming. The brain's energy budget is about 20% of the body's total, a surprisingly large amount.[15] And of this 20%, between 60% and 80% supports communication among neurons and their supporting cells (Raichle, 2006a,b; Raichle and Mintun, 2006; pp. 467–468). Yet more intriguingly, when the brain responds to the external environment only a small increment in energy consumption—less than 5% more than the brain's resting blood flow—is required. Therefore, it seems that when the brain is not responding to the world, its spontaneous, intrinsic, "resting," activity is not without purpose. It seems less like a resting and more like a preparatory or anticipatory state. In fact, with respect to overall brain function, the intrinsic activity may be far more important than evoked activity.

When people engage in goal-directed, externally oriented cognition, on the other hand, these DMN regions exhibit a distinctive pattern of deactivation. That is, when persons engage in stimulus- or task-induced activity, the DMN exhibits a decrease in metabolic activity and blood flow. The DMN then is inversely related to what is often referred to as the task-positive network (TPN), a network that includes regions like the dorsolateral prefrontal cortex (DLPFC), a network that becomes more active when attention must be distributed to tasks involving external stimuli (Northoff, 2013a, pp. 73–118).[16] In effect what Hamilton et al. (2011) discovered is that in depressed patients—but not in healthy subjects—greater DMN activity relative to TPN activity correlated with depressive rumination, but not with pondering. This discovery is important because it dovetails neatly with two converging lines of research that might be able to contribute to a theoretically motivated explanation of depression of the sort envisioned by Hempel 50 years ago.

The first of these, cognitive science research extending over three decades, has been exploring the relationship between self-focused attention and negative affect (Ingram, 1990; Mor & Winquist, 2002; Pyszczynski & Greenberg, 1987). Echoing the brooding-pondering distinction adumbrated earlier, these findings indicate that self-focus is not a unitary concept: ruminative self-focus—viz, brooding—differs from other types of self-focus in that it tends to be repetitive, unproductive, and inclined to dwell on private, negative aspects of self, thereby intensifying negative moods (Mor & Winquist, 2002). Although positive self-focus does occur, to date most research suggests that the brooding, ruminative aspects of self-focus predominate.[17]

The second line of research, that which will be considered in some detail here, concerns imaging studies of the brain's resting state that have helped illuminate how DMN dominance might be related to ruminative self-focus in the etiology of depression as well as in its resistance to therapeutic treatments.[18] Northoff (2013b, 251–327; also see Northoff & Bermpohl, 2004; Northoff et al., 2006) has argued that certain core regions of the DMN, in particular anterior cortical midline structures (aCMS) like the perigenual anterior cingulate cortex (PACC), are uniquely involved in the processing of self-related stimuli. The focus, despite being motivated by philosophical concerns (Northoff, 2012; Lane, 2012), is not on self as conventionally understood by philosophers (Lane, 2012, Lane & Liang, 2010, 2011).[19] Instead, it is on what Northoff (2013a, p. 253) refers to as "organization in relation to the organism itself," or what Lane (2014, 2015) refers to as the "subpersonal self." In short, "self"-focus so understood refers to the neuronal mechanisms in virtue of which stimuli are perceived as or judged to be related to "self" (or, "this organism"). Despite this difference in how "self" is conceived, the mental and the neuronal, the personal and the subpersonal, levels can be shown to merge in many experimental or clinical settings. Of most direct relevance to the subject at hand, ruminative self-focus and resting state activity in the PACC correlate positively with one another in patients suffering from depression (Grimm et al., 2009).

Metaphorically, the subpersonal self can be thought of as "a neuronal grid or structure" onto which stimuli are mapped (Northoff, 2013a, p. 275). When a stimulus with specific content and function, say, a baseball, is perceived, for one of the authors (Lane), it is likely to be perceived and subsequently judged as highly self-relevant; for the other author (Northoff), not. Accordingly, by hypothesis, Lane's neuronal activity should exhibit strong "overlap" with the resting state activity typically exhibited by aCMS regions (Northoff, 2013b, pp. 257–258). For Northoff, the degree of "overlap" should be considerably less.[20]

How then might the resting state's "neuronal grid" be related to the kind of self-focus that typifies depression? In order to better explain this relationship, first it should be noted that resting state activity is not confined to the DMN or the CMS (Northoff, Qin, & Nakao, 2010). Electrophysiological studies show that resting activity is prevalent throughout the entire brain: spontaneous neuronal oscillations and synchronizations have been identified in various parts of the brain, including the thalamus, the hypothalamus, the ventral tegmental area, the hippocampus, the visual cortex, and so forth. Because resting state activity is so widespread, it can influence all manner of neuronal activity that is induced by external stimuli; indeed, patterns of resting state activity in different brain regions can also directly influence one another.

Second, it should be noted that the neuroanatomy specified by DMN or CMS may have failed to identify the neural substrate of self with sufficient precision. Recent findings suggest that, although involved in self-processing, neither the DMN nor the CMS can be claimed to be uniquely involved in self-processing (Qin & Northoff, 2011). In other words, they engage in self-related, but not necessarily self-specific processing.

In order to hone in on the neural underpinnings of that which is self-specific, instead of merely emphasizing the distinction between medial and lateral regions as is done by CMS and DMN, a threefold distinction among paralimbic, medial heteromodal, and exterosensorimoter/lateral regions provides a more appropriate framework (Northoff, Wiebking,

Feinberg, & Panksepp, 2011). Not only is this distinction compatible with distinctions based upon cytoarchitecture, neurochemistry, and connectional features (Feinberg, 2009, 2011), it also links the PACC to the insula within the anterior paralimbic region as specific for the mediation of self (Northoff, 2013a, pp. 255–256), a finding that converges with important work on the neural basis of self being carried out by Craig (2009).[21] Of special relevance to our concerns here, the paralimbic regions are anatomically linked to ancient emotional and motivational networks. Given the relationship between paralimbic regions and self, along with their relationship to affect or motivation, it should not surprise that excessive self-focus can have significant consequences for mental health.

And, third, it should be noted that the resting state does not just passively respond to stimuli. Instead, it actively contributes to the constitution of mental states, which is one reason why the term "resting" state might be a misnomer. The state is more usefully regarded as the "brain's intrinsic activity."[22] Consider, for example, a study published by our group:[23] participants were asked to indicate whether emotional photos were self-related. Many of their choices struck us as odd, in that they did not comport with our intuitive assessments of participants' personalities. But we discovered that the degree of low-frequency alpha power (8–9 Hz)—even before the photos were presented—could predict the degree of self-relatedness. That is, a higher degree of alpha power disposes participants to experience pictures as more self-related; a lower degree, as less. Moreover, during the resting state, elevated levels of glutamate, which is typically associated with excitatory functions, were observed in the PACC. These findings suggest that PACC glutamate can predispose subjects to spontaneous fluctuations in frequencies, like low alpha, which in turn predisposes those subjects to perceiving stimuli as self-specific.

The "neuronal grid" idea helps explain the behavioral data, the self-relevant choices rendered by participants in the experiment. Even before the photos were shown, EEG waves in a frequency (8–9 Hz) that has previously been associated with self-relatedness were observed.[24] Moreover, during the resting state, elevated levels of glutamate in the PACC seem to predispose participants to having those spontaneous fluctuations in the 8–9 Hz frequency range. The implication seems to be that the resting and prestimulus "neuronal grid" disposes the person to perceive and judge certain stimuli to be highly self-related;[25] the specific content of a stimulus can even be well nigh irrelevant to the determination that a given photo is reported by the subject to be self-related. Inference to the best explanation suggests that elevated levels of an excitatory neurotransmitter in the PACC predispose subjects to "self-specific" frequencies, which in turn result in self-specific judgments. Succinctly, the subject is focused on self and when presented with a forced choice determination concerning an external stimulus is disposed to treat it as self-specific.

But how might these findings relate to depression? The resting state hypothesis (RSH) provides many insights. It aspires to explain MDD by bridging multiple levels, including brain networks, psychological symptoms, biochemical activity, and genetic-molecular mechanisms. The RSH aims to establish a framework that can both explain all existing data and motivate new research. As for the existing data, RSH points up that elevated resting state activity in anterior paralimbic regions—like the PACC and the anterior insula—is one among the most consistent findings in MDD research (Northoff et al., 2011; Northoff, 2013b, pp. 398–407). For this reason, and because of our intent to assess plausibility of the analytical rumination hypothesis, our discussion here is confined to brain networks (the TPN and DMN) and psychological symptoms (self-focus cum negative affect).

In addition to noting that elevated resting state in anterior paralimbic regions is characteristic of MDD, RSH further calls attention to the fact that these same regions are intimately related to basic subcortical regions that mediate processing of ancient or fundamental emotions, including physical distress, disgust, anger, fear, and sadness (Feinberg, 2009, p. 55).[26] RSH also notes that lateral regions which mediate the TPN tend to exhibit lowered resting state activity. Indeed, this contrast between medial and lateral is indicative of a perfectly general pattern of brain activity, the inverse relationship between TPN and DMN described earlier. The two networks tend to interact in an oscillatory, give-and-take, or seesaw manner: when medial regions that underlie self-related, or intereoceptive and emotional processing, undergo excitation, lateral regions that underlie the TPN tend to be inhibited. By contrast, when lateral regions are aroused, medial regions tend to be inhibited.

Concerning the medial-lateral "see-saw" one of the most important studies that sheds light on MDD was a meta-analysis conducted by Alcaro, Panksepp, Witczak, Hayes, & Northoff (2010), an analysis that included all imaging studies of human MDD focused on resting state activity. The authors found that medial regions like the PACC exhibit resting state hyperactivity; they also found that lateral regions like the DLPFC exhibit resting state hypoactivity. The relevant medial regions, in addition to exhibiting hyperactive resting states, also show structural abnormalities: reduced gray matter volume and reduced cell count markers of cellular function. Furthermore, investigations of MDD resting state in animal models reveal a similar pattern of hyperactivity.

What the findings assessed by Alcaro et al. (2010) and others (Northoff et al., 2011, pp. 1935–1945) suggest is that a neural correlate of depressive rumination, brooding, or other psychological symptoms of MDD is an imbalance between paralimbic and lateral activity. Hyperactive resting state activity in critical paralimbic regions might be that in virtue of which self-focus laden with negative affect is precipitated and sustained. This hyperactivity, accompanied by hypoactivity in lateral regions, may help explain why positive stimuli cannot easily alter an MDD patient's mood: the former, correlating with internal focus, might effectively "block" external stimuli, while the latter seems not disposed to respond to external stimuli. A diminished disposition to respond to external stimuli seems to correlate with an abnormal pattern of rest-stimulus interaction (Northoff et al., 2010), as is exhibited in MDD. In a word, when the resting state is excessively active, it blocks entry of stimuli; when excessively inactive, it is unable to respond to those stimuli.

Assuming that this view of MDD is true, why then is the self-focused rumination so intertwined with the negative affect characteristic of brooding? Why, in short, does depression "hurt?" Panksepp and Watt (2011) suggest that primary-process emotional systems, especially the separation-distress PANIC/GRIEF systems, are the major contributor to this "hurt." What seems to happen is that when PANIC/GRIEF (perhaps as well FEAR and RAGE) occur, if the paralimbic resting state hyperactivity that accompanies intense self-focus insulates the person from positive stimuli, negative emotions can "highjack" the person's overall affective and cognitive states, even the conative states. We include "conative" here because the negative affect can be consolidated and intensified by diminished SEEKING urges: that is, the person is disinclined to break out of these brooding states and seek rewarding stimuli in the external environment. In sum, when PANIC/GRIEF occur in people who exhibit the resting state imbalance described earlier, mental life can be flooded by negative affect in such a way that is aggravated by diminished inclination to go in search of rewarding stimuli.

To help understand how this "flood" of negative affect can have such an extensive impact, it is useful to distinguish between nested and control hierarchies (Feinberg, 2009, pp. 159–185). In nested hierarchies, like the brain, any given level of organization is entirely composed of its constituent parts: higher level cortical regions are not independent of the rest of the brain. Those higher levels regions physically comprise paralimbic, limbic, and other regions. Control hierarchies, on the other hand, have pyramidal structures, like an army; a general is not physically comprised by lower ranking officers and enlisted men. Accordingly, in a control hierarchy constraints can be centralized and emanate from the top; in nested hierarchies there is no centralized control and system constraints are embodied within the hierarchy itself. Although in healthy subjects the brain's nested hierarchy exhibits a pattern of mutual, more-or-less balanced modulation, for those suffering from MDD, top-down modulation is significantly diminished, thereby allowing negative affect to "flood" higher level cognition, notably brooding rumination.

On the biochemical level, what seems to be happening is that the usual excitatory-inhibitory balance that obtains between glutamate and GABA is upset. Elevated glutamate levels in critical paralimbic regions reflect decreased neural inhibition which is crucial to constraining the excessive self-focus characteristic of rumination. Excessively high levels of resting state activity in the PACC, for example, appear to be mediated by the neural excitation caused by glutamate. On the psychological level this is manifest as extreme self-focus and hopelessness. It are these findings concerning glutamate-ergic excitation in MDD that might explain why GABA-ergic drugs like ketamine can act so quickly (within 24 h) to bring relief to depressed patients who are suicidal (Niciu et al., 2014). GABA-ergic drugs can help dampen the self-focus, thereby making it possible that externally introduced positive stimuli can effectively reduce negative affect.

We regard the RSH as consistent with recent work on the neurobiology of resilience (Kalisch, Muller, & Tuscher, 2015). "Resilience" refers to the empirically observable phenomenon that not all people who are exposed to the same stressors, whether physical or social, succumb to mental health problems like MDD. Accordingly, researchers in this area do not focus on pathology per se; instead, they investigate mechanisms that prevent illness. One such mechanism, we propose, is a balanced give-and-take relationship between TPN and DMN networks. What seems to occur in MDD is that negative emotional responses to stress—say, PANIC/GRIEF or FEAR—cannot be properly adjusted because the imbalance and consequent abnormal self-focus prevents a more positive or commensurate appraisal of stressors.

The RSH hypothesis is as well compatible with work in computational neuroscience that regards the brain as an inference machine. According to the "free-energy principle" (Friston, 2009; Hohwy, 2013), for example, free energy is a quantifiable measure of surprise that can be used to model neuronal simulations of perception and action. This framework presupposes that brains employ hierarchical models dedicated to predicting sensory input with the aim of minimizing free energy, viz, surprise or predictive error. As is the case with our view of the seesaw relationship between networks, here too the idea of hierarchy is crucial: the free energy principle holds that the brain constructs sets of top-down prior expectations about sensory samples from the world. What appears to occur in MDD is "a loss of top-down control over limbic activity" (Carhart-Harris & Friston, 2010, p. 1267).[27] The flood of negative affect and the heightened self-focus as reflected in abnormally elevated paralimbic resting state activity seems to prevent the possibility of reappraising one's situation vis-à-vis stressors in a more positive light, not only because external stimuli are blocked, but also because top-down modulation of negative affect is inhibited. Baldly, the hopelessness that is symptomatic of depression might be explainable as the result of a diminution of surprise, but at the cost of depriving self of new information as well as of the capability to modulate limbic activity.

7.4.1 Other Forms of Self-Focus and Negative Affect

Still it might strike some readers as odd that self-focus as characterized here should be so strongly associated with negative affect and depression, for after all narcissists and those inclined to mind wander in the manner of James Thurber's Walter Mitty seem to be no less turned inward, yet their affective states might be largely positive. Minds insulated from the world can wander into worlds wherein self reigns narcissistically or performs heroically. And when our minds are wholly isolated from the world, as is the case when we dream, some among those dreams are infused with positive affect.

To begin with the last among these three, when the mind is severed from the external world during REM dream sleep, although dream emotion is common[28] and positive emotions are reported, negative emotions predominate (Merritt, Sickgold, Pace-Schott, Williams, & Hobson, 1994). Positive emotions (eg, joy, elation, or eroticism) account for less than one-third of emotion reports; negative emotions (eg, anxiety, fear, or sadness), more than two-thirds (Merritt et al., 1994, p. 50). Some studies even indicate that reports of negative emotions are as high as 80% of the total, and that "misfortune" is the norm for the "dream self" (Revonsuo, 2006, pp. 404–413). Moreover, although during the first half of an REM dream, the positive–negative imbalance is somewhat less, during the final half 76% of emotions are negative (Merritt et al., 1994, p. 56). Consistent with the RSH, these findings suggest that the longer self-focus persists, the more extended the period of insulation from external stimuli, the worse the mood.

Second, perhaps though the case with mind wandering or daydreaming is different? Cannot we emulate Walter Mitty? The data suggest that Walter Mitty is the exception not the rule. Carciofo, Du, Song, & Zhang (2014) report that many studies have shown there to be a link between frequent mind wandering and negative affect: Giambra and Traynor (1978) discovered correlations between frequency of mind wandering and three questionnaire measures of depression (cf., Mar, Mason, & Litvack, 2012), and Smallwood, O'Connor, Sudbery, & Obonsawin (2007) discovered that mind wandering is associated with dysphoria. Furthermore, mind wandering can predict subsequent negative affect (Killingsworth & Gilbert, 2010), and induced negative affect increases the frequency of mind wandering (Smallwood, Fitzgerald, Miles, & Phillips, 2009). It seems then that the type of self-focus associated with mind wandering resembles that found in sleep and depression.

And, third, even for narcissism there seems to be a significant relationship with depression. Kernberg and Yeomans (2013, pp. 14–15) observe that those who suffer from narcissistic personality disorder (NPD) appear to be masking "the fragmentation and weakness of their identity under a brittle and fragile grandiose self," and that they often present with "severe feelings of inferiority and failure...corresponding to depressive reactions." These observations are consistent with a case study recently reported by Saito, Kobayashi, & Kato (2013). The case concerns a man in his late twenties who exhibited a variety of narcissistic symptoms. Although the patient was treated for NPD, the authors suggest that amelioration of his symptoms was due in large part to the use of antidepressant medications. These medications, in conjunction with supportive psychotherapy, seemed simultaneously to reduce both NPD and depressive symptoms, thereby suggesting a common etiology.

But recall that not all forms of self-focus are indicative of pernicious, depressive rumination. Pondering, as opposed to brooding, can be constructive, possibly in a way that is consistent with the analytic rumination hypothesis. What might help explain the difference between these two modes of self-focused thought?

We propose that the answer is to be found in the difference between self-relatedness and self-specificity. Earlier we argued that although early discussions of the DMN and the CMS emphasized their role in mediating self or self-reference, both failed to adequately distinguish what is merely related to self, as opposed to that which is specific to self. Indeed, that concern along with a more general concern about the principal psychological roles played by DMN and CMS regions have been raised previously (Legrand & Ruby, 2009; cf., Lane, 2012). Here we conjecture that pondering of the sort conducive to dealing with social stressors implicated in the etiology of depression involves those regions of the DMN or the CMS that have not only been implicated in self-reference, they have also been implicated in the social understanding of others.

In view of the need to more clearly distinguish between that which is related to and that which is specific for self, as well as the distinction between pondering and brooding, we think it worth pointing out that one region within the DMN, the medial prefrontal cortex (mPFC), has been found to play an important role in the social understanding of others (Li, Mai, & Liu, 2014). Experimental findings concerning social tasks involving representation of the cognitive and affective states of others, attribution of mental states to others, and predicting the behaviors of others show that there is striking overlap between parts of the mPFC and other regions involved in social cognition that lie outside of the DMN or the CMS. Whereas, for example, the ventral mPFC seems more responsive to self, the dorsal mPFC seems to be involved in both self- and other- referential processing.

In sum, our prediction is that the self-focused, brooding ruminations characteristic of depression are likely to be associated with elevated levels of resting state activity in the PACC and the anterior insula, but not in the dorsal mPFC. The dorsal mPFC may, however, play a significant role in self-focused pondering. Irrespective of whether this specific hypothesis is confirmed, evidence from prior investigations of depression, REM sleep, mind wandering, and narcissism suggest a strong relationship between self-focus insulated from external stimuli and negative affect. It appears to be the case that the resting state's effectiveness at blocking external stimuli and maintaining an inward focus on self might be sufficient to strongly dispose one to experiencing negative affect.

7.5 THE RESTING STATE, DEPRESSIVE RUMINATION, AND RATIONALITY

Recall that according to the ARH, intrusive, persistent rumination is an evolutionary adaptation. It results from an evolutionary trade-off, much as is the case with fever or pain. These are not pleasant things. No one would claim that. But they are averred to be adaptations because they "proficiently promote" special effects that enhance our ability to deal with social stressors. One of the effects promoted is a coordination of body systems to facilitate rumination.

Advocates of the ARH counsel avoiding resort to medication as a way of relieving the negative affect associated with depressive ruminations. According to the ARH, it is better "to learn how to endure the pain until the problem is solved." They even suggest that their view is consistent with a "venerable philosophical tradition" which holds that pain or suffering motivates "growth and insight into oneself." The coordination of body systems that enables a closing in on self-focused, ruminative thoughts and the accompanying negative affect is something to be embraced.

The ARH and the RSH are not compatible. According to the RSH, a key to coordination of body systems is an abnormal resting state imbalance between medial and lateral regions. Lateral hypoactivity inhibits receptiveness to external stimuli and medial hyperactivity blocks the introduction of positive stimuli or top-down modulation. One probable biochemical cause for this abnormal state is an elevated level of glutamate in the PACC that aggravates the intensity of self-focus. If this view is correct, GABA-ergic drugs like ketamine can promote recovery from depression because they accomplish what the ARH advocates admonish people not to do: seek pharmaceutical relief from the ruminative thoughts and their accompanying negative affect.

The suggestion here is that the ARH conflates distinct types of self-focused thoughts and, by implication, their neural substrates. Pondering may indeed be constructive. But it is brooding, not pondering, that is associated with the self-focus and negative affect of depression. And this type of self-focus seems unlikely to promote the type of "growth and insight into oneself and the problems of life" that ARH alleges to be the functional equivalent of fever's coordination of immune responses to infection. The problem is that the hypo- and hyperresting state imbalance makes rational consideration of social stressors difficult, if not impossible, because it focuses attention exclusively onto the negative. This precipitates the hopelessness so characteristic of depression and the inability to discover positive, constructive responses while engaged in persistent, intrusive rumination.

Nozick has written (1993, p. 120) that "reasons and reasoning all would be useful to an organism facing new situations and trying to avoid future difficulties. Such a capacity for rationality...might well serve an organism in its life tasks and increase its inclusive fitness." Were the ARH to direct attention merely to the likelihood that a general-purpose capacity for rationality has been selected for, along the lines suggested by Nozick, we could endorse it.[29] The problem is that the ARH is arguing for a special purpose capacity designed to deal not with "life tasks," generally considered, but with a specific subset of life tasks, social stressors that incline persons toward depressive rumination. It is this special purpose capacity that we believe unlikely to increase the inclusive fitness of humans.

Concerning what is often called epistemic or evidential rationality, Nozick further opined that beliefs are changeable and when changes "are based upon reasons and upon reasoning to new conclusions, *on a balancing of reasons for and against*, they can be attuned to match new or changing situations and then usefully affect the behavior of an organism facing such a situation" (Nozick, 1993, p. 94).[30] In other words, epistemic rationality is concerned with holding or formulating beliefs that get things right. And this is the problem with the ARH. Depressive rumination is unlikely to contribute to the holding or formulation of belief that get things right, because it does not allow for appropriate "balancing of reasons for and against."

To see why depressive rumination is not likely to yield appropriately "balanced" reasoning, it helps to observe that epistemic rationality is consistent with a broad consensus within analytic philosophy concerning the nature of belief. The majority of analytic philosophers who investigate belief advocate some version of the idea that beliefs "aim at the truth" (Williams, 1973, pp. 137–138). Davidson (2003, pp. 366–367) emphasizes their "veridical nature"; Searle (2001, pp. 37–38) claims it is their "job to represent how things are"; Crane (2001, p. 103) says that "holding true" is a synonym for belief; Wedgwood (2002, p. 273) observes that "for every proposition p that one consciously considers, the best outcome is to believe p when p is true"; Shah and Velleman (2005, pp. 498–500; cf., Velleman, 2000, pp. 182–188) contend that beliefs are "truth-regulated acceptance"; and, Railton (2003, p. 297) holds that a belief "not only represents its propositional content as true," it "cannot represent itself as unresponsive to...truth." Although with regard to a small subset of beliefs, we think these views may be somewhat problematic (Lane, 2010; Lane &

Flanagan, 2016; Churchland, 2013, p. 81); generally speaking, we endorse the view that rational deliberations should aim at formulating beliefs that are responsive to and that aim at the truth.

Depressive rumination is not rational, and is not likely to have been rational in ancestral environments, because it lacks the type of balance that reasoning requires. Because depressive rumination is laden with negative affect, it is unable to see the good along with the bad, a state of affairs which inhibits responsiveness to the truth, and implies failure to aim at the truth. If the RSH approximates the truth, if it is indeed an accurate account of depressive rumination, then depression lacks the ability to proficiently promote responses to social stress that enhance survivability. It is highly unlikely that natural selection would design organisms with the type of self-focus characteristic of depression, even if as a trade-off, because the lack of "balance" and responsiveness to the truth is not conducive to discovery of constructive responses to social stressors.

A motivation for formulating the ARH is depression's uniqueness among mental health problems: it is so widespread. If the views expressed here are correct, however, the proper place to search for an explanation of MDD's incidence rate does not lie in our evolutionary past. Perhaps the frequency of social stressors has increased or perhaps our resilience to those stressors has been weakened.[31] Perhaps as well there might be other environmental factors that contribute to imbalances between GABA and glutamate in specific brain regions. What seems clear though is that while rationality may well be an evolved trait, the inability to access a balance of reasons when formulating or changing beliefs is not.

7.6 CONCLUSIONS

If the resting state hypothesis approximates the truth, then the analytic rumination hypothesis could not be true, because the hypo- and hyperresting state imbalance would make it impossible for the "analytic ruminations" to form beliefs that would allow for sufficiently flexible response. Turning inward, intense self-focus tends to flood the cognitive system with negative affect, while simultaneously blocking the introduction of potentially positive stimuli. Reasons and reasoning do contribute to survival, but not when the accessible reasons are so narrowly focused, and when those that are accessible are cloaked in despondence.

Jennifer Corns, writing on "hedonic rationality," has suggested that there are many instances when intervening to eliminate suffering is inappropriate, more instances than we may once have thought (Corns, 2016).[32] Simply, there are times when it is rational to suffer. Generally speaking, we are inclined to agree with Corns. But we do not think MDD is one of those instances. When patients suffer from MDD, abnormal resting state activity prevents patients from being properly responsive to reasons.

We began this essay with an epigraph penned by Aeschylus for his play *Agamemnon*. The gist of these words spoken by the Chorus is consistent with the ARH: wisdom is derived from suffering. Similar expressions of this idea appear recurrently in the writings of Aeschylus and other Greek poets and philosophers. The insight is not novel to 21st-century philosophers or scientists. Indeed, we think there are occasions when to suffer is rational and when to interfere with suffering prevents attainment of wisdom. But MDD is not one of those occasions. Medications—perhaps GABA-ergic—that adjust the resting state medial-lateral imbalance and reduce self-focus are necessary and appropriate.[33] They do not block wisdom; they make its achievement more likely.

Acknowledgments

We express heartfelt gratitude to Tim Bayne, Shaun Nichols, and Cheng Kai-Yuan for their constructive comments on previous versions of this manuscript. For much useful discussion, we are also grateful to the many other participants in Academia Sinica's *IEAS Conference on Reason and Rationality*, Taipei, Taiwan (Aug. 14–15, 2014). Funding for this research was, in part, provided by the (Ministry of Science and Technology) National Science Council of Taiwan research Grants, 102-2420-H-038-001-MY3, 104-2420-H-038-002-MY3, and 105-2632-H-038-001-MY3.

References

Alcaro, A., Panksepp, J., Witczak, J., Hayes, D. J., & Northoff, G. (2010). Is subcortical-cortical midline activity in depression mediated by glutamate and GABA? A cross-species translational approach. *Neuroscience and Biobehavioral Reviews, 34*, 592–605.

Andrews, P. W., & Thomson, J. A., Jr. (2009). The bright side of being blue: Depression as an adaptation for analyzing complex problems. *Psychological Review, 116*(3), 620–654.

Bai, Y., Nakao, T., Xu, J., Qin, P., Chaves, P., Heinzel, A., Duncan, N., Lane, T., Yen, N., Tsai, S., & Northoff, G. (2015). Resting state glutamate predicts pre-stimulus alpha. Increase during self-relatedness—A combined EEG-MRS study on rest-self overlap. *Social Neuroscience, 11*(3), 249–263.

Bar-On, E., Weigl, D., Katz, K., Weitz, R., Steinberg, T., & Parvari, R. (2002). Congenital insensitivity to pain: Orthopaedic manifestations. *The Journal of Bone and Joint Surgery, 84-B*, 252–257.

Blanco, C., Okuda, M., Wright, C., Hasin, D. S., Grant, B. F., & Liu, S. M. (2008). Mental health of college students and their non-college-attending peers: Results from the National Epidemiologic Study on alcohol and related conditions. *Archives of General Psychiatry, 65*, 1429–1437.

Brandon, R. (1990). *Adaptation and environment*. Princeton, NJ: Princeton University Press.

Buller, D. J. (2005). *Adapting minds: Evolutionary psychology and the persistent quest for human nature*. Cambridge, MA: The MIT Press.

Carciofo, R., Du, F., Song, N., & Zhang, K. (2014). Mind wandering, sleep quality, affect and chronotype : An exploratory study. *PLoS ONE, 9*(3), e91285.

Carhart-Harris, R. L., & Friston, K. J. (2010). The default-mode, ego-functions and free energy: A neurobiological account of Freudian ideas. *Brain, 133*, 1256–1283.

Churchland, P. S. (2013). *Touching a nerve: The self as brain*. New York: W. W. Norton & Company.

Corns, J. (2016). Hedonic rationality. Unpublished manuscript.

Craig, A. D. (2009). How do you feel—now? The anterior insula and human awareness. *Nature Reviews Neuroscience*, *7*, 189–195.

Crane, T. (2001). *Elements of mind: An introduction to the philosophy of mind*. New York: Oxford University Press.

Davidson, D. (2003). Thought and talk. In T. O'Connor, & D. Robb (Eds.), *Philosophy of mind: Contemporary readings* (pp. 353–369). London: Routledge.

Demertzi, A., Soddu, A., Vanhaudenhuyse, A., Schabus, M., Noirhomme, Q., Bredart, S., Boly, M., Phillips, C., Luxen, A., Moonen, G., & Laureys, S. (2011). Two distinct neuronal networks mediate the awareness of environment and of self. *Journal of Cognitive Neuroscience*, *23*, 570–578.

Diaz, B. A., Sluis, S., Moens, S., Benjamins, J. S., Migliorati, F., Stoffers, D., Braber, A., Poil, S., Hardstone, R., Van't Ent, D., Boomsma, D., De Geus, E., Mansvelder, H., Van Someren, E., & Linkenkaer-Hansen, K. (2013). The Amsterdam Resting State Questionnaire reveals multiple phenotypes of resting-state cognition. *Frontiers in Human Neuroscience*, *7*, 446.

Feinberg, T. (2009). *From axons to identity: Neurobiological explorations of the nature of self*. New York: W. W. Norton & Company.

Feinberg, T. (2011). The nested neural hierarchy and the self. *Consciousness and Cognition*, *20*, 4–15.

Foland-Ross, L. C., Hamilton, J. P., Joormann, J., Berman, M. G., Jonides, J., & Gotlib, H. (2013). The neural basis of difficulties disengaging from negative irrelevant material in major depression. *Psychological Science*, *24*(3), 334–344.

Friston, K. (2009). The free-energy principle: A rough guide to the brain? *Trends in Cognitive Science*, *13*, 293–301.

Giambra, L. M., & Traynor, T. D. (1978). Depression and daydreaming: An analysis based upon self-ratings. *Journal of Clinical Psychology*, *34*(1), 14–25.

Grimm, S., Ernst, J., Boesiger, P., Schuepback, D., Hell, D., Boeker, H., & Northoff, G. (2009). Increased self-focus in major depressive disorder is related to neural abnormalities in subcortical-cortical midline structures. *Human Brain Mapping*, *30*, 2617–2627.

Hagen, E. H. (2011). Evolutionary theories of depression. *Canadian Journal of Psychiatry*, *56*(12), 716–726.

Hamilton, E. (Trans.) 1958. *Three Greek plays: Prometheus Bound, Agamemnon, and The Trojan Woman*. New York: W. W. Norton & Company

Hamilton, J. P., Furman, D. J., Chang, C., Thomason, M. E., Dennis, E., & Gotlib, I. H. (2011). Default-mode and task positive network activity in major depressive disorder: Implications for adaptive and maladaptive rumination. *Biological Psychiatry*, *70*(4), 327–333.

Hamilton, J. P., Chen, M. C., & Gotlib, I. H. (2013). Neural systems approaches to understanding major depressive disorder: An intrinsic functional organization perspective. *Neurobiology of Diseases*, *52*, 4–11.

Hempel, C. G. (1965). *Aspects of scientific explanation*. New York: The Free Press.

Hendrie, C. A., & Pickles, A. R. (2009). Depression as an evolutionary adaptation: Implications for the development of pre-clinial models. *Medical Hypotheses*, *72*, 342–347.

Hendrie, C. A., & Pickles, A. R. (2010). Depression as an evolutionary adaptation: Anatomical organization around the third ventricle. *Medical Hypotheses*, *74*(4), 736–740.

Hohwy, J. (2013). *The predictive mind*. New York: Oxford University Press.

Ingram, R. E. (1990). Self-focused attention in clinical disorders: Review and a conceptual model. *Psychological Bulletin*, *107*, 156–176.

Kalisch, R., Muller, M. B., & Tuscher, O. (2015). A conceptual framework for the neurobiological study of resilience. *Behavioral and Brain Sciences*, *38*, e92.

Kernberg, O. F., & Yeomans, F. E. (2013). Borderline personality disorder, bipolar disorder, depression, attention deficit/hyperactivity disorder, and narcissistic personality disorder: Practical differential diagnosis. *Bulletin of the Menninger Clinic, 77*(1), 1–23.

Killingsworth, M. A., & Gilbert, D. T. (2010). A wandering mind is an unhappy mind. *Science, 330*, 932.

Kluger, M. J. (1986). Is fever beneficial? *The Yale Journal of Biology and Medicine, 59*, 89–95.

Lane, T. (2010). The ethics of false belief. *EurAmerica, 40*(3), 591–633.

Lane, T. (2012). Toward an explanatory framework for mental ownership. *Phenomenology and the Cognitive Sciences, 11*(2), 251–286.

Lane, T. (2014). When actions feel alien—An explanatory model. In T. W. Hung (Ed.), *Communicative action* (pp. 53–74). Springer Science + Business Media.

Lane, T. (2015). Self, belonging, and conscious experience: A critique of subjectivity theories of consciousness. In Rocco Gennaro (Ed.), *Disturbed consciousness: New essays on psychopathology and theories of consciousness* (pp. 103–140). Cambridge, MA: The MIT Press.

Lane, T., & Flanagan, O. (2016). Neuroexistentialism, eudaimonics, and positive illusions. In B. Kaldis (Ed.), *Mind and society: Cognitive science meets the philosophy of social sciences, Synthese Library Series of Studies in Epistemology, Logic, Methodology, and Philosophy of Science*. New York: Springer Science + Business Media.

Lane, T., & Liang, C. (2010). Mental ownership and higher-order thought. *Analysis, 70*(3), 496–501.

Lane, T., & Liang, C. (2011). Self-consciousness and immunity. *The Journal of Philosophy, 108*(2), 78–99.

Legrand, D., & Ruby, P. (2009). What is self specific? Theoretical investigation and critical review of neuroimaging results. *Psychological Review, 116*(1), 252–282.

Li, W., Mai, X., & Liu, C. (2014). The default mode network and social understanding of others: What do brain connectivity studies tell us. *Frontiers in Human Neuroscience, 8*(74), .

Mar, R. A., Mason, M. F., & Litvack, A. (2012). How daydreaming relates to life satisfaction, loneliness, and social support: The importance of gender and daydream content. *Consciousness and Cognition, 21*, 401–407.

McGuire, M., & Troisi, A. (1998). *Darwinian psychiatry*. New York: Oxford University Press.

Merritt, J. M., Sickgold, R., Pace-Schott, E., Williams, J., & Hobson, J. A. (1994). Emotion profiles in the dreams of men and women. *Consciousness and Cognition, 3*, 46–60.

Mor, N., & Winquist, J. (2002). Self-focused attention and negative affect: A meta-analysis. *Psychological Bulletin, 128*(4), 638–662.

Murphy, D., & Stich, S. (2000). Darwin in the madhouse: Evolutionary psychology and the classification of mental disorders. In P. Carruthers, & A. Chamberlain (Eds.), *Evolution and the human mind: Modularity, language and meta-cognition* (pp. 62–92). Cambridge, UK: Cambridge University Press.

Nejad, A. B., Fossati, P., & Lemogne, C. (2013). Self-referential processing, rumination, and cortical midline structures in major depression. *Frontiers in human neuroscience, 7*, 666.

Nesse, R. M. (2000). Is depression an adaptation? *Archives of General Psychiatry, 57*, 14–20.

Nettle, D. (2004). Evolutionary origins of depression: a review and reformulation. *Journal of Affective Disorders, 81*, 91–102.

Niciu, M. J., Luckenbaugh, D. A., Ionescu, D. F., Guevara, S., Machado-Vieiva, R., Richards, E. M., Brutsche, N. E., Nolan, N. M., & Zarate, C. A. (2014). Clinical predictors of ketamine response in treatment-resistant major depression. *The Journal of Clinical Psychiatry, 75*(5), e417–e423.

Nolen-Hoeksema, S., Morrow, J., & Fredrickson, B. L. (1993). Response styles and the duration of episodes of depressed mood. *Journal of Abnormal Psychology, 102*, 20–28.

Nolen-Hoeksema, S., Wisco, B. E., & Lyubomirsky, S. (2008). Rethinking rumination. *Perspectives on Psychological Science, 3*(5), 400–424.

Northoff, G. (2012). Immanuel Kant's mind and the brain's resting state. *Trends in Cognitive Sciences, 16*(7), 356–359.

Northoff, G. (2013a). *Unlocking the brain. Volume I: Coding*. New York: Oxford University Press.
Northoff, G. (2013b). *Unlocking the brain. Volume II: Consciousness*. New York: Oxford University Press.
Northoff, G., & Bermpohl, F. (2004). Cortical midline structures and the self. *Trends in Cognitive Science*, *8*(3), 102–107.
Northoff, G., Heinzel, A., de Greck, M., Bermpohl, F., Dobrowolny, H., & Panksepp, J. (2006). Self-referential processing in our brain—A meta-analysis of imaging studies on the self. *Neuroimage*, *15*(31a), 440–457.
Northoff, G., Qin, P., & Nakao, T. (2010). Rest-stimulus interaction in the bra a review. *Trends in Neuroscience*, *33*(6), 277–284.
Northoff, G., Wiebking, C., Feinberg, T., & Panksepp, J. (2011). The resting state hypothesis of major depressive disorder—A translational subcortical-cortical framework for a system disorder. *Neuroscience and Biobehavioral Reviews*, *35*(9), 1929–1945.
Nozick, R. (1993). *The nature of rationality*. Princeton, NJ: Princeton University Press.
Panksepp, J., & Watt, D. F. (2011). Why does depression hurt? Ancestral primary-process separation-distress (PANIC) and diminished brain reward (SEEKING) processes in the genesis of depressive affect. *Psychiatry*, *74*(1), 5–13.
Pyszczynski, T., & Greenberg, J. (1987). Self-regulatory perseveration and the depressive self-focusing style: A self-awareness theory of reactive depression. *Psychological Bulletin*, *102*, 122–138.
Qin, P., & Northoff, G. (2011). How is our self related to midline regions and the default mode network. *NeuroImage*, *57*, 1221–1233.
Raichle, M. E., & Mintun, M. A. (2006). Brain work and brain imaging. *Annual Review of Neuroscience*, *29*, 449–476.
Raichle, M. E. (2006a). The brain's dark energy. *Science*, *314*, 1249–1250.
Raichle, M. E. (2006b). Brain work and brain imaging. In S. E. Hyman, & T. J. et al. Jessell (Eds.), *Annual review of neuroscience* (pp. 449–476). Palo Alto, CA: Annual Reviews.
Raichle, M. E. (2010). Two views of brain function. *Trends in Cognitive Sciences*, *14*(4), 180–190.
Raichle, M. E., & Gusnard, D. A. (2002). Appraising the brain's energy budget. *Proceedings of the National Academy of Sciences*, *99*(16), 10237–10239.
Raichle, M. E., MacLeod, M. A., Snyder, A. Z., Powers, W. J., Gusnard, D. A., & Shulman, G. A. (2001). A default mode of brain function. *Proceedings of the National Academy of Sciences*, *98*(2), 676–682.
Railton, P. (2003). *Facts, values, and norms: Essays toward a morality of consequence*. Cambridge, UK: Cambridge University Press.
Raison, C. L., & Miller, A. H. (2013). The evolutionary significance of depression in pathogen host defense (Pathos-D). *Molecular Psychiatry*, *18*, 15–37.
Revonsuo, A. (2006). *Inner presence: Consciousness as a biological phenomenon*. Cambridge, MA: The MIT Press.
Saito, S., Kobayashi, T., & Kato, S. (2013). A case of major depressive disorder barely distinguishable from narcissistic personality disorder. *Seishin Shinkelgaku Zasshi*, *115*(4), 363–371.
Searle, J. (2001). *The rediscovery of mind*. Cambridge, MA: The MIT Press.
Seligman, M., & Yellen, A. (1987). What is a dream? *Behavior Research and Therapy*, *25*, 1–24.
Shah, N., & Velleman, J. (2005). Doxastic deliberation. *The Philosophical Review*, *114*, 497–534.
Smallwood, J., Fitzgerald, A., Miles, L. K., & Phillips, L. H. (2009). Shifting moods, wandering minds: Negative moods lead the mind to wander. *Emotion*, *9*(2), 271–276.
Smallwood, J., O'Connor, R. C., Sudbery, M. V., & Obonsawin, M. (2007). Mind-wandering and dysphoria. *Cognition and Emotion*, *21*(4), 816–842.
Sterelny, K. (2003). *Thought in a hostile world: The evolution of human cognition*. Malden, MA: Blackwell Publishing.
Trapnell, P. D., & Campbell, J. D. (1999). Private self-consciousness and the five-factor model of personality: Distinguishing rumination from reflection. *Journal of Personality and Social Psychology*, *76*, 284–304.

Treynor, W., Gonzalez, R., & Nolen-Hoeksema, S. (2003). Rumination reconsidered: A psychometric analysis. *Cognitive Therapy and Research, 27*, 247–259.
Velleman, J. D. (2000). *The possibility of practical reason*. New York: Oxford University Press.
Watkins, E. (2008). Constructive and unconstructive repetitive thought. *Psychological Bulletin, 134*(2), 163–206.
Watkins, E., & Moulds, M. (2005). Distinct modes of ruminative self-focus: Impact of abstract versus concrete rumination on problem solving in depression. *Emotion, 5*, 319–329.
Watson, P. J., & Andrews, P. W. (2002). Towards a revised evolutionary adaptationist analysis of depression: The social navigation hypothesis. *Journal of Affective Disorders, 72*, 1–14.
Wedgwood, R. (2002). The aim of belief. *Philosophical Perspectives, 16*, 267–297.
Williams, B. (1973). *Problems of the self*. Cambridge, UK: Cambridge University Press.
Woodward, J., & Cowie, F. (2004). The mind is not [just] a system of modules shaped [just] by natural selection. In C. Hitchcock (Ed.), *Contemporary debates in philosophy of science* (pp. 312–334). Malden, MA: Blackwell.

Endnotes

1. According to this PATHOS-D hypothesis, it is not that the alleles for depression coevolved with immunological alleles that support pathogen defense; instead, "the alleles for depression… are in fact one in the same as…" those immunological alleles (Raison & Miller, 2013, p. 16).
2. The third ventricle includes the pineal gland, the hypothalamus, and the amygdala.
3. Of course the adaptive landscape in this vicinity is likely more complex than the single peak model described here.
4. The hypothesis proposed by Andrews and Thomson concerns only unipolar depression; they do not challenge the view that bipolar differs qualitatively from unipolar depression.
5. The point is that although severe pain is aversive and disabling, it is nevertheless beneficial; so too is severe emotional response. For those who might think pain not to be beneficial, consider the suffering endured by those who are congenitally insensitive to pain (Bar-On et al., 2002).
6. Italics not contained in original.
7. Consider that people contemplating divorce might lose children, money, and home by leaving. Alternatively, by not leaving, they risk continued marital conflict. Determining the optimal solution requires extended analysis and the capacity to endure the emotional pain that supplies the motivation.
8. Functional neuroimaging during the performance of emotional working memory tasks can also be used to show that negative, irrelevant stimuli can be especially difficult for persons suffering from depression to disregard.
9. Dichotic listening probes can, eg, be used to simultaneously present positive and negative stimuli.
10. Cerebral blood flow and metabolic changes will be a focus of concern in the next section, where we discuss the resting state hypothesis.
11. Investigators using the ruminative responses scale and correlational along with principal component analysis have identified at least three distinct types of items: depressive, brooding, and self-reflective (Nolen-Hoeksema et al., 1993).
12. Italics not contained in original.
13. Among the core regions are the posterior cingulate cortex, a medial prefrontal area, and the inferior parietal lobule.
14. During functional magnetic resonance imaging (fMRI), the resting state is typically measured by asking subjects to close their eyes or fixate on a cross while lying quietly.

15. This is 10 times higher than what would be expected were calculations based upon weight alone (Raichle & Gusnard, 2002).
16. There are several different ways of drawing this distinction: some, for example, distinguish between the "internal and external awareness network" (Demertzi et al. 2011).
17. Whether this emphasis more nearly reflects a common characteristic of self-focus itself, or whether it is an artifact of researchers' selective focus remains to be seen (Watkins, 2008). We return to discussion of the link between self-focus and negative affect in the next section.
18. A recently developed resting state questionnaire that is based upon data gathered from 813 subjects indicates that "self" is one of seven distinctive dimensions of resting state cognition (Diaz et al., 2013).
19. The philosophical sense of "self" tends to emphasize self-as-subject, or the subject of experience.
20. The neuronal activity that is manifest during both the resting state and self-related processing is spatial and temporal: both functional connectivity among critical regions and strong low-frequency fluctuations are exhibited (Northoff, 2013a, pp. 299–301).
21. Paralimbic regions include lower portions of the orbitofrontal cortex, perigenual and supragenual anterior cingulate cortex, the posterior cingulate cortex, the retrosplenial cortex, the temporal pole, and the insula.
22. There are, however, important conceptual distinctions in this vicinity—intrinsic activity, resting state, and baseline—that should be preserved. For explication, see Northoff (2013a, pp. 74–76).
23. Bai et al., 2015.
24. Exaggerated emphasis on the search for neural correlates of consciousness may have been an obstacle to discovery the way in which the "neuronal grid" can structure experience. A more comprehensive understanding of conscious experience, including the pathological experiences under consideration here, will require that attention be given to the "neural predispositions of consciousness" (Northoff, 2013, pp. 541–542).
25. "Grid" should not be interpreted as something that is in any literal sense inflexible; prior interaction between stimuli and resting state activity can modulate the resting state (the "grid") such that it "prepares itself" for subsequent processing of the same or similar stimuli (Northoff, 2013a, p. 246).
26. Because primary emotions emerge by the age of one, and because they are expressed in cross-culturally stereotypical fashion, it seems they are "hardwired" into the developing nervous system.
27. The view we articulate here is in many—but not all—respects consistent with the view presented by Carhart-Harris & Friston (2010).
28. Seligman and Yellen (1987) say of dream emotion that it is a "limbic bath" that persists throughout a dream's entirety. According to the study discussed in the text (Merritt et al., 1994, p. 47, 50), 95% of dream reports were associated with emotion; only 11 of 200 indicated no emotion.
29. "General" here does not imply that mechanisms are adapted to some "general" feature of the environment; instead, what matters is that there be mechanisms of "phenotypic plasticity" which are not committed to producing any specific response before interacting with the environment. The beliefs that supervene on such a mechanism are "functionally decoupled from any specific actions, while being potentially relevant to many" (Sterelny, 2003, pp. 30–40).
30. Italics not contained in original.
31. Although we do not develop our argument here, we speculate that adequate explanation of the incidence rate will give special emphasis to a diminution of resilience. The social

stressors are not new; rather, what has changed is our capacity for dealing with those stressors.

32. In this cogent manuscript Corns argues that agents can be found to be rational, or not, simply in virtue of what they feel, the pleasantness or unpleasantness of their emotions.
33. It is not our intent to dismiss the value of cognitive therapies that can promote pondering social stressors.

PART IV

IRRATIONALITY

Is rationality a characteristic shared by all human beings? Or can human populations from diverse social backgrounds develop ways of thinking that are ontologically dissimilar from one another? While coherence is a key element in the Western notion of rationality, textual inconsistency seems much more prevalent in ancient Chinese philosophy. "Irrational" thus seems to be the first impression that ancient Chinese philosophy gives to many Western scholars. Some argue that these phenomena reveal the cultural diversity of rationality. Others hold that the alleged cultural differences have been exaggerated. Part IV considers whether ancient Chinese philosophy really does diverge substantially from Western ideas of rationality, or whether the appearance of irrationality in various classics of Chinese philosophy can be explained in some other way.

In Chapter 8, Yiu-ming Fung challenges the perceived view that ancient Chinese thinkers are nonanalytical, and that their ways of reasoning are incommensurate with thinkers in the Western philosophical tradition. He locates this view in the works of a number of scholars, including Marcel Granet, Joseph Needham, A. C. Graham, David Hall, and Roger Ames. Fung argues that this view should be rejected, not just because it contradicts ancient texts, but also because it is self-defeating.

In Chapter 9, Wai Chun Leong reviews the widespread claim that ancient Chinese philosophy features a kind of "logic" or "rationality" that is distinct from Western notions. For example, some have alleged that Chinese philosophy involves an acceptance of contradictions as if they were rational, whereas Western philosophy does not. In that case, attempting to understand Chinese philosophy in terms of current, Western notions of rationality might lead to a distortion of ancient traditions. Leong argues that the usual evidence for this claim either attributes no real contradiction to Chinese philosophy, or simply fails to make ancient Chinese philosophical texts intelligible.

In Chapter 10, Ting-mien Lee considers the cultural relativity of rationality from the viewpoint of Sinology. According to Lee, early Chinese philosophical texts are notorious for contradictions and a lack of apparent coherence. She argues that these apparently incoherent texts do not support the claim that ancient Chinese philosophy features a notion of rationality different from that operative in the Western tradition. She also provides an alternative explanation for textual incoherence, one that does not invoke a separate notion of rationality.

CHAPTER

8

Reason and Unreason in Chinese Philosophy

Y.-M. Fung
Hong Kong University of Science & Technology, Hong Kong

8.1 INCOMMENSURABILITY THESIS

Following Marcel Granet and Joseph Needham's explanation of the Chinese way of thinking, some Western scholars in the field of Chinese philosophy, including A. C. Graham, David Hall, and Roger Ames, regard the mode of thinking in some major ancient Chinese thinkers' thought as nonanalytic, correlative, or mystic, which is essentially different from or incommensurable to an analytic, causal, or rational mode of thinking in the Western philosophical tradition. Similarly, some Asian scholars, such as D. T. Suzuki (鈴木大拙) and Zongsan Mou (牟宗三) think that the Buddhist nonanalytical wisdom (prajñā, 般若) in Zen (Chan, 禪) Buddhism and the way (*dao*, 道) in ancient Daoism cannot be understood or interpreted with analytical language. They also claim that there is an essential difference between the way of thinking in Zen Buddhism or ancient Daoism, on the one side, and that in the Western philosophical tradition, on the other.

I do not think this kind of understanding or interpretation of Chinese thinking and language is accurate. It is not only because their interpretation is not in accordance with the Chinese texts, but also because they cannot explain the issue in an intelligible way without being self-defeating. In this chapter, I will provide two case studies, one in Zhuangzi's (莊子) Daoist philosophy and the other in Zen Buddhism, and try to demonstrate that the views mentioned above are self-refuting. According to Donald Davidson's principle of charity, I think, we can only explain the irrationality in the seat of rationality, or make unreason intelligible with reason.

Rationality. http://dx.doi.org/10.1016/B978-0-12-804600-5.00008-8

8.2 THE VERY IDEA OF CORRELATIVE THINKING

According to Needham's view, the major trend of Chinese thinking in the Han (漢) dynasty is correlative or associative. He says:[1]

> In correlative thinking, conceptions are not subsumed under one another, but placed side by side in a *pattern*, and things influence one another not by acts of mechanical causation, but by a kind of "inductance." ... The symbolic correlations or correspondences all formed part of one colossal pattern. Things behaved in particular ways not necessarily because of prior actions or impulsions of other things, but because their position in the ever-moving cyclical universe was such that they were endowed with intrinsic nature which made that behavior inevitable for them. If they did not behave in those particular ways they would lose their relational positions in the whole (which made them what they were), and turn into something other than themselves. They were parts in existential dependence upon the whole world-organism. And they reacted upon one another not so much by mechanical impulsion or causation as by a kind of mysterious resonance.

Needham thinks that the mode of thinking mentioned above is essentially different from that in the Western tradition. Following Needham's view and pushing further into a deep level of conceptual scheme, Graham believes that "all thinking is grounded in analogization."[2] Different cultures may have different ground of analogization or "metaphorical roots." For example, in comparison with the metaphorical root behind Westerners' "matter" and "law," that behind Chinese "*qi*" (氣), (vital force) and "*li*" (理), (pattern, order, reason, or principle) is essentially different. For the Western "outsider," unlike the Chinese "insider" who habitually thinks with their concepts, is much less conscious of the differences at the bottom or root level of thinking.

In contrast to Graham's theoretical or structural interpretation, Hall and Ames stress that the Chinese nonanalytic, correlative or nonrationalized analogical thinking "cannot be formalized or overly rationalized without violating the very premise of embedded aesthetic relatedness."[3] They reject all kinds of analytical or formal interpretation. Instead, they adopt an aesthetic or informal one. Graham does not think that there was not logical thinking other than correlative thinking in ancient China, but Hall and Ames do think that ancient Chinese thinking was dominated with this prelogical or illogical characteristic. As indicated in the following passage, they believe that there was a kind of productive vagueness in ancient Chinese thinking:[4]

> Intercultural communication patterned by productive vagueness is not a strictly rational process, but a *reasonable* one. Such communication is not logical but analogical, a clumsy process of fits and starts which involves the juxtaposition of distinctive feelings and intentions, images and actions. To communicate is to articulate differences, and the procedures involved in such articulation are themselves not wholly open to articulation.

As a matter of fact, there is not exactly the same view among these scholars when they use the term "correlative thinking" to describe the Chinese mode of thinking; but they all recognize more or less the term's implication as "nonlogical" or "prelogical," "nonrational" or "irrational," "intuitive-associative" or "beyond analytical thinking." Based on this presumption, some of them even think that there is "irreducibility" from the root level of (correlative) thinking to the upper level of (analytical) thinking or that there is "incommensurability" between correlative thinking and analytical thinking.

I think this kind of understanding or interpretation of the Chinese mode of thinking is self-refuting. According to Davidson's principle of charity, we cannot identify any thought if there is no common ground between the interpreter and the speaker. If there is any thought with the characteristic of irrationality or unreason, we can only explain their irrationality in the seat of rationality, or make unreason intelligible with reason. There is no transcendence of rationality or logic in human thought. Davidson writes:[5]

> The principle directs the interpreter to translate or interpret so as to read some of his own standards of truth into the pattern of sentences held true by the speaker. The point of the principle is to make the speaker intelligible, since too great deviations from consistency and correctness leave no common ground on which to judge either conformity or difference... From a formal point of view, the principle of charity helps solve the problem of the interaction of meaning and belief by restraining the degrees of freedom allowed belief while determining how to interpret words.

Based on this principle, Davidson thinks that "we could not understand someone whom we were forced to treat as departing radically and predominantly from all such (rational) norms. This would not be an example of irrationality, or of an alien set of standards: it would be an absence of rationality, something that could not be reckoned as thought." So, relativism or skepticism does not have a place in human thought. It is because, Davidson says, "If what we share provides a common standard of truth and objectivity, difference of opinion makes sense. But relativism about standards requires what there cannot be, a position beyond all standard."[6] In other words, relativism or skepticism which goes beyond our rational space cannot be understood as irrational, but nonrational. It means that it is not about thought and that it cannot be either true or false. Irrational thinking is false because it is qualified to be false, but nonrational thinking (if it can be called "thinking") is not false because it is not qualified to be false.

In the following I will provide two case studies to explain why unreason or irrationality must be understood in terms of reason or rationality. One is about Zhuangzi's idea of oneness (*yi*, 一) or great oneness (*tai-yi*, 太一) which is generally interpreted as an unnamable, ineffable, or indescribable entity; the other is about the public case (*ko-an/gong-an*, 公案) of

Zen Buddhism which is generally understood as a kind of collection of paradoxical expressions and as transcending rationality and logic. Based on my analyses of these two cases, I will try to demonstrate that the view of incommensurability mentioned above cannot be sustained and that irrationality or unreason must be explained in our rational space. For these purposes, I will try to use the methods of conceptual analysis and logical analysis to deal with the former problem and the speech act theory to tackle the latter one.

8.3 INEFFABILITY OF *YI* (ONENESS) IN ZHUANGZI'S DAOISM

Let us look at the first case. In chapter two (Qi-wu-lun, 齊物論) of the *Zhuangzi*, we can find a passage which seems to say that the idea of *yi* is ineffable or unnamable as follows:[7]

> Heaven, Earth, and I were produced together, and all things and I are one. Since they are one, can there be speech about them? But since they are spoken of as one, must there not be room for speech? One and Speech are two; two and one are three. Going on from this (in our enumeration), the most skilful reckoner cannot reach (the end of the necessary numbers), and how much less can ordinary people do so! Therefore from non-existence we proceed to existence till we arrive at three; proceeding from existence to existence, to how many should we reach? Let us abjure such procedure, and simply rest here. (*Zhuangzi* I 2:9)

> 天地與我並生，而萬物與我為一。既已為一矣，且得有言乎？既已謂之一矣，且得無言乎？一與言為二，二與一為三。自此以往，巧曆不能得，而況其凡乎！故自無適有，以至於三，而況自有適有乎！無適焉，因是已。

As I know, most of the Chinese scholars in the field of Daoism are inclined to interpret *yi* as identical with *dao* which is ineffable or unnamable. They even regard the ineffable *yi* or *dao* not only as transcending rationality and logic, but also as a transcendent (not transcendental in the Kantian sense) entity in terms of mysticism or ontology. On the other hand, some Western scholars do not put much emphasis on the point of ontological transcendence; they rather focus on the paradoxical character of the idea of *yi*. For example, Graham interprets Zhuangzi's view as rejecting any statement of the oneness. He thinks that the passage about "all (or ten thousand) things and I are one." (*wan-wu yu wo wei-yi*, 萬物與我為一) quoted above (*Zhuangzi* I 2: 9) is Zhuangzi's argument against Hui Shi's (惠施) claim that "everything is one" (*tian-de yi-ti*, 天地一體) (*Zhuangzi* III 11:7). He also thinks that to accept this claim about *wei-yi* (為一), (being one) or *yi-ti* (一體), (one body) will lead to a paradox similar to Plato's. According to Graham's interpretation, for Zhuangzi it is impossible to assert the oneness of all things. The reason is that "as soon as I say it there are two things, the world and my statement about it."[8] So, the statement cannot be included in the world as oneness and thus discredits the idea of oneness. In other words, the assertion of the statement itself, which requires the existence of a statement about the world or oneness, and so at least two things (ie, the world as oneness and the statement which is not included in the world as oneness), undermines the truth of the assertion.

No matter whether *yi* understood as an undifferentiated reality or the great whole of one body is Zhuangzi or Hui Shi's idea (I will explain these two senses of *yi* later), there is a consensus in the field of Daoist philosophy that *yi* is unnamable or ineffable. Based on a transcendental perspective, some Chinese scholars interpret it as Zhuangzi's own idea, which is about a transcendent entity and goes beyond rationality and logic. In contrast, Graham regards *yi* as Hui Shi's idea, which is criticized by Zhuangzi in the sense that to express it will lead to a contradiction or paradox. So, to escape from this predicament, Zhuangzi seems to suggest that one has to give up the intention to express the idea of *yi*.

8.4 IN WHAT SENSE IS *YI* INEFFABLE OR UNNAMABLE?

If, for the sake of argument, we accept Graham's interpretation, that is, that Zhuangzi rejects Hui Shi's idea of oneness (either *wei-yi* or *yi-ti*), he would assign a notorious view to Zhuangzi's criticism of Hui Shi that an indefinable or unconstructable collection as an entity is not expressible or not describable. Nevertheless, the so-called "everything" concept assigned to Hui Shi is what Georg Cantor, one of the major founders of set theory, describes as "absolute infinite." Cantor says:[9]

> A multiplicity can be such that the assumption that all its elements "are together" leads to a contradiction, so that it is impossible to conceive of the multiplicity as a unity, as "one finished thing." Such multiplicities I call absolutely infinite or inconsistent multiplicities. As we can readily see, the "totality of everything thinkable," for example, is such a multiplicity.

I think the concept of "everything" is similar to the concept of "unbound or unlimited totality" pursued by some philosophers in traditional theology. Both are not identifiable, definable, or constructable through any method of effective procedure, such as bijection (one-to-one correspondence), diagonalization, or recursive procedure used in defining the concept of "infinite" in mathematics. If what is conceived cannot be defined or constructed with a method of effective procedure in mathematics, it is highly probable that it is not an identifiable entity in any possible world: mathematical, physical, or metaphysical.

To demonstrate that to name, describe, or define the oneness or great oneness in a statement will lead to a contradiction or paradox, let us use the individual constant "k" for "the oneness" and "e^{Dk}" for "the event of Dk" (or "the event that k is namable, describable or definable"), the predicates "D" for "is namable, describable, or definable" and "T" for "is a thing or event." The argument can be formulated in a valid form as follows:

[1]	1. Dk	Assumption
	[The oneness is describable.]	
[2]	2. $(\forall x)(Tx \rightarrow x \in k)$	Definition of the oneness
	[If any x is a thing or event then x is a member of k (the oneness).]	
[1]	3. $Dk \rightarrow \sim(e^{Dk} \in k)$	1, Entailment
	[Dk entails e^{Dk} (the event of Dk) is not included in k.]	
[1]	4. $\sim(e^{Dk} \in k)$	1,3, MP
[5]	5. Te^{Dk}	A fact that e^{Dk} is a thing or event
[2]	6. $(Te^{Dk} \rightarrow e^{Dk} \in k)$	2, UE
[2,5]	7. $(e^{Dk} \in k)$	5,6, MP
[1,2,5]	8. $[(e^{Dk} \in k) \& \sim(e^{Dk} \in k)]$	4,7, Conjunction
[2,5]	9. $\sim Dk$	8, RAA

As indicated in step 8, it is obvious that to assume the statement that the oneness is namable, describable, or definable will lead to a contradiction. However, if we use Bertrand Russell's theory of definite descriptions, the story would be different. Let us use the predicate "G," instead of the individual "k" for "oneness." The above argument can be reconstructed in the following form:

1. $(\exists x)\{[Gx \,\&\, (\forall y)(Gy \rightarrow y = x)] \,\&\, Dx\}$
   [There is an oneness which is describable.]
2. $(\exists x)\{[Gx \,\&\, (\forall y)(Gy \rightarrow y = x)] \,\&\, Dx\} \rightarrow$
   $\sim \{(\exists x)[Gx \,\&\, (\forall y)(Gy \rightarrow y = x)] = (\exists x)[Gx \,\&\, (\forall y)(Gy \rightarrow y = x)]\}$
   [If there is an oneness which is describable, then the oneness (being described) is not really the oneness. (It is because the description is not included in the oneness.)]
3. $\sim \{(\exists x)[Gx \,\&\, (\forall y)(Gy \rightarrow y = x)] = (\exists x)[Gx \,\&\, (\forall y)(Gy \rightarrow y = x)]\}$
   [The oneness (being described) is not really the oneness.]
   From (1), (2), and (3), it seems that we can use the rule of *reductio ad absurdum* to conclude that (1) is false. But it is not really to prove that

"there is an entity of oneness which is indescribable" or "there is an indescribable entity of oneness" as with the following form:

4. $(\exists x)\{[Gx \,\&\, (\forall y)(Gy \rightarrow y = x)] \& \sim Dx\}$

Here, the conclusion (4) is not validly derived from the premises of this argument. But the following sentence can be derived:

5. $\sim (\exists x)\{[Gx \,\&\, (\forall y)(Gy \rightarrow y = x)] \& Dx\}$

Here, the obvious difference between (4) and (5) is that the negation sign in (4) is used as a predicate-negation while that in (5) is a sentence-negation. The sentence form (4) means that "there is an entity of oneness which is indescribable" whereas the sentence form (5) means that "there is no entity of oneness which is describable." So if we use the theory of definite descriptions to analyze the above sentences, we cannot consider (5) but (4) as a form for the sentence "the oneness is indescribable" which has an ontological commitment to the existence of oneness as an entity, whereas (5) does not have such an commitment.

The argument formulated above is quite simple. In the following I will provide two different versions of the argument to illustrate the point that there is no ontological commitment to the existence of oneness as an entity if we formulate "oneness" as a predicate. The first one is:

[1]	1. $(\exists x)\{[Gx\&(\forall y)(Gy\rightarrow y=x)]\&Dx\}$	Assumption
[2]	2. $(\forall x)(\forall z)[(Gx\&Dz)\rightarrow\sim(z=x)]$ [If anything is an oneness and any other thing is describable, then the former is not identical with the latter. (It is because the oneness does not include its description as its member.)]	Explanation of the oneness
[1]	3. $\{[Gk\&(\forall y)(Gy\rightarrow y=k)]\&Dk\}$	1, EE
[1]	4. Dk	3, Simplification
[1]	5. $[Gk\&(\forall y)(Gy\rightarrow y=k)]$	3, Simplification
[1]	6. Gk	5, Simplification
[1]	7. (Gk&Dk)	6, Conjunction
[2]	8. $(\forall z)[(Gk\&Dz)\rightarrow\sim(z=k)]$	2, UE
[2]	9. $[(Gk\&Dk)\rightarrow\sim(k=k)]$	8, UE
[1,2]	10. $\sim(k=k)$	7,9 MP
[2]	11. $\sim(\exists x)\{[Gx\&(\forall y)(Gy\rightarrow y=x)]\&Dx\}$	10, RAA

Based on (2) (what is described is not identical with its description or the oneness does not include its description), we have the conclusion in (11) that: there is no oneness which is describable or which includes its description as its member.

Based on the above analysis, we can conclude that if one describes a collective whole of infinite components as an entity of "one finished thing" or gives a name for such an entity, it is unconstructable and thus would lead to a contradiction. However, if one uses a predicative description to express a mere collection of infinite components, its description does not necessarily commit to the existence of an entity of such a collection. Hence, to describe it does not necessarily commit a contradiction which is used as an indirect proof to demonstrate that there is an entity of oneness which is indescribable, though it can be used to indirectly prove that there is no such entity of oneness which is describable. Moreover, the argument form elaborated above does not lead to a paradox in the modern sense, either a semantic or set-theoretical one, though it can be used to demonstrate that the assumption is self-refuting.[10]

If we think that the oneness is describable, that if anything is describable it is with the characteristic of being exclusive of its description, and that if it is with the characteristic of being exclusive of its description it is not the oneness or great oneness per se, then, we can derive the conclusion that it is not the case that there is an entity of oneness which is describable. Let us use the predicates "G" for "oneness," "D" for "is describable" and "E" for "is exclusive of its description." The second version of the argument can be formulated as follows:

[1]	1. $(\exists x)\{[Gx\&(\forall y)(Gy\rightarrow y=x)]\&Dx\}$	Assumption
[2]	2. $(\forall x)(Dx\rightarrow Ex)$	Assumption
[3]	3. $(\forall x)(Ex\rightarrow\sim Gx)$	Assumption
[1]	4. $\{[Gb\&(\forall y)(Gy\rightarrow y=b)]\&Db\}$	1, EE
[1]	5. Db	4, Simplification
[2]	6. $(Db\rightarrow Eb)$	2, UE
[1,2]	7. Eb	5,6, MP
[3]	8. $(Eb\rightarrow\sim Gb)$	3, UE
[1,2,3]	9. $\sim Gb$	7,8, MP
[1]	10. $[Gb\&(\forall y)(Gy\rightarrow y=b)]$	4, Simplification
[1]	11. Gb	10, Simplification
[1,2,3]	12. $(Gb\&\sim Gb)$	9,11, Conjunction
[2,3]	13. $\sim(\exists x)\{[Gx\&(\forall y)(Gy\rightarrow y=x)]\&Dx\}$	12, RAA

The strategy of the above analysis is that even though, for the sake of argument, we agree that the idea of "*wei-yi*" in Chapter 2 of the *Zhuangzi* is identical with Hui Shi's idea of "*yi-ti*" (in Chapter 33), and Zhuangzi does criticize Hui Shi's idea of oneness, it is not necessarily that to assert a statement about the oneness will lead to a paradox in the modern sense. Even if both Hui Shi and Zhuangzi regard the oneness as an entity, to assert a statement about the oneness is self-refuting, not paradoxical. Furthermore, if they do not treat the oneness as an entity referred to by a name, but as a fixing property described by a predicate, the self-refuting argument is not to assert that there is an entity of oneness which is indescribable. Instead, it is used to demonstrate that there is no such an entity of oneness which is describable. But, most importantly, as I have mentioned earlier there is no textual evidence to support the interpretation that Zhuangzi does offer a self-refuting argument to criticize Hui Shi. Here, the crucial question is: Is Zhuangzi's "*wei-yi*" (*Zhuangzi* I 2:9) identical with Hui Shi's "*yi-ti*" (*Zhuangzi* III 11:7)?

My answer is "no." Zhuangzi's "*wei-yi*" is not Hui Shi's "*yi-ti*" in the sense that the former means "all as one," whereas the latter means "all in one." If, for the sake of argument again, we interpret Zhuangzi's claim as that if the oneness is namable, describable, or definable they would commit a fallacy of asserting the unassertable or describing the indescribable, then, we have to interpret the oneness as a unity of "one finished thing," as described by Cantor. But as we can find evidence from the text, Zhuangzi does not treat *yi* as an entity. Actually, his claim is that the heaven, earth, and I can be seen as being produced together and all things and I as being one if one can transcend the mentality of linguistic construction or conceptual carving. In other words, in this spiritual vision, there is no temporal priority between heaven, earth, and me and there is also no individuality of objects and no distinction between all the things and me. When one goes beyond the relativity of language and calculation in thinking, one can entertain the spiritual vision of an undifferentiated and harmonic horizon which is chaotic (*hun-dun*, 渾沌) and ineffable.

Why do I think that Zhuangzi's "*wei-yi*" (being one) or "*tai-yi*" (great oneness) is not Hui Shi's "*yi-ti*" (one body/one as a whole)? One of the reasons can be found in the text as follows:

> Therefore his liking was one and his not liking was one. His being one was one and his not being one was one. In being one, he was acting as a companion of Heaven. In not being one, he was acting as a companion of man. When man and Heaven do not defeat each other, then we may be said to have the True Man. (*Zhuangzi* I 6:1)
>
> 故其好之也一，其弗好之也一。其一也一，其不一也一。其一，與天為徒；其不一，與人為徒。天與人不相勝也，是之謂真人。

Here, Zhuangzi's message is that there is no distinction between sameness and difference in the undifferentiated oneness. According to our ordinary thinking, there is an essential distinction between sameness and difference. But for Zhuangzi, when one goes beyond the mentality of conceptualization and calculation and becomes a True Man" (*zhen-ren*, 真人),

there would be no distinction in his mind because he is just following the natural course of Heaven or entertains a harmonic or natural state of reality.

According to Zhuangzi, all things to be the case are nothing but linguistic production. It means that in reality there is nothing in correspondence to humans' artificial making (ie, language construction or conceptual carving). Here, "nothing" means the natural state of this world (ie, reality) that is without any saying to make something to be the case, a natural state of what Zhuangzi's ancient [wise] men (*gu-zhi*-ren, 古之人) or true men know or entertain, and "something" means a thing of the case made by a particular saying or conceptual production. For Zhuangzi's ancient men, their wisdom is reflected in their entertainment of the natural state of nothing (*wei-shi yu*-wu, 未始有物) before any schematic thinking with individuation and distinction (*you*-feng, 有封) (*Zhunagzi*, I 2:7). If we try to define or describe the natural state of "*wei-yi*" (being one) with the linguistic conceptualization "*wei-zhi-yi*" (謂之一), (to name it as one, it would lead people to make different truth-claims about the "*yi*" of "*wei-zhi-yi*" and thus also lead them to use another linguistic item (ie, the third item or another something) to define or describe the meaning of the "*yi*" of "*wei-zhi-yi*" and the relation between the "*yi*" of "*wei-yi*" and the "*yi*" of "*wei-zhi-yi.*" Since people often affirm their rejection of other people's truth-claims and negate other people's assertion of a truth-claim, there will be no end for this infinite disputation. So, Zhuangzi concludes that we should not go on to do this (*wu-shi-yan*, 無適焉). Instead, we should follow what it is in nature (*yin-shi-yi*, 因是[寔]已) (*Zhuangzi* I 2:9). This is the second reason from the text to explain why "*wei-yi*" is not identical with "*yi-ti.*"

Zhuangzi does not think that there is a reality which is a correspondence base for us to use language or conceptual tools to represent. Even though we agree that what is perceived is caused by the external world, the so-called external cause is still interpreted in our language or conceptual scheme. Zhuangzi does not refute the existence of the external world or reality, but he does not buy the thesis of correspondence or representation between the reality and language. His claim is that all our distinctions and individuation, judgments, and knowledge are nothing but man-made construction. So, as another reason from the text to explain his distinct idea of "*wei-yi*," he says:

A path (or road) is formed by walking. A thing (or event) is to be the case by saying. (*Zhuangzi* I 2:6, my translation) (道行之而成，物謂之而然。).

It means that in reality (or in the original or natural state of this world) there is no path or, more correctly speaking, there is no such a thing as path before people's walking. (I think people with the experience of hiking or mountain climbing with a certain degree of difficulty would know the meaning of this sentence.) Similarly, there is also no such an object or event before people's saying. In other words, all things are reality's being conceptually or linguistically "polluted." When the original or natural state of reality is carved by a linguistic and conceptual scheme, we would enter into a world of sameness and difference, truth and falsity, love and hatred, a world in which "A path (or road) is to be formed by walking. A thing (or event) is to be the case by saying." In this situation, *dao* or the undifferentiated vision of "*wei-yi*" (being one) will be lost or, as shown by one of Zhuangzi's fables, "they dug one orifice in the *hun-dun* (chaos) every day; and at the end of seven days he died. (日鑿一竅，七日而渾沌死。) (*Zhuangzi* I 7:7). Of course, Zhuangzi does not reject there is reality; but, as I said before, it is not a reality recognized as a base of correspondence or representation. What he means by "reality" is an undifferentiated oneness, an unknown what it is, an unsayable *dao*, or the *hun-tun* which has not yet been differentiated by conceptualization into individual things or events.

Hui Shi's idea of "*yi-ti*" may not be treated as a finished individual entity; it can be understood as a description of a totality. If I am right, the problem of leading to a paradox or contradiction which can be used to reject the description of the oneness or to demonstrate that an entity of oneness exists but cannot be named or described, as interpreted by Graham, would not be obtained. More importantly, Zhuangzi's idea of "*wei-yi*" is not identical with Hui Shi's idea of "*yi-ti*" and thus cannot be understood as a target of his attack. The most important reason from the text to explain the difference between Zhuangzi's "*yi*" and Hui Shi's "*yi*" is that the relativity of distinctions mentioned in the text just before the idea of "*wei-yi*" is irrelevant to the argument against the so-called unconstructable oneness. To reject the idea of "a finished individual entity of unbound totality," it is not significant to say that "Under heaven there is nothing greater than the tip of an autumn down, and the Tai mountain is small. There is no one more long-lived than a child which dies prematurely, and Peng Zu did not live out his time. Heaven, Earth, and I were produced together, and all things and I are one" (天下莫大於秋毫之末，而太山為小；莫壽於殤子，而彭祖為夭。天地與我並生，而萬物與我為一。) (*Zhuangzi* I 2:9). It is because the idea of relativity embedded in these sentences is irrelevant to the criticism of the so-called "oneness" as referring to an individual entity of unbound totality. It is also unnecessary for Zhuangzi to mention the problem from nothing to something (*zi wu shi you*, 自無適有) at the end of this passage (*Zhuangzi* I 2:9).

Zhuangzi also makes a similar point in other places. When Zhuangzi mentions that the people who reach the ultimate *dao* are able to know how to penetrate all the things into oneness (*zhi-tong wei-yi*, 知通為一) (*Zhuangzi* I 2:6), he also explains that it is because they can think in accord with the undifferentiated reality without using different conceptual schemes to carve the reality into a nonnatural artifact or mental products. So, he concludes that we should just follow the reality (*yin-shi-yi*, 因是矣). In other words, the oneness as an undifferentiated reality (*shi*, 是/寔) or chaos (*hun-dun*) cannot be expressed without distortion by various conceptual schemes or languages.

Zhuangzi's idea of inexpressibility is used by him as a strategy to promote a kind of mental (but not ontological) transcendence or transformation in the sense that the oneness or *dao* is beyond rational conceptualization and calculation. It is not only because reasoning cannot provide an absolute standard to establish and justify an absolute truth in terms of the idea of correspondence or representation, but also because it cannot help us to escape from infinite disputation which is without final result and thus cannot help us to enter into the natural harmony of undifferentiated reality. According to Zhuangzi, the natural state of reality is without wearing any linguistic or conceptual cloth and thus does not support any truth-claim. This state can only be obtained or entertained through a kind of Daoist practice such as "the fasting or cleaning of the mind" (*xin-zhai*, 心齋) (*Zhuangzi* I 4:2) and "sitting and forgetting all things" (*zuo-wang*, 坐忘) (*Zhuangzi* I 6:9), a kind of spiritual exercise which can help us to go beyond or to transcend the rational trap of truth claiming.

In ancient Daoism, both Laozi (老子) and Zhuangzi do claim that the oneness or *dao* is unnamable or ineffable. But Laozi's thesis of ineffability is self-refuting while Zhuangzi's is intelligible. Their theses are different in the sense that Laozi's thesis is ontological or onto-cosmological while Zhuangzi's is aesthetic or spiritual. Both have the implication of mysticism. Nevertheless, Laozi's ontological or objective mysticism commits a two-world theory which invites metaphysical realism and skepticism. It maintains that something out there is ineffable because it is a realm or world which transcends the realm or world of our rational understanding, and thus there is a gap between these two realms or worlds. Zhuangzi's aesthetic or subjective mysticism does not commit a two-world theory. It means that, based on our conceptual schemes, the world can be understood as constituted of objects and events. But before our linguistic-conceptual carving of it, its original state is ineffable. It is because it is nothing before linguistic construction. Here, "nothing" means no things, and "no things" means without individuation and distinction. But it does not mean the nonexistence of the external world or reality. It is because the individuation and distinction of things or events have to be done with linguistic or conceptual tools; before linguistic or conceptual construction, the external world is nothing but an undifferentiated reality or *hun-dun*. In other words, Zhuangzi's ineffability means the state of the world before our saying on it. It is not a distinct realm that our rational thinking cannot access. For Zhuangzi, there is only one world with two states: one is the natural state without linguistic or conceptual carving; the other one is the nonnatural state of mental construction. They are the two states or aspects of the same world.

8.5 TRANSCENDENCE OF LOGIC AND RATIONALITY IN ZEN BUDDHISM

In traditional Chinese philosophy, such as Daoism, Zen Buddhism, and New Confucianism (including Sung-Ming (宋明) and contemporary Confucianism), the mind or inner experience of enlightenment is usually interpreted as "featureless self," "conceptless subject," "contentless consciousness," "absolute mind" or "no-self." This kind of idea is generally understood as a thesis of transcendence of logic and rationality.

In the field of Zen Buddhism, Suzuki is one of the major figures to promote this kind of idea. He sometimes stresses the contrast between the Western and the Asian modes of thinking. One of the major differences emphasized by him is the contrast between rationality and irrationality, or logical and illogical thinking. For example, Suzuki sometimes says that "Zen is the most irrational, inconceivable thing in the world," that it "defies all concept-making" and that the essence of Zen is satori (*dun-wu* 頓悟) the experience of "sudden enlightenment," which is irrational, inexplicable, and incommunicable.[11] He also maintains the following:[12]

> If we are to judge Zen from our common-sense view of things, we shall find the ground sinking away under our feet. Our so-called rationalistic way of thinking has apparently no use in evaluating the truth or untruth of Zen. It is altogether beyond the ken of human understanding. All that we can therefore state about Zen is that its uniqueness lies in its irrationality or its passing beyond our logical comprehension.

In response to the Chinese sinologist Hu Shih's (胡適) criticism, he says, "Zen is not explainable by mere intellectual analysis. As long as the intellect is concerned with words and ideas, it can never reach Zen."[13] Therefore, to know Zen one must give up her rational thinking and dualistic logic, and then she could be enlightened with prajñā-intuition (*bo-re zhi-guan*, 般若直觀) an unknowable knowledge."

Why does one have to give up rational thinking and dualistic logic? For Suzuki, it is because people without Zen enlightenment are living in the world of samsāra (*sheng-si*, 生死) with the sufferings generated from dualistic thinking. If one wants to be emancipated from these sufferings and to enter into Zen's nondualistic world, one is required to go beyond rational thinking. To be free from the dualistic cage and enter into this beautiful world, one must know nothing; because to fall into the dualistic abyss, one is forced to know something conceptualized. Zen or the insight of sunyata (*kong*, 空) is nothingness, because there is nothing in it which can be conceptualized. Suzuki thinks that "the dualist view of reality has been a great stumbling block to our right understanding of spiritual truth"[14] and thus "Zen is decidedly not a system founded upon logic and analysis. If anything, it is the antipode to logic, by which I mean the dualistic mode of thinking."[15] He even says, "According to the philosophy of Zen, we are too much of a slave to the conventional way of thinking, which is dualistic through and through. No 'interpenetration' is allowed, there takes place no fusing of opposites in our everyday logic."[16]

In order to deconstruct dualistic logic, Suzuki sometimes stresses the necessity for Zen masters to use some incoherent or paradoxical statements to express their insight. He thinks that the reason why Zen masters make those apparently incoherent statements is "to set the minds of their disciples or of scholars free from being oppressed by any fixed opinion or prejudices or so-called logical interpretations."[17] More theoretically speaking, "Paradoxical statements are... characteristic of prajñā-intuition. As it transcends vijnana [*shi*, 識] or logic it does not mind contradicting itself; it knows that a contradiction is the outcome of differentiation, which is the work of vijnana."[18] One of the paradoxical statements frequently used by Suzuki is "We generally reason: 'A' is 'A' because 'A' is 'A'; or 'A' is 'A', therefore, 'A' is 'A'. Zen agrees or accepts this way of reasoning, but Zen has its own way which is ordinarily not at all acceptable. Zen would say: 'A' is 'A' because 'A' is not 'A'; or 'A' is not 'A', therefore, 'A' is 'A'."[19] It seems that the way of Zen that Suzuki describes is the way to subvert, generally, the duality of "A" and "~A;" and, specifically, the dichotomy of subject and object. He believes that "in prajñā this dichotomy no longer exists," because, "[p]rajñā is not concerned with finite objects as such; it is the totality of things becoming conscious of itself as such. And this totality is not at all limited. An infinite totality is beyond our ordinary human comprehension."[20] So, he concludes, "Satori (emptiness) may be defined as an intuitive looking into the nature of things in contradistinction to the analytical or logical understanding of it."[21]

Some famous examples of paradoxical statement mentioned by Suzuki, which are called *ko-an*," are the following:

1. A monk asked Tung-shan (東山) "Who is the Buddha?" The answer is: "Three *chin* (斤) (pounds) of flax."
   問：誰是佛? 答：麻三斤。
2. When Ming the monk overtook the fugitive Hui-neng (惠能) he wanted Hui-neng to give up the secret of Zen. Hui-neng replied, "What are your original features which you have even prior to your birth?"
   什麼是父母未生前本來面目？
3. A monk asked Chao-chou (趙州) "What is the meaning of the First Patriarch's visit to China?" "The cypress tree in the front courtyard."
   問：何為祖師西來意? 答：庭前柏樹子。
4. A monk asked Yun-men (雲門) "Who is the Buddha?" The answer is: "The dried up dirt-cleaner."
   乾矢橛。
5. "If you meet the Buddha, kill him."
   見佛殺佛。

6. "What is the clap of one hand?" ("Listen to the sound of one hand.")
   單掌拍手的聲音是什麼？ (聽聽單掌的聲音)
7. "I am him and yet he is not me."
   我是他，但他不是我。
8. "What is gained is what is not gained."
   得即是失。
9. "I hold spade empty-handedly. I walk on foot and yet I ride on horseback. When I pass over the bridge, the water flows not, but the bridge does."
   空手把鋤頭，步行騎水牛；人在橋上走，橋流水不流。

Some of the above examples look contradictory or inconsistent; some others seem ridiculous or even mad. But, for Suzuki, this is the characteristic of Zen language which is necessary for enlightenment. Suzuki's explanation of the paradoxical expressions of *ko-an* is generally accepted by scholars in the field of Zen Buddhism. But is it really that Zen is a wisdom or truth transcending rationality and *ko-an* a kind of expression transcending logic? I will give a negative answer in the next section.

8.6 DOES ZEN TRANSCEND LOGIC AND RATIONALITY?

According to Suzuki's explanation, *ko-an* is significant and necessary for Zen enlightenment. He writes:[22]

> *Ko-an* literally means "a public document" or "authoritative statute" - a term coming into vogue toward the end of the T'ang dynasty, It now denotes some anecdote of an ancient master, or dialogue between a master and monks, or a statement or question put forward by a teacher, all of which are used as the means for opening one's mind to the truth of Zen. In the beginning, of course, there was no *ko-an* as we understand it now; it is a kind of artificial instrument devised out of the fullness of heart by later Zen masters, who by this means would force the evolution of Zen consciousness in the minds of their less endowed disciples.

It seems that *ko-an* in its literal sense can be understood as a statement of contradiction, absurdity, or irrelevant to the understanding of the truth of Zen and to the enlightenment of Zen. Some of the scholars even think that *ko-an*, as a specific expression of Zen teaching, cannot be understood or solved by logic or rational thinking; people of Zen training use them to cut dualistic thinking, awaken to their Buddha nature, and rid themselves of ego. This is what Suzuki calls the "Zen approach" which can be used to know or entertain the truth or wisdom of Zen. But is this approach effective to the understanding of the ultimate goal of Zen enlightenment?

I think Suzuki's thesis is inaccurate because there would be no criterion for us to identify the so-called "truth" or "wisdom" if our language of interpretation does not abide by any rational standard and there would be no teaching if *ko-an* were there not an intentional act. Nevertheless, as indicated in Suzuki's explanation, he does offer a rational explanation for the so-called "inexpressible." I think what he has done is "to express the inexpressible" and thus his view is a self-refuting. Besides, he does not reject that Zen masters did have intention to communicate or to direct their disciples to reach the ultimate goal of enlightenment. If communication is necessary for teaching, including the teaching of *ko-an*, and what Zen masters had done are intentional acts, their verbal or nonverbal behavior as described in *ko-an* cannot be understood by Suzuki as something irrational.

Although *ko-an* seems irrational in its literal sense, I think, as an intentional speech act with the function of directing mental transformation, it is not really irrational. Furthermore, Suzuki's effort of making sense of the function of *ko-an* implies that the absurdity literally reflected in *ko-an* is suggestive, if not necessary, for its function of directing enlightenment which is not literally reflected in *ko-an*. So, if Suzuki's explanation is rationally acceptable, it would contradict his antirational thesis.

I think that one of the effective and rational approaches to the understanding of the language of Zen in general or *ko-an* in particular is an approach based on a theory of speech acts.[23] It is clear that what *ko-an* means literally is not what a Zen master implicitly intends to mean or to do by *ko-an*, though the former is related to the latter in a complicated or perhaps an elusive way. So, the master's response or answer to his disciples in *ko-an* can be recognized as a peculiar sort of speech act. If we use John Searle's theory, we can say that *ko-an* is an institutional fact in Zen culture and all the expressions of *ko-an* used by Zen masters can be understood as a variety of speech acts of which the game of Zen teaching is constituted.

In the game, each expression understood in its literal sense appears to be absurd or ridiculous, but as an intentional speech act uttered by the player (Zen master) it is intended to mean (a second meaning of indirect speech act) or to do something (without second meaning, just like a metaphor in the Davidsonian sense) other than what is literally understood and it is not absurd or ridiculous. To say something literally absurd or nonsensical but nonliterally functional in a sensible way is probably to make a special kind of speech act. In this sense, *ko-an* can be recognized as a rule-governed act and can be intellectually understood by members living in Zen culture.

According to Searle's view, in order to understand metaphorical utterances, ironical utterances, indirect speech acts, etc., we have to distinguish word and sentence meaning, on the one hand, and speaker's meaning or utterance meaning, on the other. He thinks that what the sentence means may depart from what the speaker means as in the case of metaphors, ironies, and indirect speech acts. Here, I do not accept Searle's view of "meaning departure."[24] It is because "meaning departure" presupposes that a metaphor, irony, or indirect speech is used to do more than one speech act by one and only one sentence. So, there is implicit or additional meaning (or meanings) to the literal meaning of a speaker's sentence. I think there is no sentence meaning without speaker's meaning and vice versa. That is to say, what a sentence means is nothing but what the sentence used by a speaker is intended to mean. Of course, what a sentence used by a speaker is intended to mean in one context may be different from what the same sentence used by the speaker is intended to mean in another context. This is one of the reasons why we can use the same sentence to make different speech acts in different contexts. But we cannot thus claim that some implicit meaning or meanings of a speaker departs from what her sentence literally means, and this implicit meaning or meanings of the speaker is only located in the mind without some implicit sentence to match.

My view is that what the sentence means is nothing but what the sentence used by the speaker means and there is no real distinction between sentence meaning and speaker's meaning. I agree with Searle that there are at least two meanings in an indirect speech act; but I do not agree with him that there is only one sentence which has a literal meaning and a nonliteral meaning. My view is that there are two sentences, one of which (sentence A) is explicitly expressed and semantically or logically related to the other hidden one (sentence B) which is embedded in our background knowledge. Although it seems that, in addition to a literal meaning, sentence A also has an implicit meaning, actually the so-called "implicit meaning" can be expressed in sentence B which is semantically or logically related to sentence A in our background knowledge.

For example, when a wife responds to her husband's proposal of going to the movies by saying that "It is raining," the speaker's intention for communication is very clear: that is, a rejection of his proposal. Based on the speaker's intention for communication, we can say that there is some kind of speaker's meaning which is reflected in some implicit sentence, such as "I don't want to go to movies" (a sentence of rejecting the proposal). But there is no "meaning departure," for the speaker's intention for communication and the implicit sentence though there is a meaning departure for the speaker's intention for communication and the explicit sentence and its literal meaning. In other words, the so-called "nonliteral meaning" of the sentence "It is raining" is semantically related to and determined by the speaker's intention for communication and thus exactly the same as the literal meaning of the implicit sentence "I don't want to go to movies."

I think that in some cases of an indirect speech act, in addition to the literal meaning of a sentence, there is some seemingly nonliteral meaning of the sentence which can be understood as or reduced to some literal meaning of another sentence which is semantically related to and determined by some kind of intention for communication. Hence, this kind of seemingly nonliteral meaning of a sentence (say, sentence A) does not depart from the literal meaning of a second sentence (say, sentence B) though it does depart from the literal meaning of the first sentence. Here our problem is: how to identify this second sentence?

Generally, the identification of the second or implicit sentence is based on our sensibility of the built-in logical implication or contextual entailment which is embedded in our background knowledge. This background knowledge is a kind of implicit capacity or tacit knowledge shared by people living in the same language environment. In this regard, the nonliteral meaning of a sentence A can be considered as nothing but the literal meaning of another sentence B which is inferred from the literally uttered sentence A. For example, when a child of 5 years old asks her 18-year- old brother, "Let's go to the movies tonight," her brother may answer, "I have to study for an examination tomorrow." Since the child does not have the background knowledge for understanding the implicit meaning of her brother's reply, she would probably ask for an explanation about the relation between his reply and her request. I think her brother may explain in this way: "If I have to study for an examination tomorrow, I have to prepare for the examination tonight; and if I have to prepare for the examination tonight, I cannot go to the movies tonight. Since I said in (2) that I have to study for an examination tomorrow, it implies or means that I cannot go to the movies tonight." The logical relation embedded in her brother's background knowledge is that $[(p \rightarrow q) \& (q \rightarrow r),\ p\ / \therefore\ r]$. Here, the conditionals $[(p \rightarrow q) \& (q \rightarrow r)]$ are embedded in an adult's background knowledge that a child does not have. So, when she does not know her brother's reply, he has to make explicit the relation of implication from p to r.

I agree with Searle that in this case there is one sentence with two illocutionary acts on the stage; but I do not think there is not (another) a sentence behind the stage. What is behind the stage is the sentence implied by the sentence on the stage. As illustrated in the example discussed above, it is not the case that there is only one sentence "p" (I have to study for an examination tomorrow) which performs two illocutionary acts: one is about what p explicitly means and the other is about what p implicitly means. I think there are two sentences in this case: the first one (p) is used to express its literal meaning and the second one (r) is implied by the first one. The meaning of the second one seems to be the nonliteral meaning of the first one; but actually, for an adult with sufficient background knowledge, the seemingly nonliteral meaning of the first one is expressed by a hidden sentence (r) which is implied by the first one (p). It means that there are two sentences to do two illocutionary acts, though one of them is logically related to the other one and the logical relation is embedded in the relevant people's background knowledge.

There are other kinds of speech acts, such as metaphors, which can be used to illustrate this point, that is, there is no speaker's meaning without sentence meaning. I think *ko-an* cannot be understood as an indirect speech act as discussed above or understood as a metaphor as explained by Searle, that is, *ko-an* is not a dual speech act which is constituted of two illocutionary acts by one sentence. On the contrary, *ko-an* is a special kind of speech act which is constituted of one illocutionary act accompanied by some kind of perlocutionary act. Or we can say that *ko-an* mainly functions as a perlocutionary act which is supervenient on an illocutionary act.

It seems to me that *ko-an* is more like a metaphor than an indirect speech act. In this regard, I do not agree with Searle that there is a speaker's meaning other than the sentence meaning in a metaphor; and I agree with Davidson that there is only a perlocutionary effect in addition to a metaphor's literal meaning. Just like a Davidsonian metaphor, *ko-an* mainly functions as a perlocutionary act which is supervenient on an illocutionary act in a peculiar way.

Ko-an looks like an indirect speech act because the former, just like the latter, seems to have another illocutionary effect at the nonliteral level in addition to the effect produced by its speaker at the literal level. Nevertheless, if there were a second illocutionary act with an illocutionary effect in *ko-an*, we would have been able to make it explicit, that is, to paraphrase or translate it into another sentence or expression. This difficulty or impossibility of paraphrasing suggests that *ko-an* is much more like a metaphor in the Davidsonian sense than a metaphor or an indirect speech act in the Searlean sense, because we cannot have a paraphrase or translation for a metaphor or a *ko-an*.

If we accept Davidson's idea of metaphor, I think the explanation of the function of *ko-an* should be focused on its perlocutionary effect, instead of its illocutionary effect. In other words, according to Davidson, there is no second meaning or metaphorical meaning in a metaphor. For the same reason, we can say that, in addition to a literal meaning, there is no second meaning in *ko-an*. The reason offered by Davidson to explain why a metaphor does not have a second meaning is the following:[25]

> We must give up the idea that a metaphor carries a message, that it has a content or meaning (except, of course, its literal meaning). The various theories we have been considering mistake their goal. Where they think they provide a method for deciphering an encoded content, they actually tell us (or try to tell us) something about the *effects* metaphors have on us. The common error is to fasten on the contents of the thoughts a metaphor provokes and to read these contents into the metaphor itself.

Ko-an acts like a metaphor in the sense that the hidden intention of a Zen master cannot be spelled out without turning into a stiffened or dead indoctrination and losing its effect of mental transformation for enlightenment. Just like the case of uttering a literal or nonliteral speech, first of all, the Zen master who uses *ko-an* must have a reflexive intention in uttering his sentence for meaning something literally. But unlike an indirect speech act, *ko-an* does not have a second meaning or second illocutionary effect, though the master may have some kind of implicit intention. The reason why this intention cannot be spelled out as a second meaning is that when it is spelled out the function (ie, the effect of mental transformation) will have totally faded out or disappeared.

I think it is very difficult, if not impossible, to explain why different expressions of *ko-an* can do the same job of producing the same illocutionary effect if we assume there is a second illocutionary act produced; but it is quite easy for us to explain why they can have the same perlocutionary effect of mental transformation. Why, to one and the same question is a master's answer sometimes "No," sometimes "Yes"? Why can a master flourish a stick in a different way each time but they all have the same effect of directing his disciples to enlightenment? And why are two great Japanese masters, Sekito and Yakusan, who may seem to have much disagreement with each other in answering the same question, identified in Zen literature as talking about the same thing?[26] I think the answer is not due to illocutionary force, but due to perlocutionary effect. Just like the case that when there is a car running very fast on the road and, at the same time, a very old woman is going to cross the road, we may warn her by different speech acts as follows:

1. A car is coming.
2. The green light has not yet turned on.
3. Be careful!
4. Dangerous!
5. Oh, lady!
6. God is behind you!

All these sentences are speech acts with different illocutionary forces, but they have the same perlocutionary effect if the old woman is aware of the warning of not crossing the road (or is directed to not cross the road).

Furthermore, Zen masters sometimes claim that, "our everyday language fails to convey the exact meaning as conceived by Zen" and also claim that "Zen *mondoo* (問答) (ie, question and answer in *ko-an*) cannot be set aside as of no meaning," I think the seeming contradiction of these sentences can be explained away if the meaning of *ko-an* is not understood as semantic meaning but perlocutionary effect. I also think that the term "meaning" mentioned above cannot be understood as referring to a mystical entity from a perspective of antirationalism or mysticism. If the meaning cannot be understood as a semantic one or a mystical entity and also cannot be expressed by our everyday language, I think the only possible option to interpret what Zen masters mention is a kind of directive value in term of mental transformation. Suzuki's idea of "pointing" or "pointer" is another indicator of the directive function of *ko-an*. Suzuki sometimes even stresses that Zen language is "devoid of intelligible meaning" though it is able to have "psychological effect"[27] and that "No (second) meaning is to be sought in the expression itself, but within ourselves, in our own mind, which are awakened to the same experience."[28] It means that the so-called meaning of *ko-an* is not only not a semantic one but also not a mystical entity.

I agree with Suzuki that "there is in Zen nothing to explain, nothing to teach," but it is not because there is some kind of transcendental truth or mystical meaning which is inexpressible and cannot be taught. Instead, the reason of "nothing to explain" and "nothing to teach" is that there is no truth and meaning at all except the literal meaning of *ko-an*. If I am right in saying that there is no transcendental truth and mystical meaning in Zen language, including *ko-an*, the remaining question would be: how does a master do Zen with words or how can he open his disciples' minds via *ko-an*?

To answer this question, I think we should pay double attention to the view of antiintellectualism held by most scholars of Zen. According to the teaching of Buddhism in general and Zen in particular, human beings' sufferings come from their attachment to desire and being dominated by its companion, rational calculation. To be liberated from sufferings and to enter into the state of enlightenment, human beings should give up desire and calculation. As emphasized by Suzuki, rational or logical thinking is the obstruction of *satori*. So, to move this obstruction out of the mind is essential to Zen enlightenment. If we ignore the perspective of mysticism, when Suzuki says that "a *satori* turned into a concept ceases to be itself" he does have a point. The point is that to free the mind from conceptual calculation is a necessary condition of mental transformation.

In regard to the question of why ordinary people cannot but a master can be enlightened when they both "have a cup of tea," I think the answer is that the former is still in the mental state of calculation, say, to consider which tea is tasty and which cup is useful, while the latter is free from such calculation. So, in Zen Buddhism, Suzuki is right to claim that *ko-an* is generally understood as a skill "to shut up all possible avenues to rationalization."

Now, I think we are ready to recognize why most expressions of *ko-an* are expressed in a senseless or nonsensical way. The purpose for Zen masters to express their *ko-an* in a form of absurdity, contradiction, or irrelevance to their disciples' questions for enlightenment is to give them a great puzzle or to baffle, surprise, or shock. In Zen culture, there is a consensus that leading pupils to a perplexed predicament and letting them have an ever-increasing mental strain, they would face a mental crisis which may suggest an abrupt (*tun*, 頓) transformation in their mind.

In order to help his students to free themselves from mental impasse, Zen masters probably have an intention of banning rational or logical thinking, the mode of thinking in the mind of calculation; but they cannot spell it out. If they make the intention explicit, the banning function would vanish. Just like the case of paraphrasing a metaphor, if we translate a metaphor into its so-called nonmetaphorical equivalent or make it explicit, it would become a dead metaphor and thus the performative function of a specific perlocutionary effect would be disappeared.

The function of urging a child to swim faster by saying "There is a shark behind you" cannot be replaced by a description of intention like "You are urged to swim faster." The how-knowing being cultivated in a learner's mind can be stimulated by a teacher's act of making puzzles and producing shocks, but it probably cannot be indoctrinated by a teacher's act of producing some kind of that-knowing. In the case of swimming, although how-knowing cannot be replaced by that-knowing, we cannot exclude the possibility that the former may be helpful for the latter. Nevertheless, in the case of attaining Zen enlightenment, the story is extremely different. The very how-knowing is to know how to ban all that-knowing in our rational thinking because this mode of thinking goes against the essence of Zen. This is why *ko-an* being used as a pedagogic method is peculiar and is not welcome to ordinary people.

8.7 CONCLUSIONS

I have provided an intelligible interpretation and rational explanation for the idea of *yi* in Zhuangzi's Daoism and for the function of *ko-an* in Zen Buddhism in this chapter. The description of *yi* seems contradictory or paradoxical. But, for Zhuangzi, *yi* is nothing which has not yet been expressed in any language or conceptual scheme; it is the natural, original, or chaotic state of the world or reality which is in a harmonic state before any linguistic or conceptual construction. It is Zhuangzi's aesthetic vision of the same world as what we use language or conceptual schemes to express; it is not another world which is hidden as a breeding ground of skepticism or metaphysical realism. It is ineffable because it has not yet been expressed in language; it is not because it is contradictory or paradoxical.

Similarly, *ko-an* seems senseless or ridiculous in its literal meaning and some transcendental meaning or truth is hidden behind its literal meaning. Nevertheless, if all the expressions of Zen masters' *ko-an* are intentional speech acts and all expressions have the same function of promoting mental transformation for their students, I think they, just like metaphors in Davidson's sense, cannot be understood as having other meaning than their literal meaning and their major function can be understood as a kind of perlocutionary effect. So, there is no real contradiction or paradox in these expressions. We can understand all of them in an intelligible way. In this regard, the theses of antilogic and antirationality cannot be sustained.

In conclusion, all claims of real or seeming irrationality or unreason are either senseless or not senseless. If they are senseless, they cannot be located in rational space. If they are interpretable, learnable, or understandable, they have to be located in the home of rationality or reason. Without the home language of rationality or reason, there would be no thought to be recognized.

Endnotes

1. Needham, J. (1956). Science and civilisation in China. In *History of scientific thought* (2). Cambridge: Cambridge University Press.
2. Graham, A. C. (1992). *Unreason within reason: Essays on the outskirts of rationality*. Illinois: La Salle: Open Court.
3. Hall, D., & Ames, R. (1995). *Anticipating China: Thinking through the narratives of Chinese and Western culture*. Albany, NY: State University of New York Press, 141.
4. Op. cit., 179.
5. Davidson, D. (2001a). *Subjective, intersubjective, objective* (pp. 148–149). Oxford: Oxford University Press.
6. Davidson, D. (1993). Locating literary language. In R. W. Dasenbrock (Ed.), *Literary theory after Davidson* (pp. 307). University Park, PA: Pennsylvania State University Press.
7. James Legge's translation from the Chinese Text Project on http://ctext.org/daoism. Hereafter, all the quotations from the *Zhuangzi* is based on Legge's translation except my translation.
8. Graham, A. C. (1969-1970). Chuang-tzu's essay on seeing things as equal. *History of Religions*, *9*(2/3), 144–145.
9. Cantor, C. (1967). Gesammelte Abbandlungen, 443 (S. B. Mengelberg, Trans.). In J. van Heijenoort (Ed.), *From Frege to Gödel* (p. 114). Cambridge, MA: Harvard University Press.
10. A paradox (either semantic or set-theoretical one) in the modern sense has the logical form that: (1) $K \rightarrow \sim K$ and (2) $\sim K \rightarrow K$. But a self-refuting argument can have either (1) or (2), but not both.
11. Suzuki, D. T. (1996). In B. William (Ed.), *Zen Buddhism: Selected writings of D.T. Suzuki* (13). New York: Doubleday.
12. Suzuki, D. T. (1994). *Living by Zen*. York Beach, ME: Samuel Weiser.
13. Suzuki, D. T. (1953). Zen: a reply to Hu Shih. *Philosophy East and West*, 3(1).
14. Suzuki, D. T. (1994). *Living by Zen*. York Beach, ME: Samuel Weiser.
15. Suzuki, D. T. (1991). *An introduction to Zen Buddhism* (pp. 38). London: Random House.
16. Suzuki, D. T. (1996). In B. William (Ed.), *Zen Buddhism: Selected writings of D.T. Suzuki* (pp. 112). New York: Doubleday.
17. Suzuki, D. T. (1991). *An introduction to Zen Buddhism* (pp. 78–79). London: Random House.
18. Suzuki, D. T. (1955). *Studies in Zen* (pp. 94–95). New York: Dell.
19. Suzuki, D. T. (1953). Zen: a reply to Hu Shih. *Philosophy East and West*, 3(1).
20. Suzuki, D. T. (1960). Lectures on Zen Buddhism. In D. T. Suzuki, Fromm Erich, & De Martino Richard (Eds.), *Zen Buddhism and psychoanalysis* (pp. 57). New York: Harper and Row.
21. Suzuki, D. T. (1991). *An introduction to Zen Buddhism* (pp. 88). London: Random House.
22. Suzuki, D. T. (1991). *An introduction to Zen Buddhism* (pp. 102). London: Random House.

23. As I know, the first scholar to use speech act theory to deal with the *ko-an* is Henry Rosemont Jr. But I do not agree with his view that "the Zen master is not performing illocutionary but perlocutionary speech acts" in *ko-an*. It is because the illocutionary act performed by the explicit sentence is necessary for the performance of the related perlocutionary act. See his Rosemont, H., Jr. (1970). The meaning is the use: Kōan and Mondō as linguistic tools of the Zen masters. *Philosophy East and West*, 20, 117.
24. Searle, J. (1979). *Expression and meaning: Studies in the theory of speech acts*. Cambridge, MA: Cambridge University Press.
25. Davidson, D. (2001b). *Inquiries into truth and interpretation* (2nd ed.). Oxford: Oxford University Press, 261.
26. Suzuki, D. T. (1972). *Living by Zen*. York Beach, ME: Samuel Weiser.
27. Suzuki, D. T. (2000). *Essays in Zen Buddhism* (2nd ser.) (pp. 175). New Delhi: Munshiram Manoharlal.
28. Suzuki, D. T. (2000). *Essays in Zen Buddhism* (1st ser.) (pp.290). New Delhi: Munshiram Manoharlal.

CHAPTER

9

Irrationally Intelligible or Rationally Unintelligible?

W.C. Leong

Department of General Education, Macau University of Science and Technology, Macau

9.1 INTRODUCTION

Rationality seems to be such an essential feature of human beings that Aristotle thinks of it as the defining feature of humans. However, the notion of rationality seems less to be so. It is notorious in the field of ancient Chinese philosophy[1] that this notion seems to be missing. The most often cited evidence is that there is no one word which could be translated as "rationality" in any ancient Chinese philosophical texts. The closest notion may be "*li* (理), yet *li* often means the order of nature and of human beings (Hall & Ames, 1998). Due to this, perhaps, some scholars even take a step further and claim that Chinese philosophers have no rationality, or at least have a kind of rationality that differs from the "Western" understanding of rationality stemming from ancient Greece. Two prominent representatives in this tradition are David Hall and Roger Ames:

> A... philosophical argument concerning the absence of concern with strictly rational modes of argumentation is that the protorational thinking in China was itself quite different from the nascent forms of rationality in the West—so much so that even the fully developed forms supplied by later Mohism bore no strict resemblance to Western rationality. (Hall & Ames, 1998, p. 131)

For Hall and Ames, therefore, not only is the argument that Chinese philosophers are different from those of their Western counterparts, even "protorational" thinking in China, which presumably means thinking before the development of later Mohist logic in China, is also different. What is distinctive to "Western" rationality, Hall and Ames believe, is the "employment of logic in the search for necessary truths."

Rationality. http://dx.doi.org/10.1016/B978-0-12-804600-5.00009-X

(Hall & Ames, 1998, p. 131). They think Leibniz's and Hegel's taking of the principles of identity and of noncontradiction as starting points of their philosophical reflections is an illustration of the point that "Western modes of rationality have elided rational and logical discourse." (Hall & Ames, 1998, p. 131).

It is interesting that Hall and Ames use Leibniz and Hegel as examples here because they seem to suggest that the employment of logic requires awareness of explicitly formulated logical principles, and that rational thinking or discourse can be separated from any employment of logic. But the employment of logic in one's thinking of course does not require one's awareness of explicitly formulated logical principles. One can infer from the belief that snow is white to the conclusion that it is not the case that snow is not white, without any awareness of the principle of noncontradiction. Therefore, it casts doubt on the suggestion that rational thinking can be separated from the employment of logic.

One may, however, try to defend that although no awareness of any logical principle is required for rational or logical thinking, the logical principles employed in Chinese thinking are so different that it is not implausible to say that Chinese philosophy shows a different kind of rationality. Thus without assuming a particular definition of rationality, scholars who defend this view often start from the observations concerning either one of the two following notions closely related to rationality, namely, truth and contradiction. Concerning the former, the claim is that Chinese philosophy does not have the concept of truth, and therefore when the Chinese construct their arguments, they do not think of the truth of their claim; instead, they focus on the pragmatics. Their evaluation of an argument does not involve whether its premises or conclusions are true, or the validity of the argument, but whether it is beneficial or useful (Hansen, 1985). Hall and Ames, on the other hand, argue that Chinese philosophers primarily employ what they call "correlative thinking," which involves the use of analogy and other correlative procedures[2] (Hall & Ames, 1995).

The claim concerning the latter is that, perhaps related to the first claim, Chinese philosophers in some senses accept contradictions. There are various proposals on how Chinese philosophers accept contradictions, but what these proposals share in common is that contradictions are at least intelligible for Chinese philosophers. Thus, for example, Nisbett, Peng, Choi, and Norenzayan, 2001, p. 301 say that Chinese philosophy involves "transcending, accepting, or even insisting on the contradiction among premises,"[3] in the sense that contradictions can sometimes truthfully describe the way things are (Nisbett et al., 2001). As Seok (2007, p. 226) puts it, "If contradictions are a natural part of the universe, we cannot use contradiction as an indicator of falsity or irrationality." This peculiar feature of Chinese philosophy, Nisbett and his college even argue, is the root of contemporary Easterners' tendency to favor or agree with apparently contradictory statements, a tendency which contemporary Westerners do not share.

If either one of these two claims is true, Chinese philosophers indeed seem to show another kind of rationality.

I believe, however, neither of these claims are true. In this paper I argue that Chinese philosophers have the concept of truth and it is featured in their arguments. In addition, contradictions for them are not acceptable. Those paradoxical sentences which some scholars take as contradictions that Chinese philosophers accept are either not really contradictions, or are only accepted in certain interpretations which render them not as contradictions. One example I focus on here is the famous White Horse paradox in the *Gongsun Longzi*.

The central claim of the paradox is this: *baima fei ma*. Let me call this the "White Horse claim." Proposed translations of this claim include: "A white horse is not a horse," "White horses are not horses," and even "White-horseness is not horseness," as well as "White-horse-stuff is not horse-stuff," and "White horse is not horse." It is not my intention here to argue for a better or even a correct interpretation of this claim. Instead, by discussing the debate between Chad Hansen and Christopher Harbsmeier on this paradox, I examine some general criteria for a better interpretation. Two rival principles are considered: the principle of charity and the principle of humanity.

Hansen argues that we should adopt the principle of humanity. I distinguish between two versions of the principle of charity: a local version and a Davidsonian version. I argue that Hansen's attack on the principle of charity applies, at most, to the local version. Besides, the principle of humanity needs to assume a certain degree of understanding of the language being translated. The Davidsonian version of the principle of charity needs not make such an assumption, and it can accumulate the merits of the principle of humanity.

If the Davidsonian version of the principle of charity is an inevitable criterion of the interpretation of a text, we can draw two conclusions from it. First, no significantly different norm of rationality can be found in Chinese philosophy, as well as in other philosophical traditions, because the principle of charity necessarily imposes our norm of rationality on the target text and its authors. Second, consistency of the text being translated or interpreted must first be assumed at the beginning of the process of translating or interpreting the text. Attribution of contradiction or inconsistency can be made only when a large body of the text is already translated or interpreted or, to put it differently, only when there is better way to make sense of the text.

In Section 9.2 I discuss and reject the argument that ancient Chinese philosophy has no semantic concept of truth. In Section 9.3 I examine some well-known paradoxical expressions and the way we interpret them, in particular, the White Horse claim. In Section 9.4 I compare the principle of humanity and the principle of charity, and argue that we should adopt the latter instead of the former. I also consider some further implications of the principle of charity in interpreting ancient texts.

9.2 THE SEMANTIC CONCEPT OF TRUTH IN ANCIENT CHINESE PHILOSOPHY

Although Hansen intends to apply his claim that Chinese philosophy does not feature the semantic concept of truth only to the philosophical activities of the ancient Chinese, one may be tempted to generalize this claim and say that ancient Chinese do not have the semantic concept of truth at all, not even in their nonphilosophical thinking. After all, one reason ancient Chinese have not used the concept in their philosophy could be that they simply do not have the concept. As Hansen's argument partially depends on certain features of the ancient Chinese language, it may further facilitate the generalization of his claim. If they do not have the concept of truth, then they would not reason with the truth of their beliefs in mind, but think with so-called "correlative reasoning." If this is the case, then it may appear that ancient Chinese did indeed have a different norm of rationality.

But before we consider whether this generalization is warranted, we should examine whether Hansen's original claim is true. If Hansen's claim does not correctly characterize ancient Chinese philosophy, we no longer need to consider the generalization. Leong (2015) has argued that Hansen's argument cannot support his claim that Chinese philosophy does not have the semantic concept of truth, so here I only briefly recap Hansen's argument and my criticism.

Hansen's argument starts from several observations of the ancient Chinese language. He notices that, first, the ancient Chinese language is noninflectional, eg, the same character "*mei* (美) can be used as a noun, a verb, or an adjective. Second, not entirely explicated sentences appear very often in ancient Chinese text. For instance, after a sentence mentions a grammatical subject, if the subsequent sentences have the same subject, the subject is usually omitted. Since the ancient Chinese language does not have any punctuation, it is sometimes difficult to say where a sentence starts and where it ends. So a passage may look similar to this: "John appear in the court pick up a microphone drop it into a box walk out of the court." These two features lead Hansen to speculate that Chinese philosophers may not notice the significance of a sentence as a linguistic unit in their theories of language, but only focus on *ming* (名) (names). What they call a name can be a noun, a verb, or even a phrase, since they do not classify names into different word classes. This is further supported by the observation that when Chinese philosophers talk about their language, they almost exclusively talk only about names. Names, however, are not something that can be true or false, even though they can be said to be correctly applied to certain things. If Chinese philosophers think of sentences as mere strings of names, and do not distinguish them from other strings of words, they would likely miss one significant feature of sentences, namely, that they are true or false. If they talk only about names then, they seem to have no reason to introduce the semantic concept of truth to talk about their language.

Another observation of the Chinese language is that, in those contexts in which we would use beliefs to track others' mental states, Chinese philosophers would describe others' mental states in terms of how others discriminate things. So instead of saying that a person believes that A is B, Chinese philosophers would say that that a person deems A as B. This is why Hansen says that in the Chinese language belief contexts revolve around predication instead of assertion. An implication of this kind of belief context, for Hansen, is that it leads Chinese philosophers to take mind as a faculty to discriminate, rather than a repository of propositions (ie, having the belief *that p*). If this is the way Chinese philosophers think of our mind, they would not attribute beliefs to others, and would not use the semantic concept of truth to characterize beliefs or minds.

In short, Hansen thinks that in their theories of language, Chinese philosophers do not use the concept of sentence, while in their theories of mind they do not use the concept of belief. So in neither of these aspects of their theoretical considerations do they have a concept to talk about things that can be true or false, and therefore they do not have reason to introduce the semantic concept of truth.[4]

So far the evidential base of Hansen's argument is relatively weak. Besides features of the Chinese language, on which his observations are relatively uncontroversial, other evidence such as Chinese philosophers' theories of language and theories of mind depends on our interpretations of Chinese philosophical texts. As Hansen's interpretation of these texts are not uncontroversial, he needs further support for his argument.

Hansen thus appeals to the three standards of doctrine [*yan* (言)] proposed in the *Mozi*. Traditionally, these standards of doctrine are understood as tests of truth.[5] So the word *yan* is taken as something that can be true or false. Hansen, however, argues that they are not. If we interpret these standards as tests of truth, he argues, we cannot make sense of some parts of the text. So he proposes his interpretation of the three standards as standards of name use, for names cannot be true or false, but only be correctly or incorrectly applied to certain objects or events. Taking those standards as standards of names not only helps Hansen deny them as counterexamples to his argument, they can also be turned into further evidence that can support his claim on the absence of the concept of truth. The relevant passage of the standards of doctrine reads:

> 必立儀，言而毋儀，譬猶運鈞之上而立朝夕者也，是非利害之辨，不可得而明知也。故言必有三表。」何謂三表？子墨子言曰：「有本之者，有原之者，有用之者。於何本之？上本之於古者聖王之事。於何原之？下原察百姓耳目之實。於何用之？廢以為刑政，觀其中國家百姓人民之利。此所謂言有三表也。

> Some standards must be established. To say something without regard to the standards is analogous to determining the directions of sunrise and sunset on a turning potter's wheel: the distinction of being right and being wrong (*shi fei*, 是非) being beneficial and being harmful (*li hai*, 利害) cannot be obtained and clearly known. Therefore, there must be three standards of doctrine. What are the three standards? Master Mozi said, "Its root, its origin, and its utility. In where should it root? It should root above in the deeds of the ancient sage-kings. From where should it originate? It should originate below from the examination of what the common people really hear and see. To where should it be used? Declare it as laws or policies and observe its benefits to the state and the people. This is what is meant by 'doctrine has three standards' (*Mozi* 56/35/6–10, my translation).[6]

Here is Hansen's interpretation of this passage:

> The first standard is a historical criterion of appropriate usage... One social standard of language appropriateness traces conformity back to the coiners of the terms. We conform to past usage in making a discrimination—in projecting the term to new uses. Mozi also wants us to conform to past usage in linking words. That is part of getting the distinction right... [The second standard] coheres better with the context if we treat it as a social standard of appropriate usage. We should use language as ordinary people do in reporting what they see and hear....

The eyes-and-ears test, then, is a test of word application. We should not use words or make distinctions that the people do not or cannot make using their eyes and their ears. We understand the test as a test of the social applicability and hence the usefulness of terms and distinctions. If people cannot apply the terms on the evidence of their eyes and ears, then the terms are too abstruse for beneficial general use.

> [The third] standard flowers naturally out of Mozi's language utilitarianism. We must use language in ways that yield benefit. We apply the standards so we can *bian* [辨] in utilitarian ways. (Hanson, 1992, pp. 145–146)

Thus the standard about the root of a doctrine is taken as a criterion of appropriate usage of a term. Thus if someone invents a term, we should use the term in the way he uses it. It is inappropriate to use the term in a different way. The standard about the origin of a doctrine is taken as a test of word application. We should use a word in the way other members in the same linguistic community use them. For Hansen, the author of the above passage in the *Mozi* also thinks that applying a word is applying a distinction, hence the usefulness of a word is also the usefulness of a distinction. The standard about utility, for Hansen, is a utilitarian standard. The purpose of this standard is to test whether a way of using language is beneficial to us.

It is relatively uncontroversial that the standard about utility does not involve the concept of truth. The standard about origin is less uncontroversial, but Hansen's interpretation of it is not obviously implausible. The real problem, however, lies in his interpretation of the standard of root.

Besides the passage mentioned above on the standards of doctrine, in the *Mozi* one can find another passage in which the standards are actually applied to a doctrine about the existence of fate:

> However, there are gentlemen now in the world who think of fate as existing. Let us examine the deeds (*shi*, 事) of the sage-kings. In ancient times, the chaos caused by Jie (桀) was received but was turned into order by Tang (湯); the chaos caused by Zhou (紂) was received but was turned into order by King Wu (武). The times did not change and the people were the same, yet under Jie and Zhou the world was chaotic and under Tang and Wu it was orderly. How can it be said that fate exists? (*Mozi* 57/35/10–12, my translation)

This passage apparently does not seem to be about name use. If it were, it should at least mention how the sage-kings (the supposed inventors of the Chinese language for Hansen) use the term "fate." Instead, this passage describes what they do and then concludes that fate does not exist. In particular, the passage explicitly asks us to examine the deeds of the sage-kings instead of what they say. On the contrary, if we take this passage as discussing a doctrine of the existence of fate, a doctrine that can be true or false, we can make better sense of it. The author tries to show that people's well-being is not determined by fate but by their (or the sage-kings', to be precise) efforts: the chaotic status of the state caused by previous kings was turned into order by sage-kings.

Hansen's interpretation of the three standards of doctrine therefore fails to explain another passage in the same chapter in a satisfactory way. The chapter about the three standards, therefore, remains a counterexample to Hansen's claim that Chinese philosophy does not have any concepts for something that can be true of false. The term "*yan* (doctrine)" seems to refer to something truth-apt. As a result, Chinese philosophers indeed have reasons to introduce the semantic concept of truth to their philosophy. At least they can talk about the truth of a doctrine.

Attempts to identify a truth predicate in ancient Chinese language seem to be the next natural move for those who reject Hansen's view. For example, Fraser (2012) argues that the term *dang* (當) serves as a truth predicate in later Mohist logic. Leong (2015) also argues that the term *ran* (然)

is often used as a truth predicate in various Chinese philosophical texts. Other candidates include *shi* (是), *shi* (實) *cheng* (誠), etc.[7] Due to limited space I leave this issue here. Suffice it to say, there are many plausible truth predicate candidates in ancient Chinese texts. They may not correspond exactly to the truth predicate in a formal language, but neither does the predicate "is true" in English. It does not seem very plausible, therefore, to deny that Chinese philosophy has the semantic concept of truth.

As Hansen's argument does not succeed, it cannot give support to the claim that Chinese philosophy has no semantic concept of truth, or the claim that ancient Chinese philosophy shows another norm of rationality because of the absence of the concept of truth. In Section 9.3 I discuss another line of argument one may take to argue that ancient Chinese has a different norm of rationality. If ancient Chinese think that paradoxes and contradictions can be accepted in a relevant sense, it would seem that they have another kind of rationality, even though they have the semantic concept of truth.

9.3 PARADOXICAL EXPRESSIONS AND THE WHITE HORSE PARADOX

Paradoxical expressions are not uncommon in ancient Chinese texts. Quite the contrary, they are so common that it is not implausible to say that paradoxical expression forms a special kind of rhetorical expression in ancient China. Usually these paradoxes consist in two antonyms in one sentence, or two opposing attitudes (affirmative and negative) toward one term in a sentence. According to De Reu (2006), these paradoxical expressions can be classified into three kinds. The first kind involves the word *ruo* (若) to seem which indicates only similarity, for example, 大巧若拙 (the greatest skill seems clumsy). Since these kinds of paradoxical expressions do not strictly involve any contradiction, I will not discuss them here. The second kind involves implication, for example, 不言之辯 (the speechless disputation). These kinds of paradox usually contains one property or activity, in our example, 言 (speech), which is usually implied by the other property or activity in the same expression, that is, 辯 (disputation). But again, this does not involve any contradiction. An atypical activity may be referred to, for example, a kind of disputation that does not proceed with speech. The third kind of paradoxical expression involves identity, such as 上德不德 (the highest virtue is not virtuous) and 至樂無樂 (ultimate happiness is without happiness). In one reading, even this third kind of paradoxical expression does not express any contradiction. One could say, for instance, since the highest virtue is a property, and a property is not something that can have any virtue, no virtue in this sense is thus virtuous. In another equally grammatical reading, however, the expression could mean "the highest virtue is not a virtue." Although this expression per se is not a contradiction, whoever accepts it as true would accepting it as a contradiction, if he does not think that no virtue exists at all. For he would then accept that there is a virtue such that it is a virtue and, when compared to other virtues, it is in a certain sense the highest one, and yet it is not a virtue. Call such a virtue *V*. He would therefore have to accept both that *V* is a virtue (since it is the highest virtue) and that *V* is not a virtue, which results in a contradiction.

If this latter reading of this third kind of paradoxical expression is the most plausible among other readings, it would seem that Chinese philosophers indeed accept contradictions and have contradictory beliefs, and they are even aware of the contradictions and do not find them problematic. It is then highly likely that ancient Chinese philosophers have a norm of rationality radically different from ours.

The issue now is, naturally, whether the above reading is the most plausible one. Apparently De Reu does not think so. Basically he thinks that the first term and the second term in the expression refer to different concepts. To paraphrase his translation of the expression, it says "what I (the author of the text in which this expression appears) call the highest virtue is not what others call a virtue." He thinks that this expression appears in a context in which the author is in a disputation of what a virtue is. Thus putting it in this paradoxical way has the rhetorical benefit of impressing the reader, but suffers from a lack of information, for what the author call "the highest virtue" is left unexplained. He also quotes another passage on 至樂無樂 (ultimate happiness is without happiness) from *the Zhuangzi* to illustrate this point:

今俗之所為與其所樂，吾又未知樂之果樂邪？果不樂邪？... 果有樂無有哉？吾以無為誠樂矣，

又俗之所大苦也。故日：『至樂無樂，至譽無譽。』

> What today's ordinary people do and where they find happiness, once more I do not know whether their happiness is really happiness or not... Is there after all really happiness or not? I take non-action as true happiness, and yet ordinary people consider it greatly distasteful. Therefore I say: "Ultimate happiness is without happiness, ultimate praise is without praise." (*Zhuangzi* 18/47/29-48/2, De Reu's translation (De Reu, 2006, p. 287))

This passage nicely illustrates De Reu's point. The author explicitly compares where he finds happiness with where ordinary people find happiness. Naturally he finds himself in this aspect superior to ordinary people, thus what he refers to by "ultimate happiness" is what he regards as true happiness, which ordinary people consider as greatly distasteful. So, again, to paraphrase the expression: (what I take as) ultimate happiness is without (what ordinary people take as) happiness. This reading avoids taking the expression as a contradiction and it fits well with the context of the passage.[8]

Two points should be noted here. First, if De Reu's reading is correct, this seems to suggest that Chinese philosophers do not accept contradictions even though they often use paradoxical expressions. Using paradoxical expressions is but a rhetorical way to impress the reader. Second, De Reu's interpretation is supported by the fact that it renders the paradoxical expression coherent with the context in which the expression appears. The first point is related directly to whether Chinese philosophers show a norm of rationality different from ours, while the second point is related to the criteria of a better interpretation of a text. To further examine these two points, in the following I discuss the well-known White Horse paradox.

The White Horse paradox is usually attributed to Gongsun Long, who is traditionally taken as a representative of the so-called School of Names. Only a few chapters of his work survive today, and one of them is the White Horse Dialogue. In this dialogue Gongsun argues for the claim *baima fei ma* (白馬非馬). There are many renderings of this claim. As my aim here is not to argue for a better interpretation of this claim or of the whole dialogue, I am going to discuss mainly Hansen's and Christoph Harbsmeier's interpretations of it. For Hansen, a better rendering of it would be "white-horse-stuff is not horse-stuff," while for Harbsmeier, it would be "White horses are not horses." I start with Hansen's argument for his reading. But before explaining each of their interpretation of the paradox, some preliminary remarks are needed.

The White Horse paradox is not an isolated claim merely mentioned in a list without a context. From the White Horse Dialogue in the *Gongsun Longzi* and the Gongsun Long chapter of the *Kongcongzi* (孔叢子) we know that it is a well-known paradox among Gongsun Long's contemporaries, and most of them do not accept the claim "*baima fei ma*." Someone even visits Gongsun Long from another state to argue with him. It is therefore safe to say that most of Gongsun Long's contemporaries do not take the claim "*baima fei ma*" as a true one. Their responses to the paradox therefore should be taken into account when interpreting the paradox. Gongsun Long's contemporaries may not understand the claim in the way Gongsun Long intended, but at least we must explain why they have such responses and whether these responses are appropriate or result from certain misunderstandings (Harbsmeier, 1998, p. 301).

Another interesting point is that, according to the *Kongcongzi*, none of Gongsun Long's contemporaries are able to beat him at his own game. Most of them do not accept his claim, yet cannot find a way to refute his argument. This fact does not, of course, imply that his argument is flawless, but at least, it seems, that his argument is very powerful to his contemporaries.

The last remark is about the nature of the paradox for both Gongsun Long and his contemporaries. Clearly the opponents of Gongsun Long's claim do not take the claim as a mere false claim or a claim that merely does not fit reality. The evidence is that none of the opponents try to refute the white horse claim by appealing to real white horses. They argue instead by saying, for example, having a white horse implies having a horse, therefore a white horse must be a horse. Thus it seems that for the opponents, the problem of the paradox resides in Gongsun Long's argument. It is likely that the opponents take the claim as one that cannot be true, and it is needless to appeal to any empirical investigation to argue against it. At any rate, similar to the third kind of paradoxical expressions I discussed a few pages back, accepting the white horse claim (with the opponent's understanding of it) is accepting an obvious contradiction. This shows at least one instance of Chinese philosophers' attitude toward a contradiction. But does Gongsun Long mean by the white horse claim something that implies a contradiction?

Neither Hansen nor Harbsmeier think so. For Hansen, the paradox is closely related to the Neo-Mohists' analysis of compound terms (*ming*, 名) In the Neo-Mohists' analysis, compound terms can be distinguished into two kinds, those whose extension is the union of the extensions of the constitutive terms, and those whose extension is the intersection of the extensions of the constitutive terms. An example of the former is "ox-horse," such that any ox or horse is an ox-horse; while an example of the latter is "hard-white," such that only those objects which are both hard and white are hard-white. Hansen thinks that Gongsun Long constructs the paradox by taking "white horse" as an instance of the former kind of compound term, while ordinary people take it as an instance of the latter kind. Thus when Gongsun Long claims that "*baima fei ma*," he means, Hansen believes, those things which are white and those things which are horses as a whole are not those things which are horses, for there are many white things that are not horses. For his contemporaries, they understand the compound of "white horse" as one of the latter kind. So "white horses" refer to those things which are white and are horses, and "white horses are not horses" is naturally false and not acceptable (Hanson, 1992, pp. 258–259).

Harbsmeier, on the contrary, thinks that the white horse claim is true. It is Gongsun Long's opponents who misunderstand what he intends to say. The white horse claim, for Harbsmeier, should be translated as "White hors' is not horse." With the quotations "white horse" now referring not to individual horses, but to the term or the concept of horse. Understanding the claim this way, it becomes a true and plausible claim. One justification of this translation is that in the dialogue, Gongsun Long shifts from talking about having a white horse to seeking a white horse. This is a shift, according to Harbsmeier, from an extensional context to an intensional context. This shifting to the intensional context suggests that the original subject matter is intensional. This understanding of the claim can also make sense of Gongsun Long's inference in his debate: since a yellow or black horse can satisfy someone who is seeking a horse but not someone who is seeking a white horse, seeking a horse is different from seeking a white horse. What makes "seeking a horse" different from "seeking a white horse" is the difference between "horse" and "white horse." Gongsun Long concludes, therefore, "white horse" is not "horse." His opponents insist on taking the white horse claim in an extensional way, and therefore find the claim unacceptable (Harbsmeier, 1998, p. 306). Another confirmation for this reading comes from the grammatical structure of certain expressions. In the ancient Chinese language, the structure X *ze* (者) indicates that the notion/concept/term of X is the subject of the subsequent discussion, instead of what "X" refers to. When Gongsun Long tries to explain to his opponent why "white horse is not horse," he uses this structure several times to explain both "white" and "horse."

Although Harbsmeier's interpretation of the paradox seems to me a better one, it is not my intention here to try to argue for which interpretation is better. But once again, as we have seen above in De Reu's interpretation of other paradoxical expressions in other ancient Chinese texts, it seems that Chinese philosophers do not accept contradiction. Otherwise the opponents of Gongsun Long would not reject the White Horse paradox without hesitation. In particular, they all think that Gongsun Long's argument is powerful and they are not able to refute it, even though they have not the slightest doubt that the conclusion is unacceptable. This seems to mean that Gongsun Long's argument does not involve any premise that is outright ridiculous for them. Gongsun Long himself, on the other hand, does not seem to accept "*baima fei ma*" as an expression for something which implies a contradiction. He may have used a misleading expression to say his conclusion on purpose, in order to create certain rhetorical effect. But his argument for the claim "*baima fei ma*" indeed seems to be a powerful one, whether the claim is understood in either Hansen's or Harbsmeier's interpretation. But if both of the interpretations seem to be equally good, how do we choose among them? What criterion is there for us to evaluate them?

It turns out that Hansen and Harbsmeier disagree with each other also on this issue. There are basically two principles that one could adopt in interpreting a text: the principle of charity and the principle of humanity. Hansen links the former to truth and the latter to epistemic warrant. The principle of charity, in Hansen's formulation, states that one should interpret a text in a way such that the number of true sentences in it is maximized. The principle of humanity, by contrast, states that one should interpret a text in a way such that the author of the text would have maximal epistemic warrant for what he says in the text. Hansen takes the White Horse paradox as the clearest example to show the differences between the two principles, and also the superiority of the principle of humanity over the principle of charity.

As discussed above, most of Gongsun Long's contemporaries reject the claim "*baima fei ma*." From our knowledge of the ancient Chinese language, the sentence could indeed be read as a contradictory claim. For these reasons, perhaps, Hansen takes the claim as a false one. Hansen's interpretation thus starts from this and, being guided by the principle of humanity, proceeds to find Gongsun Long's epistemic warrant for making the claim. He finds hints in both later Mohist logic and the *Zhuangzi*. Later Mohist logic has a detailed analysis of compound terms and the use of examples such as "ox-horse" and "hard-white." In the *Zhuangzi*, on the other hand, he finds criticism on what appears to be the White Horse paradox, and the authors of the *Zhuangzi* show significant familiarity with the School of Names, of which Gongsun Long is usually thought to be a member. Simply put, Hansen tries to find the reason Gongsun Long can construct an argument that leads to an obviously false conclusion but still appears to be convincing for his contemporaries.

Harbsmeier, by contrast, assumes that "*baima fei ma*" is true, and attempts to find an interpretation that can both make it true and make sense of Gongsun Long's argument for it. Harbsmeier therefore takes Gongsun Long as using a sentence which in one ordinary reading means something plainly false to mean something that is true. This interpretation of the White Horse claim makes Gongsun Long's inference valid and sound, and can explain his shifting from an extensional context to an intensional context. The reason for Gongsun Long's doing so, is to provide lords in the court intellectual entertainment by using a seemingly powerful argument to defend a seemingly outright false sentence. For this motivation, Harbsmeier also has strong textual evidence.

If both principles could lead to interpretations that look equally good, why should we favor one instead of the other?

9.4 CHARITY AND HUMANITY

Hansen gives four reasons to favor the principle of humanity over the principle of charity. First, following the principle of charity may require attributing to the author of a text certain beliefs or assertions which he has no reason to hold or make. One example Hansen gives is an early interpretation of the White Horse paradox by (Feng Yu-lan, 1983, p. 203). Feng translates the White Horse claim as "White-horseness is not horseness," thus attributes to Gongsun Long the concept of universal. Whether Feng believes in the existence of universal or not, Feng cannot explain why Gongsun Long would have the concept of universal, a concept which is rather theoretical and is more familiar to thinkers which somehow have access to Platonism. Unless Feng can also show that Gongsun Long came up with a theory on universal himself, or have access to any Platonist works, there seems to be no reason to attribute to Gongsun Long the concept of universal, and Gongsun Long would not have any reason to talk about universals. So even if it is true that universals exist, and Feng believes so, interpreting the White Horse claim as true in this Platonist way is still inadequate. By contrast, Hansen argues, if we follow the principle of humanity we would always need to explain why the author has the concept he has before we can attribute it to him. Hansen's interpretation, in this aspect, relies on the later Mohist analysis of compound terms, suggesting that Gongsun Long may have access to the later Mohist texts directly, or to a common source from which those Mohist texts get their content.

Second, Hansen believes that the principle of charity could not guide us to a better interpretation among interpretations which render the same, or the same number of, sentences in a text as true. Interpretations which take the White Horse claim as saying "White horse is not horse," "the set of white horses is not the same as the set of horses," or "the mereological White-horse object is not the mereological horse object," etc., all render the White Horse claim true. Thus the principle of charity, Hansen thinks, provides us no help on choosing which one to adopt.

Third, the principle of charity, Hansen argues, fails to "establish a fact of the matter about meaning because truth is more metaphysical than epistemological or explanatory" (Hansen, 2007, p. 483). The truth of an assertion is not a reason to attribute the assertion to a person, if we do not think that the person has access to the truth of that assertion. If we attribute the concept of universal to Gongsun Long, it would seem that the concept has certain causal power to make Gongsun Long possess it, or that it is a universal concept no one can fail to acquire.

The fourth criticism of the principle of charity by Hansen is not about the principle per se, but about how the principle is often used, in particular in the field of sinology. He is critical of the fact that many scholars interpret ancient Chinese texts in a "liberal" way as long as it renders the sentences in those texts true. For example, the term "*ma*" in the White Horse claim can be translated as "a horse," "horses," "all the horse," or even "the word horse," depending on the context. But in the same context, changing the translation from one to another, Hansen thinks, requires evidence from the text, evidence which shows that the author of the text is aware of the change. He therefore also criticizes Harbsmeier's interpretation of the White Horse Dialogue, taking some instances of the term "*ma*" as "a horse," while some other as "horse" as something that features in a intensional context. For instance, Harbsmeier takes the opponents' understanding of the White Horse claim as "a white horse is not a horse," yet Gongsun Long's understanding of it as "White horse is not horse."

Also Harbsmeier thinks that Gongsun Long's shift from "having a white horse" to "seeking a white horse" is a shift from an extensional context to an intensional context. Hansen thinks that these kinds of changes of interpretation of the same term in the same text are unsupported, for there is no indication in the text that the author is aware of such change. The only support is that these changes would make the passage true, from the interpreter's perspective.

To repeat, my primary aim here is not to judge whose interpretation is better. Instead I want to focus on the principle they use in guiding their interpretation. Before I reply to Hansen's criticism of the principle of charity, let me draw a distinction on two versions of this principle: the principle of local charity (PLC), and the Davidsonian principle of charity (DPC). The PLC states that one should interpret a passage or a text in such a way that can maximize the number of true sentences in it. The DPC states that, roughly, one should interpret a passage or a text in such a way that can optimize both the number of true sentences in it and the author's beliefs. Apparently DPC is based on Donald Davidson's version of the principle of charity.

There are two major differences between PLC and DPC. First, PLC applies only to sentences in a text, while DPC applies to both the sentences in a text and to the beliefs of the authors of the text. In some cases, therefore, DPC may require us to take some of the sentences in a text as false in order to attribute certain true beliefs to the authors. PLC, on the other hand, does not require one to optimize the authors' beliefs, so it would not require, so to speak, sacrificing the truth of the sentences for the authors' beliefs.

Second, PLC asks us to maximize the number of true sentences in a text, but DPC requires us to optimize the truth of the sentences and the authors' belief. One reason for shifting from maximization to optimization is that, since beliefs are infinite in number, talk of maximization may not make too much sense. But a more crucial reason is that optimization is not a mere attempt to maximize the number of true sentences, it also takes into account the meaning of the sentences attributed by an interpretation. So for instance, if the White Horse claim is taken to mean "white horse is a not horse," then the principle of charity would require us to prefer this interpretation over another interpretation which takes it as "a white-horse is not a horse," in which "a white-horse" is taken to mean a kind of ritual artifact. The latter interpretation may explain that Gongsun Long for some obviously strange reasons (eg, these artifacts can give birth to horses) thinks that those artifacts are called "white-horses" and most of his contemporaries do not know about them, while in fact they are well-known among people but no one calls them "white-horses," or believes that they give birth to horses. This interpretation renders the White Horse claim true (those artifacts are not horses) but attribute an unreasonable belief to Gongsun Long (that they give birth to horses and are called "white-horses."). Thus optimization also measures the weight of beliefs. Measuring the weight of a belief is, however, a tricky matter. There is no clear way to perform such a measuring. But we can give more weight to those beliefs which we would have if we were under similar circumstances. This is actually what Davidson calls the Principle of Correspondence:

> [T]he Principle of Correspondence prompts the interpreter to take the speaker to be responding to the same features of the world that he (the interpreter) would be responding to under similar circumstances... [It] endows him [the speaker] with a degree of what the interpreter takes to be true belief about the world. (Davidson, 1991, p. 211)

Since we would call a white horse a horse, we would attribute this belief to Gongsun Long, unless there is some powerful counter-evidence. Because the belief that an artifact can give birth to horses is so ridiculous to us, the Principle of Correspondence requires us to avoid interpretation of the White Horse claim which requires us to attribute such as a belief to Gongsun Long.

Besides the Principle of Correspondence, another principle involved in the optimization of true assertions and beliefs is the Principle of Coherence:

> The Principle of Coherence prompts the interpreter to discover a degree of logical consistency in the thought of the speaker; ... [it] endows the speaker with a modicum of logic. (Davidson, 1991, p. 211)

The attribution of a modicum of logic is required for interpretation because the content of beliefs, as well as the semantics of one's language, is partially determined by their logical relations to each other. That is, for Davidson, the holistic nature of beliefs:

> Because of the fact that beliefs are individuated and identified by their relations to other beliefs, one must have a large number of beliefs if one is to have any. Beliefs support one another, and give each other content. Beliefs also have logical relations to one another. As a result, unless one's beliefs are roughly consistent with each other, there is no identifying the contents of beliefs. A degree of rationality or consistency is therefore a condition for having beliefs. (Davidson, 1997, p. 124)

Therefore, not only the attribution of a modicum of logic is required, attribution of certain evidential relations is also needed. For example, if one has the belief that apples are fruits, then one must also have a lot of other beliefs concerning apples and fruits, say, that apples have peel, that they grow on trees, that most fruits are edible, that fruits are not meats, etc. There is no fixed list of beliefs one must have in order to have a particular belief, but one must have many other beliefs related by logical or evidential relations in order to have a particular belief. This is also the reason why we would not attribute a belief about laptop to the tribute member in the *lapatai* example discussed earlier: because we do not think that he has any other beliefs about what a laptop is.

DPC involves both of these two principles, while PLC aims only to maximize the number of true sentences in a text. After we make this distinction between DPC and PLC, we can reply to Hansen's criticisms of the principle of charity. I think his criticisms apply only to PLC. DPC not only is not subjected to these criticisms, it can also accommodate the advantages of the principle of humanity over PLC, and is free from a certain circularity of the principle of humanity.

Given the holistic nature of beliefs, DPC would not require attributing to an author a belief of which he does not already have a certain amount of related beliefs. Thus Feng's attribution of the belief of universals to Gongsun Long would be a deviation of DPC since there is no textual evidence to suggest that Gongsun Long has any belief about universals, or any concept logically or evidentially related to the concept of universals.

DPC could also solve the situation mentioned in Hansen's second criticism. Even though various interpretations may equally take the White Horse claim to be true, they would not therefore comply with DPC to the same degree. The degree they optimize the beliefs attributed to the authors and the interpretation given to the text according to the Principle of Coherence and the Principle of Correspondence would not be the same. There are many more factors than mere the number of true sentence in a text that are relevant to an interpretation according to DPC.

Hansen's third criticism seems to suggest that meaning is more epistemological or explanatory than metaphysical. Although it is not exactly clear what he means, DPC would not allow an attribution of belief or interpretation simply because the belief or a sentence under the interpretation is true. As stated above, the Principle of Correspondence would prompt the interpreter to take the speaker to be responding to the same features of the world that the interpreter himself would be responding to under similar circumstances. If under similar circumstances the interpreter would respond to certain aspects of reality, then the interpreter must have certain epistemological access to them. Of course a great deal depends on what features of the circumstances count as relevantly similar: what we, the interpreters, think the author knows, what we think would be obvious to the author under those circumstances, etc. This aspect of DPC alone is worth a separate discussion. But the same is true for the principle of humanity. The principle of humanity emphasizes the epistemic warrant an author has, and requires the interpreter to attribute to the author beliefs and assertions for which he has epistemic warrant. But for the interpreter to find out for what the author has epistemic warrant essentially depends on, again, factors such as what we think the author knows and what we think would be obvious to the author, etc. At any rate, the principle of humanity and DPC do not seem to be so different on this aspect.

Although Hansen's criticism on the application of the principle of charity does not apply to DPC per se, DPC seems to be able to mitigate the problem. DPC requires the interpreter to take into account the author's perspective. Interpretation that involves the changing of meaning with the same term in a passage would be allowed only when the interpreter finds the change reasonable, if the interpreter is under similar circumstances.

I agree with Hansen on his criticism of PLC. But so far my reply to these criticisms does not suggest anything against the principle of humanity. Why then not simply adopt the principle of humanity instead of DPC? At the heart of the principle of humanity is epistemic warrant. But how could an interpreter know what is epistemically warranted for an author? Among other aspects, the author's beliefs seem to be the most crucial. But as an interpreter, how could we have access to the author's beliefs, besides interpreting the author's assertions in those texts? Of course, in principle and in fact, we have a lot of other circumstantial evidence, such as excavated artifacts, historical structures, human/nonhuman remains, etc. This is why archaeology is highly relevant to interpreting texts. But our primary access to the beliefs of the author of a text is still the text itself and other relevant ancient texts. Access to the author's beliefs already assumes, therefore, an interpretation of the same text or some other texts. If this interpretation is also guided by the principle of humanity, we would eventually come back in a circle. In Hansen's interpretation of the White Horse paradox, Gongsun Long's inference depends on the analysis of compound terms found in later Mohist works, that is, taking the compound "white-horse" as having the extension of all white things and all horses, similar to the compound "ox-horse." But how do we know Gongsun Long thought of the compound "white-horse" in the way later Mohists thought of the compound "ox-horse"? To know about this, first we must know how later Mohists thought of the compound "ox-horse," which, again, depends on our interpretation of the later Mohist texts. Hansen would need to employ the principle of humanity once more. Similarly, to interpret the later Mohist texts, he must rely on evidence from other texts, and continue the use of the principle of humanity. The end result would be a coherent interpretation of the text in question and of those relevant texts, but a coherent yet detached-from-reality interpretation would also satisfy the principle of humanity. At the end of the day, the principle of humanity simply asks us to give a generally coherent interpretation.

But mere coherence is not enough. Thus the principle of charity is what is needed. Optimizing truth is what anchors our beliefs to reality, so to speak, since the latter is what most of our beliefs are about, and where our beliefs get their content from. The situation of sinologists is similar to that of the radical interpreter in Davidson's radical interpretation, only that we already have a lot of beliefs about the ancient Chinese people, their language, the environment they were in, and testimonial beliefs about what those texts say passed down by generations of teachers. But the situation is not essentially different. One piece of evidence is that none of the beliefs just mentioned is, in principle, completely immune to revision. So sinologists can follow the imagined radical interpreter and assume the truth of the assertions in a text and start to construct a theory about both what the assertions mean and what the asserters' beliefs are. Thus, unlike the principle of humanity, DPC has an extra constraint: the interpreter should optimize also the truth of the assertions in a text, instead of the mere epistemic warrant the asserters have for such assertions.

There is another difference between DPC and PLC. PLC does not require the interpreter to assume the truth of the assertions; it requires only that the final interpretation given to the text can maximize the number of true sentence in the text. DPC, by contrast, requires the interpreter initially to assume the truth of the assertions, and then go on to try to figure out what the assertions mean. In a later stage, the interpreter may revise his initial attribution of truth to some of the assertions, if doing so would actually better optimize the overall truth of the assertions and of the beliefs of the author. This turns out to be a difference particularly relevant to sinologists.

Many of the extant ancient texts were probably not written by a single author, nor have they remained intact throughout the transmission from ancient times. A text may be actually just a collection of sayings circulating at the time of the authors, and they may be edited and reorganized decades or even centuries later, without any indication of what was changed. This may result in a text inconsistent not only in style but also in content. Later commenters and scholars often needed to make changes to the text in order to make sense of the text. Fortunately, after some time they started to add notes on the changes they made. But still, there are probably many alterations of the original text which we do not know of (in the field of sinology, many relatively recently excavated texts are sufficiently similar to an extant text to be identified as being the "same" text, but with enough differences to be treated as a different version). Many sinologists therefore suggest that we should not interpret these ancient texts as being consistent, for they are not, given their history of edition and transmission.[9] But the problem is, no one knows where and what those editors changed. So even if we agree that a particular text as a whole is probably inconsistent, we have no idea which passage is inconsistent with which. This greatly hinders our success of interpretation. But if one follows DPC one would have a reason to justify attributing inconsistency to a text: if by doing so could optimize the truth of the assertions and the authors' beliefs. See, for a more detailed discussion.

To conclude, rationality in ancient China cannot be significantly different from ours. They may favor a certain kind of argument form or rhetoric, or use certain kind of inferences more often than others. But these preferences do not make their rationality different from ours. For if my argument is correct, DPC requires us to impose a certain degree of rationality on the authors of the ancient Chinese texts, of which we could not make sense without DPC. Not only do we need to discover a modicum of logical and evidential relations between the beliefs of the author of a text (the Principle of Coherence), but also a degree of what the interpreter takes to be true beliefs in the author (the Principle of Correspondence). In short, the intelligibility of a text depends on the rationality we find in it. For those who think that we can find a different rationality in ancient Chinese texts, they now face this dilemma: either they can try to find a significantly different kind of (ir)rationality in a text, then struggle with the intelligibility of their interpretation of the text, or they can argue that using our standard of rationality to interpret a text would only make the text unintelligible. But neither of these two choices is, given the relation between rationality and intelligibility, rational.

References

Davidson, D. (1991). Three varieties of knowledge. *Subjective, intersubjective, objective.* Oxford: Clarendon Press, pp. 205–220.

Davidson, D. (1997). The emergence of thought. *Subjective, intersubjective, objective.* Oxford: Clarendon Press, pp. 123–134.

De Reu, W. (2006). Right words seem wrong: neglected paradoxes in early Chinese philosophical texts. *Philosophy East and West, 56*, 281–300.

Defoort, C. (2008). The profit that does not profit: paradoxes with *"li"* in early Chinese texts. *Asia Major, 21*(1), 29.

Feng, Y. (1983). *A history of Chinese philosophy* (D. Bodde, Trans.). Princeton, NJ: Princeton University Press.

Fraser, C. (2012). Truth in moist dialectics. *Journal of Chinese Philosophy, 39*(3), 351–368.

Hall, D. L., & Ames, R. T. (1995). *Anticipating China: Thinking through the narratives of Chinese and Western culture.* Albany, NY: State University of New York Press.

Hall, D. L., & Ames, R. T. (1998). *Thinking from the Han: Self, truth, and transcendence in Chinese and Western culture.* Albany, NY: State University of New York Press.

Hansen, C. (1985). Chinese language, Chinese philosophy, and "Truth". *The Journal of Asian Studies, 44*(03), 491–519.

Hansen, C. (2007). Prolegomena to future solutions to "white-horse not horse". *Journal of Chinese Philosophy, 34*(4), 473–491.

Hanson, C. (1992). *A Daoist theory of Chinese thought.* New York: Oxford University Press.

Harbsmeier, C. (1998). *Science and civilisation in China, Vol. 7, Part 1. Language and logic.* New York: Cambridge University Press.

Hu, S. (1922). *The development of the logical method in ancient China.* Shanghai, China: The Oriental Book Company.

Jiang, X. (2002). Zhang Dongsun: pluralist epistemology and Chinese philosophy. In Cheng Chung-Ying, & Nicholas Bunnin (Eds.), *Contemporary Chinese philosophy* (pp. 57–81). Oxford: Blackwell Publishers Ltd.

Lau, D. C., & Chen, F. C. (2000). *A concordance to the Zhuangzi.* Hong Kong: The Commercial Press.

Leong, W. C. (2015). The semantic concept of truth in pre-Han Chinese philosophy. *Dao, 14*(1), 55–74.

Mozi (1956). *Harvard-Yenching Institute Sinological Index Series Supplement* (Vol. 21). Cambridge, MA: Harvard University Press.

Nisbett, R. E., Peng, K., Choi, I., & Norenzayan, A. (2001). Culture and systems of thought: holistic versus analytic cognition. *Psychological Review, 108*(2), 291.

Seok, B. (2007). Change, contradiction, and overconfidence: Chinese philosophy and cognitive peculiarities of Asians. *Dao, 6*(3), 221–237.

Endnotes

1. In this paper, by "ancient Chinese" I mean pre-Han Chinese.
2. Zhang Dongsun is perhaps the first scholar who argues that Chinese philosophy features correlative thinking and a different kind of logic (Jiang, 2002) for discussion.
3. Interested reader can see their paper for a list of contemporary philosophers who share the same view. Seok (2007) seems to agree with Nisbett and his colleges' view that this is indeed a peculiar feature of Chinese philosophy, although he thinks that this alleged feature has a different root.
4. Hansen is not trying to argue that Chinese philosophers' theories of language and theories of mind are true of their language or of their minds. He simply intends to argue why they construct their theories in the way they do.
5. This view is popularized by Hu (1922).
6. All passages from classic Chinese texts are referred to by page/book/line to the respective concordance (Lau and Chen, 2000; Mozi, 1956).
7. See Harbsmeier (1998) for discussions on passages containing these candidates.
8. See also Defoort (2008) for a detailed discussion on a similar expression *Dali bu li* (大利不利) "great profit is not profit."
9. Of course we do not have to accept that these ancient texts are inconsistent. A typical example is the case of Wikipedia. Most of the entries of Wikipedia have multiple authors, but not many of them are inconsistent.

CHAPTER

10

Does Classical Chinese Philosophy Reveal Alternative Rationalities?

T.M. Lee

Department of Philosophy, Tunghai University, Taichung, Taiwan

10.1 INTRODUCTION

The issue of rationality has received significant attention in the study of classical Chinese philosophy from comparative perspectives. As classical Chinese philosophy is considered fundamentally different from Western philosophy, it is believed to hold potentials for gaining insights on the limitations of Western understandings of the nature of rationality (Clarke, 2000, p. 13; Hall & Ames, 1995, p. 114). Based on observations of the differences between Chinese and Western philosophies in reasoning and argumentation, some scholars have come to the conclusion that ancient Chinese philosophy did not have rationality or, less radically, at least had a different paradigm of rationality. Roger T. Ames (1992), for example, argues that Chinese philosophy does not accord with the Western standard of rationality. Detailed elaborations of this theory are offered by David L. Hall and Ames. According to them, rationality emerged once but did not survive in China; and even the Chinese protorational thinking did not resemble Western rationality. The Western paradigm of rationality, Hall and Ames argue, is marked by the use of logical arguments, which is nonetheless absent in Chinese philosophy (Hall & Ames, 1995, pp. 54, 65; 1998, pp. 130–131).

The theory that Chinese philosophy is nonrational or that it features a different kind of rationality yields the perspective that rationality may not be universal: it may be culturally relative or a product of historical contingence (Hall & Ames, 1995, p. 114). If this is the case, we should then rethink the norm of rationality and reflect upon the cultural or historical

Rationality. http://dx.doi.org/10.1016/B978-0-12-804600-5.00010-6

limitations of the proposed characterizations of rationality through reconstructing "Chinese rationality."

In this chapter, however, I do not attempt to examine what "Chinese rationality" might be or in what ways Chinese philosophy may challenge the current scholarship of rationality, nor do I try to argue for or against the theory that Chinese philosophy is nonrational or exemplifies an alternative paradigm of rationality. Instead, I focus on the methodology of identifying a different rationality. I will first explain why classical Chinese philosophy, the *Zhuangzi*'s philosophy in particular, is often judged to be lacking in rationality or representing an alternative paradigm of rationality. I will then argue that these reasons are methodologically questionable.

10.2 IDENTIFYING DIFFERENT RATIONALITY BY IDENTIFYING DIFFERENT LOGIC

The thesis that ancient Chinese philosophers did not have rationality or had a uniquely different rationality is grounded on the theory that Chinese philosophers reasoned in a way different from the Western mode of rational thinking. According to this theory, the major feature of the Chinese way of thinking is the dominance of "correlative" or "analogical" thinking in contrast with Western analytic and logical thinking (Ames, 1992; Graham, 1989, pp. 319–324; Hall & Ames, 1995, pp. 54, 123–141, 256–168).[1] This mode of thinking is depicted as reasoning by analogical associations rather than by truth functional logic or propositional coherence (Hall & Ames, 1995, p. 124, 1998, pp. 123–135).

As the Western paradigm of rationality is characterized by the employment of logic, the Chinese way of thinking, according to the previous depiction, does not use logic, that is, ancient Chinese did not follow logical rules in reasoning and argumentation. Some scholars argue more specifically and explicitly that ancient Chinese philosophers had a special logic that did not follow the law of noncontradiction. Adopting this special logic, ancient Chinese philosophers accepted contradictions and did not consider being inconsistent irrational (Liu, 1974; Zhou, 1990).

The theory that ancient Chinese had a different logic ("different-logic theory" hereafter) is inspired by the common impression that Chinese philosophical texts are often inconsistent. A widespread interpretation has it that Chinese philosophical texts, especially those affiliated with Daoism such as the *Zhuangzi*, have inconsistent statements or present contradictory thoughts.[2] Under this interpretation, Zhuangzi's philosophy is described as a philosophical tradition that differs remarkably from Western thought in that it accepts inconsistencies. Huang Hanqing, for example, asserts that Zhuangzi intended to offer mystical intuitions instead of consistent thought, so one should not assess Zhuangzi's philosophy in terms of Western philosophical traditions (Huang, 2007, p. 104). Deng Xiaomang claims, similarly, that Zhuangzi was fond of making paradoxes and proud of being self-contradictory (Deng, 2003, p. 9). Adopting a sceptic reading of the *Zhuangzi*, Deng therefore concludes that whereas Western scepticism is rational and provides logically valid arguments, Chinese scepticism is nonrational and contradictory.

Following this line of interpretation, many contend that Chinese philosophy should be understood with special Chinese logic and cannot be assessed in terms of the Western notion of rationality. Ye Shuxian, for example, claims that Zhuangzi subscribed to the monistic view that all things, including the contradictory, are one, namely the ineffable Dao, so Zhuangzi's philosophy does not parallel Western dualistic thinking and conceptual discrimination resulted from "analytic rationality" (Ye, 2005, p. 37). Ye thus complains that contemporary scholars are too much influenced by "Western logical thinking"; they thus fail to recognize the incompatibility of "analytic rationality" and Zhuangzi's "poetic wisdom" and tend to attribute contradictory opinions in the *Zhuangzi* to different thinkers. For Ye, those who try to solve the contradictions in the *Zhuangzi* wrongly presuppose the logical rules Zhuangzi did not follow.

The interpretation of an inconsistent *Zhuangzi* encourages the idea that ancient Chinese thinkers reasoned in a special logic that tolerates or even endorses contradictions (Hansen, 1992, pp. 10, 201; 2010). It is thus believed that the contribution of Zhuangzi's philosophy (or Daoism) to contemporary philosophy lies in its potential of offering a different mode of reasoning and exposing the limits of our contemporary understanding of rationality.

As we have seen thus far, the attribution of irrationality or a different rationality to the philosopher Zhuangzi (the alleged author of the text, the *Zhuangzi*) is grounded on the attribution of a different logic to the *Zhuangzi*; and the attribution of a different logic depends on the attribution of inconsistency to the text. Yet it remains unclear as to what interpretive methodologies one can legitimately adopt to interpret the *Zhuangzi* as making inconsistent statements or expressing contradictory thoughts. As it will be argued in the next section, proponents of the different-logic theory are often circular in presupposing that the *Zhuangzi*, or classical Chinese philosophical texts in general, is inconsistent.

10.3 ATTRIBUTION OF INCONSISTENCY AND DIFFERENT LOGIC: A CIRCULAR ARGUMENT

Proponents of the different-logic theory generally assume that Chinese philosophical texts, especially the *Zhuangzi*, have inconsistencies—an assumption I call the "assumption of inconsistency"—they, however, do not give an explicit and noncircular explanation on the methodological ground on which one can justifiably attribute inconsistencies to the texts.

The assumption of inconsistency has encouraged and is encouraged by the methodological prescription that interpreters should avoid reading the *Zhuangzi* as though it is consistent. This prescription, clearly, presupposes that there are inconsistences in the *Zhuangzi*. This presupposition has been taken for granted[3] and has added to the prevalence of the view that an eligible interpretation of the *Zhuangzi* must acknowledge, not dissolve, the contradictions in the text. Sydney Morrow (Morrow, 2015), for example, credits Steve Coutinho (2013)'s *An Introduction to Daoist Philosophies* for characterizing the *Zhuangzi*'s philosophical implications by keeping its contradictions intact.[4] This methodological tendency encourages interpreters to attribute inconsistencies to the *Zhuangzi*; as a result, it reinforces the view that the *Zhuangzi*'s contribution to comparative philosophy lies in its special logic, nonrational wisdom, or a different rationality. As the assumption of inconsistency is widespread, some come to accept the "different-logic theory" as an explanation for the presupposed inconsistencies in Zhuangzi's philosophy.

While the different-logic theory may be able to explain why the *Zhuangzi* is inconsistent (if it is indeed so), it will be circular to use the very same theory to justify attributing inconsistencies to the *Zhuangzi* or to criticize consistent readings of the text; as an explanation, the different-logic theory has already put the inconsistencies as its explanandum. A natural question, therefore, is how proponents of the different-logic theory defend attribution of inconsistencies to the *Zhuangzi* or why they disagree with those who attempt to interpret the text as consistent in content?

Intriguingly, advocates of the different-logic theory seem to be disinterested in questioning the assumption of inconsistency. Furthermore, they often use the different-logic theory circularly to challenge interpreters who try to read the *Zhuangzi* text as expressing consistent thoughts. The circularity is even more prominent in cases where proponents of the different-logic theory, or different-rationality theory, criticize interpretations that do not attribute a different logic to the texts for failing to recognize the different way of thinking in the texts.

Despite the long-entrenched perception that the *Zhuangzi* is not a consistent text, some interpreters try to show that the alleged "inconsistencies" in the *Zhuangzi* are not irreconcilable (Van Norden, 1996). They argue that although many statements in the text seem to be inconsistent, one can still dissolve the inconsistencies by examining what the author(s) actually believed and intended to do with those statements. One of the most prominent scholars who objects attribution of contradictions to the *Zhuangzi* is Chad Hansen, whose experimental interpretation of the

Zhuangzi and other philosophical texts is considered the most vehement expression against the attribution of a special logic and nonrational way of thinking to Chinese philosophy (Clarke, 2000, p. 168). Hansen argues that the alleged contradictions in the *Zhuangzi* are introduced by the traditional interpretation (Hansen, 1992, p. 10), which makes some assumptions that inevitably render Zhuangzi's philosophy contradictory. One of the assumptions is that the *Zhuangzi* is a metaphysical theory of the ultimate, overarching, mystical, and absolute entity—the Dao—that no one can know or speak of (Hansen, 2010). The *Zhuangzi*, however, discusses and claims to know something about the ineffable and unknowable "Dao." As Hansen points out, the *Zhuangzi* would not have such contradictions if this assumption was not being made in the first place. Hansen indicates, additionally, that no statement in the *Zhuangzi* explicitly suggests that the *Zhuangzi* author(s) permitted contradictions (Hansen, 2010, p. 30). In other words, the claim that the *Zhuangzi* author(s) reasoned in a special logic that endorsed contradictions has no direct evidence, and it is a result of ungrounded attribution of contradictions. For this reason, Hansen tries to provide an alternative interpretation that can read the *Zhuangzi* consistently.

Hansen's attempt at reading the *Zhuangzi* as a consistent philosophy are challenged by scholars who attribute to the text contradictions, a different rationality, or a special logic that tolerate contradictions. The major criticism is that the methodological assumption of consistency—the principle that an interpreter should assume the consistency of the text when interpreting the text—is inappropriate in the case of Chinese philosophy. An underlying reason is defended by Hall and Ames, who suggest that Chinese philosophers did not pay attention to propositional coherence and are not interested in building systematic thoughts (Hall & Ames, 1998, pp. 124–126). It is therefore an inappropriate expectation that there are consistent thoughts to be found in Chinese philosophy. A stronger expression of such criticisms is that any interpretation that reads the *Zhuangzi* as a consistent text must be wrong. Youru Wang, for instance, criticizes Hansen for intentionally neglecting the contradictions in the *Zhuangzi* (Wang, 2003, p. 95). This criticism clearly begs the question against Hansen as it has already presupposed that there are contradictions in the *Zhuangzi*. In a similar vein, proponents of the different-logic theory, or the different-rationality theory, question Hansen's approach by presupposing a lack of ordinary logic or rationality in Chinese philosophy. They argue that Hansen uncritically assumes Western analytic rationality and logic as guiding criteria in interpreting Daoist philosophy (Ames, 1994; Clarke, 2000, p. 170; Hall & Ames, 1995, pp. 149–152), while the belief in the universality of rationality and logic is an expression of Western ethnocentrism (Hall & Ames, 1995, p. 182). Clarke thus criticizes Hansen, saying that although Hansen stresses the radical differences of Chinese philosophy, he himself uncritically accepts the priority of the Western rational way of thinking and accordingly undermines his own interpretation. Due to this oversight, Hansen fails to appreciate the richness and uniqueness of Chinese philosophy and ignores the distinct spiritual and metaphysical implications of Daoist writings (Clarke, 2000, p. 170).

It is clear from aforementioned that the critics of Hansen's approach are circular in presupposing that Zhuangzi's philosophy, or Chinese philosophy in general, has radically different logic or rationality. Some might, in line with Clarke, argue that using this presupposition to challenge Hansen's approach does not have the problem of circularity since Hansen himself admits that Chinese philosophy differs radically from Western traditions. Nonetheless, as Hansen indicates, there are several ways in which Chinese philosophy can differ from Western philosophy: it may be that Chinese thinkers reasoned differently or that they simply did philosophy with a very different set of assumption about language and mind (Hansen, 2010, p. 28). The advocates of the different-logic theory, however, never explain why the uniqueness of Chinese philosophy must lie in its peculiar way of reasoning.

It should also be noted that Hansen does not deny the possibility that ancient Chinese thinkers had a very different logic or that they did not have rationality at all (Hansen, 1992, pp. 198–199). His point is rather that even if that is the case, we can still only try to understand the Chinese philosophical texts according to ordinary logic that we can access since we cannot apprehend what our rationality does not allow us to. More importantly, before claiming that a text adopts a radically different logic and features a very distinct kind of rationality, we should first test all available interpretations on the table until we can confidently conclude that there is no way to make sense of the text by any other ways of reasoning (Hansen, 1992, p. 10). Nonetheless, to make such a claim is to admit that we cannot understand the text and we should give up trying because we can only understand the thoughts of creatures who share rationality with us to a certain extent (Hansen, 1992, p. 199).[5]

While the different-logic theory might be correct, as I have argued so far, proponents of it cannot defend it as they have not answered this crucial methodological question: on what basis can we ascertain that there are contradictions and special ways of reasoning in Chinese philosophical texts, and how can we understand those texts if they are so contradictory and so different in terms of logic? After all, we cannot identify inconsistencies or different logic without having already understood something consistent and logical to us in the texts. Even if we have already experimented with all possible interpretations and found it impossible to interpret the texts as consistent in accordance with ordinary logic, this still cannot justify the claim that ancient Chinese philosophers reasoned in a radically different logic and that they have another kind of rationality that differs radically from ours. The most we can say is that they are not intelligible to us. An attribution of massive contradictions or different rationalities to a text would not be plausible if the interpreter could not explain how he or she identified these contradictions and alternative rationalities when he or she found nothing consistent and logical in the text.

10.4 ATTRIBUTION OF INCONSISTENCIES AND DIFFERENT PARADIGM OF RATIONALITY: AN ALTERNATIVE DEFENCE

Another theory, the multiple-author theory, is constructed for defending the attribution of inconsistency to the *Zhuangzi* and other classical philosophical texts. It holds that a classical text is inevitably inconsistent since it was not written by a single author: it is a gradual historical accretion or a collection of divergent materials that reflect the ideas of more than one thinker. This theory is not only intended as an explanation of the presence of inconsistencies but also as a justification for attributing contradictions to classical Chinese texts. Similar to the different-logic theory, it presupposes the existence of inconsistencies in Chinese philosophy and adheres to the methodological prescription that an eligible interpretation of a classical philosophical text should preserve the inconsistencies in the text. The multiple-author theory, therefore, has similar implications for the issue of Chinese rationality. If it is right in presupposing that a text written and edited by multiple authors is inevitably inconsistent, then the thought as presented in the *Zhuangzi*, not the philosopher Zhuangzi, may well reveal a different paradigm of rationality. Moreover, the *Zhuangzi*'s alleged inconsistent thought has inspired and was appreciated by later generations of Chinese. This may suggest that Chinese people, compared with Western people, are generally more open to contradictions or that they reason in a logic that does not follow the law of noncontradiction (Nisbett, 2010, pp. 25–28; Seok, 2007).

The multiple-author theory has been considered a reasonable explanation for the inconsistencies in the *Zhuangzi* (Fraser, 1997). As an explanation of inconsistency, it is better than the different-logic theory in that it does not claim circularly that the *Zhuangzi* is inconsistent because its author(s) reasoned inconsistently. More importantly, it has textual evidence. Philological surveys of the *Zhuangzi* have shown the incongruity of the lexicons, genres, and literary styles in different parts of the *Zhuangzi* (Liu, 1994). These observations support the common sense view that the received *Zhuangzi*, although attributed to an individual Zhuangzi, "is not a homogeneous collection made by a single author" (Loewe, 1993, p. 56). Based on this view, the multiple-author theory contends that the *Zhuangzi* had gone through many hands (of authors or editors) and as a result, it became inconsistent.

Beyond the philological basis, the multiple-author theory has another explanatory advantage. It does not resort to a hypothesis that has not yet been well defended in a noncircular manner, that is, the hypothesis that Zhuangzi, or any ancient Chinese thinkers, had a radically different logic. The multiple-author theory does not need to explain why modern readers, Western or Chinese, can still understand the text if it was written by a thinker with a distinctively different rationality or even without rationality. It solves the problem of inconsistency in Chinese philosophy by holding that the inconsistent ideas were in fact held by different thinkers (authors or editors).

The multiple-author theory too has implications for the issue of Chinese rationality. If it is proven better than the different-logic theory in terms of explanatory power, then the theory that Chinese philosophers had no or had alternative rationalities should be nuanced. According to the multiple-author theory, the existence of inconsistencies in the *Zhuangzi* does not indicate that the philosopher Zhuangzi lacked rationality or had a distinctively different rationality; instead, it resulted from having multiple authors. This suggests that the statements recorded in the *Zhuangzi*, when put together, make up a thought that reveals a different paradigm of rationality or collective rationality. Thus, one may say, the Chinese, especially the Daoist, philosophical culture presents an alternative rationality, which does not consider accepting contradictions irrational. For this reason, some argue that, immersed in this philosophical culture, Chinese people are generally more open to or even inclined to endorse paradoxical and contradictory statements (Nisbett, 2010; Seok, 2007).

As we have seen thus far, although the multiple-author and different-logic theories focus on different aspects of Chinese philosophical literature, both yield the view that the standard of rationality may be culturally specific. Both theories are not only used by scholars as explanations of the inconsistencies in the Chinese philosophical texts but also as justification for the attribution of inconsistency to the texts. Similar to the different-logic theory, the multiple-author theory presupposes the existence of inconsistencies; it also supports the methodological prescription that interpreters must resist the temptation to read the *Zhuangzi* as though it is consistent and that a responsible interpretation of the *Zhuangzi* should reflect the text's contradictions (Fleming, 1998). Sydney Morrow, for example, states, "Anyone engaged for any time studying the *Zhuangzi* must acknowledge the inconsistencies, which indicate more than one author" (Morrow, 2015, p. 624). Some even state that unconvincing interpretations of the *Zhuangzi* are acceptable since the *Zhuangzi* text is a collection of divergent materials and it is fragmentary and inconsistent (Richey, 2011, p. 498).

Despite the explanatory advantages, the multiple-author theory shares with the different-logic theory the predicament of question begging when it is employed to defend the attribution of inconsistencies to the *Zhuangzi* or other classical texts. As mentioned earlier, any attribution of inconsistencies must depend on some recognized consistencies; that is, one cannot detect inconsistencies if one does not grasp an overall consistency in the text. Being aware of this paradox—one must acknowledge the inconsistencies while there must be some sort of consistency discernible in the text—some speculate that the overall consistency one finds in the *Zhuangzi* might be imposed by later-day editors (Klein, 2011). Yet, collective authorship or editorship is supposed to reflect collective rationality, let alone in the alleged case that there were editors who saw to it that the text being edited would look consistent. That the group of authors or editors had tried to make the text consistent but failed to remove inconsistencies is something that needs to be explained. One might explain that these authors or editors were neither careful nor sophisticated, so they overlooked some inconsistencies. Yet, by adopting this explanation, one still begs the question if he or she cannot explain why it is more plausible to say that those authors or editors were muddle-headed than to say that his or her interpretation is simply wrong.

Moreover, proponents of the multiple-author theory sometimes make assumptions that have not been convincingly defended or clearly articulated. They, for example, seem to assume that inconsistency of lexicon and writing style implies multiple authorship or that multiple authorship implies inconsistency of thought. Such assumptions do not clearly distinguish among various aspects of consistency.[6] Additionally, as Hansen points out, "A text may be coherent even if worked on by multiple authors. It may be incoherent if written by a single author" (Hansen, 1992, p. 399). In other words, the assumption that the *Zhuangzi* was not authored by a single person does not imply that the *Zhuangzi* has inconsistent thought and cannot justify reading the text as having inconsistent thought.

To sum up, the multiple-author theory can serve, at best, as an explanation for inconsistencies if there is indeed any, but it is methodologically problematic to use it to justify attributing inconsistencies to a text. Whether an attribution of inconsistencies to a text is plausible is a question that the multiple-author theory cannot provide any direct answer. The same goes for the different-logic theory. Suppose my interpretation is that the first statement contradicts with the second and coheres with the third, and your interpretation is that the first contradicts with the third but coheres with the second. Can both of us invoke the multiple-author or different-logic theory to justify our attributions of "inconsistencies"? In other words, even if we accept a very strong assumption that a text made by plural authors must be inconsistent or that ancient Chinese thinkers endorsed contradictions, this assumption is still methodologically unhelpful: it cannot help us determine which parts of the text are inconsistent with which other parts. We still need to interpret the entire text in order to determine what the inconsistencies are. After all, what statements contradict with what other statements is subject to interpretation.

10.5 ASSUMPTION OF CONSISTENCY IN THE INTERPRETATION OF MULTIPLE AUTHORS TEXTS

Some might argue that although the multiple-author theory cannot justify attributing contradictories to a text, it at least indicates the implausibility of the methodological assumption of consistency and urges interpreters to reflect upon the unrealistic expectation that the classical text they are interpreting present a consistent thought. Yet, I will continue to argue, the multiple-author theory does not play such a significant role in the methodology of interpreting the thought of the *Zhuangzi* or other ancient Chinese texts.

Some might find it implausible to methodologically assume that a classical Chinese text is consistent, since it may reflect different intellectual stages of the same author, or it may be authored by different persons; it may also be compiled gradually during a long period of time, or contain a wide range of textual sources of various origins. These possibilities (conveniently put together under the label of "multiple-author theory"), however, would not undermine the plausibility of the assumption of consistency. I will first argue that these possibilities do not have much effect on whether a text is to be interpreted as consistent or not. I will then argue that assuming otherwise (namely, assuming that a text is inconsistent) is detrimental to the enterprise of text interpretation.

The assumption that an ancient Chinese text was very likely written, compiled, edited, or reedited by different persons contributes little to our interpretive methodology concerning consistency. To see why, let us consider two cases. In the first case, the assumption might be thought to have a categorical effect on an interpretation, that is, if a text was not written by a single author, we should rule out all those interpretations that attribute to the text's generally consistent content. This alleged effect, apparently, does not follow from that assumption, as a single author may make contradictory statements, and the statements by different authors may happen to be consistent on certain aspects. Methodologically speaking, the assumption of multiple authorship does not help us determine whether a text is consistent or not. In order to make this judgment, we need to interpret the text. As an illustration, we can think of Wikipedia as an example. We all know that most Wikipedia entries have multiple editors. But when we are reading a Wikipedia entry, we still assume that the statements in an entry are consistent unless we discover that some of them are not. We must try first to understand all the statements before judging whether some of them contradict with each other. Suppose that we are told in advance, "The entry you are reading is edited and reedited by dozens of people," the situation would not change much. Whether we are to interpret it as consistent or not, our interpretation will not contradict the assumption that this entry is edited and reedited by dozens of people.

In the second case I consider, one may concede that the possibility of multiple authorship does not have a categorical effect on our interpretation, but, one continues, it may raise the chance of a text being inconsistent. Following this line of reasoning, one may perhaps accept this methodological assumption: the probability of the text being inconsistent is raised on the fact that this text was authored by different people. Yet this methodological assumption too makes no significant difference, since we still need to interpret all the discourses in a text before judging whether this text is consistent. Even if our conclusion is that this text is perfectly consistent, this conclusion would not contradict that assumption.

After arguing that the multiple-author theory has no significant effect on whether the text is to be interpreted as consistent, I will continue to argue that it will not undermine the methodological assumption of consistency. Some might believe that given the possibility that the *Zhuangzi* has multiple authors and is a collection of divergent materials from different periods and of different origins, a plausible interpretive methodology should reject the methodological assumption that the text is consistent. While this possibility can indeed rationalize an interpretation that reads inconsistencies into the *Zhuangzi* (when it is supported by textual evidence), as I will argue, it will not render the assumption of consistency implausible. Moreover, discarding the assumption of consistency is denying the intelligibility of the *Zhuangzi* and risks leading to interpretive anarchy: a lack of criteria of determining whether an interpretation is justified.

That the *Zhuangzi* may possibly be a historical accretion that had gone through many authorial and editorial hands would not undermine the assumption of consistency because the assumption of consistency is a methodological assumption instead of an interpretive conclusion (namely, a conclusion being drawn from an interpretation; see Chapter 9).[7] The assumption of consistency does not suggest that the text being interpreted must be consistent, or that one cannot argue that the text is inconsistent; rather, it suggests only that one must methodologically assume that a text is consistent when he or she is interpreting it and that he or she must try to achieve an interpretation that can optimize the consistency of the text. This assumption is methodologically fundamental because it is also the assumption that the text expresses something interpreters can possibly apprehend and the principle that interpreters must not assign meanings arbitrarily to the text.

The assumption of consistency is essential to interpretive activity since it is an assumption concerning the intelligibility of the text. If the interpreters do not find the text consistent to a certain degree, they cannot understand it, let alone discover its inconsistency. The plausibility of an attribution of inconsistency depends on an attribution of a large degree of consistency to the text; otherwise the text would not be intelligible to the interpreters. It is because the alleged inconsistent statements already presuppose an interpretation of them, and an interpretation, in turn, requires an attribution of a certain degree of consistency among related statements.[8] Thus assuming that the *Zhuangzi* is consistent during our process of interpretation does not imply that the text is in fact consistent, it is about treating the text as expressing something we could understand. Rejecting this assumption amounts to saying that we cannot possibly understand the text, or that it is not something that can be called a text at all.

Moreover, the assumption of consistency is methodologically crucial because it attends to the normative consideration of the interpreters' justification. Methodological assumption is about what reasons we have to believe an interpretation to be correct, or how we can justify an interpretation. Some ancient Chinese authors and editors might in some places be clumsy in reasoning or unconsciously make contradictory statements, but as interpreters we can only claim so when we have already interpreted the texts and had justifications. It may be true that many ancient Chinese texts are likely or arguably inconsistent, but any judgment of this kind must be an interpretive conclusion; it cannot be taken as a methodological assumption in a helpful way.

More importantly, the assumption of consistency is the basis of the most fundamental interpretive criterion—the criterion of context—that is, reading a statement against its previous and subsequent statements. There is no methodology for interpreting a single statement in a written text (or a single utterance in a speech) without referring to its context, especially in the case of decoding pragmatics. Since the meaning of every single statement is partially determined by its place in the meaning network of other statements, one cannot understand or even justify an interpretation of a statement without considering or referring to that network.

The assumption of consistency is necessary in this regard: it puts necessary constraints on text interpretation by requiring interpreters to test and adapt their interpretive theories in light of the discourses from the same context, namely the totality of textual evidence available rather than any single discourse. Rejecting the assumption of consistency is tantamount to refusing to interpret the sentences of a text against their context—since without the assumption, the sentences may be taken as unrelated and do not form a unified context—and will lead to the danger of interpretive anarchy, namely a lack of justificatory criteria. Suppose that someone gives me this methodological instruction: "The text you are interpreting is a collection of statements written by different people and thus the text is very likely inconsistent, so you better read it as inconsistent." This instruction would amount to licensing me to read every single statement of the text as isolated, since I do not need to care about the context, that is, whether the statements in the text are consistent. Accordingly, I can read it as inconsistent on whatever aspect I can think of, such as the aspect of literal meaning, pragmatic meaning, belief, and intention. I can interpret all the statements in the text as mutually unrelated and contradictory in terms of not only what is literally said but also of what topic it is about and what beliefs and perspectives are expressed. The person who instructs me to interpret the text inconsistently henceforth cannot criticize my interpretation for failing to read these statements against their "context"—because any attempt to read a statement against its preceding and subsequent statements must presuppose the consistency of these statements on certain aspects. By assuming beforehand that the text being interpreted is inconsistent, one can no longer appeal to the criterion of context to judge whether an interpretation is plausible.

It is therefore unreasonable to accept any methodological theory that rejects the assumption of consistency, unless we are to welcome interpretive anarchy. Assuming that a text is inconsistent is tantamount to giving up all evidence resorting to the context. Therefore, before or during the process of interpreting a text, we must methodologically assume that it is consistent, if we wish to retain some basic criteria for interpretation. This is a methodological assumption, not an interpretive conclusion. After having tried to interpret a text, we might reach at the conclusion that there is no possible way to read the text as consistent. We could then argue that this text is inconsistent by precisely indicating which sentences are inconsistent with which other sentences.[9] It is at this rather late stage of interpretation that we are allowed to resort to the multiple-author theory or the different-logic theory to explain the inconsistencies. It is also at this interpretive stage that we can reasonably defend the thesis that classical Chinese philosophy reveals a distinct paradigm of rationality or that ancient Chinese thinkers did not have rationality at all.

10.6 CONCLUSIONS

Classical Chinese philosophical texts, especially the *Zhuangzi*, are often interpreted as expressing inconsistent thoughts. To explain the lack of consistency, some speculate that ancient Chinese thinkers reasoned in a special logic that tolerated and even endorsed contradictions. Derived from the different-logic theory is the theory that ancient Chinese philosophers did not have rationality or had a distinctively different rationality. This chapter argued that the different-rationality theory has not been defended in a methodologically responsible way.

I first argued that the different-rationality theory presupposed the different-logic theory, which, in turn, presupposed the inconsistencies attributed by traditional interpretations to the Chinese philosophical texts, especially the *Zhuangzi*. Methodologically speaking, therefore, the different-rationality theory has to provide additional justifications when it is challenged by interpreters who find it more plausible to read the classical

Chinese philosophical texts as having consistent content according to ordinary logic.

Nonetheless, proponents of the different-rationality theory often beg the question by employing the different-logic theory and the alleged inconsistencies in their defence, and even criticize interpreters who read consistent thoughts into Chinese texts for failing to recognize the special logic and contradictions. Beyond the problem of question begging, proponents of different-rationality theory have not provided any answer to the question of how one can understand ancient Chinese thought if it is so different in logic and full of contradictions.

Next, I considered another theory—the multiple-author theory—which is also often used to defend the attribution of inconsistency to classical Chinese philosophy. It holds that due to having multiple authors and editors, a classical Chinese philosophical text is inevitably inconsistent. This theory has similar implications for the issue of rationality. It does not suggest that ancient Chinese thinkers reasoned differently, but rather that Chinese philosophical texts present contradictory thoughts and, as a result, Chinese philosophical culture does not exemplify the norm of rationality. Likewise, however, the multiple-author theory errs in taking an explanation of inconsistencies (if there are indeed any) as a justification for attributing inconsistencies to Chinese philosophical texts. The theory can serve at best as an explanation instead of a justification because the fact that the text being interpreted was gradually written and compiled and edited by different people does not entail that the text is inconsistent.

More importantly, the different-logic theory and multiple-author theory share similar methodological predicaments as both prescribe discarding the methodological assumption that the text being interpreted is consistent. As I argued in the final section, the methodological assumption that the text we are interpreting is consistent and that we should try to optimize its consistency is a basic requirement for interpretation. Giving up this assumption is tantamount to giving up essential constraints on interpretive attempts: it means giving up the constraint to assign meaning to the text as a whole. Presupposing that a classical Chinese text does not have generally consistent content amounts to presupposing that it is futile to try to interpret its statements against each other. As a result, there would be no criteria to judge if an interpretation is justified. In other words, if we are methodologically permitted to interpret a text as inconsistent, we can literally attribute any kind of reading to it as long as we read it grammatically. It is therefore unclear as to how the proponents of the different-logic theory or multiple-author theory can justify their interpretations of Chinese thought when they reject the assumption of consistency and presuppose that one should not interpret ancient Chinese thought as consistent in content.

Therefore, one can only argue that a text is inconsistent after he or she has already tried to interpret it and realized that there was no way to read it consistently. Only when one is at this rather late interpretive stage can he or she invoke the different-logic theory or the multiple-author theory to explain why attributing inconsistencies to the text is not entirely problematic. It is also at this later stage that one can responsibly defend the different-rationality theory. As interpreters who claim that there are inconsistencies in the *Zhuangzi* (or in other Chinese philosophical texts) generally do not explain why the inconsistencies cannot be resolved and why alternative consistent readings are impossible, their interpretations fail to support the claim that ancient Chinese thinkers were not rational or had distinctly different rationalities. As no satisfactory methodology has been developed to defend an inconsistent reading of the *Zhuangzi* or any other ancient Chinese philosophical text, the claim that the *Zhuangzi* author(s) or other ancient thinkers reasoned in a different logic or represented an alternative rationality does not seem to be well-grounded.

References

Ames, R. T. (1992). Chinese rationality: An oxymoron? *Journal of Indian Council of Philosophical Research*, *9*(2), 95–119.

Ames, R. T. (1994). Review: A Daoist theory of Chinese philosophy: a philosophical interpretation by Chad Hansen. *Harvard Journal of Asiatic Studies*, *54*(2), 553–561.

Clarke, J. J. (2000). *The tao of the west: western transformations of Taoist thought*. New York: Routledge.

Coutinho, S. (2013). *An introduction to Daoist philosophies*. New York: Columbia University Press.

Davidson, D. (1973). On the very idea of a conceptual scheme. *Proceedings and addresses of the American Philosophical Association*, 47, 5–20.

Deng, X. (2003). Lun zhongxi huaiyilun de chayi. *Fujian Luntan: Renwen Shehui Kexue Ban*(1), 2–9.

Fleming, J. (1998). On translation of Taoist philosophical texts: Preservation of ambiguity and contradiction. *Journal of Chinese Philosophy*, *25*(1), 147–156.

Fraser, C. (1997). Review of classifying the Zhuangzi chapters, by Liu Xiaogan. *Asian Philosophy*, *7*(2), 155–159.

Graham, A. C. (1989). *Disputers of the Tao: Philosophical argument in ancient China*. La Salle, IL: Open Court.

Hall, D. L., & Ames, R. T. (1995). *Anticipating China: Thinking through the narratives of Chinese and Western culture*. Albany, NY: SUNY Press.

Hall, D. L., & Ames, R. T. (1998). *Thinking from the Han: Self, truth, and transcendence in Chinese and Western culture*. Albany, NY: SUNY Press.

Hansen, C. (1992). *A Daoist theory of Chinese thought: A philosophical interpretation*. New York, NY: Oxford University Press.

Hansen, C. (2010). A Dao of "Dao" in Zhuangzi. In V. H. Mair (Ed.), *Experimental essays on Zhuangzi* (pp. 23–55). Dunedin, FL: Three Pines Press.

Huang, H. (2007). *Zhuangzi sixiang de xiandai quanshi*. Taipei, Taiwan: Wunan tushu.

Klein, E. (2011). Were there Inner Chapters in the Warring States? A new examination of evidence about the Zhuangzi. *T'oung Pao*, *96*, 299–369.

Liu, S. -H. (1974). The use of analogy and symbolism in traditional Chinese philosophy. *Journal of Chinese Philosophy*, *1*(3–4), 313–338.

Liu, X. (1994). *Classifying the Zhuangzi chapters*. Ann Arbor, MI: Center for Chinese Studies, University of Michigan.
Loewe, M. (1993). *Early Chinese texts: A bibliographical guide*. Berkeley, CA: University of California, 1993.
Morrow, S. (2015). Review: An introduction to Daoist philosophies by Steve Coutinho. *Philosophy East and West, 65*(2), 623–625.
Nisbett, R. (2010). *The geography of thought: How Asians and Westerners think differently—and why*. New York: Simon and Schuster.
Richey, J. L. (2011). Review: Individualism in early China: Human agency and the self in thought and Politics, By Erica Fox Brindley. *Journal of Chinese Philosophy, 38*(3), 495–498.
Rošker, J. S. (2013). *Traditional Chinese philosophy and the paradigm of structure (Li)*. Newcastle upon Tyne, England: Cambridge Scholars Publishing.
Seok, B. (2007). Change, contradiction, and overconfidence: Chinese philosophy and cognitive peculiarities of Asians. *Dao, 6*(3), 221–237.
Van Norden, B. W. (1996). Competing interpretations of the inner chapters of the"Zhuangzi". *Philosophy East and West, 46*(2), 247–268.
Vrubliauskaitė, A. (2014). Language in Zhuangzi: How to say without saying? *International Journal of Area Studies, 9*(1), 75–90.
Wang, M., Yu, X., & McLean, G. F. (1997). *Beyond modernization: Chinese roots for global awareness*. Washington, DC: The Council for Research in Value and Philosophy.
Wang, Y. (2003). *Linguistic strategies in Daoist Zhuangzi and Chan Buddhism: The other way of speaking*. London: Routledge.
Watson, B. (2013). *The complete works of Zhuangzi*. New York: Columbia University Press.
Ye, S. (2005). Zhuangzi de wenhua jiexi: Qian gudian yu hou xiandai de shijie ronghe. Taiyuan, China: Shanxi renmin chubanshe.
Zhou, G. X. (1990). *Chinese traditional philosophy*. Beijing: Beijing Normal University Press.

Endnotes

1. Fu Jizhong and Zhou Shan characterize the Chinese way of thinking, stating "while Westerners attach great importance to deduction, the Chinese give priority to analogy" (Wang, Yu, & McLean, 1997, p. 53). For related discussions, see, for example, Clarke (2000, pp. 72–73) and Rošker (2013, pp. 32–35).
2. About the inconsistencies of the *Zhuangzi*, the standard account is that the contents of the "Outer Chapters" and "Miscellaneous Chapters" contradict those of the "Inner Chapters" (Watson, 2013, p. xxi). While many scholars believe that the "Inner Chapters" present a more-or-less consistent thought, some argue that the "Inner Chapters" contain inconsistencies as well (Liu, 1994, p. 25; Van Norden, 1996).
3. As an example, see Vrubliauskait (2014).
4. To quote it at length: "The comparison of several contemporary voices in the field defending different interpretations of this convoluted text is quite a treat. This adds depth to the phenomenological, hermeneutic approach of interpreting the *Zhuangzi* by keeping its paradoxes and contradictions intact. The author is not looking to explain away the plethora of limits and dead ends, or the vagueness and indeterminacy that skew the view of a concrete, existential goal. Keeping them intact, he stays true to the fluid, unpredictable spirit that characterizes the philosophical implications of the *Zhuangzi* text" (Morrow, 2015, p. 624).
5. This argument echoes Davidson's thesis that there is no such thing as a different conceptual scheme: if there is something radically different from our conceptual scheme, we would have no reason to say that it is a conceptual scheme at all (Davidson, 1973).
6. It should be noted that there are two kinds of inconsistencies attributed to the *Zhuangzi*. One is that the *Zhuangzi* contains inconsistent statements; the other is that the philosophy

of the *Zhuangzi* is intrinsically inconsistent. Many scholars of the *Zhuangzi*, however, do not clearly distinguish the two.

7. It is a methodological assumption in the sense that it can be reasonably made at an early stage of interpretation, that is, it does not ultimately depend on any particular interpretation of the text. For example, if someone assumes that the inner chapters (*nei pian*, 內篇) of the *Zhuangzi* present more consistent philosophical theory than other chapters, and he tries to reconstruct the philosophical theory of the inner chapters, then he begins an interpretive inquiry at a middle, not the earliest, stage—because he has already assumed certain interpretations of the *Zhuangzi*, such as the interpretation that the inner chapters contradict with other chapters. That a text is inconsistent is an interpretive conclusion, so it cannot be taken as a methodological assumption. Nonetheless, that a text is consistent can be a methodological assumption. I will give my arguments in the following passages.
8. See also Leong, 2016 in the same volume.
9. It should be emphasized that the assumption of consistency does not imply that every interpretation that reads a text consistently is plausible. If an interpretation imposes upon a text what this text does not say, it is problematic whether it reads the text as coherent or not. The assumption of consistency does not cause this problem, but reading the text without sufficient textual evidence does.

PART V

NONHUMAN

Part V focuses on reason and rationality in nonhuman systems. While Descartes famously denied that nonhuman animals could be rational, recent evidence shows that highly intelligent nonhuman beings behave in ways that could be interpreted as approximating rationality. Descartes also thought language to be an indicator of rationality, which raises the possibility that a machine would be rational if it could, for instance, pass the Turing test. Would attributing rationality to nonhuman systems be to commit the fallacy of personification? Or, rather, does recent data show that human beings are not alone in being the only ones capable of being rational? If machines are to be rational thinkers, how should they be designed? Can logic-based and probability-based approaches to artificial intelligence be used to understand the rationality of human (and perhaps also nonhuman) animals? And if we admit that some highly intelligent nonhuman animals are rational, must we admit that much simpler organisms are rational as well? Part V examines these questions regarding the rationality of nonhuman systems.

In Chapter 11, Hanti Lin integrates two main approaches to the study of reasoning in artificial systems. The logic-based approach to artificial intelligence presupposes a binary conception of belief, while the probability-based approach presupposes a probabilistic conception of belief. These two approaches concern two distinct kinds of cognitive systems, and Lin shows how a binary system and a probabilistic system can work together coherently as two subsystems of a single agent's cognitive system. The way they work together bridges the two approaches to artificial intelligence.

In Chapter 12, Tzu-Wei Hung focuses on descriptive-practical-procedural rationality, according to which one's action is described as rational if it is determined by internal processes that conform to logical or Bayesian rules. He argues that this rationality can be found in all organisms, including unicellular bacteria. To this end, he first reviews three seemingly true claims and explains why they lead to an inconsistency. He argues that we should reject one of the claims in light of the fact that recent microbiological data on *Escherichia coli* suggests that, to some extent, they satisfy the criteria for this type of rationality. Rather than concluding that humans and bacteria are therefore equally rational, Hung argues that rationality consists of varying degrees.

CHAPTER

11

Bridging the Logic-Based and Probability-Based Approaches to Artificial Intelligence

H. Lin

Department of Philosophy, University of California, Davis, CA, United States

11.1 INTRODUCTION

There are two ways of attributing belief to an agent: "she *believes* that proposition *A* is true" versus "she is *a% confident* that *A* is true." The second way is quantitative, and I will assume it be not only quantitative but also probabilistic. In other words, degrees of confidence, also called credences, should take probabilistic values. The first way is qualitative; in fact, it involves binary values: either one believes *A*, or one does not. So we have two ways to attribute belief: one binary and the other probabilistic.

If we take binary attribution of belief seriously, we will work on traditional epistemology and/or logic-based artificial intelligence (depending on whether we are interested in human agents and/or machine agents). Then we will want to know, for example, when an agent is supposed to believe which propositions, how she should revise her binary beliefs in response to new information, how she should infer from some of her binary beliefs to new defeasible conclusions, and how she should employ her binary beliefs to work out a plan for achieving a goal (Minker, 2000).

Similarly, if we take probabilistic attribution of belief seriously, we will work on Bayesian epistemology and/or probability-based artificial intelligence. Then we will want to know, for example, when an agent is supposed to have such and such probabilistic credence in such and such

Rationality. http://dx.doi.org/10.1016/B978-0-12-804600-5.00011-8

proposition, how she should revise her credences in response to new information, and how she should make a decision given her credences and desires (Pearl, 1988).

I take both kinds of belief attribution seriously, because I think that it is potentially advantageous for an agent to possess both kinds of belief, as I will explain in Section 11.2. If so, then we need an epistemological theory for agents who possess both kinds of belief. And I will take a first step to develop such a theory in Sections 11.3–11.6.

11.2 TWO SYSTEMS TO SWITCH BETWEEN

Consider an agent whose belief can be modeled by probabilistic credences. Let $\mathbb{P}$ be her (subjective) probability function; namely, she is $a\%$ confident in A if $\mathbb{P}(A) = a\%$. Although the agent already possesses the probabilistic credences that $\mathbb{P}$ assigns, those credences might not be "usable" immediately. For example, given that $\mathbb{P}(A) = .9274...$ and $\mathbb{P}(A \mid E) = .0361...$, it does not mean that these credences have already had an impact on the agent's behavior or thought. For these credences might be stored in a way that requires them to be decoded before they can have any impact on behavior or thought. Such a decoding process might correspond to, for example, retrieval of memory or deliberation over the evidence available. Partially decoded results, such as those represented by "$\mathbb{P}(A) \in [.9,1]$" and "$\mathbb{P}(A \mid E) \in [0, .1]$," can be more or less easily obtained. But the agent might need to have more digits decoded before those credences can have any significant impact, such as the act of preparing for going grocery shopping tonight, or the decision to invest in stock X rather than stock Y. Even if enough digits of the probability values have been decoded, it still takes time for them to actually generate significant impacts. For such a generation process might involve (conscious or unconscious) computation of probability intervals in order to estimate the relevant expected utilities.

When the agent is solving a relatively simple problem—say, about grocery shopping rather than about stock investment—then it might be advantageous for the agent to possess and process the binary representations of belief. Suppose the following:

> A says: "The grocery store is still open."
> E says: "It's already passed 7 pm." (Oops! Too late!)

Further that the agent believes that A is true, and believes that A is false given that E is true. She recognizes that she is uncertain, namely that $\mathbb{P}(A)$ and $\mathbb{P}(A \mid B)$ do not take extremal values 0 or 1. To solve this particular problem, her brain might just work with her binary beliefs without pursuing the digits in $\mathbb{P}(A) = .9274...$ and $\mathbb{P}(A \mid E) = .0361...$ And this might be advantageous to her. If the agent implements a suitable planning algorithm that makes use of those binary beliefs (rather than probabilistic credences), it might take a relatively short time for her to arrive at a quite reasonable solution, such as: "check the time; if it's already passed 7 pm, stay at home; if not, decide whether to rush to the grocery store or take my time."

If a problem can be solved by a computation process that is more efficient because it works with the simpler, binary representations, then let the problem be solved that way. Reserve probabilistic representations for harder problems, such as those about stock investment. The agent needs the system that uses binary beliefs and implements something like classical planning, and she also needs the system that uses probabilistic credences and implements something like maximization of expected utility.[1] The challenge for the agent is to switch between those two systems aptly.

The idea that an agent can, or does, have two different systems for problem solving is not new. Kahneman (2011) argues that human beings have two systems. What he calls System 1 is fast, automatic, frequent, and emotional. System 2 is slow, effortful, infrequent, and sophisticated. Recognition of those two systems actually opens the doors to multiple systems.[2] Let the fastest system be System 1.0, which would probably be based solely on one's intuitive responses. Let the slowest, most sophisticated system be 2.0, which we may identify with the Bayesian ideal of probabilistic reasoning and maximization of expected utility. The system that uses binary beliefs and implements classical planning is a system in between, which we may call System 1.5. This intermediate system is slower and more sophisticated than the intuition-based System 1.0, because it requires reasoning from one's old binary beliefs to new binary beliefs in a way governed by logics, perhaps classical logic for conclusive reasoning plus a suitable nonmonotonic logic for defeasible reasoning. But this intermediate system is faster and less sophisticated than the probability-based System 2.0, because it works with relatively coarse-grained representations of belief, which are binary rather than probabilistic.

My focus here will be placed on the relationship between Systems 1.5 and 2.0. There must be some other systems in between (called Systems 1.6 or 1.9 if you wish), which might involve, for example, both one's believing that $A \vee B$ is true and one's taking A to be more probable than B, without taking "how much more probable" into account. My investigation into Systems 1.5 and 2.0 is intended to serve as a case study, which I hope to be instructive for obtaining a clearer idea about the intermediate Systems 1.6–1.9 and their relations.

The challenge for the agent is to switch between Systems 1.5 and 2.0 aptly, as we have noted. The challenge for us is different, and this is a quite unexplored area of research. There are questions about the mechanism that triggers the switch from System 1.5 to 2.0 or the other way round:

Conceptual Question: What does it mean for a switching mechanism to be apt?

Normative Question: When should the agent switch?

Computational Question: How to efficiently implement an apt switching mechanism, at least in a way that costs less than persistent adherence to one and the same system?

I am unable to answer these questions here, nor do I know any work devoted to answering any of those questions. The reason, I think, is that there is a big question that has to be answered first.

The ability to switch between the two systems presupposes that the agent can have both of the systems coherently. Is it OK to have System 1.5 in which one believes that A is false and, simultaneously, have System 2.0 in which $\mathbb{P}(A) \geq .99$? No, it is not OK. I would add: it is not rationally permissible to have both systems that way.

That is an easy question. Here is a more difficult one: Given that one has credence $\mathbb{P}(A) \geq .99$, is it always rationally required to believe A? No, thanks to the lottery paradox (Kyburg, 1961). Consider a lottery that is fair and has 100 tickets, and the agent knows that for sure. Now consider the following propositions:

Ticket no. 1 will lose.

Ticket no. 2 will lose.

⋮

Ticket no. 100 will lose.

One of those one hundred tickets will win (ie, not lose).

Then the agent assigns probabilities of least .99 to all the above propositions. (To be precise, she assigns 1 to the last proposition and .99 to all the others). But the above propositions are jointly inconsistent, so the agent is not rationally required to believe each of them or so it is typically assumed in logic-based artificial intelligence. In general, for any threshold $t < 1$, an agent is not always rationally required to believe every proposition to which she assigns a credence $\geq t$. Just use a fair lottery with n tickets such that $(n-1)/n \geq t$.

What we need is a systematic theory that answers to questions of the following form:

The Big Question: Given that one has System 2.0 with such and such credences, is one rationally permissible to have System 1.5 with such and such binary beliefs?

Answers to the Big Question constrain answers to the Normative Question about the mechanism that triggers the switch. If an agent should switch between System 2.0 with such and such probabilistic credences on the one hand, and System 1.5 with such and such binary beliefs on the other hand, then the latter has to be rationally permissible given the former.

The rest of this paper is devoted to taking a first step toward answering the Big Question.

11.3 MODELING SYSTEMS 1.5 AND 2.0

To model the two systems, suppose that the agent needs to distinguish a number of mutually exclusive possibilities for her present purposes. Call those possibilities possible worlds and let them form a set W. Note that a possible world w in W need not be very specific about every imaginable detail of how things might be; w can be, for example, an assignment of truth values only to the atomic sentences that are relevant to the agent's present purposes. A proposition (relevant to the agent's present purposes) is a subset of W; a proposition is true at a world if it contains that world. Assume, for simplification, that W is finite.

The more sophisticated System 2.0 contains a belief representation based on subjective probabilities. A probabilistic credal state (relevant to the agent's present purposes) is a probability distribution over W, that is, a function $\mathbb{P} : W \rightarrow [0,1]$ such that $\sum_{w \in W} \mathbb{P}(w) = 1$. If the agent were to have probabilistic credal state $\mathbb{P}$, then the probabilistic credence that the agent would have in proposition A is defined by $\mathbb{P}(A) =_{df} \sum_{w \in A} \mathbb{P}(w)$. Assume that learning follows conditionalization. That is, if the agent having $\mathbb{P}$ were to receive new information that E is true, and if $\mathbb{P}(E) > 0$, then she would come to have $\mathbb{P}_E$, which is defined by conditionalization on E:

$$\mathbb{P}_E(X) =_{df} \frac{\mathbb{P}(X \cap E)}{\mathbb{P}(E)}.$$

$\mathbb{P}_E$ is undefined if $\mathbb{P}(E) = 0$.

The less sophisticated but faster System 1.5 is supposed to contain the propositions that one believes, called binary beliefs, as the qualitative counterparts of probabilistic credences. But, since we assume that change of probabilistic credences follows conditionalization, a probability distribution represents not only one's belief but also one's policy of belief change. So the qualitative counterparts of probability distributions should represent not only one's binary beliefs, but also one's policies for changing binary beliefs. Such qualitative representations are required for building System 1.5. And I propose that they are just something that can represent nonmonotonic/defeasible reasoning, which I make precise below.

A consequence operator (relevant to the agent's present purposes) is a function $\mathbb{C}$ that maps each proposition E to a set $\mathbb{C}(E)$ of propositions, taken as the defeasible consequences of E. Formally, $\mathbb{C}$ is a function from $\wp(W)$ to $\wp(\wp(W))$. For example, let:

B: Twitty is a bird.
F: Twitty can fly.
P: Twitty is a penguin.

Then consider a consequence operator with the following properties:

$$F \in \mathbb{C}(B).$$
$$\neg F \in \mathbb{C}(B \wedge P).$$

This particular $\mathbb{C}$ allows one to infer from "being a bird" to "being able to fly", and infer from "being a bird and a penguin" to "being not able to fly." In general, $\mathbb{C}$ licenses defeasible inference from E to all and only the propositions in $\mathbb{C}(E)$. That is, $\mathbb{C}$ allows one to draw A as a defeasible consequence of E iff $A \in \mathbb{C}(E)$.

A consequence operator $\mathbb{C}$ guides what propositions to believe: given information E, to believe all and only the defeasible consequences of E that $\mathbb{C}$ licenses. That is, to believe all and only the propositions in $\mathbb{C}(E)$. Given no information, that is, given the most uninformative T ($=_{df} W$), $\mathbb{C}$ tells one to believe just the propositions in $\mathbb{C}$(T). Consequence operator $\mathbb{C}$ also guides revision of binary beliefs. Suppose that one's binary beliefs are persistently guided by $\mathbb{C}$ when one receives a sequence of successive information E_1, E_2, E_3, etc. Then the set of one's binary beliefs will start as $\mathbb{C}$(T), then change to $\mathbb{C}(E_1)$, then to $\mathbb{C}(E_1 \cap E_2)$, then to $\mathbb{C}(E_1 \cap E_2 \cap E_3)$, etc., assuming that information accumulates without inconsistency. So, a consequence operator guides what binary beliefs to have, and it also guides how to revise those binary beliefs.

When an agent's binary beliefs are persistently guided by one and the same consequence operator $\mathbb{C}$, this agent can be equivalently understood as revising $\mathbb{C}$ systematically in response to new information. To be precise, suppose that the agent starts with $\mathbb{C}$ and then receives information E. Then, what consequences would she draw given further information X? She would infer all and only the propositions in $\mathbb{C}(E \cap X)$. Define a new consequence operator $\mathbb{C}_E$ as follows:

$$\mathbb{C}_E(X) =_{df} \mathbb{C}(E \cap X).$$

So, after receipt of information E, she can be understood as being prepared to apply the new consequence operator $\mathbb{C}_E$ to the next information X. Receipt of information E prompts change in one's binary beliefs from $\mathbb{C}$(T) to $\mathbb{C}(E)$, and it also prompts change in one's defeasible reasoning policy from $\mathbb{C}$ to $\mathbb{C}_E$. Call $\mathbb{C}_E$ the result of conditionalizing $\mathbb{C}$ on E, in comparison to $\mathbb{P}_E$ as the result of conditionalizing $\mathbb{P}$ on E.

In sum: suppose that an agent has System 1.5, which contains a consequence operator $\mathbb{C}$, and that she has System 2.0, which contains a probability distribution $\mathbb{P}$. They represent one's belief as follows. For each proposition $A \subseteq W$:

- the agent believes that A is true if $A \in \mathbb{C}(\mathrm{T})$;
- the agent is $a\%$ confident that A is true if $\mathbb{P}(A) = a\%$.

Both systems are responsive to receipt of information E:

- $\mathbb{C}$ will then be replaced by $\mathbb{C}_E$;
- $\mathbb{P}$ will then be replaced by $\mathbb{P}_E$.

11.4 WHAT RATIONALITY PERMITS

Let $\mathrm{R}(\mathbb{P},\mathbb{C})$ mean that, given that one has System 2.0 with $\mathbb{P}$, it is rationally permissible for one to have System 1.5 with $\mathbb{C}$. The goal of this section is to list some plausible axioms to constrain relation R.

Let $\mathcal{P}$ be the set of all probability distributions over W. Let $\mathcal{C}$ be the set of all "reasonable" consequence operators over W. The term 'reasonable' is a place holder that invites us to give a list of axioms that constrain the consequence operators that are to be judged reasonable. We will do that in the next section. Here are some quite basic constraints on relation R:

Domain. $\mathrm{R} \subseteq \mathcal{P} \times \mathcal{C}$.

Consistency. If $\mathrm{R}(\mathbb{P},\mathbb{C})$, then $\bot \notin \mathbb{C}(\mathrm{T})$.

Probability 1/2 Rule. If $\mathrm{R}(\mathbb{P},\mathbb{C})$ then, for all propositions $A, E \subseteq W$, if $A \in \mathbb{C}(E)$ then $\mathbb{P}(A \mid E) > 1/2$.

Probability 1 Rule. If $\mathbb{P}(w) = 1$, then:

- for some $\mathbb{C} \in \mathcal{C}$, $\mathrm{R}(\mathbb{P},\mathbb{C})$ and $\{w\} \in \mathbb{C}(\mathrm{T})$;
- for each $\mathbb{C} \in \mathcal{C}$, if $\mathrm{R}(\mathbb{P},\mathbb{C})$ then $\{w\} \in \mathbb{C}(\mathrm{T})$.

Nonskepticism. It is not the case that, whenever $\mathrm{R}(\mathbb{P},\mathbb{C})$ and $\{w\} \in \mathbb{C}(\mathrm{T})$, then $\mathbb{P}(w) = 1$.

Suppose that the agent has an underlying probability distribution $\mathbb{P}$. Upon receipt of new information E such that $\mathbb{P}(E) > 0$, we want to find the consequence operators that she is rationally permitted to "settle with," namely, to incorporate into her System 1.5. There are two ways to find them.

Probabilistic, Diligent Way: Start from $\mathbb{P}$. Conditionalize $\mathbb{P}$ on E to obtain $\mathbb{P}_E$. Then find a $\mathbb{C}' \in \mathcal{C}$ such that $\mathrm{R}(\mathbb{P}_E,\mathbb{C}')$. Settle with $\mathbb{C}'$.

Binary, Easy Way: Start from $\mathbb{P}$. Then find a $\mathbb{C} \in \mathcal{C}$ such that $\mathrm{R}(\mathbb{P},\mathbb{C})$. Then conditionalize $\mathbb{C}$ on E to obtain $\mathbb{C}_E$. Settle with $\mathbb{C}_E$.

The binary, easy way is "sound" if it only produces things that can be produced by the probabilistic, diligent way; namely:

Forward Tracking. Whenever $\mathrm{R}(\mathbb{P},\mathbb{C})$ then $\mathrm{R}(\mathbb{P}_E,\mathbb{C}_E)$, for any new information $E \subseteq W$ such that $\mathbb{P}(E) > 0$.

The binary, easy way is "complete" if it can produce everything that can be produced by the probabilistic, diligent way, namely:

Backward Tracking. Whenever $\mathrm{R}(\mathbb{P}_E,\mathbb{C}')$ then $\mathrm{R}(\mathbb{P},\mathbb{C})$ for some $\mathbb{C}$ such that $\mathbb{C}_E = \mathbb{C}'$.

Both of the tracking conditions hold if what the easy way can produce is exactly the same as what the diligent way can produce. We can express this in an elegant way. Define the set of consequence operators that are R-related to $\mathbb{P}$ as follows:

$$\mathrm{R}(\mathbb{P}) =_{df} \{\mathbb{C} \in C : \mathrm{R}(\mathbb{P},\mathbb{C})\}.$$

To conditionalize a set S of consequence operators on E is to conditionalize each member on E, respectively:

$$S_E =_{df} \{\mathbb{C}_E : \mathbb{C} \in S\}.$$

So we have

$$\begin{aligned}(\mathrm{R}(\mathbb{P}))_E &= \{\mathbb{C}_E : \mathbb{C} \in \mathrm{R}(\mathbb{P})\} \\ &= \{\mathbb{C}_E : \mathbb{C} \in C \text{ and } \mathrm{R}(\mathbb{P},\mathbb{C})\}\end{aligned}$$

Then the forward and backward tracking conditions can be jointly expressed in an elegant form:

Forward + Backward Tracking. $\mathrm{R}(\mathbb{P}_E) = \mathrm{R}(\mathbb{P})_E$, for any new information $E \subseteq W$ such that $\mathbb{P}(E) > 0$.

11.5 REASONABLE NONMONOTONIC LOGIC?

In the nonmonotonic logic literature, it is usually assumed that a reasonable consequence operator should satisfy the following axioms, where $X \vdash_{\mathbb{C}} Y$ abbreviates $Y \in \mathbb{C}(X)$:

Reflexivity

$A \vdash_{\mathbb{C}} A.$

Left Weakening

$$A \vdash_{\mathbb{C}} B \text{ and } B \subseteq C \Rightarrow A \vdash_{\mathbb{C}} C.$$

And

$$A \vdash_{\mathbb{C}} B \text{ and } A \vdash_{\mathbb{C}} C \Rightarrow A \vdash_{\mathbb{C}} B \wedge C.$$

Or

$$A \vdash_{\mathbb{C}} B \text{ and } C \vdash_{\mathbb{C}} B \Rightarrow A \vee C \vdash_{\mathbb{C}} B.$$

Cautious Monotonicity

$$A \vdash_{\mathbb{C}} B \text{ and } A \vdash_{\mathbb{C}} C \Rightarrow A \wedge C \vdash_{\mathbb{C}} B.$$

The above axioms are jointly called axiom system P, where P stands for "preferential" because of a sound and complete representation in terms of preferential orders (Kraus, Lehmann, & Magidor 1990). Let $\mathbb{C}_{\text{Pref}}$ be the set of consequence operators (over *W*) that satisfy this axiom system.

Another standard axiom is Rational Monotonicity:

$$A \vdash_{\mathbb{C}} B, A \nvdash_{\mathbb{C}} C \Rightarrow A \wedge C \vdash_{\mathbb{C}} B.$$

Axiom system P plus Rational Monotonicity is called axiom system R, where R stands for "rankable" because of a sound and complete representation in terms of rankable orders (Kraus et al., 1990). Let $\mathbb{C}_{\text{Rank}}$ be the set of consequence operators (over *W*) that satisfy this axiom system.

11.6 MAIN RESULTS

Let me start with a negative result:

Proposition 1. There is no relation R that satisfies all the constraints listed in Section 11.4, given that $\mathbb{C} = \mathbb{C}_{\text{Rank}}$.

This is an immediate corollary of the theorem in Lin & Kelly (2013). Fortunately, a positive result can be obtained by weakening the nonmonotonic logic from "Rankable" to "Preferential:"

Proposition 2. There is a relation R that satisfies all the constraints listed in Section 4, given that $\mathbb{C} = \mathbb{C}_{\text{Pref}}$.

Proof. Let > be an order over the set *W* of possible worlds. Understand $w > u$ as saying that world w is more plausible world u. Define the set of >-maximal elements (ie, most plausible worlds) given *E* as follows:

$$\max(>, E) =_{df} \{w \in E : \neg \exists u \in E (u > w)\}.$$

Then, let $\mathbb{C}^{>}$ be the consequence operator that licenses defeasible inference from E to the conclusion that one of the most plausible worlds is true, namely, from E to max(>, E). To be more specific, let $\mathbb{C}^{>}$ license defeasible inference from E to all and only the logical consequences of max(>, E). In symbols:

$$\mathbb{C}^{>}(E) =_{df} \{A \subseteq W : \max(>, E) \subseteq A\}.$$

It is a well-known result in nonmonotonic logic that whenever > is a strict partial order, then $\mathbb{C}^{>}$ satisfies axiom system P, that is, $\mathbb{C}^{>} \in C_{\text{Pref}}$ (Shoham, 1987; Kraus et al., 1990). Now, understand relative plausibility relation > from a probabilistic perspective: roughly, $w > u$ iff w is at least k-times as probable as u, where k is a large real number. To be more precise, for each probability distribution $\mathbb{P}$ and each threshold $k > 1$, define the strict partial order $>^{\mathbb{P},k}$ as follows:

$$w >^{\mathbb{P},k} u \text{ iff } \mathbb{P}(w) \geq k \cdot \mathbb{P}(u).$$

Then use this strict partial order $>^{\mathbb{P},k}$ to generate a consequence relation in the way defined above: $\mathbb{C}^{>^{\mathbb{P},k}}$, which is a cumbersome notation and will be denoted simply by $\mathbb{C}^{\mathbb{P},k}$. So, in sum, we have

$$\mathbb{C}^{\mathbb{P},k}(E) = \{A \subseteq W : \max(>^{\mathbb{P},k}, E) \subseteq A\}.$$

As the last step, define relation R^k as follows:

$$\mathrm{R}^k(\mathbb{P}, \mathbb{C}) \text{ iff } \mathbb{C} = \mathbb{C}^{\mathbb{P},k}.$$

It is a routine to verify that relation R^k satisfies all the constraints listed in Section 4, except possibly the Probability 1/2 Rule. Let $k > |W| - 1$, then the Probability 1/2 Rule is guaranteed to be satisfied. This proves the proposition.

Discussion. R^k has the property that every $\mathbb{P}$ is related to a unique $\mathbb{C}$. This means: R^k requires that, given any probabilistic credal state, there is only one rationally permissible consequence operator. Well, this seems quite strong. This bug is easy to fix. One might be undecided about which precise k-value to use, except that it has to be greater than $|W| - 1$. In that case, just use an interval (a, b) of k-values:

$$\mathrm{R}^{(a,b)} =_{df} \bigcup_{a<k<b} \mathrm{R}^k.$$

It is routine to verify that, whenever $|W| - 1 < a < b$, then $\mathrm{R}^{(a,b)}$ satisfies all the constraints listed in Section 4.

11.7 CONCLUDING REMARKS

This is just a prolegomena to a general theory that answers to the Big Question. There is still a long way toward answering the Conceptual, Normative, and Computational Questions about the mechanism that triggers the switch between Systems 1.5 and 2.0. Answers to those four questions require collaboration among philosophers, logicians, computer scientists, and psychologists. I hope I have achieved the goal to this paper: to articulate those four questions, to suggest that those questions are really important and deserve more attention, and to take a first step toward answering those questions, at least to give some evidence that those questions are answerable.

Acknowledgments

I am indebted to Jui-Lin Lee for his detailed comments on an earlier draft of this paper. I am also indebted to the School of Philosophy at the Australian National University, where this work was completed during my stay in 2013–14—I especially thank Alan Hájek for the numerous discussions with him.

References

Evans, J. S. (2008). Dual-processing accounts of reasoning, judgment, and social cognition. *Annual Review of Psychology, 59*, 255–278.

Kahneman, D. (2011). *Thinking, fast and slow*. New York: Farrar, Straus and Giroux.

Kraus, S., Lehmann, D., & Magidor, M. (1990). Nonmonotonic reasoning, preferential models and cumulative logics. *Artificial Intelligence, 44*, 167–207.

Kyburg, H. (1961). *Probability and the logic of rational belief*. Middletown, CT: Wesleyan University Press.

Lin, H., & Kelly, K.T. (2013). Comments on Leitgeb's stability theory of belief. In *Logic across the university: Foundations and applications, Studies in logic: Vol. 47*. London: College Publications.

Minker, J. (Ed.). (2000). *Logic-based artificial intelligence*. Boston, MA: Kluwer Academic Publishers.

Pearl, J. (1988). *Probabilistic reasoning in intelligent systems: Networks of plausible inference*. San Mateo, CA: Morgan Kaufmann.

Russell, S., & Norvig, P. (2010). *Artificial intelligence: A modern approach* (3rd ed.). Englewood Cliffs, NJ: Prentice Hall.

Shoham, Y. (1987). A semantical approach to nonmonotonic logics. In M. Ginsberg (Ed.), *Readings in nonmonotonic reasoning*. Los Altos, CA: Morgan Kauffman.

Endnotes

1. See Russell and Norvig, 2010 for an overview of AI planning theory and theory of expected utility maximization.
2. This view is usually referred to as a dual process theory. Evans (2008) for a review.

CHAPTER

12

Rationality and *Escherichia Coli*

T.-W. Hung

Institute of European and American Studies Academia Sinica, Taipei, Taiwan

12.1 INTRODUCTION

Rationality, generally speaking, has long been viewed as a capacity exclusively belonging to the human species, according to the Western tradition. This view was proposed by Aristotle[1] and followed by Descartes[2] and Kant. This is because only human beings have language and reason. In his *Lectures on Anthropology* (Kant, 2013, p. 7, 127), Kant holds that "The fact that the human being can have the representation 'I' raises him infinitely above all the other beings on earth. By this he is a person...that is, a being altogether different in rank and dignity from things, such as irrational animals...." However, if rationality is such a unique characteristic and is shared among human beings, it should likely be identified by many cultures in history, as well. However, in fact, there is no such tradition in the East. First, unlike the terms "language" and "mind," there was no direct translation of "rationality" in the Japanese, Korean, and Chinese languages before modernization in the 19th century. Second, although there are relevant words for "soul," "thought," and "intelligence," these concepts usually do not categorically distinguish humans from other creatures. In Buddhism, all sentient beings may have a Buddhist nature and therefore can attain enlightenment. Unlike in Christianity, all creatures are equal. In the Chinese classic *Shang Shu*, animals do possess intelligence, although, "of all creatures man is the most highly endowed" (*Great Declaration I*). Humans and other animals differ in degree rather than in kind. In *Mengzi*, Mencius also says, "that whereby man differs from the lower animals is but small" (*Li-Lou II*). If a man withdraws himself from morality, he literally becomes a beast. In other words, there is no consensus about the uniqueness of human rationality according to the Eastern tradition.

Rationality. http://dx.doi.org/10.1016/B978-0-12-804600-5.00012-X

More specifically, in what ways might rationality not be exclusive to humans? Inquiry on rationality includes two main aspects: descriptive study concerns what rationality actually is, while normative study concerns what it should ideally be. Regarding the descriptive aspect, rationality can be divided into theoretical and practical. The former is about what it is rational to believe, while the latter is about how it is rational to act (Mele & Rawling, 2004). Practical rationality further decomposes into behavioral (if the agent's external actions conform to certain criteria, such as maximin or fitness) and procedural (if the actions are determined by internal processes conforming to logical or Bayesian rules). Scientists of animal cognition have frequently reported that nonhuman animals also exhibit behavioral rationality in various problem-solving cases, including tools used by New Caledonian crows (Hunt, 1996; Klump, van der Wal, St. Clair, & Rutz, 2015; Logan, Breen, Taylor, Gray, & Hoppitt, 2015; Weir, Chappell, & Kacelnik, 2002; Wimpenny, Weir, & Kacelnik, 2011) and Goffin cockatoos (Auersperg et al., 2012, 2014; O'Hara, Auersperg, Bugnyar, & Huber, 2015). Conversely, procedural rationality is more difficult to observe. It is unclear whether nonhuman animals may possibly have procedural rationality, let alone nonanimal organisms. This chapter focuses on *descriptive-practical-procedural* rationality (rationality, hereafter, except where otherwise stated). That is, one's action is described as rational if it is determined by internal processes that conform to logical or Bayesian rules.

This chapter aims to argue for the degree of rationality: organisms exhibiting different levels of computational power for reasoning and decision-making also exhibit different levels of rationality. This view applies to *Escherichia coli,* too. To this end, Section 12.2 reviews three claims and argues that although each of these claims seems to hold, they cannot all be true at once and will lead to an inconsistency. Section 12.3 explains the reasons to reject the claim that *E. coli* are not a type of creature that can be rational or irrational. By appealing to recent microbiological data, this section examines in what ways *E. coli* is capable of reasoning, decision-making, and cross-cell communication. Section 12.4 evaluates and replies to some possible objections. The final section concludes that humans and *E. coli* do have different levels of rationality.

12.2 THREE THESES AND THEIR INCONSISTENCY

Each of the following three claims seems to be true, but together they lead to an inconsistency. We review the three claims in turn.

(1) *E. coli* are computational systems in a nontrivial sense.
(2) *E. coli* are not the types of creatures that can be rational or irrational.

(3) Rationality is a matter of computational facts in that nontrivial sense, and organisms of the same computation are creatures that can be rational or irrational.

To evaluate claim (1), one needs to know what the term "computational" means. Piccinini (2007, 2008a) distinguishes three main senses in which a system can be computational: (i) a system's behavior is modeled by the output of a computational system, but the target system itself need not be computational (eg, meteorological systems); (ii) a system's internal states are modeled by a computational system's internal states, and the system need not be computational either (eg, bodily movements simulated by a forward model); and (iii) a system's behavior is described by its own computational processes and their properties. According to Piccinini (2007), only computation in this strict sense is nontrivial and relevant to the philosophy of mind. Piccinini (2008b; Piccinini & Bahar, 2013) maintains that not all neural cells perform computation in the (iii) sense, but in neural cells that do compute, their computation falls under three categories: (iiia) classical computation, which is realized in networks of logic gates; (iiib) nonclassical computation, which transforms input into output through continuous dynamics that cannot be divided into intermediate steps; and (iiic) sui generis computation, which cannot be captured by both the mathematics of digital and analog computation but requires specially designed mathematical tools. Piccinini and Bahar, 2013 argue that as the human brain's neural spike trains are constituted by discrete spikes but graded as continuous signals, the activity of brain neurons can only be computational in the (iiic) sense.

E. coli cells evolve with no nerve systems but can nevertheless be computational in either the (iiia) or (iiic) sense, depending on what stance one takes in describing their internal processes. On the one hand, an *E. coli* bacterium has various protein-made receptors on its surface to detect nutrients and toxins in the environment. When nutrients are detected, chemical signals from receptors are sent to the biochemical mechanism inside the cell in which a lock-and-key mechanism is used to recognize various types of amino acids (Liu et al., 2006). Only chemical substrates that fit into the binding site inside the cell lead to reactions. This site functions as a logic gate with variable input sensitivity, and the output of the chemical reaction is identified by mechanical procedures, which is a typical example of Turing's computability (Magnasco, 1997; Shapiro, 2012). Thus *E. coli* do compute in the (iiia) sense. On the other hand, if one holds that the distribution/transmission of input is also part of the computational procedures, then the floating of chemical substrates inside the *E. coli* cells is not discrete but continuous. This feature resembles Piccinini and Bahar, 2013 analysis on neural cells and can only be captured by a sui generis computation (iiic). Accordingly, regardless of whether (iiia) or (iiic) is adopted in explaining *E.coli*'s internal processing, claim (1) is true.[3]

Claim (2) seems to hold. It was assumed in the past that not all creatures, but only a small set of species, are rational beings. Aristotle and Descartes believed that the human species is the only member of that set. However, recently it has been reported that some highly intelligent animals, such as chimpanzees (Povinelli & Vonk, 2006; Tomasello & Call, 2006), dolphins (Tschudin, 2006), and birds (Dretske, 2006), behave in ways that would be regarded as more or less behaviorally rational. These reports show that the size of the set is still under debate, but humans are no longer the sole members of this set. However, although it is difficult to draw a line distinguishing behaviorally rational beings from those who are not, unicellular bacteria are less likely to be borderline cases and are not the types of creatures that can be behaviorally rational or irrational. Likewise, unicellular bacteria are less likely to be procedurally rational. Procedural rationality is more difficult to observe than behavioral rationality, and there is no direct evidence showing that *E. coli* bacteria are behaviorally rational. Therefore, it seems plausible to hold that *E. coli* cannot be rational or irrational in both behavioral and procedural senses. Therefore, claim (2) is true.

Claim (3) seems to also be true, but requires elaboration. Claim (3) contains two clauses. The former clause may have two interpretations. For those believing that the mind is computational in the (iiia) sense (Crane, 2003; Fodor, 2008; Gallistel & King, 2009; Schneider, 2011), procedural rationality amounts to the properties of the collective behavior of logical gates, while for those believing that brain neurons are computational in the (iiic) sense (Ermentrout & Terman, 2010; Piccinini & Bahar, 2013), procedural rationality involves the processing of inputs in a sui generis way. However, no matter which reading is taken, one must be consistent with both brain cells and *E. coli* cells. This is because, although brain cells rely on electrochemical reactions and *E.coli* cells on biochemical reaction, they share similar computational features: their information processing is discrete but their information transmission is continuous. Regardless of whether (iiia) or (iiic) is adopted, procedural rationality is a matter of computational facts in the (iii) sense. Thus claim (3)'s first clause is true.

The second clause seems to hold, too. It is an overgeneralization to claim that all computational systems can be procedurally rational or irrational. Both Block (1980) and Dennett (1987) describe the processing chips in a vending machine in ways satisfying computation in the (iiia) sense. However, a vending machine cannot operate without a human designer (to initial the program) and an instructor (to give commands by pressing a button). This machine cannot be rational or irrational because it is not autonomous. Autonomy is necessary to a rational agent in both human and robotic domains. Not only do Wallace's (1999) three concepts of human rational agency (agents motivated by desire, by higher order disposition, and by volition) involve autonomy, agent-based AI scientist Russell (1997, 2014) also regards the rational agent as an automated entity that can be defined through agent function $f\colon O^* \rightarrow A$, (where O^* is the set of observable sequences and A is the set of performable actions), which is evaluated by its performance that the designer defined. Therefore, while autonomy does not imply rationality, rationality requires autonomy.

Unlike vending machines, organisms are autonomous adaptive systems. They are autonomous because their behaviors can be driven by their own internal states (hunger for nutrition or any essential elements of life). They are adaptive because their behaviors are intended for surviving, and scientists have reported that even prokaryotes display high intelligence in solving environmental challenges (Richardson, 2012, 2013). If one holds that the human mind meets (iiia) and can be procedurally rational or irrational, then the second clause holds. After all, if we admit that organisms with n number of logical gates can be procedurally rational or irrational (eg, humans), so can those with n–1, n–2,... logical gates. Therefore, an organism with only a few logical gates (*E. coli*) can also be procedurally rational or irrational. Alternatively, if what one believes is not (iiia) but (iiic), then the second clause holds because the size of the network only affects the power of computation (I return to this point in the next section). Hence, because both clauses hold, so does claim (3).

However, if (3) is true, from (1) and (3) one can derive that *E. coli* could be rational, which contradicts (2). Therefore, an inconsistency occurs.

12.3 POSSIBLE SOLUTIONS AND *E. COLI'S* RATIONALITY

Due to the conjunction of the three claims leads to an inconsistency, at least one claim should be false. Here, seven options are available to solve the inconsistency:

a. reject claim (1)
b. reject claim (2)
c. reject claim (3)
d. reject claims (1), (2), and (3)
e. reject claims (1) and (2)
f. reject claims (2) and (3)
g. reject claims (3) and (1)

However, claim (1) is a plain fact if a specific sense of computation is defined [eg, either (iiia) or (iiib)]. Because it cannot be rejected, options *a*, *d*, *e*, and *g* are ruled out. We next examine whether claim (3) is deniable by taking a further look at the notion of rationality.

Skeptics may argue that claim (3) is false because its second clause is true only if one accepts that rationality is gradually aggregated, where complex rationality is continuously evolved from more primitive rationality (known as the accumulation view). However, one needs not accept this view. Rather, rationality can emerge only if a certain threshold of computational power is met (known as the emergence view). Hence, when the emergence view is chosen, an organism can be computational without being rational or irrational. In this case, claim (3) is false.

A quick reply is as follows. There has been no decisive evidence yet showing whether either the emergence or accumulation view is correct, but there are reasons why the latter is better: broadly speaking, rationality has a close relationship to intelligence (though how the two concepts are read as well as how they are related remain the subject of disagreement among researchers).[4] If intelligence varies in degree, then it is likely that rationality does too. In microbiology, for example, the shared physiology and behavioral traits of a eukaryotic living system may enable some primitive form of intelligence (Calvo & Baluška, 2015; LeDoux, 2012). In AI, Rodney Brooks' (2014) behavior-based robotic system is labeled as exhibiting "insect-level intelligence" (Adams & Aizawa, 2009; Dejohn, 2004; Pfeifer, 2001) as opposed to "human-level intelligence." In both natural and artificial cases, there is a continuous progression from simpler to more complex intelligence. Because intelligence is this way, complex rationality is likely to aggregate from simpler forms as well.

In contrast, if rationality emerges at a certain point, then some sufficient condition must be satisfied at this point. However, whether there is such a sufficient condition of human rationality and whether it is identifiable are themselves subjects of a long debate (Foley, 1990; Fumerton, 1990; Ye, 2015). Even if we can satisfy this condition, it is unclear whether it provides clarification in emerging fields such as animal rationality. In other words, the accumulation view is comparatively promising. Accordingly, claim (3) is unlikely to be rejected, and hence options *c* and *f* are also ruled out; thus we only have option *b* at hand. However, can claim (2) not to be true?

It appears to be ridiculous to reject claim (2) and concede that *E. coli* could possibly be rational and irrational. However, it is not.

Unicellular bacteria such as *E. coli* evolve with no brains or nervous systems, but they can nevertheless perform highly complex tasks, such as sensory integration, motor control, reasoning, decision-making, or even social behavior, such as cell-to-cell communication and cooperation (Allman, 2000; Bayliss et al., 2012, Ben-Jacob, Becker, Shapira, & Levine, 2004; Hellingwerf, 2005; Koraimann & Wagner, 2014; Lyon, 2007; Perkins & Peter, 2009; Shapiro, 2007; Ben-Jacob, 2014; Refardt, Bergmiller, & Kümmerli, 2013). For example, *E. coli* bacteria are capable of reasoning by inducting one type of information (where nutrition is) from another (variation of concentration). An *E. coli* bacterium's receptors can sense surrounding chemicals. The detected chemicals are compared with signals received seconds earlier to decide whether the concentration of nutrients is increasing. If it is, the biochemical mechanisms inside the cell will send feedback signals to the receptors to alter the structure of the inside loop of the receptor protein, amplifying the strength of the next signal from the receptor. Using the same lock-and-key mechanism, the bacterium can control flagellar motors by either amplifying or decreasing the signals from receptors. When the signals are amplified, the *E. coli*'s flagella will gather to form a propeller for forward swimming. Otherwise, these flagella will tumble to change direction (Allman, 2000). Furthermore, if we define decision-making as the act of choosing between possible outputs that may lead to different results, then we can conclude that *E. coli* are capable of decision-making, too. Suppose that the concentration of toxins is simultaneously increasing with that of nutrition. Whether *E. coli* bacteria decide to take risks to obtain the resources is also determined by biochemical reactions inside the cell (Allman, 2000; Adler & Tso, 1974; Balaban, Merrin, Chait, Kowalik, & Leibler, 2004). Aidelberg et al. (2014) found that the mechanism underlying *E. coli* decisions is quite subtle and can differentiate at least six types of nonglucose carbon sources.

However, skeptics may argue that this is not genuine decision-making, but merely a stimulus-response reaction because *E. coli* cannot freely choose to approach toxins if the receptors have already indicated that their concentration is increasing. However, this criticism ignores the fact that humans always face similar situations. In fight-or-flight cases, running seems to be the only option for most people when great danger is perceived. Of course, skeptics may argue that humans can choose to sacrifice themselves if others' lives are in danger; even if it seems to be irrational with respect to self-preservation, it is a real decision-making process.

However, surprisingly, some *E. coli* bacteria also commit suicide for altruistic purposes. Refardt et al. (2013) discovered that among two strains of *E. coli* bacteria, one strain self-destructs when infected with a lethal virus and the other does not. Unless it kills itself first, an infected bacterium not only dies but also serves as an incubator for some 300 new virus particles. Refardt et al. (2013) argue that when two types of *E. coli* and the virus were mixed together under varying conditions, the suicidal strain fared better than the nonsuicidal strain. Robb and Shahrezaei (2014) further offer a stochastic model explaining how *E. coli*'s sacrifice may depend on not only viral concentration but also on the number of infecting phages. In this case, *E. coli* do make decisions to maximize the colony's overall fitness.

More surprisingly, although for many years bacteria were considered autonomous organisms with little collective behavior, they are highly communicative. They can use a mechanism called "quorum sensing" to coordinate gene expression and to synthesize small molecules diffusing in and out of the cells, which make cross-cell communications possible (Williams et al., 2007). All these data show that it is not absurd to hold that *E. coli* may have some minimal rationality. The resulting conclusion is that humans and *E. coli* do have different levels of rationality. Organisms exhibiting different levels of computational power for reasoning and decision-making also exhibit different levels of rationality.

A very short diagnosis of why people are loath to reject claim (2) is probably because, in the past, the concept of rationality was usually tangled with noble concepts, such as soul, spirit, and humanity. A dictator's cruelty to people is considered not only irrational/mad but also inhuman. This tangle makes the denial of claim (2) emotionally unacceptable.

12.4 OBJECTIONS AND REPLIES

Microbiological studies have indicated that *E. coli* bacteria are more intelligent than people thought. However, some may refuse to think that the capacities render them as rational beings. This section discusses some of these objections, including: (1) rationality involves not merely reasoning capacity, it requires consciousness, too; (2) the view commits the fallacy of personification; and (3) the three claims are not inconsistent but are vague/ambiguous. I explain and reply to these objections as follows.

12.4.1 Rationality and Consciousness

Skeptics may argue that having reasoning capacities is far from being rational or irrational because rationality requires consciousness. Without consciousness, reasoning is merely an automatic processing similar to vending machine processes. Because *E. coli* bacteria have no consciousness, they cannot be rational at all.

A reply is that according to the definition offered at the opening section, consciousness is not a prerequisite for descriptive-practical-procedural rationality. However, even it was, it would not imply that *E. coli* could not have this rationality. There is no decisive evidence showing that *E. coli* have or do not have consciousness. However, there is reason to believe that *E. coli* may be conscious. For example, David Chalmers (2015) argues for a view called panpsychism, in which all (or at least some) fundamental physical entities are conscious. To support this view, Chalmers proposes a dialectical argument in which the thesis (dualism is true), antithesis (materialism is true), and synthesis (panpsychism is true) are presented in turn.

Chalmers first offers the conceivability argument against the material view that everything, including consciousness, is physical. The conceivability argument runs as follows. Let P be the conjunction of all microphysical truths about the universe and Q an arbitrary phenomenal truth (eg, I am conscious). P&~Q is conceivable; and if P&~Q is conceivable then P&~Q is metaphysically possible; and if P&~Q is metaphysically possible, materialism is false; therefore, materialism is false.

However, Chalmers then offers the causal argument against the dualist view that some things are physical but others are mental. The causal argument goes like this. Phenomenal properties are causally relevant to physical events. Every caused physical event has a full causal explanation in physical terms. If every caused physical event has a full causal explanation in physical terms, every property causally relevant to the physical is itself grounded in physical properties. If phenomenal properties are grounded in physical properties, materialism is true. Therefore, materialism is true.

Chalmers (2015, p. 249) contends the aforementioned two arguments provide strong bases against and for materialism and dualism and motivate a particular view "that captures the virtue of both view and vices of neither." That is, every fundamental physical entity is conscious. If Chalmers' argument for panpsychism holds, them *E. coli* can possibly be conscious and therefore possibly rational.

Furthermore, as seen in Section 12.3, the internal procedure in *E. coli* is not merely automatic but controlled; an *E. coli* bacterium may choose to output an altruistic behavior even if this behavior will eventually lead to its own death.

12.4.2 Anthropomorphism

Skeptics may argue that granting bacteria rationality commits the anthropomorphism (personification) fallacy: misattribution of human traits to nonhuman organisms or inanimate objects.

A reply is that the proposed view is neutralized rather than anthropomorphist. The anthropomorphist perspective is to first characterize a feature (eg, rationality and intelligence) that humans exhibit and then apply it to nonhuman entities. This perspective may suit the study of primates and mammals but could be misleading in studying simple creatures. For example, Wystrach (2013) maintains that assuming that ants, the smallest insect with a brain, require a cognitive map as humans do is a mistake. Ants need not bind all their information into a holist representation of the world. Instead, different modules (eg, odors, visual scenery, and backtracking) are responsible for different navigation tasks.

Conversely, a neutralized approach first characterizes the shared traits among all organisms and then applies it to both human and nonhuman organisms for calibration. This approach starts with simple explanations of complex behavior in simple computational systems, and then adds complex behaviors. If we humans do not measure the rationality of other organisms in terms of the criterion of our own, we may have a better understanding of rationality. Holding that rationality is universal but comes in degrees lifts the limits of the anthropomorphist perspective.

12.4.3 Vagueness and Ambiguity

Skeptics may suspect that the argument of inconsistency fails to hold because the concept of rationality involved in its premises is either vague or ambiguous. If "rationality" is a vague term and cannot be adequately applied, then the truth values of the second and third premises are undetermined, and thus no inconsistency occurs. Alternatively, if the term is ambiguous, then the inconsistency can easily be solved by offering suitable contexts (eg, "rational" in the second premise refers to the anthropomorphist reading, while that in the third refers to the nonanthropomorphist reading).

The reply involves two different attitudes toward the concept of rationality. First, if "rationality" is vague, then because vagueness cannot be eliminated by further defining the term (Williamson, 2002), the term should be avoided in serious research. One may reserve the terminology for everyday conversation but replace it with more specific notions in academic studies. This attitude is often adapted when an old term provides more confusion than clarification. For example, "innateness" has been avoided in many nature-nurture debates because it has at least nine different meanings (Samuels, Stich, & Faucher, 2004), including nonacquisition, genetic determination, presence at birth, and consequence of inner causes. Academic researchers may use gain-loss calculation, probabilistic-based optimization, or insect-level intelligence to describe the features that an organism exhibits when making decisions or solving problems in various situations. Abandoning rationality helps us focus more on the causal relationship between phenomena than on rhetorical disputes.

On the other hand, if rationality is used ambiguously, then it may reflect the fact that academic professionals are using the same term in rather different ways, which may lead to confusion in interdisciplinary conversation. If this is the case, we need to expand (or neutralize) rationality to encompass new phenomena discovered in animal cognition and artificial intelligence to find an accurate characterization within this scope. This approach is frequently seen in the history of physics and biology. Scientific terminology such as mass, organic, and evolution are ever changing, such that their current meanings stray far beyond their original uses. This second attitude conforms to the central proposal because they both allow human and nonhuman beings to be rational with diverse levels and evaluations of rationality. In other words, if the concept of rationality is still regarded as illuminating to a certain degree, then we should expand the notion to capture newly found phenomena in emerging sciences, or at least allow the term to indicate different facets of the phenomenon without rendering any inconsistency. Otherwise, we should abandon it in serious research.

12.5 FURTHER QUESTIONS

A frequently asked question is what the moral implication is once we grant bacteria rationality. I am not a moral philosopher and currently have no specific answer, but two (opposite) ways of thinking can be imagined. The first way is admitting that moral responsibility also comes in degrees (either in the human-bacteria or bacteria-bacteria relationship). The other perspective, which I prefer, is to stop connecting the notion of rationality with morality because sometimes how an object should be treated is irrelevant to its capacity to be rational/irrational (eg, its environment). For example, Haidt (2012) holds that in everyday life our moral judgment responds to our intuitions or emotions instead of rationality. Thus there might be no moral implication at all. Still, both lines of thought need to be explored seriously.

To summarize, I first explained why, although each of the three claims seems to be plausible, they cannot be true at once and lead to inconsistency. Then I discussed possible solutions and suggested replacing claim (2) with the view that rationality is universal but varies among organisms. I next discussed some objections and explained why they fail to hold.

To conclude, I reiterate that this paper does not aim to argue that *E. coli* and human beings are both rational at the same level, but that rationality comes in degrees. Thinking that simple organisms, such as bacteria are rational seems to be counterintuitive and could be distressing to the dignity of human beings at first glance. However, by granting bacteria rationality, we may achieve a wider and better perspective in the interdisciplinary study of rationality.

References

Adams, F., & Aizawa, K. (2009). Embodied cognition and the extended mind. In P. Calvo, & J. Symons (Eds.), *The Routledge companion to philosophy of psychology* (pp. 193). New York: Routledge.

Adler, J., & Tso, W. W. (1974). Decision-making in bacteria: chemotactic response of *Escherichia coli* to conflicting stimuli. *Science, 184,* 1292–1294.

Aidelberg, G., Towbin, B. D., Rothschild, D., Dekel, E., Bren, A., & Alon, U. (2014). Hierarchy of non-glucose sugars in *Escherichia coli*. *BMC Systems Biology, 8*(1), 133.

Allman, J. (2000). *Evolving brains*. New York: Scientific American Library.

Auersperg, A. M. I., von Bayern, A. M. I., Weber, S., Szabadvari, A., Bugnyar, T., & Kacelnik, A. (2014). Social transmission of tool use and tool manufacture in Goffin cockatoos (*Cacatua goffini*). *Proceedings of the Royal Society of London B: Biological Sciences, 281*(1793), 20140972.

Balaban, N. Q., Merrin, J., Chait, R., Kowalik, L., & Leibler, S. (2004). Bacterial persistence as a phenotypic switch. *Science, 305*(5690), 1622–1625.

Bayliss, D. L., Walsh, J. L., Iza, F., Shama, G., Holah, J., & Kong, M. G. (2012). Complex responses of microorganisms as a community to a flowing atmospheric plasma. *Plasma Processes and Polymers, 9*(6), 597–611.

Ben-Jacob, E. (2014). My encounters with bacteria—Learning about communication, cooperation and choice. *Physical Biology, 11*(5), 11.

Ben-Jacob, E., Becker, I., Shapira, Y., & Levine, H. (2004). Bacterial linguistic communication and social intelligence. *Trends in Microbiology, 12*, 366–372.

Block, N. (1980). What is functionalism? In N. Block (Ed.), *Readings in philosophy of psychology* (pp. 171–184). Cambridge, MA: Harvard University Press.

Brooks, R. A. (2014). Cognitive simulators. In *Architectures for intelligence: The 22nd Carnegie Mellon Symposium on cognition* (pp. 225). Abingdon, England: Psychology Press.

Calvo, P., & Baluška, F. (2015). Conditions for minimal intelligence across eukaryota: a cognitive science perspective. *Frontiers in Psychology, 6*, 1329.

Chalmers, D. J. (2015). Panpsychism and Panprotopsychism. Consciousness in the Physical World: Perspectives on Russellian Monism, 246.

Crane, T. (2003). The mechanical mind: A philosophical introduction to minds, machines and mental representation. *Presbyterian Publishing Corp.*

Dejohn, J. (2004). Where are all the cockroaches? *Journal of Experimental & Theoretical Artificial Intelligence, 16*(1), 1–3.

Dennett, D. C. (1989). *The intentional stance.* Cambridge, MA: MIT Press.

Descartes, R., & Maclean, Ian. (2006). *Discourse on the method of rightly conducting the reason and seeking truth in the sciences.* Oxford: Oxford University Press.

Dretske, F. (2006). Minimal rationality. In L. In Susan, Hurley, & Matthew Nudds (Eds.), *Rational animals?*. Oxford: Oxford University Press (2006).

Ermentrout, G. B., & Terman, D. H. (2010). *Mathematical foundations of neuroscience* (35). New York: Springer Science & Business Media.

Fodor, J. A. (2008). *LOT 2: The language of thought revisited: The language of thought revisited.* Oxford: Oxford University Press.

Foley, R. (1990). Fumerton's puzzle. *Journal of Philosophical Research, 15*, 109–113.

Fumerton, R. (1990). Reasons and Morality: A Defense of the Egocentric Perspective.

Gallistel, C. R., & King, A. P. (2011). *Memory and the computational brain: Why cognitive science will transform neuroscience* (6). Hoboken, NJ: John Wiley & Sons.

Haidt, J. (2012). *The righteous mind: Why good people are divided by politics and religion.* New York: Pantheon Books.

Hellingwerf, K. J. (2005). Bacterial observations: a rudimentary form of intelligence? *Trends in Microbiology, 13*, 152–158.

Hunt, G. R. (1996). Manufacture and use of hook-tools by New Caledonian crows. *Nature, 379*(6562), 249–251.

Kant, I. (2013). *Lectures on anthropology.* Ed. Wood, A. & Louden, R. Cambridge: Cambridge University Press.

Klump, B. C., van der Wal, J. E., St Clair, J. J., & Rutz, C. (2015). Context-dependent 'safekeeping' of foraging tools in New Caledonian crows. *Proceedings of the Royal Society of London B: Biological Sciences, 282*(1808), 20150278.

Koraimann, G., & Wagner, M. A. (2014). Social behavior and decision making in bacterial conjugation. *Frontiers in Cellular and Infection Microbiology, 4*(54), 4.

LeDoux, J. (2012). Rethinking the emotional brain. *Neuron, 73*, 653–676.

Liu, Y., Liao, J., Zhu, B., Wang, E., & Ding, J. (2006). Crystal structures of the editing domain of *Escherichia coli* leucyl-tRNA synthetase and its complexes with Met and Ile reveal a lock-and-key mechanism for amino acid discrimination. *Biochemical Journal, 394*, 399–407.

Logan, C. J., Breen, A. J., Taylor, A. H., Gray, R. D., & Hoppitt, W. J. (2015). How New Caledonian crows solve novel foraging problems and what it means for cumulative culture. *Learning & Behavior*, *44*(1), 1–11.

Lyon, P. (2007). From quorum to cooperation: Lessons from bacterial sociality for evolutionary theory. *Studies in History and Philosophy of Biological and Biomedical Sciences*, *38*, 820–833.

Magnasco, M. O. (1997). Chemical kinetics is Turing universal. *Physical Review Letters*, *78*(6), 1190.

Mele, A. R., & Rawling, P. (2004). Introduction: Aspects of rationality. In A. R. Mele, & P. Rawling (Eds.), *The Oxford handbook of rationality*. New York: Oxford University Press.

O'Hara, M., Auersperg, A. M., Bugnyar, T., & Huber, L. (2015). Inference by exclusion in Goffin cockatoos (Cacatua goffini). *PloS One*, *10*(8), e0134894.

Perkins, T. J., & Peter, S. S. (2009). Strategies for cellular decision making. *Molecular Systems Biology*, *5*(1), 326.

Pfeifer, R. (2001). *Embodied artificial intelligence: 10 years back, 10 years forward* (pp. 294–310). Lecture Notes in Computer Science, 2000.

Piccinini, G. (2007). Computational modelling vs. computational explanation: Is everything a Turing machine, and does it matter to the philosophy of mind? *Australasian Journal of Philosophy*, *85*(1), 93–115.

Piccinini, G. (2008a). Computation without representation. *Philosophical Studies*, *137*(2), 205–241.

Piccinini, G. (2008b). Some neural networks compute, others don't. *Neural Networks*, *21*(2), 311–321.

Piccinini, G., & Bahar, S. (2013). Neural computation and the computational theory of cognition. *Cognitive Science*, *37*(3), 453–488.

Povinelli, D., & Vonk, J. (2006). We don't need a microscope to explore the chimpanzee's mind. In S. L. Hurley, & M. Nudds (Eds.), *Rational animals?* (pp. 385–412). New York: Oxford University Press.

Refardt, D., Bergmiller, T., & Kümmerli, R. (2013). Altruism can evolve when relatedness is low: Evidence from bacteria committing suicide upon phage infection. *Proceedings of the Royal Society B: Biological Sciences*, *280*(1759), 20123035.

Richardson, K. (2012). Heritability lost; intelligence found. Intelligence is integral to the adaptation and survival of all organisms faced with changing environments. *EMBO Reports*, *13*, 591–595.

Richardson, K. (2013). The evolution of intelligent developmental systems. *Advances in Child Development and Behavior*, *44*, 127–159.

Robb, M. L., & Shahrezaei, V (2014). Stochastic cellular fate decision making by multiple infecting lambda phage. *PLoS One*, *9*(8), .

Russell, S. (1997). Rationality and intelligence. *Artificial Intelligence Journal*, *94*(1–2), 57–77.

Russell, S. (2014). Rationality and intelligence: A brief update. In C. Vincent, & Müller (Eds.), *Fundamental issues of artificial intelligence (Synthese Library)*. Berlin: Springer.

Samuels, R., Stich, S., & Faucher, L. (2004). Reason and rationality. In *Handbook of epistemology* (pp. 131–179). Dordrecht, The Netherlands: Springer.

Schneider, S. (2011). *The language of thought: A new philosophical direction*. MIT Press: Cambridge, MA.

Shapiro, J. A. (2007). Bacteria are small but not stupid: Cognition, natural genetic engineering and socio-bacteriology. *Studies in History and Philosophy of Biological and Biomedical Sciences*, *38*, 807–819.

Shapiro, E. (2012). A mechanical Turing machine: Blueprint for a biomolecular computer. *Interface Focus*, *2*(4), 497–503.

Stanovich, K. E. (2012). On the distinction between rationality and intelligence: Implications for understanding individual differences in reasoning. The Oxford handbook of thinking and reasoning, 343–365. New York: Oxford University Press.

Todd, P. M., & Gigerenzer, G. (2012). What is ecological rationality. Ecological rationality: Intelligence in the world, 3–30. New York: Oxford University Press.
Tomasello, M., & Call, J. (2006). Do chimpanzees know what others see, or only what they are looking at? In S. L. Hurley & M. Nudds (Eds.), *Rational animals?* (pp. 371–384). New York: Oxford University Press.
Tschudin, A. J.-P. C. (2006). Belief attribution tasks with dolphins: What social minds can reveal about animal rationality. In S.L. Hurley & M. Nudds (Eds.), *Rational animals?* (pp. 413–436). New York: Oxford University Press.
Wallace, R. J. (1999). Three conceptions of rational agency. *Ethical Theory and Moral Practice, 2*(3), 217–242.
Wechsler, D (1944). *The measurement of adult intelligence*. Baltimore: Williams & Wilkins.
Weir, A. A., Chappell, J., & Kacelnik, A. (2002). Shaping of hooks in New Caledonian crows. *Science, 297*(5583), 981–1981.
Williams, P., Winzer, K., Chan, W. C., & Camara, M. (2007). Look who's talking: Communication and quorum sensing in the bacterial world. *Philosophical Transactions of the Royal Society B: Biological Sciences, 362*(1483), 1119–1134.
Williamson, T. (2002). *Knowledge and its limits*. New York: Oxford University Press.
Wimpenny, J. H., Weir, A. A., & Kacelnik, A. (2011). New Caledonian crows use tools for non-foraging activities. *Animal Cognition, 14*(3), 459–464.
Wystrach, A. (2013). We've been looking at ant intelligence the wrong way. https://74.50.56.43/profiles/antoine-wystrach-102485/articles
Ye, R. (2015). Fumerton's puzzle for theories of rationality. *Australasian Journal of Philosophy, 93*(1), 93–108.

Endnotes

1. See Aristotle's *Topics* I.5 and VI. 4, 1984 translation.
2. Descartes (Descartes & Maclean, 2006, p. 46) explains, "if there were such machines having the organs and outward shape of a monkey or any other irrational animal, we would have no means of knowing that they are not of exactly the same nature as these animals, whereas, if any such machines resembled us in body and imitated our actions insofar as this was practically possible, we should still have two very certain means of recognizing that there were not, for all that, real human beings."
3. An *E. coli* bacterium may also be computational in the (i) and (ii) senses, because its whole-cell behaviors and in-cell biochemical functions can respectively be simulated by a model and part of a model. However, as almost all physical systems can be computational in the (i) sense and many in the (ii) sense, I only discuss computation in the (iii) sense to avoid triviality.
4. For example, Some hold that intelligence can be defined by rational agent (Russell, 1997) or rational thinking (Wechsler, 1944); some hold that ecological rationality can be understood as the fit between intelligence and the environment (Todd & Gigerenzer, 2012); and some hold that intelligence and rationality can be partly disassociated (Stanovich, 2012).

PART VI

COMMUNICATION AND EMOTION

Rationality is part of the social survival kit for our interpersonal interactions. It shapes and fine-tunes our beliefs and actions. It thus plays a role in determining how we assess the credibility of information derived from everyday conversation, as well as how we interact with other rational agents in morally relevant situations. Part VI explores two themes regarding the ways in which rationality plays this role: how knowledge is formed through verbal communication, and how ethics is shaped by the interplay between emotion and reason.

In Chapter 13, Eric McCready focuses on theoretical rationality. The question of when it is rational to believe something is a perennial problem in epistemology, and to a lesser extent, moral philosophy. McCready contributes to this debate by approaching it from the perspective of linguistics and the philosophy of language. There has been a substantial amount of research in the philosophy of language concerning the effects of information transfer on the beliefs of communicators. Such information transfer has been modeled in possible world semantics by using contractions of the sets of worlds that correspond to belief states. While much has been learned as a result, the question of when individuals should rationally accept the content proffered to them by their interlocutors remains understudied. McCready uses a repeated game model to show that rational update policies can be constructed on the basis of reputational considerations. Moreover, this model is a special case of information acquisition, and similar considerations can be developed with respect to evidence sources for a more general model of rational, evidence-based belief.

In Chapter 14, Ellie Hua Wang explores the roles that reason and emotion play in Xunzi's ethics. She first reviews Soek's and Slingerland's analyses of Xunzi. Whereas Soek regards Confucian ethics as generally operating with an emotion-based model, Slingerland categorizes Xunzi's moral psychology as a theory that presumes what he calls the "high reason model." This model significantly resembles the reason-based model developed in Soek's account. Wang also argues that Xunzi's ethics can be captured by neither of these models; instead, she develops a hybrid model that emphasizes ritual practices in the cultivation of *xin* 心 and *qing* 情 as a means of approaching sagehood, which sheds light on a possible interplay between reason and emotion in ideal moral judgments. Wang's discussion inspires further consideration of what a moral rationalist might be, and the extent to which Xunzi might be considered as one.

CHAPTER

13

Rational Belief and Evidence-Based Update

E. McCready

Department of English, Aoyama Gakuin University, Shibuya, Tokyo, Japan

13.1 INTRODUCTION

The question of when it is rational to believe some piece of content is a perennial problem in epistemology, and, to a lesser extent, moral philosophy and the theory of value. The goal of this chapter is to contribute to this debate by approaching it from the perspective of linguistics and the philosophy of language.

The starting point for my investigation of rational belief will be communicative acts. Suppose that you are engaged in conversation with a person who makes a claim to you. Should you believe this claim? Or should you disregard what they say? In other words, is it rational to believe what is asserted? One can find various answers to this question in the philosophical literature, the most extreme coming from Hume and Reid in the 18th century. Hume takes the content of communication (hereafter called testimony) to be universally in need of other justification, while Reid takes it to be universally reliable in the absence of reasons to the contrary. A more nuanced answer to this question depends on a variety of factors: the identity of the agent, the content of the communication, your prior beliefs, and so on. Some of these factors are enumerated in Section 13.2, together with a brief discussion of the two main views of testimonial reliability.

The main goal of this chapter is to provide a formal model of belief change suitable for the analysis of the testimonial case, and general enough to provide a basis for a more universal basis for justifiable change in beliefs. It is thus necessary to put the discussion on a formal footing. The usual model of belief change in modern linguistics and philosophy is dynamic semantics; Section 13.4 explicates a relatively simple version of this

Rationality. http://dx.doi.org/10.1016/B978-0-12-804600-5.00013-1

theory, giving its main formal characteristics. But dynamic semantics is, as its name implies, a semantic theory rather than a pragmatic one; as such, it does not have much to say in most formulations about when a particular change in belief is rational, instead focusing on the semantic consequences of changes in belief. This gap is filled in Section 13.3, which provides a formal model of rationality in belief change. The main idea here is to assume that communicative acts are situated within longer term interactions with agents who can be characterized as reliable or not depending on their characteristics, including their prior communicative behavior. The literature on repeated games makes it straightforward to characterize optimal—rational—behavior in such a setting, given certain assumptions: a rational update is one made on the basis of a communicative event of an agent with (among other properties) a sufficiently high proportion of past reliability.

This model (as I will show in Section 13.3) indicates when it is rational to accept a proposal for update made by a communicative act (at least given the definition of rational update I will propose). However, this story does not generalize in a fully obvious way to other kinds of belief. What about instances of new potential beliefs that arise via inference or via sensory input, for example? The main task of Section 13.4 is to show how the model integrates with a general picture of evidence-based update formulated in dynamic semantics. There, I will sketch the dynamic model of updates made on the basis of evidential observations proposed in McCready (2015) and show in Section 13.5 how the earlier, reputation-based part of the proposal can be integrated into it. This section brings the two proposals together in terms of a "reputational" constraint on the dynamic model, and also concludes the chapter.

13.2 RELIABILITY OF TESTIMONY

The main focus of this chapter is the question of when it is rational to believe what is said to one in conversation. The main issue is thus the reliability of information acquired through testimony. This topic has received a good deal of recent attention within epistemology, though most of the work on the topic concentrates on when knowledge is transmitted by testimonial means, rather than on the question of the rationality of belief in testimony. Because of this focus, much of the literature is not very useful to the purposes of this chapter. However, many of the conditions that people have proposed concerning when a particular instance of testimony is to be regarded as knowledge transmitting can also be viewed as conditions on when a particular instance of testimony should be judged reliable, and thus a good candidate for rational belief. It will therefore be useful to examine some of this work.

The literature is huge, however.[1] In this chapter, I will restrict myself to a brief discussion of Hume and Reid, with an eye to the extraction of some elements relevant for the analysis I will propose in the next section, which, as we will see, in some sense combines aspects of Humean and Reidian views. A fuller treatment can be found in McCready (2015).

As I mentioned in the introduction, Hume and Reid are usually taken to exemplify two main strands in the analysis of testimony: the reductionist position and the antireductionist, respectively. According to the reductionists, justification for belief in testimony is acquired via extratestimonial factors. Hume has it (in the "On Miracles" section of Hume, 1977) that (paraphrasing) we believe given instances of testimony because the testimonial agent has a sufficiently good track record of success. This idea can be generalized or restricted in various ways, for instance, by restricting it to particular kinds of content, or generalizing over the track records of some larger group of speakers. But one thing is obvious from even this brief statement: it is necessary to have some means of modeling a testimonial agent's past performance in order to justify believing any instance of future testimony. This idea will play a key role in what follows.

The contrasting position comes from a passage in Reid (1997) where he takes belief in testimony to be justified on the grounds that the social nature of human beings leads to propensities to speak truly and to believe what is said, which taken jointly lead to testimony working properly as a means of transmitting information. A version of this position is adopted by Burge (1993) who, however, also notes that it must be defeasible, as many factors can lead us to discount particular instances of testimony. Even for the reductionist, it must be acknowledged that in situations where we have little reason to trust our interlocutors, it is often the case that we do so, and also often the case that we are justified in doing so. The resulting (apparent) need for a kind of mix of reductionist and antireductionist views has prompted a wide range of positions on testimonial knowledge in the literature. The proposal I will develop in the next section also is such a mix of reductionism and antireductionism, though one that limits its antireductionist quality to highly specific situations.

13.3 RATIONAL ACCEPTANCE

How and when is it justified to accept information proffered by a testimonial agent? My strategy here will be to propose a class of testimonial interactions that can be categorized as cooperative, and then to consider such interactions in the light of research on cooperativity and altruism that has been carried out within theoretical biology and game theory. One result of this research is that a class of "best strategies" has been found for cooperative games with certain properties; given that testimonial situations have these properties, the game-theoretic results can be carried over directly. I will show that such is indeed the case, and that the resulting optimal strategies more or less directly correspond to reductionist and antireductionist views that make reference to reputation.

The picture sketched in the previous paragraph requires viewing communication as a cooperative interaction, to be realized formally as a game akin to the prisoner's dilemma, which admits cooperative moves but does not require them for payoff maximality in certain situations. Is it reasonable to view the transmission of information by testimony as requiring cooperation? Traditionally, it seems so; the highly influential Grice (1975) even proposes a "Cooperative Principle" which normatively requires speakers to speak the truth as they best understand it, among other things, something codified in most (linguistic) game-theoretic treatments of communication (as in, eg, the chapters in Benz, Jager, & van Rooij, 2006). For the purposes of this chapter, I will assume that an utterance by a speaker is cooperative if it is truth tracking, putting aside considerations of intentionality.[2] However, what about the hearer? Most proposals about communicative norms do not have much to say about the role of the hearer, focusing instead on truth-related conditions on assertion (cf. Brown & Cappelen, 2011).

The hearer is not obligation free in communicative interactions. The speaker who takes the trouble to make an assertion and attempts to transmit some information will be justifiably displeased if the hearer ignores her without remark. In general, the hearer is normatively required to respond in some way to the communicative act. Normally, this will involve uptake of the transmitted content, as evidenced by the fact that if an assertion is made, the speaker will take it to have been added to the common ground if it is treated as uncontroversial by the hearer (Stalnaker, 1978, 1999). I will assume that a hearer who takes her interlocutor to be cooperative will accept the information proffered, for if the speaker is cooperative, he should be doing his best to tell the truth, and thus the information he is trying to transmit is likely to be truth tracking if he has the normal capacities of a rational agent. We thus expect cooperative interaction on both sides in the absence of defeaters (Pollock & Cruz, 1999).

On the basis of the aforementioned considerations, I will assume in the following that communication is a cooperative endeavor on both sides of the communicative equation. Let us now put this into a game-theoretic formulation. In game theory, games are viewed as mathematical objects consisting of a set of players, a set of moves for each player, and a set of outcomes given the particular moves selected by each player. The outcomes are stated in terms of utilities as in standard utility theory.[3] The cases of communication under consideration can be modeled as two-player games with players S and H. S can select from a variety of discourse moves[4] which can be placed into two categories: moves which are truthful, which I will dub T, and moves which are not, which will be collectively called F. S can thus be viewed as selecting between truth-tracking and nontruth-tracking moves, and so to draw actions from a set $A = \{T, F\}$. I will call a play of T a cooperative move of S, and a play of F an uncooperative move. By the same token, H also has cooperative and uncooperative moves available: a cooperative move is one which results in a belief of H in the communicated content, and an uncooperative one which does not. These moves will be called B and D respectively, meaning that H draws moves from $A' = \{B, D\}$.

To round off the game description, it remains to address the payoff structure. Most standard views in linguistics let the two players each receive equal utility when communication is successful, that is, when H successfully arrives at S's intended meaning. However, in the present context this is not appropriate, as we are concerned with cases where a speaker might be intentionally transmitting inaccurate content. Instead, I will allow four possible outcomes, stated as follows:

	B	D
T	1,1	−2,2
F	2,−2	−1,−1

These payoffs can be motivated as follows. In (*T*, *B*) both players gain something; *S* because *H* has acquired some content he was willing to transmit, and perhaps *S* has also gained some "face" from the transaction (cf. McCready, Asher, & Soumya, 2013), and *H* because she has learned something true. In (*F*, *D*) *S* has said something false and *H* has ignored him, meaning that both players have wasted their time and must pay some penalty. The more interesting cases, perhaps, are the asymmetrical ones. In (*F*, *B*) *S* has tried to pass a lie, and it has worked: *H* has accepted what he said. We can assume that in some cases—say when *S* is trying to sell a used car with some undisclosed faults—*S* accrues an advantage from this transaction and *H* loses out, as represented in the payoffs. Finally, (*T*, *D*) is a case where *S* says something true yet is disbelieved, and thus both wastes time and loses some face, while *H* gains in face by the transaction by showing her power.[5]

As the reader may already have observed, this game has the structure of a prisoner's dilemma. A prisoner's dilemma is a game where each player's payoffs exhibit the following structure, where *c* indicates a cooperative move and *d* a noncooperative move:

	c	d
c	γ,γ	α,β
d	β,α	δ,δ

where, $\beta > \gamma > \delta > \alpha$. In such games, the best joint outcome for the two players is achieved if each cooperate, but each player does better if they "defect."

The result is that given the standard metric of utility maximization, each player defects and both end up in a situation worse than that arrived at if they had cooperated.

This situation arises for one-off games,[6] but changes when repeated games are considered. In such games, players have the option to punish other players for noncooperation. Suppose that the game of communication discussed earlier is played more than once. Each player has the option to play cooperatively by using *T* and *B*. Suppose that *H* plays *B* but *S* plays *F*. Then, intuitively, it is likely that *H* may not cooperate on the next turn, having already been "burned." Then the maximum utility *S* can receive when the game is repeated is −1, which already cancels out his gain from playing *F* in the first round of play. Depending on *H*'s further actions, *S* may never be able to do better than −1 again, for instance, if *H* plays what is called a grim strategy which disallows further cooperation after being "tricked" (Mailath & Samuelson, 2006).[7] *H* may also be playing a so-called tit for tat (TFT) strategy where she plays the same type of move as *S* played in the previous turn, in which case *S* can repair the damage by playing *T* thereafter.

There are a very wide range of strategies discussed in the literature on the iterated prisoner's dilemma, but researchers have isolated several kinds of optimal strategies, which differ in the resources available to the players. One which does not require much beyond a one-round memory is so-called generous TFT (Nowak, 2006). This strategy is a version of TFT with two special features: (1) it begins with a cooperative move in the first round, and (2) even when normal TFT indicates a noncooperative play, the generous version plays a cooperative move with some positive probability. These two conditions have straightforward motivations: the first maximizes chances of ongoing cooperative play by taking a chance in the first game iteration, for if the other player is also playing TFT, an initial uncooperative move may shift play into a cycle of noncooperation, and the second allows play to exit any cycles of noncooperative play caused by the interaction of TFT strategies.

In the present context, this strategy has further significance. Consider the case of games of communication. Generous TFT advocates the play of a cooperative move in the initial stage of play, as a way to raise the likelihood of further payoffs. For the case of the hearer, this amounts to an initial move of trust in the speaker; but this is precisely what is advocated by antireductionist approaches to testimony. It is worth noting that initial moves can be problematic for reductionist strategies, as there may not be enough information available to warrant trust. Thus we see that considerations about rational strategy selection in repeated games warrant antireductionist views on testimony for at least a subclass of possible situations.[8]

The reader might now wonder whether there is anything in this general picture that corresponds to a reductionist theory. The answer is positive, and indeed gives results better than those found for simple generous TFT. However, additional resources are required. In particular, it is necessary to make reference to a notion of *reputation*. Nowak and Sigmund (1998a,b) proposed a theory in which individual agents are associated with reputational indices, "image scores" which indicate how cooperative they have been in previous iterations of the game. Such indices are updated based on the moves of that agent. One simple sort of mechanism might assign individuals scores between 0 and 5, and then update these scores as follows: given an agent a with image score n at game iteration i, let a have score $n + 1$ at $i + 1$ if her move at i is cooperative, and $n - 1$ at $i + 1$ otherwise. Thus a sequence of cooperative moves will increase a's score up to the maximum available 5, and a sequence of uncooperative moves will eventually decrease it to the minimum 0. Within this model, the decision of whether or not to cooperate with an agent will depend on that agent's image score. Nowak and Sigmund explore a number of possible strategies (viewed as functions from image scores to moves). For example, one might cooperate with agents whose score exceeds some base level, say 3 or 4, or one might cooperate with those agents whose image score exceeds one's own. They show that each of these strategies yields high payoffs.

For the case of games of communication, it is clear how the notion of image score ought to be implemented. Agents can be associated with scores which are augmented for cooperative behavior and decreased for uncooperative behavior. From the perspective of someone observing an instance of testimony, whether to believe that testimony or not should depend on the image score of the speaker; if the speaker's score is sufficiently high, the hearer should come to believe the utterance, and otherwise not. This is plainly an instance of a reductionist strategy, for the question of whether a given instance of testimony is reliable depends entirely on the speaker's image score, which in turn depends on the agent's past reliability and on whatever the agent's initial score was, something which must be assigned on the basis of external considerations. Thus there is good game-theoretic motivation to think that reductionist strategies are also rational.

A more complex version of this analysis is proposed by McCready (2015), who makes use of a notion of reputation. Like image scores, reputations are derived from past speaker behavior with respect to truth telling, but unlike image scores, other aspects of the speaker's behavior are also tracked, for instance, properties of the speech situation and utterance content which allow restriction of reputational histories to those communicative moves relevant for judging reliability in the current interaction. These models also differ from that of Nowak and Sigmund in allowing a wider range of reputational values, indeed any value in the range [0,1]; doing so allows a direct identification of the agent's reputational reliability with the probability that the agent is currently being cooperative and thus truth telling. Each agent is further associated with an initial probability of reliability based on external considerations, which are then altered via conditionalization on the basis of the current move. McCready then proposes that a given instance of testimony is to be judged worthy of belief if the speaker's reputational index lies above a certain standard located in [0,1]; this standard is to be determined by contextual factors in the manner that Kennedy (2007) proposes for thresholds in vague predicates. Thus it is rational to believe an instance of testimony if $Rel(a) \succ s$, for s the contextual standard, with the proviso that if no information about reliability is available, the testimony ought to be accepted (as with generous TFT). This theory thus is a more sophisticated version of the Nowak–Sigmund model, which retains its positive features while introducing extra functionality. It also makes the same commitment to the reductionist stance that the Nowak–Sigmund theory does, but its assumption of initial cooperation brings in antireductionist features.

13.4 RELIABILITY AND UPDATE

The aforementioned seems a reasonable analysis of the rationality of belief update on the basis of testimony. Still, testimony is only one way by which speakers acquire new information. Is there a more general model in which the above could be embedded? This section will claim that there is, and propose a model beginning with a dynamic semantic picture of information acquisition, proceeding to generalize that picture to source-based reasoning, and concluding by situating testimony within the model. The analysis, again, closely follows that of McCready (2015).

The usual picture of information transmission used in linguistics and also philosophy is that of dynamic semantics (Stalnaker, 1978, 1999; Groenendijk & Stokhof, 1991; Veltman, 1996). The details of the models vary from theory to theory, but the basic picture is as follows. Agents are associated with information states, which consist in their most basic form of sets of possible worlds, those worlds which the agent takes to be live possibilities at the present moment.[9] Adding new information to such states amounts to restricting the set of worlds to those worlds that also verify the new information; so updating an information state σ with a proposition φ (also viewed as a set of worlds) gives $\sigma \cap \varphi$; if the result of such an update is the empty set, the discourse is inconsistent, and update fails.[10] Clauses for the logical connectives complete this basic picture.

Within this sort of analysis, the kinds of considerations about rational belief discussed in the previous section can be restated as questions about when it is rational to update with a proposition presented to one via testimonial means. It is common in recent work on dynamic semantics (at least within linguistics) to take assertions to be proposals for update which proffer potential updates to their targets, which can then be accepted or not by interlocutors (Murray, 2010, for a recent example, but the basic idea goes back to Stalnaker). The analysis of the previous section, then, can be understood as a metric for when it is rational to accept an update proposal, namely when either (1) the reliability of the agent proffering the update exceeds the contextual standard *s*, or (2) when the proposal comes in the initial stage of an interaction where there are not defeaters for the belief that the agent might be cooperative.

To extend this picture to one which takes into consideration when it is rational to believe potential updates from other nontestimonial sources, several ingredients are required. First, how can one judge the reliability of such sources? For the testimonial case, the reputational history of the agent was key, as was the "generosity" of the initial move; how does this carry over to other sources? Second, what is to be done in the case of conflict between information sources? For example, it often happens that someone tells us something that conflicts with a belief we have on the basis of some other source of information, such as visual evidence or inference. How are such conflicts to be adjudicated? And, finally, how does all this relate to formal models of update like that found in dynamic semantics?

The first question has a straightforward answer. The reliability of sources other than testimony can be gauged in just the same way that testimonial reliability is judged: by examination of the history of how well information provided by that source tracks truth. To implement this idea, it is necessary to have histories of nontestimonial information acquisition available. This can be done by placing the reputational histories of the previous section into a larger context. Suppose that each event of information acquisition of φ has the logical form $E_i\varphi$, where E essentially marks a Quinean observation sentence (Quine, 1960), and *i* is an index associated with a particular information source. The available sources will be just those that need to be distinguished within the model, and are drawn from a set *S* which includes the available testimonial agents and a set of more purely evidential sources, taken by McCready (2015) to track the sources that are referenced by evidential constructions in natural language (Aikhenvald, 2004). The entire sequence of information acquisition events can then be denoted *H*; *H* can be restricted to "evidential events" of a particular sort *i* by picking out only those elements of *H* which are indexed with *i*. It is then possible to derive a reliability index from the resulting subsequence in the way discussed in Section 12.3: by checking what proportion of those events are truth tracking.[11] An information source will be deemed reliable if its reliability index exceeds the contextual standard *s*, just as in Section 12.3.

Now let us turn to the second question. How is one to decide which source to believe in case of conflict between information sources? The theory as currently constructed provides a ready-made answer to this question. Each evidence source is associated with a reliability index which tracks how the source has performed in terms of providing accurate information. The higher the index, the more likely it is that the information the source provides is correct. Thus when weighing which source to believe in cases of conflict, the safest strategy is to go with the higher ranked source, as realized in the indices. Since the indices themselves lie in the connected interval [0,1], they will all be mutually ranked, and it will be rare that indecision results given the highly fine grained nature of the possible indices.[12]

In the context of dynamic semantics, all this can be spelled out as follows (though I will keep the discussion relatively informal). Let information states σ be collections of substates σ_i, rather than "flat" sets of worlds.[13] Now let an update of σ with an observation sentence $E_i\varphi$ update the substate σ_i rather than the "global state" σ, where the update itself is just restriction as discussed earlier in the section. The result of this change is that the global state is never updated, but instead only the substates; even in cases of conflict, then, update takes place as usual, but may result in a global information state that contains mutually inconsistent substates. But this does not result in genuinely inconsistent belief, but rather in what one might call inconsistent evidential belief; the agent has access to the information that the evidence sources are mutually inconsistent. We would then like to say that the agent's beliefs should depend on the information provided by the more reliable index. This can be ensured by letting "genuine" belief depend on a derived information state (call it σ_T, the "total" information state) which in turn is arrived at via a merge operation over substates. Two cases arise in substate merge. In the first, the two states are consistent; in this case, we simply intersect them, yielding $\sigma_i \otimes \sigma_j = \sigma_i \cap \sigma_j$. In the second, the two are inconsistent, so $\sigma_i \cap \sigma_j = \varnothing$. In this case, we can assume that the more reliable substate takes precedence, so $\sigma_i \otimes \sigma_j = \sigma_i$ if $Rel(i) \succ Rel(j)$.[14] We thus end up with consistent genuine beliefs, which are arrived at via a process founded on observation of the performance of various different kinds of information sources.

Can the resulting beliefs be regarded as rational? The answer depends on our view of the relationship between rationality and reliability. According to the analysis I have sketched here, an update with an observation sentence $E_i\varphi$ will result in a belief that φ just in case the source i is ranked sufficiently high in the reliability ordering over source types. For this to be the case, it must be relatively reliable compared with other sources in cases of conflict; in the absence of conflict, however, the condition I have imposed is fairly weak. It seems that more is required for beliefs acquired in the manner I have described to be genuinely rational. However, the requisite condition is already present in the theory. I will show how rationality can be achieved in the next section.

13.5 RATIONAL UPDATE

In the preceding sections, I have outlined a dynamic semantic model for source-based information acquisition, with testimony as a special case. I began with a consideration of the kinds of conditions under which agents can be viewed as cooperative communicators, claiming that, for speakers, cooperativity requires truth telling, and, for hearers, that cooperativity requires (normative) belief. I then discussed some optimal strategies that can be deployed in situations where the interests of all agents are not aligned, but where their choices and desires form a prisoner's dilemma: for such situations, the best strategies involve a kind of "cooperation with punishment," according to which it is best to cooperate within reason. Two such strategies were shown to be generous TFT and a strategy choosing to cooperate or not based on the reputation of the other player: I claimed that these two instantiate, respectively, antireductionist and reductionist strategies in the domain of the epistemology of testimony. The result of making use of reputation indices was that speakers can be ranked for reliability, and that such rankings can be extended to other information sources, resulting in a notion of what amounts to defeasible update.

However, the result is not completely satisfactory with respect to genuinely rational belief, though it may be satisfactory with respect to the linguistic facts which it was originally intended to model. To see the issue, consider the following case. Suppose that agent a updates her information state with $E_i\varphi$, resulting in $\sigma_i \cap \varphi$, for $\sigma_i \in \sigma^a$. What contribution does this make to a's total information state σ^a_T? Let i be minimally ranked with respect to reliability, so $i < j$ for all sources j such that $j \neq i$. Then any other information source will override i, and the information φ will not survive into σ^a_T in the presence of any conflicting information from another source. However, suppose that there is no such conflicting information. Then φ will survive into σ^a_T, as will any other consistent information in σ_i. But surely one would not want to regard the resulting belief in φ as a rational one. Is there a way to address this problem in the present framework?

I believe that the answer is positive, though it is neglected by McCready (2015) due mostly to the linguistic focus of that work. The challenge raised by this case is to unify the reputation-based view of warranted belief with the dynamic evidence model. According to the initial reputation-based view (or at least one version thereof, as discussed in Section 12.3), a proposal should be accepted if its author's reliability index exceeds a minimal standard of reliability s set by context, as with other vague predicates. In the second, a proposal is accepted in the absence of conflicting information. The two can be unified by reintroducing the quantitative, standard-based aspects to the evidence model, which at present makes only purely ordinal comparisons between indices. Concretely, if $Rel(i) < s$ for some standard s, then the substate σ_i should simply be left out of the unification process, regardless of whether information from any other source conflicts with the information provided by σ_i. The idea is that sufficiently unreliable sources are just not proper candidates for merging to form global beliefs, as the information they carry can rationally be discounted. This brings the two aspects of the model together and yields a full model of rational evidence-based update.

The resulting system allows a characterization of rational belief: it is rational to believe something if it is learned on the basis of a sufficiently reliable source. According to the present theory, those sources that count as "sufficiently reliable" are those whose reliability exceeds a contextually set standard, together with being relatively reliable as compared with other sources. Rational belief is thus, on this view, in part a context-relative notion, a result which seems likely to interact in interesting ways with recent theories of epistemology which take knowledge, and belief, to be context sensitive (Rysiew, 2011; Kim, 2012).

Let me close the chapter with two potential difficulties for the approach.[15] The first worry involves situations in which two sources are extremely close in their probability of reliability, perhaps even indistinguishable from the perspective of a normal human agent, as often found in cases of vagueness (cf., Fara, 2000). Suppose that two such sources are in conflict on some proposition. In such cases, the information carried by the higher ranked source will be retained in the total information state, in the absence of other conflicts; but, given that the two sources do not significantly differ in their reliability, can it be rational to select one with such certainty? Probably not. There are various responses that can be made to this issue. The one I would like to support here involves setting equivalence classes of sources with respect to reliability, and allowing conflicts within the equivalence class to result in a withholding of judgement about the source of the conflict.[16] The second sort of case is more problematic. Consider a situation in which a high-ranked source carries the information that ϕ, while eight relatively low-ranked sources (though still reasonably reliable) have it that ϕ. On the current theory, ϕ is carried over to the total information state. Is this rational? It is not easy to say, and the answer to the question itself looks to be context dependent. It is likely in some cases one would like to believe the high-ranked source and in others allow the other sources to trump it; in general, the problem of voting effects like these is a familiar but extremely difficult one for theories of preference aggregation (Nitzan, 2009), which provides a formal basis for the present enterprise. The problem is raised already in McCready (2015), but no solution is proposed there, for the reason that no obvious and fully general solution presents itself within the framework. This problem is one I will have to leave for future research.

Acknowledgments

Thanks to the audience of IEAS for helpful comments, to the organizers for making the opportunity available, and especially to Wen-Fang Wang for his comments on this chapter and to Linton Wang for extensive discussion.

References

Adler, J. (2013). Epistemological problems of testimony. *The Stanford Encyclopedia of Philosophy*. Spring, 2013.

Aikhenvald, A. (2004). *Evidentiality*. Oxford: Oxford University Press.

Andreka, H., Ryan, M., & Schobbens, P. -Y. (2002). Operators and laws for combining preference relations. *Journal of Logic and Computation, 12*, 13–53.

Baltag, A., & Smets, S. (2008). A qualitative theory of dynamic belief revision. In G. Bonanno, W. van der Hoek, & M. Wooldridge (Eds.), *Logic and the foundations of game and decision theory, No. 3 in Texts in logic and games* (pp. 13–60). Amsterdam, The Netherlands: Amsterdam University Press.

Baltag, A., Smets, S. (2009). Talking your way into agreement: Belief merge by persuasive communication. In: *MALLOW, vol. 494 CEUR Workshop Proceedings.*.

Benz, A., Jager, G., van Rooij, R. (Eds.), (2006). *Game theory and pragmatics*. New York: Palgrave.

Brown, J., & Cappelen, H. (Eds.). (2011). *Assertion*. Oxford: Oxford University Press.

Burge, T. (1993). Content preservation. *The Philosophical Review, 102*(4), 457–488.

Craig, E. (1990). *Knowledge and the state of nature*. Oxford: Oxford.

Fara, D. G. (2000). Shifting sands: An interest-relative theory of vagueness. *Philosophical Topics, 28*, 45–81.

Gardenfors, P. (1988). *Knowledge in flux*. Cambridge, MA: MIT Press.

Grice, H. P. (1975). Logic and conversation. In P. Cole, & J. Morgan (Eds.), *Syntax and semantics III: Speech acts* (pp. 41–58). New York: Academic Press.

Groenendijk, J., & Stokhof, M. (1991). Dynamic predicate logic. *Linguistics and Philosophy, 14*, 39–100.

Hume, D. (1977). *An enquiry concerning human understanding*. Indianapolis, IN: Hackett (First published 1748).

Kennedy, C. (2007). Vagueness and gradability: The semantics of relative and absolute gradable predicates. *Linguistics and Philosophy, 30*(1), 1–45.

Kim, Hyun, B. (2012). *The context-sensitivity of rationality and knowledge* (PhD thesis). Columbia University, New York, NY.

Lewis, D. (1973). *Counterfactuals*. Oxford: Oxford: Basil Blackwell.

Mailath, G., & Samuelson, L. (2006). *Repeated games and reputations: Long-run relationships*. Oxford: Oxford.

McCready, E. (2015). *Reliability in pragmatics*. Oxford: Oxford University Press.

McCready, E., Asher, N., Soumya, P. (2013). Winning strategies in politeness. In Y. Motomura, A. Butler, D. Bekki (Eds.), *New Frontiers in artificial intelligence, Vol. 7856, Lecture in computer science* (pp. 87–95). Berlin: Springer.

Murray, S. (2010). *Evidentiality and the structure of speech acts* (Ph.D. thesis). Rutgers University, New Brunswick, NJ.

Muskens, R., Johan van, B., & Albert, V. (1997). Dynamics. In J. van Benthem, & A. ter Meulen (Eds.), *Handbook of logic and language* (pp. 587–648). Amsterdam, the Netherlands: Elsevier.

Nitzan, S. (2009). *Collective preference and choice*. Cambridge: Cambridge University Press.

Nowak, M. (2006). *Evolutionary dynamics*. Cambridge, MA: Belknap Press.

Nowak, M., & Sigmund, K. (1998a). The dynamics of indirect reciprocity. *Journal of Theoretical Biology, 194*, 561–574.

Nowak, M., & Sigmund, K. (1998b). Evolution of indirect reciprocity by image scoring. *Nature, 393*, 573–577.

Pollock, J., & Cruz, J. (1999). *Contemporary theories of knowledge*. Lanham, MD: Rowman Littlefield.

Quine, W. V. O. (1960). *Word and object*. Cambridge, MA: MIT Press.

Reid, T. (1997). *An Inquiry into the human mind on the principles of common sense*. University Park, PA: Pennsylvania State University Press, Originally published 1764.

Rysiew, P. (2011). Epistemic contextualism. *The Stanford Encyclopedia of Philosophy*. Winter, 2011.

Stalnaker, R. C. (1978). Assertion. In P. Cole (Ed.), *Syntax and semantics* (pp. 315–322). New York: Academic Press.

Stalnaker, R. C. (1999). *Context and content: Essays on intentionality in speech and thought*. Oxford: Oxford University Press.

Veltman, F. (1996). Defaults in update semantics. *Journal of Philosophical Logic, 25*, 221–261.

Endnotes

1. See Adler, 2013 for discussion of extant positions, together with references.
2. I think this is sufficient for my purposes here, though it certainly is not for deciding whether a speaker is genuinely cooperative.
3. More sophisticated formulations also make use of probabilities and sometimes other elements, but I will leave these aside for the simple structures I discuss here.
4. Indeed, the number of possible moves is so large that the abstraction to categories carried out immediately below is crucial for the tractability of the analysis.
5. The payoffs in the asymmetrical cases do not represent what happens in every instance of such transactions, but rather some percentage of cases which I assume to be high enough to motivate this structure. The particular payoffs in this game are also open to debate, as only the proportions matter, as usual in game theory.
6. At least, when no other complications—communication, prior agreement, and external norms—are introduced. I will leave such considerations out of this discussion.
7. The reason for using scare quotes in the previous sentence is that it is not necessary to anthropomorphize; game theory solution concepts involve maximizing the values of functions, not genuine reasoning about outcomes by agents.
8. To the extent that game-theoretic considerations can be thought of as properly modeling evolutionary processes and behavior, the analysis suggested here might also be compatible with a more general evolutionary approach to the epistemology of testimony and how it interacts with considerations of knowledge (cf. Craig, 1990).
9. This picture can be enriched in various ways. For example, the analysis of discourse anaphora requires making use of discourse referents and ways to assign objects to such referents, so information states can be viewed as sets of possible worlds and assignment functions. See Muskens et al. (1997) for an informative survey.
10. Alternatively, updates yielding inconsistency can result in revision of the information state (Gardenfors, 1988). This decision depends on precisely whether the semantics is supposed to model discourse update or genuine change of belief. I will not pursue this issue further here as it will not be crucial to my discussion.
11. As in the case of testimonial sources, however, each source will be provided with an initial probability of reliability, which is then modified by observation of further truth-tracking, or nontruth-tracking, events.
12. This holds for the full ranking, but may not hold for cases where the ranking is derived for subsequences, for instance, only those events relating to a particular kind of information or context. There, we may assume that ties in the ranking require consideration of the broader context after all; if worries about possible failures in ordering remain,

one may introduce a kind of analogue of the Lewisean Limit Assumption for rankings (Lewis, 1973) and claim that each source is always mutually ranked, even if the ranking requires a coin flip.

13. In the model of McCready (2015), this picture is slightly complicated: information states (including substates) consist of pairs of sets of worlds and orderings over those worlds. The reason is that McCready (2015) assumes a different notion of update than the one sketched in the main text, for reasons having to do with the necessity of revision (the particular kind of update is the priority update of Baltag & Smets, 2008, 2009). I will put these complications aside for the purposes of the present chapter.
14. This move might seem to make problems when one wants to leave out only some information from σ_j; this problem is resolved in the full theory involving priority update, and consequently a merge operation amounting to a genuine kind of preference upgrade (Andreka, Ryan, & Schobbens, 2002).
15. These problems were raised in the useful comments by Wen-Fang Wang.
16. This strategy of course requires the ability to withhold judgement in the first place, something not discussed in the "official" theory given by McCready (2015), but certainly compatible with it.

CHAPTER

14

Reason and Emotion in Xunzi's Moral Psychology

E.H. Wang

Department of Philosophy, National ChenChi University, Taipei City, Taiwan

14.1 SOEK'S TWO MODELS

Soek recently characterized two contrasting models of moral psychology: "reason based" and "emotion based." The reason-based model takes the often presumed canonical rational abilities, such as the reflective and conscious reasoning ability to be the essence of one's moral judgment and action. In this model, the emotions and the affective mechanisms play only minor roles (if any), and often times they are merely distractions that bias one's otherwise cool and deliberate moral reasoning. The emotion-based model, on the other hand, takes one's emotional dispositions to be an essential or at least necessary component of one's moral judgment and action.[1]

What is the relation between emotion and moral judgment/decision in Xunzi's view? Soek understands Confucian ethics in general to operate with the emotion-based model, but his argument mainly concerns Mencius' work.[2] There are, moreover, reasons to doubt that Xunzi's moral psychology operates with the emotion-based model. First, the emotion-based theories Soek mentioned (eg, moral sentimentalist theories and Mencius theory) all consider our affective natural inclinations to be the foundation of our moral judgments and actions, while Xunzi considers our natural affective inclinations, such as *qing* 情 and *yu* 欲 to be not ideal in their original state, but something to be nurtured and reformed. Second, unlike the emotion-based theories Soek mentioned, in Xunzi's account the participation of one's *xin* 心 (often translated as the "heartmind"), such as thinking (慮)[3] and permission (可), which Xunzi differentiates from the effects of *qing* 情 and *yu* 欲, is considered crucial in moral judgment and action.[4] He even clearly urges one to deliberate carefully when one sees

Rationality. http://dx.doi.org/10.1016/B978-0-12-804600-5.00014-3

something desirable, and to maturely calculate the relative merits of alternative courses of action before one makes a decision.[5] Moreover, crucial to Xunzi's view of moral cultivation, and especially the way to restore order, is to render one's *xin* 心 as able to make decisions in accordance with *li* 理 the objective order/pattern of the world or the "rational principles."[6] It is not about changing one's natural emotions, such as desires.[7] (I will elaborate on these points later.) Xunzi's emphasis on thinking and the ability to make decisions according to li renders it doubtful that Xunzi's moral psychology can be captured by the emotion-based model.

One may also consider whether Xunzi's view presumes the reason-based model. Slingerland (2010) puts Xunzi's view in this category.[8] In his work, however, he uses a slightly different name for the model: the high reason model. Examining Slingerland's depiction of the high reason model and his criticism of it gives us a concrete understanding of the implications of the reason-based model. In the following I thus examine the high reason model and argue that this model also does not capture Xunzi's moral psychology.

14.2 THE HIGH REASON MODEL

Inspired by A. Damasio's work,[9] Slingerland (2010, 2011) cited recent empirical studies to criticize a model of moral reasoning (resulting in moral judgment and decision/action),[10] which they call the "high reason model."[11] This model assumes ideal moral reasoning to be a process that is conscious, calm, and deliberative: one simply considers all possible scenarios and performs reasoning in a form close to a cost-benefit analysis. According to Slingerland, this model presumes that moral reasoning should be under conscious control, where one is aware of all the relevant factors of this process; moreover, rational faculties and emotional faculties (and bodily functions) are essentially competitive during the reasoning process, and rational faculties should take priority: one is required to suppress one's emotional (and bodily) reactions and not let personal feelings bias one's judgment.[12] (Slingerland does not explicitly list the rational faculties and emotional faculties or the bodily functions he has in mind, but from the context we may infer that the rational faculties he has in mind involve narrowly defined[13] cognitive abilities and processes, such as deliberative, reflective, and inferential abilities, while emotional faculties and bodily functions involve emotions, implicit skills, or unconscious habits). One aims at arriving at a rational, objective decision through this reasoning process; cognitive embodiment and emotional faculties play no role in this ideal process.[14]

We can see that the high reason model in Slingerland's account makes several distinctive claims.[15]

1. Ideal moral reasoning is conscious and deliberative.
2. Rational faculties and emotional faculties (and other bodily functions, implicit skills, etc.) are competitive in the moral reasoning process, and emotional responses should be suppressed and overridden.
3. Cognitive embodiment and emotional faculties play no essential role in the ideal moral reasoning process.

The similarity between the high reason model and Soek's reason-based model should be apparent. Both of them take the often assumed canonical rational abilities, such as conscious deliberation and reflection to be essential in moral judgment and action. Emotions and affective mechanisms only play a minor role if any, and they are often considered as a distraction interfering with ideal moral judgment and action.

In his criticism, Slingerland cites recent studies to point out that, on the one hand, conscious self-control must occur rarely, since it consumes significant amounts of time and already limited cognitive resources; and on the other hand, automatic processes involving emotional faculties, bodily functions, implicit skills, and heuristics in fact pervade our everyday decision-making and action. These processes are shown to be fast, computationally frugal, and reliable. Conscious interventions in these processes can in fact be counterproductive, and even misleading.[16] Even though these studies do not dismiss the possibility of conscious, rational control, we should still consider what our reasonable expectation of it should be. On the other hand, emotional faculties and bodily functions need not always be suppressed; in fact, they may be very helpful in reaching good judgment and decision.

The criticism above addresses the first two claims of the high reason model, but more argument is required to criticize the third claim of this model. After all, the supporter of this model may grant that cognitive embodiment and emotional faculties may be marginally helpful in moral reasoning and play only a minor role in the reasoning process, and argue that they are not essential to the reasoning process.

The studies Slingerland cites do provide a challenge to this third claim as well. He points out that the automatic processes pervasive in our decision process in fact play crucial roles in human cognition. For example, studies by Damasio show that emotional and bodily functions help prioritize certain options (through forming emotional and bodily reactions called "somatic markers"), and thus allow people to take the consequence of alternative courses of actions into consideration and make choices effectively (or make choices at all).[17] Based on these studies (and others), Slingerland shows that cognitive embodiment and emotional faculties in fact play crucial roles in the moral reasoning process. He thus rejects the high reason model, and finds a model of ethics "that does not rely primarily on active cognitive control and algorithmic reasoning but instead aims to cultivate self-activating, automatic, effortless dispositions to act in virtuous manner" more convincing.

14.3 THE HIGH REASON MODEL AND XUNZI'S MORAL PSYCHOLOGY

Slingerland categorizes Xunzi's moral psychology as a theory that presumes the high reason model. He takes Xunzi to prioritize the rational faculties, with the view that they can and should monitor emotional responses, and override them when needed.[18] He does not explain in detail why he takes Xunzi's view to presume this model, but we might see a prima facie reason.[19]

As mentioned earlier, Xunzi does urge one to deliberate and calculate the relative merits of alternative courses of action before one makes a decision. This may suggest that, according to Xunzi, conscious deliberation in a form close to a cost-benefit analysis is the ideal form of moral reasoning, and that during the reasoning process it is this cool deliberation that should suppress and override one's emotional responses. This view may be further buttressed by one common interpretation of Xunzi's action theory: one's emotional states (*qing* 情 and *yu* 欲) potentially bring about action, and one's *xin* 心 can and should monitor and control *qing* 情 and yu 欲 by determining whether the action that is to be brought about by *qing* 情 and *yu* 欲 is permissible; when the action is impermissible, it controls *qing* 情 and *yu* 欲 by stopping their bringing about the action, or channeling them so that they bring about another action. This interpretation may sound similar to the high reason model: rational faculties and emotional faculties are competitive in the moral reasoning process, and rational faculties *can* and *should* supervise and, when appropriate, override the reactions of our more emotional faculties.[20]

In the following I examine Xunzi's moral psychology, with special attention to the roles *xin* 心 and *qing* 情 (and *yu* 欲) play in the moral reasoning process that results in moral judgment and action. Based on this discussion, I will argue that Xunzi's moral psychology does not presume the high reason model, and also propose a way *qing* 情 (and *yu* 欲) functions in moral reasoning. I argue that, based on this proposal, Xunzi's moral psychology is at least compatible with the view that emotions and cognitive embodiment play an essential role in moral reasoning.

14.4 CLARIFICATION OF THE CONCEPTS: *XIN* 心 AND *QING* 情

Before I move to examine the roles that *xin* 心 and *qing* 情 (and *yu* 欲) play in the moral reasoning process in Xunzi's view, a clarification of the relevant concepts is in order. Xunzi understands *xin* to possess narrowly defined cognitive abilities, such as "thinking",[21] "being aware of the defining characteristics and make distinctions",[22] "making inferences"[23] (especially analogical inferences),[24] "evaluating and deciding whether a pursuit is possible/permissible",[25] etc. We should not, however, identify *xin* with the rational faculties, as Slingerland understands them. *Xin* should not be understood as an ability or a mere faculty; rather, it stands for the subject, the agential faculty that possesses abilities and makes use of sub-agential faculties. According to Xunzi, *xin* 心 is the "lord" of the body[26] and the "spirit".[27] It issues commands but does not receive commands.[28] Moreover, *xin* also has emotional faculties, such as likes and dislikes,[29] and it is *xin* that can feel and differentiate emotions, such as pleasure and anger, sorrow and joy, love and hate, and desires.

Xunzi understands *qing* 情 to be emotions and sentiments, such as "love and hate, delight and anger, sorrow and joy."[30] *Qing* closely connects with the concept of desire yu 欲 (and the pair 情欲 is often used together in Xunzi's text), which is a specific emotional response that arises due to the subject's interaction with an object.[31] In the following I sometimes refer to *yu* 欲 as a state of *qing* 情. Xunzi understands bodily functions to provide sense contact, including the eye, ear, nose, mouth, and body, which are called "the faculties given us by nature."[32] Since *xin* 心 is the "lord" of the body[33] and the "spirit," we can expect that in some sense *xin* rules the body and the sentiments. How does it rule? Here my focus is on whether or not *xin* rules the body and the sentiments by online, conscious control, having its rational faculties suppress and override emotional and bodily responses during the moral reasoning process, as the high reason model presumes. Now we turn to examine the roles *xin* and *qing* play in the moral reasoning process in Xunzi's view.

14.5 THE ROLES *XIN* 心 AND *QING* 情 PLAY IN MORAL REASONING

As I mentioned earlier, one common interpretation of Xunzi's action theory is that a state of *qing* 情 (such as desire) is able, by itself, to bring about action (such as the action of pursuing the object of desire); however, since the action so brought about may not be permissible (the object of desire may not be possible for pursuit, or the pursuit itself may not be permissible), we need *xin* (given its rational abilities) to monitor and control *qing* by determining whether to allow this action to be brought about. Whenever an impermissible action is motivated and about to be brought about, *xin* controls *qing* by stopping its bringing about the action, or channeling it so that it brings about another action. A Xunzi scholar W. Sung gives a vivid water analogy for this common view: desire is like water flowing in a drain, and the object of desire is analogous to the destination. *Xin* is like the valve(s) or pipes that can affect the flow of water, changing its path or its destination.[34] Is this common interpretation an apt understanding of Xunzi's action theory? In the following I examine some of Xunzi's passages and argue that it is not.

14.5.1 Xunzi 22.1

To start, regarding the roles *xin* and qing play in decision (and action) processes, Xunzi said, "(1) The feelings of liking and disliking, of delight and anger, and of sorrow and joy that are inborn in our nature are called qing. (2) The *qing* being so and *xin* chooses, this is called thinking 慮. (3) *Xin* thinks and so its faculties act on it, this is called *wei* 偽. (4) When thoughts are accumulated and *xin*'s faculties have been practiced and act to complete something, this is called *wei* 偽."[35] My focus here is on (2) and (3), but (4) is also of importance here and I will start with it.

Notice that the term "*wei* 偽" appears in both (3) and (4). From the passage, it should be clear that these two *wei*'s have different meanings besides the often observed commonality that they both involve something "artificial"[36]: the former [the "*wei*" in (3)] refers to the process leading to action/decision or the action itself, where, even though *xin* plays the crucial part in thinking and acting, the thoughts and the faculties involved are not necessarily results of moral education. (Xunzi often uses the idea of accumulation and practice to refer to the hard work required in moral education and moral development).[37] The latter [the "*wei*" in (4)], on the other hand, refers to the process of an achievement or completion, or an achievement or completion itself, given the accumulated thoughts and cultivated faculties through practice (this is often translated as "exertion" or "accumulative, deliberate effort"). From this passage, we can see that Xunzi uses "*wei*" in two senses: action/action process (where *xin* plays an essential role) and achievement/cultivation process.[38]

With this clarification, we now see that in the action/decision process, *xin* makes certain choices given a particular state of *qing* (eg, anger or desire). A particular state of *qing* may initiate *xin*'s thinking and choosing. What kind of choice? What is the object of choice? (Also, how does *qing* initiate the thinking and choosing? I will leave this question for later.) Based on the common interpretation earlier, since the object of control is *qing*, the object of choice will be *qing*, or "whether allowing *qing* to bring about action". We thus interpret (2) to be: "*qing* is in a state that brings about a certain action, and *xin* chooses 'whether to allow qing to bring about that action'." Let us call this interpretation (2)*. However, if we follow this interpretation, it is difficult to understand (3). In sentence (3), *xin*'s thinking and choosing is a necessary condition for its faculties to act.[39] That is, without *xin*'s thinking and choosing, actions will not be initiated. In this case, *qing* by itself will not be sufficient to bring about action. This renders (2)* and also the common interpretation questionable. Since *qing* itself does not bring about action, the object of choice for *xin* will not be *qing*, or "whether to allow *qing* to bring about action." Rather, it should be "whether the action (or the object of pursuit) is permissible/good."[40]

One may wonder, it is possible that Xunzi in 22.1 only talks about the sort of judgment *xin* makes, and the sort of action *xin* initiates; maybe there are other sorts of judgments of actions that do not require *xin* to take part in, but can be initiated by a state of *qing*, such as a desire. Another passage in Xunzi (Xunzi 22.11) clearly rejects this possibility and supports the previous reading.

14.5.2 Xunzi 22.11

Following the Confucian thinkers before him, Xunzi's primary concern is also with restoring order to promote the interests and well-being of people. His view of the human condition is that men are born with desires which, if not satisfied, will lead to contention, and this in the end leads to disorder.[41] To restore order, however, Xunzi does not think we should try to rid ourselves of desires. He makes this point clearly in 22.11: this is because desires come from human nature. Whether people have desires, and how many desires they have, depends on human nature. Due to human nature, desire exists whether the object of desire may or may not be pursued. However, whether people will actually take action and pursue their object of desire does depend on whether the object of desire, is judged possible/permissible to be pursued, and this judgment is made by *xin*. Indeed, Xunzi thinks that *xin* plays a crucial role in judgment and action, and thus "order and disorder lie in what *xin* permits and not with the desires," and moral education lies in getting what *xin* permits to coincide with *li* 理.[42]

Here we see Xunzi's view again that the judgment (permission) made by *xin* is required for the initiation of action. *Xin* thus plays the necessary role in the action/decision process, and a particular state of *qing* (eg, desire) by itself is insufficient to initiate action.[43] Moreover, there is also reason to think that, on Xunzi's account, a particular state of *qing*, such as desire, is not necessary for action initiation. This is made clear in Xunzi 21.9 and 22.11. In 21.9, Xunzi said, "*xin* is the lord of the body and master of the spirit. It issues commands but does not receive commands. On its own authority it forbids or orders, renounces or selects, initiates or stops (judgment or action)."[44] Specifically, *xin* does not require a particular state of *qing*, such as desire to initiate or stop action. In 22.11, Xunzi said, "Although the desires are not strong enough to motivate a person, his actions may exceed his desires because *xin* has ordered them to do so. If what *xin* permits conflicts with what is reasonable, then although the desires be few, how could it stop at disorder?"[45]

It should now be clear that a particular state of *qing*, such as desire, it is neither necessary nor sufficient to bring about action (or judgment). This shows the problem with the common interpretation of Xunzi mentioned earlier. Particular states of *qing* do not by themselves bring about action (or judgment). In moral reasoning, the object of choice/judgment is the action, or whether the object of pursuit is possible/permissible (instead of "whether to allow desire to bring about action"), and the object of control is the action itself. Recall the water analogy; it may be closer to Xunzi's view to say that *xin* also plays the role of water: xin by itself is able to bring about action. Particular states of *qing* by themselves do not even have the potential to cause action.[46]

What role do particular states of *qing* play in reasoning processes? As mentioned earlier, Xunzi thinks that *xin* makes certain choices "given" the particular state of *qing*. Since *xin* takes no command and it always needs to go through the judgment of permission before decision/action, we should not think that *qing* causes *xin* to make a certain choice. I propose that a more apt understanding is that particular states of *qing* may initiate *xin*'s thinking and choosing; it may also help to present options to *xin*. *Xin* in turn considers whether it is permissible/possible to pursue the object of desire, whether to act, and how to act. *Xin* may even make choices "in light of" *qing*: *qing* may present to *xin* options of choice in a weighted manner. We may thus think that, in Xunzi's account, *qing* not only initiates *xin*'s thinking and choosing, but it may strongly affect this thinking and choosing as well.[47]

This is a crude proposal. I will come back to elaborate on it and develop it further in Section 14.7. What should be clear by now is this: since the object of online control of *xin* is not *qing*, but the judgment and action itself, *qing* by itself does not bring about action, but helps to present to *xin* options of choice; in an important sense the emotional faculties and the rational faculty of *xin* are not competitive in the reasoning process, they in fact play different roles in the process. (In Section 14.7, I will come back to address the sense in which they may be considered to be "indirectly"competitive). For the same reason, it is not the case that, on Xunzi's account of moral reasoning, emotional responses should be suppressed and overridden.

This is a relevant point: notice that so far the concern is with the object (or the content) of choice or permission *xin* makes (through thinking and choosing) to initiate action. Based on the previous discussion, particular states of *qing* are neither necessary nor sufficient for action initiation. Thus the object of choice or permission is not "whether to allow qing to bring about action", but the action (or the object of pursuit) itself, deciding whether it is permissible. This discussion, however, does not address the issue of whether particular states of desire can "motivate" action in the sense that is different from "bring about" action. For example, A. Ben-Ze'ev (2000) thinks that some emotions have a motivational component: to have the emotion, such as a desire, is partly to intend certain actions to be executed, or to be ready to act.[48] My view is that Xunzi's view may accommodate this view of emotions, but I do not argue for this point here.

14.6 MORAL REASONING AS CONSCIOUS COST-BENEFIT ANALYSIS

I have presented a basic idea of the roles *xin* and *qing* play in the moral reasoning process, and I have argued that, in an important sense, on Xunzi's account the rational faculties and the emotional faculties are not competitive, and that emotional responses are relevant and need not be suppressed (even when it is an untutored emotional reaction from nature, such as a natural desire for profit). Now I come back to consider whether, on Xunzi's account, moral reasoning is necessarily a conscious, full-fledged deliberative process that is like a cost-benefit analysis.

Xunzi does not discuss the issue of whether the activities of *xin*, including making moral judgments, are always conscious. Based on the previous discussion, we can infer Xunzi's view to be that *xin* always issues judgments (eg, permission) before it initiates or stops an action. However, he does not describe the reasoning process in detail, and does not consider whether consciousness necessarily plays a role, or what role it plays if it does, in this process. Conceivably this judgment may take an unconscious form, or take a form of a conscious decision; even if the latter, this decision may result from a conscious but quick and intuitive judgment, rather than a full-fledged cost-benefit analysis.

As mentioned earlier, Xunzi does make remarks urging careful deliberation when one sees something desirable, but he also treats fast and accurate responses (especially at the time of changes) as ideal. For example, he said, "In his responses to evolving phenomena, [the gentlemen] is quick and alert, prompt and agile, but is not deluded."[49] As studies show, conscious, careful deliberation is a process that requires a lot of time and cognitive resources, while fast and accurate responsiveness is the manifestation of mature ability of judgment that is not necessarily deliberative or based on conscious calculation. There is thus no reason to interpret Xunzi to presume moral reasoning as necessarily a conscious process that is like a cost-benefit analysis. Xunzi's view so far is compatible with the empirical studies Slingerland considered.

At this point of discussion, a question may arise; as mentioned, Xunzi understands *xin* as the ruler of body and the spirit, it should thus have a certain kind of control over bodily and emotional faculties. From the previous discussion we know that the rational faculties of *xin* need not directly monitor and control emotional responses at the point of decision/action. What sort of control and rulership does *xin* then have? My view is that this control is rather indirect, manifesting in the education process toward sagehood Xunzi articulates, that is, through "purifying one's natural lord (xin)," "rectifying one's natural faculties", and "nourishing one's natural emotions."[50] I will elaborate on this point in the following section.

14.7 MORE ON THE ROLE QING PLAYS IN THE REASONING PROCESS

I have argued that Xunzi does not presume the first two claims of the high reason model, now I turn to the third claim: cognitive embodiment and emotional faculties play no essential role in the ideal moral reasoning process.

According to Xunzi, emotions resulting from our nature interact with the world, and are thus affected by the world. For example, we naturally desire beautiful things and profit, etc. Some philosophers before his time thus adopt a cautious attitude toward emotion and try to resist it or control it. Xunzi criticizes these philosophers for not noticing the fact that *qing* can be educated and developed.[51] He argues that moral education is not through controlling and resisting one's natural emotions, but through nourishing and regulating them through ritual practices and music.[52] Xunzi thinks that the education of *qing* can help change people's behavior and eventually help restore order. For example, "Music was enjoyed by the sage kings; it can make the hearts of the people good; it deeply stirs men, and it alters their manners and changes their customs. Thus, the ancient kings guided the people with ritual and music, and the people became harmonious and friendly" (20.6). It should be clear that, on Xunzi's account, *qing* not only may be educated, but this education helps to change people's actions. Given that the education of *qing* is through ritual practices and music, that this education is crucial for changing people's actions, and that people's actions result from the thinking and choosing of *xin* (recall from the previous discussion that the thinking and choosing, and the permission of *xin* is the necessary condition of decision/action), we may infer that, on Xunzi's account, emotional faculties and embodiment play an important role in one's reasoning process. Unlike the high reason model, Xunzi's moral psychology does not rely primarily on active cognitive control, such as conscious deliberation, but also attends to the importance of bodily and emotional cultivation. Now we naturally ask: on Xunzi's account, what role do emotional faculties play in the moral reasoning process?

From the previous discussion, we know that particular states of *qing* (eg, a particular desire) cannot bring about an action, and that rational faculties and emotional faculties are not competitive in the sense that *xin* does not apply its rational faculties to monitor, control, or suppress the emotional responses at the time of decision/action. I then proposed a way *qing* may function: it may initiate *xin*'s thinking and also present to *xin* options for its evaluation and judgment. Here a distinction is helpful for developing my proposal further.

Given Xunzi's view that *qing* from nature can and should be nurtured and educated or there will be disorder, and that the sage's *qing* can be satisfied without leading to disorder (21.12), it makes sense to distinguish between natural emotion and educated emotion in Xunzi's theory. Before moral education, we already have natural emotion that initiates *xin*'s thinking and presents *xin* with the option to pursue the object of one's natural and uneducated desire. At this point because *xin* is also not educated and has not internalized reason (through following a teacher's guidance and the study of the classics, learning and practicing ritual and music, reaching the state of openness, unity, and stillness, etc.), it does not have a lot of resources to entertain options other than the ones presented by the natural emotions. *Xin*'s thinking, at this point, will thus easily be limited by natural emotions. However, after education, not only does *xin* develop abilities to entertain options other than the ones presented by *qing*, but educated emotions may also present options that compete with the options presented by natural emotions.[53] These options may also be presented in a weighted manner based on the intensity of the emotions at play, and some options may even be silenced in the process.[54] Given the limited space here, I just give one example in Xunzi's text that seems to support the view that ritual practices, by affecting one's emotions, help change the cognition and evaluation in one's moral reasoning.

Xunzi especially emphasizes the importance of funeral and mourning rites in ritual practices, and describes them in detail. The point worth noting here is that, according to Xunzi, the purpose of these rites is not just helping to put people in the proper mood to see the dead off with grief and reverence, but to make the significance of life and death clear.[55] This is important since, according to Xunzi, appreciation of the significance of life and death is crucial to the ultimate wisdom, *dao*.[56] Moreover, the way this significance is made clear that is emphasized here is not by studying classics or abstract deliberation, but through ritual practices, where one, by following the rites, is lead to be immersed emotionally in the process. This emotional immersion helps one appreciate wisdom in life, which plausibly shapes one's cognitive and evaluative structure by assigning certain options certain weights or the way it may be presented, and thus affects one's later judgments and choices.[57]

Conceivably, these weights will significantly affect the reasoning process, especially when it is not a conscious cost-benefit deliberation. This explains why Xunzi urges people to deliberate carefully when they see something desirable; in an uneducated mind, natural emotions may be the most intense, and thus the option it presents is the most weighted.[58] On the other hand, when in an urgent situation or when emotion is stirred up and becomes overly intense, the possible options *xin* can present to itself are significantly limited because in these situations *xin* may not have the cognitive resources or time to consider carefully, or may be blinded by the option weighted by the overly intense emotion. Considering this, it should be clear that a well-developed emotion is indeed crucial for correct judgment.

Earlier in Section 14.7, I proposed that based on my interpretation of Xunzi's account, in an important sense the emotional faculties and the rational faculties of *xin* are not competitive in the reasoning process, but rather play different roles in the process. Here I revise this view. Interestingly, based on my further development of the proposal in this section, *xin* and *qing* do compete in a rather indirect way: natural emotion competes with both the rational faculties of *xin* and educated emotion (resulting from the guidance of *xin* and accumulated effort) when it presents the option to be considered. This is because the rational faculties and the educated emotions may present competing options or the same options in the opposite way at the same time. This, however, is very different from the sort of competition envisioned in the high reason model. By now, it should be clear that Xunzi's theory does not presume the high reason model. Emotions and cognitive embodiment in fact play an essential role in Xunzi's view of moral reasoning.

14.8 XUNZI'S HYBRID MODEL AND HIS CONCEPTION OF MORAL REASON

I hope that by now I have shown that Xunzi's moral psychology does not presume either the emotion-based model or the high reason model. On the one hand, it recognizes the importance of rational capacities, such as conscious deliberation, and emphasizes the essential role *xin* (especially its choosing and thinking) plays in moral reasoning; on the other hand, it does not recognize exclusively or even prioritize the often presumed canonical rational capacities over educated emotional faculties and bodily functions in ideal moral reasoning. Based on my examination of Xunzi's view, I proposed a possible way for *qing* to function in moral reasoning that is compatible with the current empirical research. Indeed, we have reason to believe that emotions and cognitive embodiment play an essential role in Xunzi's view of moral reasoning.

Xunzi's account thus presents a third alternative to Soek's two models. I call it the hybrid model. In this model, both the often presumed canonical rational capacities and educated emotional dispositions (and bodily functions) play crucial roles in ideal moral reasoning, crucial for *xin* to achieve the state where its permissions are always in accordance with *li* 理. This hybrid model, I suggest, stems from Xunzi's conception of moral reason. In the end of this paper, I briefly elaborate on this point.

As I have mentioned earlier, Xunzi believes that there are objective, rational principles or a pattern called *li* 理, and human mind, through proper moral education, is able to know this principle and make judgments and act accordingly. One may wonder: if Xunzi, as I have argued, does not presume the high reason model, is he still a rationalist? To answer this question, first we need to know what moral rationalism is.

Nichols (2004) distinguishes two rationalist claims: the conceptual and the empirical.[59] I focus on the empirical claim as it is more pertinent.[60] The empirical rationalist claim is this: it is an empirical fact that our moral judgments derive from our rational faculties or capacities. Is Xunzi an empirical rationalist in Nichol's account? This, of course, depends on what rational faculties are. I have been using the term "rational faculties" in the way Slingerland uses it, which refers to the often assumed canonical rational abilities, such as conscious and reflective deliberation. However, we may wonder whether rational faculties should be so restricted; rather, rational faculties may be broadly understood as the faculties that are "aptly responsive" to reasons or *li* 理.[61] For Xunzi, the goal of moral education is to attain such faculties to know and act according to *li* 理. This cultivated ability constitutes the moral reason in Xunzi's account, and it is an ability manifested by well-cultivated cognitive, evaluative, and affective mechanisms. If we allow this broad understanding of "rational faculties," given Xunzi's view of *xin* and its capacities to grasp *li* 理 Xunzi may be considered an empirical rationalist after all.

Tiberius (2014) understands moral rationalism to be about justification: moral judgments are justified and give us normative reasons in so far as they conform to moral principles.[62] Since Xunzi takes one's choices and action matching *li* 理 as the goal for the cultivation of *xin* and *qing*, we reasonably think that *li* 理 grounds judgments and actions in Xunzi's account. This seems to render him a moral rationalist in Tiberius's account.

Furthermore, I am interested in exploring whether Xunzi is rationalist in the sense that he conceives rational principles, such as *li* 理 as an abstract and external standard by which emotions are judged (eg, whether emotions are appropriate or whether they are helpful instrumentally for one to meet the requirement of rationality), or whether he may think that emotion actually (also) grounds rational principles, or, as R. Solomon puts it, "emotions constitute the framework of rationality itself… together our emotions dictate the context, the character, the culture in which some values take priority, serve as ultimate ends, provide the criteria for rationality and reasonable behavior."[63]

The fact that Xunzi puts so much emphasis on the education of emotion and bodily functions through ritual practices (and music) may shed light on this question. Scholars have pointed out that, in Xunzi's view, ritual practices are designed to socialize and enculturate people.[64] They help establish proper relationships (and thus order) among people through educating not only people's deliberative abilities, but also importantly, people's emotional and bodily faculties. Only through this socializing and enculturating education can people finally know moral truth (*Dao*) and *li* 理 in its concrete entirety. And what are "proper relationships"? What is *Dao*? Is it an abstract standard external to our emotions? Interestingly, the path toward sagehood Xunzi envisioned is not to turn our backs against our emotions, but to nurture and fulfill them. As David L. Hall and Roger T. Ames nicely put, "Rationality for Xunzi is formed dialectically amid cultural, social and natural forces, both shaping and being shaped by them."[65] We may now see, for Xunzi, what our emotions are and that they indeed can be grounded rationality and shape concretely what rationality is.

Acknowledgments

This paper is a revision of the conference paper presented at the IEAS Conference on Reason and Rationality in 2014. I want to express special thanks to my commentator, Wang-Chung Fang, who provided thoughtful and helpful remarks for my revision. I am also grateful for the audience at the conference, whose questions and comments gave me new ideas to think about.

References

Ben-Ze'ev, A. (2000). *The subtlety of emotions*. Cambridge, MA: MIT Press.
Chong, K. (2007). *Early Confucian ethics: Concepts and arguments*. Chicago: Open Court.
Damasio, A. (1994). *Descartes' error*. New York: Putnam.
Nichols, S. (2004). *Sentimental rules: On the natural foundations of moral judgment*. Oxford: Oxford University Press.
Railton, P. (2006). Normative guidance. In R. Shafer-Landau (Ed.), *Oxford studies in metaethics* (Vol. 1). Oxford: Oxford University Press.
Slingerland, E. (2010). Toward an empirically responsible ethics: Cognitive science, virtue ethics, and effortless attention in early Chinese thought. In B. Bruya (Ed.), *Effortless attention: A new perspective in the cognitive science of attention and action* (pp. 247–286). Cambridge, MA: MIT Press.
Slingerland, E. (2011). Of what use are the odes? Cognitive science, virtue ethics, and early Confucian ethics. *Philosophy East and West*, *61*(1), 80–109.
Seok, B. (2013). *Embodied moral psychology and Confucian philosophy*. Lanham, MD: Lexington Books.
Sung, W. (2012). *Yu* in the *Xunzi*: Can desire by itself motivate action? *Dao*, *11*, 369–388.
Tiberius, V. (2014). *Moral psychology: A contemporary introduction*. New York: Routledge.
《大中華文庫漢英對照 – 荀子》, (in English: Library of Chinese Classics: Xunzi.) 2003, 湖南人民出版社.
Xianqian Wang,《荀子集解》, (Xunzi Jijie) 藝文印書館, 1973
Anthony C. Yu, 2004,《重讀石頭記》(in English: *Rereading the stone : Desire and the making of fiction in Dream of the Red Chamber*.).
《荀子今註今譯》, (Xunzi Jinzhu Jinyi) 2010, 商務
Zao-ying Chen, 2005,「『情』概念從孔孟到荀子的轉化」 (in English: The Conceptual Change of Qing from Confucius, Mencius, to Xunzi),《儒家美學與經典詮釋》(in English: Confucian Aesthetics and Interpretations of Classics)

Endnotes

1. Seok, B. (2013). *Embodied moral psychology and Confucian philosophy* (pp. 96–98). Lexington Books.
2. Soek makes this clear on p. 71. I do not comment on Soek's work on Mencius in this paper, but focus on exploring how we should think of Xunzi's account.
3. In Xunzi 22.1, Xunzi explains lu 慮 a "xin 心 makes a choice given the condition of qing 情 (or in light of qing)." Lu 慮 is also understood as thinking, eg, Xunzi 19.8. Since "deliberation" is often used to refer to the fully conscious, full-fledged all things considered reasoning and decision process, while "lu 慮" is not clearly restricted to this kind of reasoning, but may also include speedier thinking and choosing. Here I follow Knoblock 22.1 and translate lu 慮 to be "thinking" (and "choosing" in the particular way spelled out in this paper). Also note that the passage numberings of *Xunzi* in this paper are all from *Library of Chinese Classics: Xunzi* (《大中華文庫漢英對照 – 荀子》, 2003).
4. See Xunzi 22.1 and 22.11.
5. See Xunzi 3.13.
6. *Li* 理 can be known and acted in accordance with by humans. It is often understood as the objective order/pattern of the world, and it is also translated as the "rational principles" by Knoblock. Xunzi thinks that *li* 理 is something one can guide one's *xin* with (eg, 21.11).
7. See Xunzi 22.11.
8. Slingerland, E. (2010). Toward an empirically responsible ethics: Cognitive science, virtue ethics, and effortless attention in early Chinese thought. In B. Bruya (Ed.), *Effortless attention: A new perspective in the cognitive science of attention and action* (pp. 247–286). Cambridge, MA: MIT Press.
9. Descartes' Error, 1994.
10. Clearly, certain moral reasoning may necessarily involve conscious deliberation or reflection. It should be noted that the sort of moral reasoning Slingerland considers is not limited to this sort, but is generally about all sorts that result in moral judgment or action/decision.
11. In his book, Damasio calls this model the "high reason model." This is in contrast to his own "somatic marker model." Slingerland sometimes uses the terms the "high reason model" and the "cognitive control model" interchangeably.
12. Slingerland, p. 264: "the 'high-reason' conviction … [is] that the rational faculties *can* and *should* supervise and—when appropriate—override the reactions of our more emotional faculties."
13. A broad understanding includes affective, perceptual, and bodily functions and processes that underlie the abilities of decision-making and action.
14. Slingerland (2010, p. 247): This model requires one "to be consciously aware of all the relevant factors, to suppress emotional reactions and social biases, and to arrive at and carry out an objective, dispassionately rational decision. … [The] entire process of moral reasoning is transparent and under our cognitive control and has nothing to do with the details of our embodiment, or with emotions, implicit skills, or unconscious habits." Also see Damasio (1994, p. 171): "when we are at our decision-making best, we are the pride and joy of Plato, Descartes, and Kant. Formal logic will, by itself, get us to the best available solution for any problem. An important aspect of the rationalist conception is that to obtain the best results, emotions must be kept out. Rational processing must be unencumbered by passion. Basically, in the high-reason view, you take the different scenarios and … perform a cost-benefit analysis of each of them."
15. I do not discuss exhaustively all the claims one may see in the cognitive control model (Slingerland himself does not list the claims), but only focus on the ones that are essential to the model and pertinent to my discussion of Xunzi's moral psychology. I leave out at least one essential claim of this model addressed by Slingerland, that is, the presumption that self is a unitary consciousness: "This model … involves conceiving of the self as a …

unitary consciousness." (Slingerland, 2010, p. 248). "The objectivist model of reasoning and conscious decision making assumes the presence of a unitary, conscious self—the locus of rationality and will—whose job is to evaluate incoming sense data, classify it, and enforce appropriate conclusions and behavioral decisions on the dumb, recalcitrant emotions or body." (Slingerland, 2010, p. 252). A discussion of this claim involves a broader issue that is beyond the scope of this paper; I will thus not address this claim here.

16. Slingerland, 2010, pp. 251, 252, and 265.
17. Slingerland 258–263; Damasio (1994).
18. Slingerland 264: "The 'high-reason' conviction, endorsed by philosophers since the time of Plato and Xunzi, [is] that the rational faculties *can* and *should* supervise and—when appropriate—override the reactions of our more emotional faculties."
19. Slingerland may also be influenced by Dai zhen 戴震 criticism of Xunzi, which makes a similar complaint. This possibility came up as Ming-Zao Ling (林明照 my translation) introduced Dai zhen's criticism of Xunzi to me.
20. Slingerland. p. 264.
21. Xunzi 22.1.
22. Xunzi 22.5.
23. Xunzi 22.8.
24. For example, A.C. Cua argues that ethical reasoning involves backward-looking analogical projection in《倫理論辯：荀子道德認識論之研究》(1985).
25. Xunzi 22.11.
26. Xunzi 17.4.
27. Xunzi 21.9.
28. Xunzi 21.9.
29. For example, see Xunzi 11.6 and 23.7: "*xin* is fond of profit." The commentator of this paper, Wang-Chung Fang, wonders whether it is possible that actually there are two senses of *xin* in operation here: the one that is fond of profit, and the one the lord of the body and the spirit. This is indeed a possibility worth considering. Instead of understanding "*xin*" to have different meanings in these passages, my position is to understand *xin* to stand for the subject, which possesses agential abilities and also has natural inclinations (such as the fondness of profit). The idea that *xin* possesses different abilities is also argued by other Xunzian scholars, for example, Ho, Shu-Ching (2014).
30. Categorizing *qing* as emotional faculties and sentiments is accepted by many Xunzi scholars. For example, see "The conceptual change of *qing* from Confucius, Mencius, to Xunzi" (「情」概念從孔孟到荀子的轉化, 2004, 2005 my translation), *Early Confucian ethics* by Kim-chong Chong, and chapter two of *Rereading the stone : desire and the making of fiction in Dream of the Red Chamber.* Besides pointing out the emotive aspect of the concept *qing*, the scholar also mention other uses of "*qing*," including facts, the human condition, and an aspect of moral agency. I focus on the emotive aspect in this paper.
31. See Xunzi 22.12: "desire is the response of the emotions". The relation between the two is explained clearly in "The conceptual change of qing from Confucius, Mencius, to Xunzi."
32. Xunzi 17.4, ref. Knoblock's translations.
33. Xunzi 17.4.
34. Please see W. Sung (2012). According to Sung, Lee Yearly (1980), David Nivison (1996), Cua (2005) and Kline (2006) all adopt this interpretation. Sung discusses their respective arguments in her paper.
35. See 22.1. My translation is based on the translation widely accepted and used among Xunzi' scholars: Wang's《荀子集解》(1973) and a contemporary translation:《荀子今註今譯》(2010).
36. Thanks to Wang-Chung Fang for reminding me to make this commonality clear.
37. For example, see Xunzi 22 and 23.
38. This reading can be seen in Wang's《荀子集解》(1973) 以及《荀子今註今譯》(2010). A Xunzi scholar, Yiu-ming Fung gives this passage a slightly different reading in his 2005 paper. He understands the first 偽 to be about *xin*'s natural capacity, while the second

about *xin*'s achievement. My worry is that this reading will render the nature/exertion distinction Xunzi emphasizes less clear, since *xin*'s natural capacity should be counted as part of nature. Moreover, in the text the first 偽 is clearly about action or the decision/action process, limiting it to *xin*'s capacity may be unnecessarily narrow.

39. An issue worth pursuing arises: under this interpretation, Xunzi's theory does not seem to allow room for "weakness of the will," since all actions are generated from the permission of *xin*. If this is the case, does Xunzi's theory provide the resources to explain the phenomena? This investigation requires a further discussion of the concept of *xin* and its faculties, and I leave it for a later time.
40. Sung (2012) provides a different interpretation: she thinks that the object of choice here is *qing* (not the action itself), and this choice is a form of evaluation, a choice about whether to allow this *qing* to be the reason for action. This interpretation, however, faces a difficulty in my view: according to Xunzi's text, action stems from this choice of *xin*. If we follow Sung's interpretation, then in cases where *xin* does not consider *qing* to be a good reason for action, but considers there to be other good reasons, action will not be initiated. These cases may indeed happen: *qing* may have certain desires and motivate certain actions (eg, helping others for the love of fame), but it is possible that even though the action (helping others) itself is good, the desire/motivation (desiring fame) is not a good reason. Sung (2012, p. 376) may provide a different interpretation of her view. *Xin*'s choices are of two sorts: the evaluation of *qing* as a reason for action, and whether to initiate action itself. Not only does this interpretation face the difficulty I just explained, but it also needs to provide further explanation to justify this seeming extensive interpretation of the text, since Xunzi's original sentence does not state that there are two objects of choice.
41. Xunzi 19.1.
42. Xunzi 22.11.
43. It is worth noting that Xunzi's comment here seems to be a description of decision/action process, not a prescriptive claim about the ideal we should aim at.
44. Xunzi 21.9, ref. Knoblock's translation.
45. Xunzi 22.11, ref. Knoblock's translation.
46. Sung (2012) argues for a similar view, but I disagree with her in textual interpretation. Please see endnote ll.
47. But there is no reason to think that, on Xunzi's account, *xin*'s thinking/choosing "requires" *qing* being in a certain state. *Xin* may initiate thinking without the stimulation of *qing*.
48. The subtlety of emotions by Aaron Ben-Ze'ev. pp. 61–62.
49. Xunzi 12.3.
50. Xunzi 17.4.
51. Xunzi 21.12.
52. Xunzi's emphasis on ritual and music follows from Confucius' view of the importance of poetry, ritual, and music in cultivation of moral and aesthetic character. Also, the nurturing of *qing*, ultimately, is to achieve the *qing* of the sages, who's desires can be followed and emotions be fulfilled (Xunzi 21.12).
53. The nature of the educated emotion and the natural emotion needs to be spelled out further. Are they completely different or do they share some similarities? This is related to the question of whether the sages still keep the natural *qing* (天情) and natural desires. I address this issue in another paper.
54. The distinction between the occurrent emotion vs. dispositional emotion is also helpful. Occurrent state is not necessary or sufficient for thinking/action initiation, but dispositional emotion, given its role in initiating *xin*'s thinking and choosing, and more importantly, in presenting options, may be considered constitutive of the thinking/moral reasoning process. I elaborate on this point in another paper.
55. Xunzi 19.16.

56. Xunzi 19.10.
57. It will be interesting to discuss whether this may be the sort of training that helps develop the "somatic markers" in Damasio's account. I do this in another paper.
58. It is worth exploring whether the educated emotional faculties also plays an important role in dispelling blindness (解蔽). It is conceivable that the educated emotional faculties reach a significant relative reliability, which is not easily "tilted" by external things. One may wonder whether the requirement of stillness 靜, one crucial ability of *xin* to dispel blindness and know *Dao*, is at odds with the idea that emotions play a significant role in *xin*'s judgment. However, stillness 靜 need not be understood as "dispassionate", but it simply means "not allowing dreams and fantasies to bring disorder to awareness" (Xunzi 21.8). I explore this issue in my other work.
59. Sentimental Rules. p. 67.
60. The conceptual rationalist claim in Nichols' account is this: it is a conceptual truth that a moral requirement is a reason for action. Since it is unclear to me whether Xunzi thinks that we have a "concept of moral requirement" or, if yes, what Xunzi takes it to be, more work is required to analyze whether Xunzi is a conceptual rationalist. I leave this issue for another time.
61. Railton (2006) recently suggested a broad conception of rationality: "a capacity to be *aptly responsive to reasons*". My view of rationality here is also a broad conception in this sense, even though, of course, Xunzi's idea of reason is different from Railton's consequentialist conception.
62. *Moral Psychology* by V. Tiberius.
63. *The Joy of Philosophy*. p. 85.
64. Eg, see Kim-chong Chong, *Early Confucian Ethics: Concepts and Arguments*.
65. Chinese philosophy: Routledge Encyclopedia of Philosophy Online: http://www.rep.routledge.com/article/G001SECT7.

Index

S

T

MIX
Papier | Fördert gute Waldnutzung
FSC® C083411

Kolibri 360 GmbH
Ferdinand-Jühlke-Straße 7
99095 Erfurt, Deutschland
produktsicherheit@kolibri360.de